ILL II 1099

W9-AFB-126

THE RIGHTEOUSNESS
OF GOD

THE RIGHTEOUSNESS OF GOD

Luther Studies

by

GORDON⌐RUPP

BR
333.2
R9

The Birkbeck Lectures in Ecclesiastical History
Delivered in the University of Cambridge, 1947

ST. JOSEPH'S UNIVERSITY   STX
BR333.2.R9
The righteousness of God: Luther studies

3 9353 00005 2306

HODDER AND STOUGHTON

125293

First printed 1953
Third Impression 1968

Printed in Great Britain for
HODDER AND STOUGHTON LIMITED, St. Paul's House,
Warwick Lane, London, E.C.4, by LOWE AND
BRYDONE (PRINTERS) LIMITED, London, N.W.10

To

W. F. FLEMINGTON

and

R. NEWTON FLEW

CONTENTS

PREFACE

IT is now a century since Julius Hare published his " Vindication of
Luther," a work eminent in learning and in judgment among English
writings about the Reformer. Hare's own splendid collection of Luther
first editions is preserved in the Library of Trinity College, Cambridge,
a permanent reminder of the importance attached to Reformation
studies by that great Fellow of Trinity. It was perhaps fitting that
when a series of public lectures in Cambridge should be devoted to
Luther's life and thought (the first, in that place, in four centuries to
be devoted exclusively to him?), they should be under the auspices of
that College. It was a great honour for me to be invited by the Council
of Trinity College to deliver the Birkbeck Lectures in Ecclesiastical
History in April and May 1947. It was perhaps also a recognition
that in this country we have some leeway to make up in our study of
the Continental Reformation, and particularly in awareness of the .
intricate field known as " Luther Research."

Two paramount considerations have governed the revision and
expansion of those lectures. First, at the present time, any work on
Luther which is to be of use to English readers must aim to make
known some of the methods, themes and findings of modern German
and Scandinavian studies: it must, therefore, be to an almost regrettable
extent a work of vulgarization, descriptive rather than interpretative.
Second, it must enable readers to listen to Luther himself. The treatment of detailed misconceptions and controversial matters is an indispensable task of the historian, and certainly no writer on Luther can
hope to evade this duty. I have felt it right to deal with some recent
misapprehension, as it seems to me, of Luther's doctrine and to give
an outline of the ancient polemical environment of Luther studies.
I hope readers will remember that, even in regard to Denifle, I have
had less severe things to say than are expressed by modern Catholic
writers like Joseph Lortz and Adolf Herte. And yet there is a more
excellent way: the royal way is not that of polemical divinity but the
positive presentation in a coherent form, of Luther's teaching, the
gathering together, as consistently as may be, of evidence from different
levels of the material, and from different dates in his career.

Of course, no amount of evidence will convince those with strong
enough vested interests to refuse the demonstration. But I believe
it is possible to present a reasonable case capable of convincing reason-

able men. And I have thought, that if five quotations may be open to the charge of arbitrary selection, let us try what fifty will do, and if fifty are insufficient, let them have five hundred.

The historians' Luther is itself an element in the making of history, and nearly as much can be learned about history from the history of historians as from the attempt to discover " history as it really is." An outline of the story of Protestant and Catholic interpretation of Luther explains why most of us in Western Christendom come to him with certain predispositions. The sketch of " Luther in England " explains that we have escaped the bitterly polemical dialectic of Continental study, while the curiously intermittent character of our interest in him partly explains why opinion in this country has lagged, even behind informed Catholic studies in Germany.

Captain Henry Bell began with a walk-on part, but stole a whole scene, and as well as a good deal of my time, some of my affection: his story is an interesting side-light on the story of Luther in England. No doubt it is a side-light on other things as well, but I have not drawn the moral, nor hinted that, in the end, the truth about the seventeenth century will be found nearer the despised "Whig Interpretation" than its more recent substitutes, or that nothing shows up the real character of tyranny than when, stripped of glamour and romanticism, it is shown doing mean and shabby things to little people.

One of the original lectures, on "Luther and the Righteousness of God," becomes a main section of the book. The theme is fundamental to the interpretation of the Protestant Tradition, and of the sixteenth century, and germane to the ecumenical conversation. To examine, with the help of secondary studies, the movement and consolidation of Luther's doctrine of Justification in formative years, and to view it from the angle of his vocabulary, seemed to me important as well as delicate and dangerous. I believe very surely that historical theology must always be related to the historical context, and in a little book, "Luther's Progress to the Diet of Worms," I have tried to provide the interested reader with the historical framework of this discussion.

I have many debts to acknowledge, and hope the conventional phrases may not appear to rob warm feeling of sincerity. Professor Herbert Butterfield has treated me with characteristic and generous kindness. His advice and criticism, in correspondence and in the "Cambridge Review," I have deeply valued and pondered long. Even when, now and again, I have ventured to go my own way, it has been with the uneasy feeling that no doubt he will be right after all. To Dr. Newton Flew I owe my original impetus towards Reformation studies, and his encouraging prodding was sustained until the time when I could go of my own cheerful volition. He generously allowed me time (while I was his Assistant at Wesley House, Cambridge, 1946-7) to prepare these lectures. W. F. Flemington gave me all the comfort and encouragement which an ideal colleague can give. Of the students then at Wesley House (surely a "vintage year") I shall always have grateful and affectionate remembrance.

Einar Molland, Professor of Church History and Dean of the Theological Faculty in Oslo, read through such portions as relate to Scandinavian studies. I owe much to him for his fine example of scholar and Church historian. I owe him also a thought which I have guarded through all my studies of the sixteenth century, for when, fifteen years ago, I asked him, as a Norwegian Lutheran, to tell me whether an Englishman could write a good book about Martin Luther, he returned a swift and unhesitating "No!" It has been for me a salutary and chastening reminder that the true insights come from within a household of faith, that continuing community which is the holy tradition. All I have dreamed to do, is play the rôle of the child in Hans Andersen's parable of the "Emperor's Clothes" and to cry out certain simplicities unnoticed, or at least unrehearsed by the wise and prudent. It may be, after all, that Englishmen may see truths about Luther different from those discussed in those incredibly learned, detailed and profound Continental Luther studies. But in truth my friend Principal Philip S. Watson's Fernley-Hartley Lecture, delivered in July 1947, showed that an Englishman may write a very good book indeed on Luther. And perhaps it is more than accidental that two sets of lectures on Luther's thought should be given by members of the People called Methodists, for if

> "We were the first that ever burst
> Into that silent sea,"

it was because there are elements in that tradition more congenial than Anglicanism or Dissent to the original ferment of the Reformation.

Two facts have prolonged the decent interval before publication. In the first place, the post-war situation in Europe has made it exceedingly difficult to obtain copies of even indispensable secondary studies. I am grateful to my dear friend, Rudolf Weckerling, of Spandau, who generously gave me his own copies of Luther's works, and who, in 1947, took me to rummage among the salvaged stocks of blitzed publishers in Berlin. Horst Flachsmeier, recently one of my own students, was indefatigable in his efforts on my behalf. I give thanks for the ready loan of books by Dr. Friedrich Wunderlich, Professors H. Bornkamm and E. Wolf, and Hanns Iwand. The other reason for delay has been that, as originally delivered, my lectures could show no first-hand knowledge of Scandinavian studies, and I have thought fit to wait until, from my own reading, I could take account of this important field.

Three volumes reached me too late to be considered in the text of this volume: the extremely interesting 1823 edition of Luther's " De Servo Arbitrio " translated by E. T. Vaughan (sometime Fellow of Trinity College, Cambridge); the posthumous study by Dr. K. A. Meissinger, "Das katholische Luther" (Munich, 1952); and "Recht-fertigung und Heiligung " by Axel Gyllenkrok (Uppsala, 1952)—the last a provocative essay which does not, in my opinion, sustain its criticism of the work of Prenter and von Loewenich.

Professor Norman Sykes has been my constant benefactor with encouragement, criticism, advice in that fine English tradition of generosity towards old pupils. Canon Charles Smyth has shown me continuing kindness and, in his official capacity as Rector of St. Margaret's, Westminster, practical assistance. It was a privilege to taste the hospitality of a noble college, and the Senior Tutor of Trinity, Mr. R. M. Rattenbury, gave generously of time and interest.

Two distinguished historians, Fellows of Trinity, Mr. G. S. R. Kitson Clark and Mr. H. O. Evenett, watched over me with benevolent and unobtrusive kindness and, heard me out to the end with good-humoured fortitude. I am grateful to the officials of the Public Record Office, London, the British Museum, the London Library, Dr. Williams' Library, the Evangelical Library, and the Verger of St. Martin in the Fields. Mr. Leonard Cutts of Hodder and Stoughton has been exemplary in patience and forbearance. My wife has turned this whole work into typescript, and only she knows, and only my friends can imagine, what it means to accomplish the task of solving the manifold enigmas of my unusual handwriting, with cheerful patience and unruffled calm.

All Saints' Eve,   RICHMOND COLLEGE,

1951.   SURREY.

ABBREVIATIONS

A.A.S.F.	Annales Academiae Scientiarum Fennicae.
Archiv für Ref.	Archiv für Reformationsgeschichte.
C.R.	Corpus Reformatorum.
Dict. Théol. Cath.	Dictionnaire de Théologie Catholique, Paris.
D.N.B.	The Dictionary of National Biography.
Eras. Epist.	Opus Epistolarum Des. Erasmi Roterodami. Ed. P. S. Allen, 1906-38.
Ev. Theol.	Evangelische Theologie (Munich).
Franz. Stud.	Franziskanische Studien (Werl. i. W.).
P.L.	Migne. Patrologiae Cursus Completus, Series Latina.
Rev. d'Hist. et de Phil. Rel.	Revue d'Histoire et de Philosophie religieuses (Strasbourg).
Rev. d'Hist. Eccl.	Revue d'Histoire Ecclésiastique (Louvain).
S.J.T.	Scottish Journal of Theology (Edinburgh).
Schriften des Ver. Ref.	Schriften des Vereins für Reformationsgeschichte.
Schw. Z. für Psych.	Schweizerische Zeitschrift für Psychologie.
S.P.Dom.	Calendar of State Papers (Domestic).
Th. Lit. Z.	Theologische Literaturzeitung (Berlin).
Th. St. und Kr.	Theologische Studien und Kritiken (Hamburg).
Z. für Syst. Theol.	Zeitschrift für Systematische Theologie.
Z. für Th. u. K.	Zeitschrift für Theologie und Kirche.

EDITIONS OF LUTHER

W.A.	Luther's Works (Weimarer Ausgabe).
W.A.Br.	Luther's Letters (Briefwechsel, Weimarer Ausgabe).
TR.	Luther's Table Talk (Tischreden, Weimarer Ausgabe).
Werke (Munich).	Martin Luthers Ausgewählte Werke. Munich, 1948-
Works (Clemen).	Luthers Werke in Auswahl (Otto Clemen). Berlin, 1933.
W.M.L.	Works of Martin Luther. 6 vols. Philadelphia, 1943.
D.M.L. Ev. Auslegung.	D. Martin Luthers Evangelienauslegung ed. E. Mülhaupt. Göttingen, 1939.
Hirsch-Rückert.	Luthers Vorlesung über den Hebräerbrief. Ed. E. Hirsch und Hanns Rückert. Berlin, 1929.
Vogelsang.	Luthers Hebräerbrief Vorlesung, 1517-18. Deutsche Übersetzung. Berlin, 1930.

PART

I

THE HISTORIANS' LUTHER

Chapter

1

THE LUTHER OF MYTH AND THE LUTHER OF HISTORY

"Perhaps there is no one in the whole history of the world against whom such a host of implacable prejudices and antipathies have been permanently engaged, as against Luther."
    JULIUS HARE. "Vindication of Luther."

IT was a critical moment during the Leipzig Disputation (1519) when Martin Luther, out-manœuvred by his opponent, Dr. Eck, was goaded into declaring that "among the articles of John Huss . . . which were condemned, are many which are truly Christian." The audience was horrified, and perhaps Luther himself was a little shocked. For he had grown to accept the judgment of contemporary opinion against the heretic of a former generation. "I used to abhor the very name of Huss. So zealous was I for the Pope that I would have helped to bring iron and fire to kill Huss, if not in very deed, at least with a consenting mind." [1] In this verdict faith and party loyalty combined, for the Erfurt Augustinians were proud that a member of their own order, John Zachariae, had earned the title "Scourge of Huss" and his tomb bore in effigy the Golden Rose bestowed upon him by a grateful Pope. [2] It was not until Luther himself entered a similar context of Papal condemnation that he turned to examine the writings of Huss, and to criticize this unexamined assumption. Then indeed he could cry to Spalatin, "We are all Hussites, without knowing it . . . even Paul and Augustine !" [3]

Luther did not know that in later centuries, a similar weight of received opinion would lie against himself, and that faith and party loyalty, formidable vested interests of the mind, would come to obscure the truth about himself. To every age there belong mental patterns, involving assumptions about causes and persons, for the most part accepted without reference to the canons of historical criticism, and even the expert in one particular field of historical investigation is bound to take over certain general assumptions when he considers

[1] O. Scheel. Dokumente zu Luthers Entwicklung. Tübingen, 1929, No. 165.
[2] O. Scheel. Martin Luther. Tübingen, 1921, vol. ii. 64.
[3] W.A.Br. 2.42.24. (Feb. 1520).

matters beyond his own exact knowledge. Yet it is needful for the
soul's health of any culture that there should exist places where these
assumptions may be roughly handled. Above all, it would seem that
Universities might be centres of vigorous and unremitting self criticism,
where there are few closed questions, and where at any time a case
may be heard afresh, if it can reasonably be shown that evidence has
been ignored, or that new facts have been brought to light.

There are reasons why a good deal of received academic opinion
should be unfriendly towards Martin Luther. There is the modern
reaction against the judgments of the Victorian Age, not least among
those who have shed the Protestantism of their fathers. The virile
theological tradition deriving from the Oxford Movement has made
great and positive theological contributions to English religion, but
from the time of Hurrell Froude onwards, its "blind spot" has been
a rigid, narrow and wooden hostility towards the Reformers and their
works. Then there is the tradition of the liberal historians with their
wistful preference for a Reformation "along Erasmian lines" which,
they consider, might have been, but for the violent intervention of
Luther and his friends. To the liberal historians and theologians, aloof
from theology and dogma, Martin Luther could hardly be a congenial
figure. The events of our generation have hardly disposed us to a
sympathetic judgment of the course of German history, and made only
too plausible the arguments of those who derive all our ills from the
Reformation, and not a few from the influence of Martin Luther.

The case for the reconsideration of Luther is that all these judgments,
good or ill, rest upon an insufficient consideration of facts. Of the
many thousands of Luther's writings, hardly more than a score have
been available in English throughout the greater part of four centuries.
There has been little awareness of the problems and discoveries of
modern Luther study which both in detail and in principle have been
of a quality and intricacy high among historical disciplines, second only,
it may be, to that of Biblical criticism.

Reconsideration must not prejudge the issue. It must be confessed
that so much of the writing about Luther in four centuries has been
polemical that it is very difficult not to be on the defensive, or offensive,
about him. When Protestants admit faults, and Catholics virtues, in
his character, these concessions are bound to be taken from their
context and used for polemical purposes. Yet we have the soundest
reasons for supposing that an infallible Luther is no part of any Protestant confession. It was a disciple of Melanchthon, Joachim Camerarius,
who wrote, "Those who count it a reproach to great and famous people
when anything blameworthy is found in them, have too soft a con-

ception of the position of such people. For only God has this privilege, to be without a fault: human nature is not capable of it." When we have confessed that loyalty and party judgment are inevitably involved, we must face more formidable difficulties. There is first, the vastness of the material to be mastered. Let him who would write a history of the sixteenth century sit down and count the cost, whether he be able to finish, and let him remember the succession of scholars, P. S. Allen, Charles Beard, Heinrich Denifle, Preserved Smith, who have left broken monuments. A sound historical background: familiarity with secular and ecclesiastical history, and with dogmatic theology, including a more than nodding acquaintance with late scholasticism: a knowledge of Protestant theology in its origin and development. These are essential preliminaries. Then, leaving out of account secondary studies (in half a dozen languages) which run into thousands, there remain the works of Luther himself.

We know that at the Diet of Worms, the Emperor Charles V and the Papal Nuncio, Aleander, were reluctant to believe that the pile of Luther's works heaped before them could have been the work of one man in a few months. Yet that man continued to produce something like a treatise a fortnight over the next twenty-five years. As the great Weimar edition with ninety-four folio volumes draws within sight of completion,[1] we admire a feat of theological engineering, but we remember that such engineering achievements are never finished, always under repair, and that often the beginning is in need of amendment while the work is being finished. So it seems to be with the works of Luther. Dr. K. A. Meissinger reports upwards of 1400 important textual misreadings in vol. 3 (Dictata super Psalterium), and at least vols. 1, 4 and 9 appear to need similar thorough revision.[2]

If the historian has a mass of material of undoubted authenticity, there is a penumbra which is his titillation and despair. There are many volumes of sermons and lectures by Luther which we possess only in their reported form, and some, like a great part of the Genesis commentary, were published only after Luther's death. The historian is constantly tempted to have his cake, and eat it. But if he rejects the "Sermon on Marriage" (1519) for the sound reason that it is a pirated version very strongly repudiated by Luther, then he has also to admit that Luther did not sponsor the most famous of all sayings attributed to him, the famous "Hier stehe ich: ich kann nicht anders." [3]

Above all, there is the nice problem of the Table Talk. One hardly

[1] R. Jauernig. Die Weimarer Lutherausgabe. Zeichen der Zeit, 1952, 56 ff.
[2] Th. Lit. Z., 1948. Nr. 3.170.
[3] Mackinnon. Luther, ii. 302, n.

knows whether to be grateful or not for that hospitality of Luther which allowed a motley club of inferior Boswells to frequent his table, and that their garbled remembrances have, in sundry portions and in divers manners, been transmitted to posterity. We know how it irked Frau Luther to play Martha to half a dozen male Marys who made Luther talk while the food got cold. And we know how they intruded into the most domestic privacies, as in that solemn hour when Luther's beloved Magdalena lay dying in her father's arms. But they were all made welcome: the Wittenberg theologians as and when they could come: including, of course, the Melanchthons, though Frau Luther seldom could forget that while she was a Von Bora, Frau Melanchthon was the daughter of a small town mayor. There came travelling scholars and distinguished refugees, and the students. And then, from 1530 onwards, the reporters. Cordatus perhaps, seven years the senior of Luther, irascible and ungracious, a teutonic Crawley of Hogglestock: or the melancholy Schlaginhaufen, always in the dumps, but who softened Kate Luther's tongue because, really, he was wonderful with the children. And Mathesius, that enterprising young usher who smuggled some of his pupils to Luther's table until the master of the house decided that this was a little too much, even for Liberty Hall.

It is very tantalizing. Here is richly personal material, offering again and again to fill critical gaps in our knowledge. We are tempted to select what suits us, and to complain when others do the same. Moreover, while the conscious mind may reject testimony, or suspend judgment, the mind is subtly influenced by reading. Not that we need to be too sceptical. Enough of the real Luther has got into even the most dubious collections. But on the whole it is safer to use the Table Talk to confirm rather than to establish, and not to use it as a sufficient source for Luther's exact words or technical vocabulary. Modern research has established a pedigree of the sources, and brought to light some of the original note-books, so that the Weimar edition has a careful compilation in six volumes.[1] But there it all is: letters, sermons, tracts, commentaries, polemic, Table Talk providing material so heterogeneous that select quotation can support the most varied and opposite interpretations.

Luther's method aggravates the difficulty. In a preface to the Book of Exodus Luther has words about Moses, and his apparent inconsistencies, which apply also to himself. "Moses writes as the case demands, so that his book is a picture and illustration of government and life. For this is what happens when things are moving . . . now

[1] Preserved Smith. Luther's Table Talk. (A Critical Study.) Columbia Univ., 1907.

this work has to be done, and now that . . . and a man must be ready every hour for anything, and do the first thing that comes to hand. The books of Moses are mixed up in just this way." [1] Luther's writing is invariably called forth by a concrete, particular historical occasion: he had neither the leisure nor the talent to produce a systematized text-book, after the manner of the "Loci Communes" of Melanchthon, or the "Institutes" of Calvin. When we consider how for Luther, as for Moses, things were moving (between 1517 and 1546), we need not wonder that historians and theologians have found it hard to reconcile apparent differences, or driven wedges between various sections of his life.

Then there is the difficulty of Luther's personal character. When Frederick the Wise met Erasmus at Cologne in November 1520 and asked for a plain judgment on Luther, he got instead an enigmatic epigram which drove him to complain, "What a wonderful little man that is! You never know where you are with him." That kind of reticence was completely foreign to Luther, about whom even his enemy Duke George had to admit "those people at Wittenberg are at least not mealy-mouthed. They do say what they really mean, frankly and straightforwardly." The result is that for good and ill, what Luther thought came straight out, and his few attempts to be subtle, or to restrain himself, usually ended in tragi-comedy. Like St. Jerome, Luther had a physical excuse, especially in his last years, for his tantrums. But some of his best, as well as his worst, writing was done in the heat of righteous anger. When his blood was up, he would charge into battle, and when he did, his pen was not so much a sword as the spiked club with which Holbein pictures him as the Hercules Germanicus. And when the first impetus had spent itself, sheer pig-headedness might keep him going, while on such occasions he delighted to greet the scared expostulations of his timid friends with something really shocking. For he was a thorough polemic divine, and not Rabelais or Sir Thomas More had more violent and varied ways of calling a spade a spade. His sense of humour was elephantine, large and clumsy, and since it was often misunderstood by his contemporaries, it can be imagined what a mine of potential misconception it bequeathed to owl-like theologians fumbling with what is called "the jocular element in Luther."

There is a good deal in the controversial writings of Luther which repels and disgusts, and polemic has made the most of it.[2] Yet to

[1] W.M.L., vol. 6.373.
[2] The problem is not to be disposed of by speaking of the general coarseness of the age, but a picture like Brueghel's " Flemish Proverbs " is a striking illumination of common proverbial speech in the sixteenth century.

concentrate the muck in a few pages is to give a completely false impression. Certainly the Luther of the polemical writings is not the whole Luther. We must turn elsewhere to find the surprising reticences, the unexpected mildness, the swift contritions, and the melancholy so close related to his fun. He had no sympathy with the obscenities of humanist literature.

Finally, there is the whole matter of the Reformation. We read our Luther according to our interpretation of the sixteenth century. "Luther apart from the Reformation would cease to be Luther," wrote Hare. "His work was not something external to him. . . . It was his own very self, that grew out of him, while he grew out of his work. Wherefore they who do not rightly estimate the Reformation cannot rightly understand Luther." [1] But "rightly to understand the Reformation" is a great complexity.

The distinction is capital between the historical Luther—what Luther was, and did, and said: and the Luther myth—what men have believed he said, and did, and was. The historical Luther made an abiding impress on European history, and the story of the Western Church. But what men have believed about Luther throughout four centuries is itself a "factor in modern history." And the Luther of this creative tradition is a different Luther from the figure with whom a modern historian grapples from within an elaborate critical apparatus. The modern historian is confronted with the whole range of Luther's writings, but over most of four centuries very much of this material has been inert, dormant, unknown to more than a tiny band of scholars. Those early Latin commentaries, so precious to modern scholarship, were unheeded for many generations, and their influence on history has been far less than the garbled collection of Aurifaber's Table Talk, with its numerous editions and translations. Nobody can weigh imponderables, but it is possible that "Eyn feste Burg" and the little Catechism have influenced history more profoundly than all the rest of Luther's writings. And we have not only to ask what men read of Luther, but we have to remember what they neglected. We have to ask not only how well they understood him, but where they misunderstood him. Leaving on one side the perennial question whether Melanchthon is the great expositor or perverter of the legacy of Martin Luther, there is much evidence that generations of Court chaplains expounded Luther's doctrine of "Obrigkeit" for the benefit of Protestant Princes and their subjects in a way which disastrously over-simplified Luther's profound and subtle teaching, and with far-reaching practical result. Thus the Luther myth, of legend and of caricature,

[1] Julius Hare. Vindication of Luther, 1855, p. 3.

many-sided, taking form and colour from the changing mental environment, has itself become a creative historical force. No interpretation of Luther can afford to ignore what Lutherans have believed about Martin Luther.[1]

At the close of his great history of dogma, which he conceived to have been brought to an end by Luther, Adolf Harnack wrote, "Catholicism is not the Pope, neither is it the worship of saints, or the Mass, but it is the slavish dependence on tradition, and the false doctrines of sacrament, of repentance and of faith." [2] But in Luther's own estimate of his work, the Pope occupied a more important place, to which the famous epitaph of the Reformer bears witness:

"Pestis eram vivus, moriens ero mors tua, papa." [3]

If we are to understand Luther's violence against the papacy we must treat this inscription seriously, and recognize that for the sixteenth century Lutherans, Luther and the Pope are "apocalyptic figures within the action of the history of salvation." [4]

Luther prided himself on the fact that while others had attacked the manners and the morals of particular popes, or the abuses and corruptions of the Curia, he had begun with doctrine. We know that in its essentials Luther's theology existed before the opening of the Church struggle in 1517, and that it was not an improvization devised in the course of that conflict. Nevertheless, it was as the conflict developed out of the Indulgence controversy that he began to question the basis of the Papal power, and turned to the issues raised in a preceding generation by the theologians of the Conciliar movement, the question whether the Papacy were of divine or of human institution. Early in 1519 he could still write "If unfortunately there are such things in Rome as might be improved, there neither is, nor can be, any reason that one should tear oneself away from the Church in schism. Rather, the worse things become, the more a man should help, and cling to her, for by schism and contempt nothing can be mended." [5] In fateful weeks before the Leipzig Disputation, Luther studied church history

---

[1] In the next pages I have borrowed heavily from the valuable survey by E. W. Zeeden. Martin Luther und die Reformation im Urteil des deutschen Luthertums Freiburg, 1950. Also E. Wolf. Luthers Erbe? Ev. Theol., Aug. 1946, 82-115. Nov. 310-312. E. Wolf. Th. Lit. Z., 1951, 271. H. Stephan. Luther in den Wandlungen seiner Kirche, 1951.
[2] A. Harnack. History of Dogma, vol. 7, p. 265 (Eng. Tr.).
[3] " Living I was thy plague, dying I shall be thy death, O Pope." The lines probably derive from Luther himself, though they do not appear on the epitaph until 1572. Cf. Schubart. Die Berichte über Luthers Tod und Begräbnis. Weimar, 1917, p. 127, n. The couplet is printed in a broadsheet which was in circulation in 1547, and a copy may be seen in the Museum of the Public Record Office in London.
[4] Zeeden, p. 27.
[5] Unterricht auf etliche Artikel. W.A. 2.72.35.

and the papal decretals. On 13th March 1519 he wrote to his friend Spalatin, "I do not know whether the Pope is Anti-Christ himself, or only his apostle, so grievously is Christ, i.e. Truth, manhandled and crucified by him in these decretals." [1]

The Leipzig Disputation forced Luther to face the implications of his revolt, and made him realize that he could not come so far, without going further in repudiation of papal authority. Then, early in 1520, he read Hutten's edition of Valla's exposure of the " Donation of Constantine," and he wrote in disgust, "I have hardly any doubt left that the Pope is the very Anti-Christ himself, whom the common report expects, so well do all the things he lives, does, speaks, ordains, fit the picture." [2]

In June 1520 he wrote solemn, final words, in a writing of exceptional vehemence. "Farewell, unhappy, hopeless, blasphemous Rome! The wrath of God is come upon thee, as thou deservest. . . . We have cared for Babylon, and she is not healed: let us leave her then, that she may be the habitation of dragons, spectres and witches, and true to her name of Babel, an everlasting confusion, a new pantheon of wickedness." [3]

There are battles of the mind which most men cannot go on fighting again and again. We make up our minds, as we say, and the account is settled. Thereafter we reopen that particular issue only with great reluctance. No doubt this is a weakness of our spirit, though to be able to keep an open mind requires perhaps detachment from the hurly-burly of decision, and is more easily achieved in academic groves than in the battlefield or market-place or temple. Luther's words here perhaps show us the point at which he hardened his mind with terrible finality against the Papacy, as later on he reached a point at which Zwingli and Erasmus were to him as heathen men and publicans. He had become convinced that the Papacy had become the tool of the Devil, that it was blasphemous . . . "possessed and oppressed by Satan, the damned seat of Anti-Christ." [4]

The papacy which Luther attacked was not the Post-Tridentine papacy. On the other hand, he meant something more when he called it "Anti-Christ" than we mean by the adjective "Anti-Christian." Like many great Christians from St. Cyprian to Lord Shaftesbury, Luther believed himself to be living in the last age of the world, on the very edge of time. He believed that the papacy was toppling to

---

[1] W.A.Br. 1.359.29. On Luther's preoccupation in these months with the relation of Truth, Christ and the Church, see E. Vogelsang. Unbekannte Fragmente aus Luthers Zweiter Psalmenvorlesung. 1518. Berlin, 1940, 17ff.
[2] W.A.Br. 2.48.26.
[3] W.A. 6.329.17.
[4] Adversus execrabilem Antichristi bullam. W.A. 6.604.27.

its doom, and that this fate was a merited judgment upon a perversion of spiritual power to which there could be no parallel in the temporal realm, and for which only one category would serve, the Biblical category of Anti-Christ.

There are striking words in his "Of Good Works" (1520) which go to the root of this conviction. "There is not such great danger in the temporal power as in the spiritual, when it does wrong. For the temporal power can do no harm, since it has nothing to do with preaching and faith, and the first three commandments. But the spiritual power does harm not only when it does wrong, but also when it neglects its duty and busies itself with other things, even if they were better than the very best works of the temporal power."[1] For Luther the blessed thing for men and institutions is that they should be where God intends them, doing what God has called them to do, and the cursed thing for men and institutions is when they run amok in God's ordered creation, going where God has not sent them,[2] and occupied with other things than their divine vocation.

The papacy had become entangled in diplomatic, juridical, political, financial pressure. Its crime was not that these things were necessarily bad in themselves, but that for their sake the awful supreme, God-given task of the pastoral care and the cure of souls had been neglected and forsaken. Two consequences had followed. In the first place, it had become a tyranny, like any other institution which succumbs before the temptation of power. In that exposition of the Magnificat, which was interrupted by the famous journey to Worms in 1521, Luther had profoundly diagnosed this corrupting effect of power upon institutions. The tract embodies Luther's reflections upon the fate of great Empires in the Bible and in secular history. It is not empire, but the abuse of it which is wrong. "For while the earth remains authority, rule, power . . . must needs remain. But God will not suffer men to abuse them. He puts down one kingdom, and exalts another: increases one people and destroys another: as he did with Assyria, Babylon, Persia, Greece and Rome, though they thought they should sit in their seats forever."[3]

But when empire is abused, then power becomes an incentive to arrogance, and a terrible inflation begins. These institutions or individuals swell and stretch their authority with a curious bubble-like, balloon-like quality. Outwardly they seem omnipotent, and those who take them at their face value can be paralysed and brought into

[1] W.M.L. 1.263.
[2] W.A. 56.349.15. "Sic enim diabolus omne ingenium versat, ut vocationem uniuscujusque irritam faciat et ad id sollicitet seducendo, ad quod vocatus non est, quasi stultus sit Deus aut ignorans, quo eum vocare voluerit."
[3] W.M.L. 3.183.

C

bondage to them. But in fact they are hollow shams, corroded from within, so that doom comes upon them, that swift collapse so often the fate of tyrants and empires. "When their bubble is full blown, and everyone supposes them to have won and overcome, and they feel themselves safe and secure, then God pricks the bubble . . . and it is all over . . . therefore their prosperity has its day, disappears like a bubble, and is as if it had never been." [1] It is interesting that Shakespeare turns to the same metaphor when he describes the fall of Wolsey:

> "I have ventured,
> Like little wanton boys that swim on bladders,
> This many summers in a sea of glory,
> But far beyond my depth: my high blown pride
> At length broke under me." [2]

Luther is fond of punning on the double meaning of the Latin word "Bulla," which means bubble, but also the papal bull.[3]

It may well be that Luther's meditation on this quality of tyranny derives from his own experiences, 1517-20. The initial threat of excommunication, and the final promulgation of the papal bull had a deep significance for him. These were the challenge which focussed all his doubts and fears, and evoked his courage at a time when he had no reason to anticipate anything but the dire fate prophesied for him by friends and foes. But, in fact, these papal sanctions led to the revelation of the weakness of the papal authority, a revelation of immense significance, from which all over Christendom (not forgetting the England of Henry VIII) men could draw their own conclusions. It was not that a man could defy the papacy and get away with it. After all, Wyclif had died in his bed, and throughout most of the Middle Ages there were parts of Europe where heresy flourished openly. But there was a new background which echoed and reverberated Luther's defiance, and a concentration of public attention on it which rallied great historical forces.

For centuries the papal sanctions had been as thunder and lightning, and there had been times and places when princes and peoples had cowered before them. Even now the sonorous phrases, the hallowed ritual, did not lack of menacing effect and struck deep into Luther's mind, always hypersensitive to words. The extraordinary agitation of his sermon, "On the Power of Excommunication" (1518), an utterance so outspoken that it was perhaps more effectual than the Ninety-five

---

[1] W.M.L. 3.179.
[2] Henry VIII, Act III, Sc. ii.
[3] W.M.L. 2.241. "This manner of life has no warrant in Scripture . . . but is puffed up solely by the bulls (and they truly are "bulls") of human popes (solis hominum pontificum bullis, et vere bullis est inflatum)." Also W.A. 5.278.24 (1519-21).

Theses in securing his impeachment, reveals the tension in his mind. It is noticeable that in the printed elaboration of this sermon he turns to the "bladder" motif. "They say . . . our Ban must be feared, right or wrong. With this saying they insolently comfort themselves, swell their chests, and puff themselves up like adders, and almost dare to defy heaven, and to threaten the whole world: with this bugaboo they have made a deep and mighty impression, imagining that there is more in these words than there really is. Therefore we would explain them more fully, and prick this bladder which with its three peas makes such a frightful noise." [1] The publication of the Bull in 1520 evoked the same tension, and in his writings against it he affirms, "The Truth is asserting itself and will burst all the bladders of the Papists." [2]

Only gradually did Luther and his friends realize how the world had changed since the days of Huss, that the Diet of Worms would not be as the Council of Constance, though the devout Charles V might be as anxious to dispose of heretics as any Emperor Sigismund. Now the accumulated weight of the past intervened, with paralysing effect. An enormous moral prestige had been frittered away, and the papal authority was revealed as a weak thing in comparison with the deep moving tide of anti-clericalism, nationalism and the fierce energies of a changing society.

But the papacy is for Luther not simply a tyranny, which can be described, as a liberal historian might describe it, in terms of the corrupting influence of power. Its tyranny is of a unique kind, for which there can only be one category, the demonic, Biblical category of Anti-Christ. By its entanglement with law and politics, the papacy has brought the souls of men and women into bondage, has confused disastrously the Law and Gospel, has become the antithesis of the Word of God which comes to free and liberate men's souls. Thus he cannot regard the papacy simply as a corrupt institution, as did the mediaeval moralists and the heretics.[3] In Luther's later writings the papacy is included along with the Law, Sin and Death among the tyrants who beset the Christians, and is part of a view of salvation which demands an apocalyptic interpretation of history.

Two sets of Luther's writings are of special virulence: those against the Jews, the apostates of the Old Israel, and those against the Pope, the apostate of the New. Against what he considered the capital sin of blasphemy Luther turned all his invective. It is noticeable that like Ezekiel, he turned to an imagery of physical repulsion. Blasphemy and

---

[1] W.M.L. 2.43-4.   [2] W.A. 6.590.13.
[3] G. Jacob. Der Gewissensbegriff in der Theologie Luthers. Tübingen, 1929, 55-64. W.A. 40.1.178. "We oppose the Pope, not as Müntzer does 'propter personam' but 'propter Deum.'"

apostasy are not simply evil: they are filthy things, which must be
described in language coarse enough and repulsive enough to nauseate
the reader. That is not in any sense to excuse Luther's language, or
to justify his reading of the papacy. But those sadly over-simplify
who see in these tracts the vapourings of a dirty mind.

Luther's epitaph was premature. He had indeed plagued the papacy.
He could say, "While I slept or drank Wittenberg beer with my Philip
and my Amsdorf, the Word so greatly weakened the Papacy that never
Prince or Emperor inflicted such damage on it." [1] He did not kill the
papacy, but in strange partnership with Ignatius Loyola, the Popes of
the Counter-Reformation, the Society of Jesus, not to mention the
Anabaptists, he had provoked a new historical pattern which made an
end, for good and all, of the peculiar perversions of the later Middle
Ages. But I think we can understand how it seemed to him that the
papacy was doomed and dying, how it seemed to him the engine of
Satan, the embodiment of Anti-Christ in what he believed to be the
closing act of the human drama.[2]

If the papacy belongs to the dramatic, dualistic, apocalyptic view of
history, the rôle of Luther himself belonged to the same setting. It is
the rôle commemorated in a Saxon medal of the period:

"Mart. Luther. Elias ultimi saeculi." [3]

It goes back to the moment when Melanchthon broke the news of
Luther's death to the students at Wittenberg with "Alas, gone is the
horseman and the chariots of Israel." [4]

For this first generation (which included the first sketches of Luther's
career by Melanchthon, Bugenhagen, Jonas, Mathesius), Luther is,
as for Coelius, " a veritable Elijah and a John the Baptist, whom God
has sent before the Great Day." Both Melanchthon and Mathesius
drew upon Luther's own interpretation of history, the conception of
the "Wundermann," the inspired hero, and the theme of the Word
going forth conquering and to conquer. For Melanchthon, Luther
stands within a long succession which began with the patriarchs and

[1] W.M.L. 2.399.
[2] H. Obendiek. Der Teufel bei Martin Luther. Berlin, 1931, 253.
[3] Spalatin had likened Luther to Elijah as early as 1522. Schubart. Berichte über
Luthers Tod, 125-6. See also the hymn of N. Hermann (1561):

" Elias vor dem jüngsten Tag
Soll wiederkommen auf Erden,
Dass er der bösen Welt absag,
Dass Christus kommen werde.
Aber der teure Gottesmann
Hat sich längst hören und sehen lahn,
Drum ist das End nicht ferne."

2 Kings 2[12].

which includes the great Fathers of the Church, men sent by God, one after another, "just as those who fall in an order of battle, are replaced by others." [1]

We should expect, that as the contemporaries of Luther passed from the scene, there should be a diminishing sense of the personality of the Reformer. The change was accelerated by the fact that the Lutheran Churches were now fighting for their existence, and finding a dogmatic norm in their great Confessional Documents (which included the Catechisms, and the Schmalkaldic Articles of Luther). The result was an emphasis upon those confessional documents and upon the pure doctrine to which they witnessed which led in the seventeenth century to a remarkable neglect of the writings of Luther himself. This was the period of fierce dogmatic strife between disparate elements within the Lutheran tradition, evoking Shakespeare's reference to "spleeny Lutherans," and reaching comedy when Cyriacus Spangenberg interpreted Luther's famous hymn:

> "Erhalt uns, Herr, bei deinem Wort,
> Und steur des Papsts und Türken Mord "

to mean "all our enemies are to be understood by these two titles (Papists and Turks) . . . Interimists, Adiaphorists, Sacramentarians, Anabaptists, Calvinists, Osiandrists, Schwenckfeldists, Stancarists, Servetianists, Sabbatarians, Davidists, Majorists, Synergists, etc., etc."!

The emphasis is exemplified by the famous phrase on a coin of Joachim II (1564):

> "Gottes Wort und Luthers Lehr
> Wird vergehen nimmermehr."

Luther's teaching, reflected by the Confessions, became more important than Luther. "He acquired his own stereotyped work, which belonged to him, like the Wheel of St. Catherine, or the Dragon of St. George. . . . He lost his individual proportions and grew into the superhuman and mythical . . . the greatness of his work pushed him into the background." [2]

The polemic of the Counter Reformation did useful service in preventing the Luther myth from escaping altogether from its connection with history. A century after the beginning of the Reformation Johann Gerard disputed with Becanus and Bellarmine about the "Vocation of Luther" and had to admit the test of accuracy "if Luther's writings can be shown to be lying, erroneous and false, then we shall at once recognize that Luther was no prophet." [3] But if Lutheran orthodoxy exalted the Luther myth, and dangerously elevated dogmatic orthodoxy by the side of Holy Scripture, these limitations must not be pressed

[1] Zeeden, p. 31. A. L. Drummond. German Protestantism since Luther. London. 1951, 1 ff.
[2] Zeeden, p. 69.   [3] Ibid. p. 91.

too far. When all is said and done, there is very much to be said for
the modern verdict that "this view of Luther is one-sided. But it is
also profound and religious, and perhaps with all its one-sidedness, it
comes fundamentally closer to the real Luther than all the modern
'Luther Renaissance' with its many-sided source criticism, and refined
historical and psychological methods. For the orthodox view of Luther
in the seventeenth century did remain in an unbroken tradition of
faith, with the age of the Reformation." [1]

In the great "Historia Lutheranismi" of Veit Ludwig von Seckendorf (1626-92) we can sense a changing mood. He brought to the study
of Luther methods more genuinely historical than his predecessors, and
though he had no thought or desire to change the orthodox interpretation, he had deeply studied the Reformer's own writings, and been
impressed by Luther as a great religious person, and one whose greatness consisted in his "fides, agnitio veritatis, und pietas." [2] It was
natural that in an age of abortive ecumenical movements Seckendorf
should show a new sense of the evils wrought by the divisions within
the Christian world, but he held firmly to a view of Providence which
enabled him to see in the work of the Reformation not only "agente
Luthero, sed et hoc dirigente Deo." [3] The great Leibniz (1646-1716)
saw in Luther the champion of conscience, but he had little sympathy
with Luther's concern for what he regarded as trivial differences of
dogma. Philip Jacob Spener (1635-1705) heralds the advent of Pietism,
with the return to what in England was called "inward religion," and
a new emphasis on Biblical study and on philanthropic action. For
Spener, pure doctrine is replaced by pure faith, and Luther is the
champion of the freedom of conscience. Nevertheless, he could say,
"Though I rate Luther highly, I recognize he was a man, and I rate
him, far, far below the Apostles." [4]

Gottfried Arnold (1666-1714) broke new ground with a great history
of the Church and of the heresies, and turned attention to the young
Luther rather than the churchman of Luther's later years. He sharply
criticized the "subtle idolatry" of an exaggerated reverence for Luther
which sought to elevate him beyond criticism.[5] Johann Georg Walch
(1693-1775), by his editions of Luther's works, drew attention even
more sharply to the Luther of history, and prepared the way for an
assessment based upon the primary theological and historical documents. He, too, attacked the superstitious cult about Luther and denied
that he had any supernatural powers. "God gave him no gifts to work
miracles with. They were not necessary for the work he had to do." [6]

---

[1] Ibid. p. 100.   [2] Ibid. p. 119.   [3] Ibid. p. 123.
[4] Ibid. p. 155.   [5] Ibid. p. 178.   [6] Ibid. p. 215.

On the whole he gives a picture of a natural, and human Luther, a preference for the historical Luther as against the devout myth. Johann Salomo Semler (1725-91) anticipates the coming generation of the Enlightenment. He was far more enthusiastic about Erasmus than about Luther, and in fact found more in Luther to criticize than to praise. With Semler, the old apocalyptic view of Luther within the history of Salvation is finally dissolved, and the Reformer becomes a factor in modern history, in that developing story of human freedom which would have gone on, even had there been no Luther.[1]

For the thinkers of the succeeding age, Luther brought, not the light of the gospel, but the enlightenment of pure reason. Lessing (1729-81) was fascinated by Luther and in his later years thought of compiling a Luther Dictionary. For him Luther was the architect of freedom. "You have freed us from the yoke of tradition, from the unsupportable yoke of the dead letter." [2] For Frederick the Great, Luther was a "blustering" and a "raving monk," but also the man who freed the Fatherland. The eighteenth century loved to stress Luther's emphasis upon obedience, and his good citizenship. It was not a novel theme. The court chaplains of the Lutheran principalities had made the most of Luther's teaching about reverence for rulers with an effect which must be seriously pondered by those who discuss the influence of Luther upon modern German history. The eighteenth century went even further. Justus Möser (1720-94) gives us a very bourgeois Luther indeed, and speaks of this "peaceful man" who went about quietly preaching the true gospel. Johann Matthias Schröckh (1733-1808) saw a supreme fruit of the Reformation in the fact that "Religion is no more touched with any taint of revolution, and that the Rule of our Princes can be free from the orders and threats, the excommunications and unashamed tyranny of an Italian bishop: this is without doubt Luther's work." [3]

At the end of the eighteenth century stand two important figures. For Johann Gottfried Herder (1744-1803) Luther was "our heart quickening Luther . . . a true son of St. Paul." [4] Herder held a dynamic view of human history, and the story of Salvation dissolves into the world of self-contained historicism and progress. Luther becomes the founder of real freedom of thought and of religious individualism. "Simple, unlettered (!) Luther, how dear was the Word of God to you," he cried. Stronger than any previous writer, and perhaps ominous, is his patriotic emphasis, a kind of "Luther, thou shouldst be living at this hour, Germans have need of thee!" So he

---

[1] Ibid. p. 229.
[2] Ibid. p. 269.
[3] Ibid. p. 371.
[4] Ibid. p. 318.

apostrophized the Reformer. "Be yet the instructor of thy Nation, her prophet and her preacher . . . perhaps Germany will hear . . . Luther, thou! Great, misunderstood man." But despite Herder's reverence for Luther, whom he ranks with Gustavus Adolphus and Peter the Great (!), it is not the Reformation, but the processes of historical change which are his main concern.[1] For him the Christianity of dogma must yield to a free Christian spirit, as in the following remarkable dialogue, which English Christians will read with special interest:

> *Dietrich :* Luther. Alas, that the great man could not achieve that consummation devoutly to be wished, a Church of the Nation, a German Church !
>
> *Winnfried :* A German Church, Dietrich? That would have been unworthy of that great man. Look at what happened to the English Church under Henry VIII as to every other schismatic Church. She decayed, cut off from the living Body. But religion, the pure, free religion of conscience, reason and the heart, that is what Luther wanted to give his Germans . . . and has given them. . . .[2]

Very different is the return to the historical Luther in the work of Johann Georg Hamann (1730-88). He had been converted as a young man during the Evangelical Revival in London, and began to read the Scriptures with poignant intensity. Then, later, he turned to Luther first in the Jena edition and then in the edition by Walch. He soaked himself in the writings of Luther until he could write "Luther's writings are my staple reading . . . my pium desiderium! my ultimum visibile!" Like John Bunyan before him, Hamann found that his own experience seemed to have been anticipated in Luther's own struggles and discoveries. But if Hamann returned to certain elements in Orthodoxy and even in Pietism, there is a difference, and he looks forward to the developments of Luther interpretation in the nineteenth century.[3]

Thus between 1500 and 1800 the Luther myth had taken many forms, all related to the temper of their changing age, all profoundly affected by wider intellectual and even sociological pressures. But this very movement prevented an ossification of any one view of Luther, while the constant pressure of polemic forced Protestants back again and again to the Luther of history.

Catholic interpretation of Luther has also been many-sided, and without an extended survey of it, we may attempt to indicate the influence of it upon Luther study, not least by provoking Protestant theologians to jealousy, and forcing them again and again to more careful attention to the historical evidence.

Luther presents special problems to Catholics. It is unlikely that

---

[1] Ibid. p. 335.   [2] Ibid. p. 343.
[3] Ibid. p. 354. Drummond, 96-7. Th. Lit. Z., 1951, 275.

any Catholic scholar will write of him as sympathetically as M. Imbart de la Tour has written about Calvin. For Luther was a religious who apostatized, renouncing the most sacred vows, and he married a runaway nun. He initiated the most disastrous series of events in the history of the Western Church, and he attacked the most revered authorities, the most hallowed rites with outrageous and insulting vehemence. His teachings have been repeatedly and authoritatively condemned. A Catholic caricature of Luther was inevitable, and within a few years of his death the wildest stories were circulating, how in despair he had taken his own life, how his body had been snatched from the coffin by a whole posse of devils who had swept down upon the funeral procession. A more sober picture of Luther had been sketched during the Reformer's lifetime by a succession of his Catholic opponents. There was no doughtier champion of orthodoxy than the former humanist, Johannes Cochlaeus.[1] His "Commentaria de Actis et Scriptis Martini Lutheri" (1549) set the pace for Catholic interpretation of Luther in the succeeding generations. He dismisses, wistfully, the suggestion that Luther was "the offspring of an infernal spirit, in the form of an incubus,"[2] but he reports that as a novice, Luther had a wild look, said to be derived "from secret communion with a certain demon." Luther has plenty of vices, including the usual moral perquisites of heresy; pride, avarice, blasphemy. But on the whole Cochlaeus is not concerned with Luther's inner struggles and secret motives. For him the story begins with the Indulgence controversy. This he attributes to the plain venality of two Augustinians, Staupitz and Luther, against their successful rival, the Dominican Tetzel. Luther attacked Indulgences for the sake of forty-two guilders, with which he bought a new cowl. His doctrinal aberrations are a minor theme compared with the three great crimes, the rebellion against Rome, the apostasy from his vows, and his marriage with a former nun.[3]

---

[1] Adolf Herte. Das katholische Lutherbild im Bann der Lutherkommentare des Cochlaeus. Münster, 1943. 3 vols. This work is a counterpart to E. W. Zeeden's survey of Protestant writing on Luther. Herte presents the results of an analysis of some 500 Catholic books on Luther and confirms our estimate of the normative influence of Cochlaeus. He states that almost the whole Catholic literature about Luther until well into the twentieth century is in a tradition made coherent by the work of Cochlaeus. In consequence he claims for it an importance in historiography greater than any other single work, Catholic or Protestant, including the famous sketches by Melanchthon and Mathesius. (Vol. 1, IX, XV).

[2] Historia Johannis Cochlaei de Actis et Scriptis Martini Lutheri. Paris, 1565, 1.

[3] For a sympathetic treatment of Cochlaeus see J. Lortz. Die Reformation in Deutschland. Freiburg, 1948, 261-3. Less sympathetic but extremely vivid is the description given of him by the English exiles, Roye and Barlow :

> " A littell pratye foolysshe poade
> But although his stature be small
> Yet men say he lacketh no gall."

> (Rede me and be not wroth, 43.)

The century of polemic which followed is perhaps the least edifying chapter in the long history of Christian controversy. The best that can be said of it is that it was a conflict of words, against a more sinister background of sticks and stones, and broken bones, and all the savagery of the Wars of Religion. Luther's successors borrowed more easily from his epithets than his theology, as regards the papacy, and the investigation of the history of the Roman Church which had begun with the English exile Robert Barnes, and his "Lives of the Popes," now included the gleanings of many Lutherans from the seamy side of church history, and a highly coloured version of the story of Pope Joan.[1] Within the Protestant states a generation was growing up which had been sheltered from first-hand knowledge of Catholic teaching, and amid the alarming successes of the Counter-Reformation the most extravagant libels and misstatements circulated, and handbooks such as the notorious "Bienenkorb" (1579) of John Fischart.

As often, the most bitter writing came from converts and apostates. In 1564 the Protestant court chaplain, Jerome Rauscher, emitted a volume entitled "One Hundred Select, Great, Shameless, Fat, Well-Swilled, Stinking, Papistical Lies," in which Popery was depicted with the diablerie, imagery and verve of a Jerome Bosch. To this replied a Catholic turned Lutheran turned Franciscan, John Nas.

Nas discovered within himself a fatal flair for religious Billingsgate, and produced a series of scurrilities (not without incitement and pro-vocation) which culminated in his "Anatomy of Lutheranism as it was instituted by the Devil." The importance of it lies in the fact that he quoted extensively from Luther's writings, and ended with a biograph-ical sketch of the Reformer. There followed a more formidable writing in this new genre, from the pen of Johann Pistorius, physician and counsellor to the Margrave of Baden. He claimed to have read all Luther's writings three times. From them he had collected not only every obvious impropriety of speech and metaphor, but everything that could in any way be pressed into a base interpretation. The result was the "Anatomy of Luther," of which the first part, some 550 pages, was published in Cologne in 1595.[2] He offered a dissection of Luther into the Seven Devils who had possessed him, and the first part dealt accordingly with the Spirits of Whoredom, Blasphemy and Lewdness. Each of the Three Spirits, in imitation of the Koran, was sub-divided into seven sections or "Alzoars." The work was greeted with howls of rage from the Protestants, who were not a little disconcerted at this assault upon the Luther legend by innumerable citations taken from

---

[1] Janssen. History of the German People. Eng. tr. Vol. 10.32.
[2] J. Pistorius. Anatomiae Lutheri. Pars Prima. Cologne, 1595. Janssen, 10.90-150.

the writings of Luther. It is perhaps the measure of the success of Pistorius that Protestant replies concentrated rather on the papal record than the explanation of Luther. Such was Huber's method in diagnosing the Devils (Swine Spirit, Goat Spirit and Hound Spirit) of the Papacy. It must be said that on both sides, Jesuits and Lutherans protested against such methods, which lapsed because, in the end, they were offensive to pious ears.[1]

In comparison, the writings of Becanus, Bellarmine and Bossuet seem restrained and were in fact concentrated upon weighty matters of theological controversy and historical interpretation. In the early nineteenth century John Adam Möhler produced an impressive critique of Protestant theology, from the angle of his own blend of Catholic orthodoxy and German idealism, in the famous "Symbolik" (1832).[2]

[1] This bitter seventeenth century polemic can almost be described in Hegelian dialectical terms as : Catholic work evoked Protestant counterblast, which in turn gave rise to another Catholic exposition. It is in the seventeenth century that what Cochlaeus left as hints and insinuations are developed by theologians and dignitaries into explicit claims. These centre in the traditional Billingsgate manner on Luther's parentage (e.g. his mother was a public bath attendant who had intercourse with a demon) : and on his probable end (that he died after a drunken orgy, in bed with a nun : that he committed suicide : that he died shamefully in the manner of Arius : that he was choked by the Devil) : and Luther's wife. It is strange that it should be the eighteenth century which should bring forth the worst libel about Katherine von Bora. The life of Katherine by Michael Kuen is a book in which, as Herte says, Catholic Luther literature touched its lowest depths. (Vol. 1.203.) In a century and a half of polemic, only the treatment of the Reformer by St. Francis of Sales bears the marks of charity rather than hatred.
[2] The Doctrine of the Unity of the Church in the Works of Khomyakov and Möhler. Bolshakoff. London, 1946, ch. 6. The "Symbolik" was translated into English by J. B. Robertson (1843) and has had some influence on English interpretation of Protestantism. The treatment of Luther by N. P. Williams (Ideas of the Fall and of Original Sin, 1927, 427-30) seems to be taken entirely from Möhler, but Williams makes inferences which Möhler was too careful to make. Thus : Möhler, 1.85. To Luther . . . the human race had lost an integral part of its spiritual existence : but . . . in man the opposite essence had been substituted in its room . . . and then evil was converted into something substantial ! . . . Luther here touched on the borders of Manichaeism if he did not actually overstep the frontier. Williams, 429. Luther . . . seems to infer that the annihilation of the moral and religious faculties of the soul must have been followed by the substitution in their place of . . . contrarily oriented powers . . . what might be called immoral or irreligious faculties . . . it is difficult to avoid the conclusion that Luther has plunged headlong into the abyss of Manichaeanism. Perhaps only in England could such sweeping generalizations have been extended on such slender basis of proof. In fact what Luther meant by using "substantia" in relation to "peccatum" he had made clear in his "Contra Latomum" (W.A. 8.36-128). See W.A. 8.77.8.19, 88.9 ff., esp. l. 15, "Substantiam hic accipio non more Aristotelis." Luther's problem was to affirm the positive character of sin against the "sophists" without falling back into Aristotelianism. (His own Nominalist background must be remembered when considering his conception of "substantia.") Lutheran orthodoxy came to reject even this use of "substantia" when it was carried to the point of heresy by Flacius Illyricus. E. Schlink. Theologie der lutherischen Bekenntnisschriften, 1946, 78-9. Dr. Williams' addition to Möhler is an apocryphal story about Luther, rejected by all reputable modern historians, which is then equated with the Damascus Road experience of St. Paul, and St. Augustine's in the Milanese garden, and offered as a clue to the whole religious development of Luther.

His colleague and half-rival, Dr. Döllinger, championed the traditional repudiation of Luther, but less harshly, for, as Lord Acton says, "he would not have the most powerful conductor of religion that Christianity has produced in eighteen centuries condemned for two pages in a hundred volumes." [1]

The new historical studies of the nineteenth century associated with the name of von Ranke produced on the Catholic side the massive "History of the German People at the close of the Middle Ages," by Johannes Janssen (1876). This was a work of great erudition which challenged Protestantism by offering a coherent and documented interpretation of the sixteenth century. It depicted the mediaeval Church with its own surging, vigorous life, aware of its inner weaknesses, but actively grappling with them, when disastrously interrupted by the Protestant Reformation. [2]

The Luther Jubilee of 1833 saw the launching of the definitive Weimar edition of Luther's works [3] (let it be accounted to them for righteousness—with the active patronage of a Prussian government, and a Hohenzollern Prince) and the inauguration of the Verein für Reformationsgeschichte. In the next few years a number of notable sources were printed, and technical studies from a growing number of scholars, including Köstlin, Enders, Brieger, Buchwald. [4] In 1899 Dr. Ficker began to edit Luther's Lectures on Romans (1515-16), a copy of which had been found in the Vatican, while by a freak of research, Luther's own manuscript was found publicly displayed in a case in the Royal Library in Berlin.

Into this amiable and optimistic concentration, there burst a bombshell, "Luther und Luthertum in der ersten Entwicklung" from the archivist of the Vatican, the Dominican Heinrich Denifle. [5] The detonator was in the sub-title "quellenmässig dargestellt." Not since the time of Pistorius had there been an attack on Luther by one deeply grounded in Luther's own writings, and Denifle had the advantage over Protestant scholars that he had been able to make use of the unpublished Lectures on Romans. "My sole source for the study of Luther was Luther," he declared. "At the outset I used no other

[1] Lord Acton, " Essays on Liberty," p. 396. Herte, ii. 244 ff., ii. 146 ff.
[2] Reu. Thirty-five Years of Luther Research. Chicago, 1917, ch. 1. H. Strohl. L'évolution religieuse de Luther. Strasbourg, 1922, 9. Herte, ii. 149 ff. C. Stange. Z. für Syst. Theol., 1943, 332.
[3] The Erlangen Edition of Luther's works (German works, 1826-57 : Latin works, 1829-86) preceded it.
[4] Reu, op. cit. Strohl, op. cit. W. Friedensberg. Fortschritte in Kenntnis und Verständnis der Reformationsgeschichte. (Ver. Ref. Ges., 1910.) O. Scheel. Die Entwicklung Luthers, 1910, 66 ff. Preserved Smith. Decade of Luther Study. Harvard Theol. Rev., 1921. J. P. Whitney. Reformation Essays, 1939, ch 3.
[5] Mainz, 1904.

exposition of Luther's life and teachings: those I studied only when my own conclusions were firmly established." [1] It would be mistaken to suppose that Denifle brought to this first-hand study an open mind. Later he was to see in his work a most needful protest against a dangerous eclecticism among Catholics and Protestants. "Once admit that Protestantism and Catholicism are two equally authorized religious convictions which are complementary in their inner life," he warned, "and which represent at the most two different aspects of the Christian life, then if one of the sides is heretical, so is the other." [2]

But at the outset his main business was simple, the demolition of the Luther legend. He thrust through that stained-glass window a fist as rough as Luther's own, and shattered it beyond repair.

It is difficult even to begin to describe a work which changed its plan between volumes, and even between editions, and was never intended as a biography. Yet Denifle's thesis was clear enough. He took a more serious view than Janssen of the plight of the late mediaeval Church. But he saw in it two currents, one of renewal and the other of decadence ("die Strömung der Erneuerung," "die Strömung des Niedergangs"), two strains corresponding to the Pauline dichotomy, "Spirit" and "Flesh." Luther, said Denifle, began in the stream of renewal, but passed over into the current of decadence, of which he became chief apostle. His great sin was pride, but it is well known that God visits on pride the judgment of fleshly sin, and pride led Luther to spiritual negligence, and then to gross intemperance and unchastity. Faced with moral failure, powerless to overcome temptation, Luther abandoned himself to the full tide of his passions. In this moral bankruptcy he fathered his own shortcomings on the Church, and in particular upon the monastic life. His attack on the Church, the lying legend he deliberately invented about the monastic life, was simply the projection of Luther's own diseased soul. Denifle pursued this thesis through one dissertation after another, but the climax of the work is the cry, "Luther, there is nothing of God in you!" The trouble is, that by the time Denifle has done with him, there is nothing of man in Luther either. His caricature, liar, blackguard, clown, sot, lecher, knave is a monster fit only for the records of criminal pathology.

Denifle counter-attacked with great gusto the "furor Protestanticus" which his work aroused. He had some great initial victories. His own vast knowledge of the Middle Ages, his own experience of the religious life was in striking contrast to the easy-going ignorance and misunderstanding of many Protestant scholars. Denifle was able to criticize

[1] Ibid., 26.
[2] Denifle. Luther. 2nd ed. Preface, xxxi-xxxiii. Ed. Paquier. Paris, 1910.

effectively the first volumes of the Weimar edition, and to show that the Commentary on Judges was not the work of Luther, but a collection of quotations from St. Augustine! Moreover, his marshalling of evidence made a reconstruction of the traditional view of Luther imperative. If Luther were not, as Denifle claimed, a deliberate liar, then the statements of Luther had to be reconciled with all the evidence which Denifle brought forward from the theologians of the mediaeval church. Unfortunately, Denifle did not stop there; if his handling of Luther was rough, his manners with Protestant scholars were deplorable.[1] He did not refrain from the most personal taunts at the "inferior mentality" of his opponents. He accused Harnack of disregard for truth in words more insulting than those with which Charles Kingsley called forth Newman's "Apologia." He concluded, "My defence has been too easy: the attacks of Harnack, Seeberg and others mark the bankruptcy of Protestant Science." [2] Denifle continued compiling learned appendices and planning new editions until the summer of 1905. He died at Munich on 10th June,[3] three days before he was due to receive an honorary degree at Cambridge in company with Paul Vinogradoff and Frederic Harrison. What should have been his encomium was printed as an obituary notice in the " University Reporter " for 17th June, and since in that notice the Public Orator explicitly, but discreetly, noticed his work on Luther, there was some ground for the Lutheran enquiry whether the degree was being granted because of the attack on Luther.[4] There can be no doubt of Denifle's great learning, his enduring services to scholarship worthy the most signal tributes, or of his complete integrity. Yet on the whole we may be thankful that Cambridge University did not sponsor the accuracy of his work on Luther.[5]

In fact, Denifle's work had been received by some Catholics with a coolness which moved him to indignant asperity.[6] The second edition of the work had some notable modifications and omissions. The editors of the French edition were constrained to add a series of footnotes which indicated growing embarrassment. There were two reasons. In 1908 W. Braun produced an important technical examination of Luther's use of the word "Concupiscentia," especially in the Lectures

[1] " More like the pamphlet of a violent contemporary than a serious history." (P. Smith. Luther's Table Talk, p. 100.)
[2] Denifle. Ed. Paquier, 4.124.
[3] In his " Reformation Essays," 1939, p. 8, Dr. J. P. Whitney said that Denifle published his book while *en route* to Cambridge. This is corrected in the 1940 ed.
[4] CUR, 1905, 1113. " Martinum Lutherum ad fidem monumentorum nuper depictum."
[5] P. Vignaux. Luther Commentateur, p. 1. "Denifle a secoué . . . la somnolence des luthérologues; il a aussi posé avec force le problème des sources médiévales." Herte. Das katholische Lutherbild, ii. 328 ff.
[6] Denifle. Ed. Paquier. 1.xxix.

on Romans. Braun showed that Denifle had rightly drawn attention
to the great importance of this word for Luther, but that Denifle had
completely misinterpreted its real meaning, by confining its meaning
to sensual lust. More important, an enormous biography of Luther
had now appeared from the Jesuit, Hartmann Grisar. "In general,"
admitted Denifle's French editors, "Grisar is much less hard on Luther
than Denifle: he is the calm after the storm." [1]

Grisar demolished two major points in the thesis of Denifle. He was
not at all disposed to credit the tale of Luther's moral turpitude. He
stated emphatically that "the only arguments on which the assertions
of great inward corruption could be based, viz. actual texts and facts
capable of convincing anyone . . . simply are not forthcoming." [2] He
admitted that Denifle's interpretation of "concupiscence" would not
bear examination. "Nor does the manner in which Luther represents
concupiscence prove his inward corruption. He does not make it
consist merely in the concupiscence of the flesh." [3] He can pay tribute
to Luther's minor virtues, as when he admits that "Of Christian
Liberty" "does in fact present his wrong ideas in a mystical garb which
appeals strongly to the heart." [4]

Grisar dismisses and even goes out of his way to refute innumerable
fables and calumnies. But there are still very many which he is careful
to report at length, and one or two elderly calumnies into which he
contrives to breathe fresh life. Yet, on the whole, he may be said to
have done good service even in these cases by provoking more accurate
investigation. Thus, there was the old story that Luther's father had
killed a man, which led to investigation which showed that there were
two brothers Luther in Mansfeld, one Big Hans and the other Little
Hans. Protestants and Catholics, for what it is worth, may now reflect
equally on the truth that while Luther's father was an honest citizen,
his uncle was an unconscionable knave. [5]

Yet, as M. Strohl observes, "Grisar does not differ fundamentally
from Denifle." [6] Both writers speak of the Fall of Luther: and compared with that fact, the infralapsarian and supralapsarian divergences
are of secondary import. For Grisar propounded an alternative deni-
gration. He found the root of Luther's heresy in the Reformer's
hatred of good works, and in a domestic quarrel between the Observants ("the Little Saints") and the Conventuals within the Augustinian

[1] Denifle. Ed. Paquier. Vol. 2.5.
[2] Grisar. Luther. Eng. tr. London, 1913, vol. 1.111. G. Kawerau. Luther in
katholischer Beleuchtung. Ver. Ref. Ges., 1911. Herte, ii. 351 ff.
[3] Grisar, 1.112.   [4] Ibid. 2.28.
[5] Boehmer. Luther in the Light of Modern Research. London, 1930. App. C,
357 ff.   [6] H. Strohl, op. cit., 21.

order. "The real origin of Luther's teaching must be sought in a
fundamental principle . . . his unfavourable estimate of good works." [1]
"His estrangement from what he was pleased to call 'holiness by works'
always remained Luther's ruling idea, just as it had been the starting
point of his change of mind in his monastic days." [2] Thus, the cumu-
lative impression of Grisar's work is not much more flattering to Luther
than that of Denifle. Between them, Grisar and Denifle present a
documented indictment for which all students must be grateful. Anybody who cares to work through their thousands of pages will emerge
knowing that he has heard all that can plausibly be said against the
character and work of Martin Luther.

Since the publication of Grisar's Luther a generation of Luther study
of the most intensive kind has intervened. Moreover, the crowded
political events of those thirty years have made Christian men aware
of grim and deadly perils, and of deeper gulfs even than that which
separates Catholics and Protestants. These things account for the
change in method and temper displayed in "Die Reformation in
Deutschland," by Joseph Lortz.[3] The work is not a history of the
Reformation, as that is generally understood, but it is an extremely
interesting interpretation of the sixteenth century by one who has taken
into account what Protestant scholarship has to say. It is significant
that Lortz returns to an ancient Catholic view, put forward by Aleander
in 1520, that the really dangerous enemy to the Church was not Luther,
but Erasmus. Erasmus is for him "the culmination of the attractive
but disastrous Socratic error, that the Scholar is the Good Man, and
that with knowledge comes reform." [4] "With Erasmus—not with
Luther, the individual conscience comes to its destructive dominance
in the modern age." [5] He criticizes severely the superficiality of the
programme of theological simplification adumbrated in Erasmus's
"philosophy of Christ." He concludes, "Erasmus was the real threat
of dogmatic dissolution within the Church. Luther forced it rather
to confession. He called it to arms!"

Lortz has studied carefully what Lutheran scholarship has to say
about Luther. He will have nothing to do with the theory of moral
depravity. Of Luther's interpretation of his monastic career he says

---

[1] Grisar. Luther, 1.117.
[2] Ibid. vol. 4.450.
[3] 2 vols. Freiburg, 3rd ed., 1948.   [4] Vol. 1.126-8.
[5] Ibid. 128. Lortz provides, if it were needed, the refutation of that interpretation
of Luther in terms of egocentric individualism put forward by J. Maritain in " Three
Reformers " (1932). It is perhaps sufficient comment on that essay to observe the
author's naïve statement that he has gone for his facts to Grisar and Denifle, and
that he juggles with genuine and false portraits of Luther (a tactic which Denifle had
dropped after the first edition of his Luther).

"we no longer call this a pack of lies, as did Denifle," [1] and he concedes that "Luther's behaviour in the monastery until 1517 . . . was correct." [2] Lortz is concerned to stress the dogmatic uncertainty prevailing in the Church, especially in Germany, on the eve of the Reformation, and sees a sign of this in the hesitancy of the Universities and the humanists in condemning Luther's doctrines. To ascribe Luther's revolt to base motives would be, according to Lortz, grievously to under-estimate the depth of the tragedy of the Reformation. "In Luther's search for a gracious God he came to stand outside the Church without intending to do so. And it was no prearranged revolutionary pro-gramme, and no ignoble impulses and desires which led him to desire or seek a break with the Church." [3] He has severe words about the preoccupation of the curia with its own diplomacy and politics, and the levity with which those in Rome under-estimated the peril of heresy to the Church. In his criticism of Occamism, perhaps Lortz goes too far, and is hardly abreast of the more sympathetic studies by Ph. Böhner and P. Vignaux. More than any previous Catholic writer, Lortz recognizes the genius and originality of Luther. "Luther did not express many thoughts which have no parallel in earlier theologians and reformers. Nevertheless, Luther is new." [4] Even with regard to the vexed question of Luther's understanding of Rom. 1[17], he affirms "Luther discovered the saving Righteousness of God afresh. It was something new for himself." He pays repeated tribute to Luther's creative energy, to the vast, genial flood of his conceptions, unco-ordinated jumbles of paradox and insight, unrestrained and toppling over into the subjectivism and one-sidedness which are for him the key to Luther's error.[5] He shows rare appreciation of Luther's doctrine of assurance, "Luther's doctrine of assurance is not to be separated from his theology of the Cross. Only the epigoni have separated the two, or rather trodden under the profound theology of the Cross." [6]

Lortz has no doubt that Luther was justly condemned as a heretic. "But what earnestness! Luther had experienced the enormity of Sin in all its destructive fury, as few others have done. This consciousness of the reality of evil in the world becomes the centre of his thinking. . . . But what power! It is neither good scholarship, nor good Chris-tianity when one refuses to recognize this expressly, on the ground of his false dogmatic position." [7]

[1] Ibid. 419
[2] Ibid. 159, but see also 160.
[3] Ibid. 191.
[4] Ibid. 147.
[5] The charge of subjectivism ignores the christological setting of Luther's doctrine of Justification, and the magisterial doctrine of the Word.
[6] Ibid. 184.
[7] Ibid. 192.

D

Thus the Catholic interpretation of Luther has provoked, and been in turn affected by, the more accurate historical investigation of the historical sources. No doubt it will continue to benefit Luther study in this way.[1] Yet it may well be that its greatest service will be in clarifying the teachings of the doctors of the Conciliar Movement and of the "Via Moderna," by the preparation of those critical editions of texts, and learned monographs which are the indispensable basis of all interpretation. Already the essays and articles of P. Vignaux have proved how illuminating such studies may be, in a field where French Catholic scholarship displays its own superb clarity and genius.

But the "Luther Renaissance" is something richer and wider than the field of polemic and of controversy. It represents a concentration of historical criticism and theological interpretation around the focal point of Luther and his writings, to which there is no real parallel in English historical and theological investigation. It ranges from intricate discussion of textual criticism (as in the assessment of the Table Talk, or the discussion of the so-called "break-through" of Luther during the "Dictata Super Psalterium"), to the theological investigation of Luther's relation to the "Devotio Moderna" or to the Ockhamists, or the profound matter of Justification by Faith, or the issues raised by Luther's "De Servo Arbitrio." It is as though a field of English historical scholarship—say the constitutional studies of Maitland and Stubbs, or the chain of investigations into mediaeval constitutional development carried through by the Manchester school of history, were bound together with a coherent theological tradition like that deriving from the Oxford Movement. For "Luther Research" (Lutherforschung) and "Luther interpretation" (Lutherdeutung) have become inseparable in modern times. For good and ill, moreover, no single person dominates the English sixteenth century scene as does Luther in Germany. So that there is no English subject which, like Luther in Germany, can attract to itself a whole network of related subjects, turning sixteenth century Reformation history and theology into something like a vast "project," as that word is used in educational theory. That is why the best English parallel to Luther study is to be found, not in specialized historical work, but in Biblical theology and Biblical criticism (not always recognized by professional historians

[1] Dr. J. Hessen in " Luther in katholischer Sicht," 1949, goes even further than J. Lortz in his appreciation of Luther, whom he calls the " greatest of the spiritual sons of St. Augustine." He defends Luther from the charge of subjectivism and, like Lortz, rejects the polemical caricatures of Denifle and Grisar. Dr. Hessen's work is a remarkable instance of how far an eirenical and ecumenical intention can bring Catholics into awareness of and appreciation of the prophetic greatness of Luther and his work.

as presenting an exacting field demanding all the standards and canons of historical discipline). For it is here, too, that the range of investigation leads from textual criticism to the evaluation of historical evidence, while at the same time forming part of a whole nexus of theological interpretation. The quest of the historical Jesus, and the attempt to separate historic Christianity from creative Christian tradition, have real parallels in the problems of Luther study. Finally, it may be said that modern Luther studies have been astonishingly varied, and freed from the rigidities of any particular interpretation. To say that German scholars have never been afraid to differ from one another will be recognized as an understatement. But there has been untold value in this ferment of discussion and criticism.

In the nineteenth century the great theologians kept pace with "Luther research." Schleiermacher is said to have stimulated the study of Luther.[1] The theological studies of the Erlangen theologian, Hofmann, by refusing to be bound to the canons of Lutheran orthodoxy, anticipated a good deal of modern interpretation. The two volumes of Theodosius Harnack, "Luthers Theologie" (1862), have enduring value by reason of their deep sensitiveness to certain of Luther's doctrines. Their great limitation is a use of the sources now completely outmoded by modern critical apparatus. Moreover, Harnack abandoned the attempt to find a coherent unity in Luther's thought, and Wolff says of the second volume, on Luther's doctrine of Redemption, that "this book points backwards not forwards":[2] its view of Luther's doctrine of Atonement is now generally seen to be defective. It was Harnack's opponent Ritschl who encouraged historical investigation of Luther, though his own emphasis on the primacy of the ethical motive dominated and perverted his own evaluation of Luther. Reinhold Seeberg, the "learned but colourless"[3] historian of dogma, has been said to represent a synthesis of the legacy of idealism with that of Luther, and to have imported his own "transcendentalism" into the thought of the Reformer. For Adolf Harnack, Luther meant the end of the history of dogma. Luther's faith meant the dissolution of that Hellenization of Christianity which had banefully begun with the Apostolic Age. "In Luther's Reformation, the old dogmatic Christianity was discarded and a new evangelical view was substituted for it."[4] Harnack was not

---

[1] F. Kattenbusch. "Hundert Jahre," Th. St. und Kr., 1927-8, xiv. For a less favourable estimate of the influence of Schleiermacher, O. Wolff, Haupttypen der neueren Lutherdeutung. Stuttgart, 1938. Stephan, 68 ff.
[2] O. Wolff, 63 ff.
[3] E. Wolf. Luthers Erbe. Ev. Theol., 1946, 93.
[4] A. Harnack. History of Dogma. Eng. tr., 7.227.

uncritical of Luther and believed that he persisted with elements of mediaeval religion which were really incompatible with his own revolution. Troeltsch was even stronger in his affirmation of the mediaeval element in Luther, and put forward the view that the sixteenth century Reformers as a whole were too entangled in the mediaeval world, and saw the real break-through of the modern world view as occurring in the eighteenth century.[1]

But it was the great work of Karl Holl to show that Luther research and Luther interpretation belong inseparably together.[2] Holl was a great Church historian at home in many fields of ecclesiastical history, and his knowledge of Luther was profound and detailed. Lietzmann described the publication of his essays on Luther as "like a sudden and mighty revelation," while Harnack called him "the renewer of Lutheranism."[3] Ernst Wolf has summarized his achievements in three directions.[4] First, he made it plain that the basis of all Luther study must be the exact, historical and philological examination of the sources. Next, from his own wide knowledge of Church history, he was able to relate Luther to the whole spiritual development of the West, and to show the relevance of Luther to many important modern problems, because in fact it had been the historical work of Luther to raise them, and to point forward to their solution. Third, he showed the religion of Luther to be the theology of conscience, and that this was no relapse into subjectivism, but part of a genuinely theocentric religion based on personal relations between man and God.

Holl is very far from saying the last word about Luther. He had to meet strong criticism from his contemporaries, among others from the disciples of Troeltsch and Gogarten. Franz Lau has directed an impressive criticism against Holl's exposition of Luther's conception of creation and of Natural Law.[5] Holl reacted against some of the doctrines of traditional Lutheran orthodoxy, and notably the forensic view of justification. In his reaction against Ritschl's christocentric conception of Luther's doctrine, Holl's emphasis on its theocentric character has been said to show traces of the influence of Kant, and of his own interest in the work of Calvin. It has been alleged that Holl exaggerates the place of "You ought" as a divine imperative in the

[1] There is valuable criticism of Troeltsch's handling of Luther in K. Holl's essays.
[2] K. Holl. Gesammelte Aufsätze. 3 vols. Tübingen, 1927.
[3] There have been many such tributes, e.g. E. Sormunen calls Holl " the renewer of Luther studies," and Hermelink described his work as the " turning point."
[4] E. Wolf. Luthers Erbe, 94 ff.
[5] Fr. Lau. " Äusserliche Ordnung " und " Weltlich Ding " in Luthers Theologie. Göttingen, 1933.

development of Luther, and that he gives too great a place to the First Commandment in the thought of the Reformer.[1]

Moreover, Holl has been accused of paying too much attention to the early sources and to the thought of the Young Luther, and Hermelink remarked, "It is hardly possible to exaggerate the value of Luther's Lectures on Romans, but has it not occurred with Holl?" More important than these criticisms is the charge made in recent years with increasing clarity in Germany and Scandinavia, that Holl has imported a Ritschlian confusion of ethics and religion into Luther's doctrine of Justification, and so let in the Catholic conception of salvation by a back door. Holl had met the charges of Denifle and Grisar by giving prominence to the ethical motive behind Luther's search for a gracious God, and had emphasized, as nobody before, the innumerable passages in Luther's Psalms and Romans in which he describes the transformation in the life of the believer, by the work of the Spirit. Holl had sharply criticized the forensic doctrines of imputation as they had been formulated by Melanchthon, and following him, later orthodoxy. In so doing, it has been plausibly argued, he had come near to regarding the "making righteous" of the sinner as of decisive importance, so that Justification becomes merely the initial groundwork for God's continuing dealing with men. This would seem to be a serious oversimplification of Luther's teaching, and though the matter is too intricate to be dismissed in a couple of lines, it is probable that some of this criticism can be sustained. Certainly the more recent Scandinavian monographs on Luther's doctrine of salvation have set out a profound view of Luther's doctrine of Justification which does more justice to all the elements in Luther's thought, and especially to his anthropology of "the whole man" (totus homo).[2]

It is well that English students should heed this criticism, for of all works by Continental scholars, those of Holl are likely to seem most impressive and congenial to English readers. Our own endemic English misconceptions of Luther's teaching have been clear-cut, that he is at heart an antinomian, that he has no doctrine of sanctification, and that he leaves Christian ethics hanging in the air. It is because Holl's exposition defends Luther at precisely these points that some may be tempted to accept it uncritically. Here is an important matter where German and Scandinavian research has moved beyond Holl,

---

[1] Holl. Ges. Aufs. Luther, and refs. ad loc. E. Schott. Th. Lit. Z., 1948, Nr. 4, 199 ff. Luthers Verständnis des ersten Gebots, and refs. ad loc. That the First Commandment was an important element in Luther's moral theology of " Anfechtung " is shown by such passages as W.A. 5.171-2.

[2] R. Prenter. Spiritus Creator, 60 ff. G. Ljunggren. Synd och skuld i Luthers teologi (1928).

in a series of learned monographs by such scholars as E. Hirsch, E. Vogelsang, H. Boehmer, C. Stange, E. Wolf, J. Iwand and H. Bornkamm (a list that could be trebled, of significant writers).

There is a Luther about whom the Germans have most right to speak. He was a patriot, at a time when the national self-consciousness was becoming intensified, and his writings and his rebellion expressed the pent-up grievances of the German nation against an Italian Papacy. Luther loved Germany, and whom he loved he chastened, for he had a shrewd eye and a sharp tongue for the vices of his own nation. But there can be no doubt of his influence upon the German language, and upon German history. Here, again, there is no real English parallel of religious leader and national hero combined: had John Wesley won the Battle of Plassey, or had Nelson written the "Hymns for the People called Methodists," we might have produced such a composite figure. It was therefore natural and inevitable that nineteenth and twentieth century German historians should give prominence to "Luther, the hero of the German Nation." The emphasis of Holl, and of the next generation on the "Relevance of Luther" to the modern situation led indeed to certain writings which read strangely to English readers, in the light of two world wars. Yet it would be foolish, because we deprecate a baneful and excessive nationalism, to deny the value of German patriotism, and its insight into the life and achievement of one of the greatest Germans. Some recent historians, with a keen eye for the sinister, have thought to trace, in the course of modern German history, the baneful result of the theology of Luther. We should be more inclined to take them seriously if they ever faced the question why these influences have not been still more obvious in those Scandinavian countries which have been more consistently and whole-heartedly Lutheran than Germany has ever been. Not that this disposes of the question, for it could still be true that the decisive differences lie in a different historical context, in the impact of completely different sets of events and persons. Yet those have hardly the right to indulge in sweeping generalizations who have made no attempt to wrestle with this fact. The Scandinavian Lutheran interpretation of Luther is therefore important. It is made doubly important by reason of the "Swedish Luther Renaissance" of the last fifty years, and a series of works of theological scholarship of such high value that no modern discussion of Luther can be adequate which has not reckoned with their methods and their findings.

If Scandinavian Lutherans have not been distracted by some aspects of Luther, this does not mean that he is less significant for them. On the contrary, it has been suggested that "the rise of a distinctive theology

in Sweden is virtually synonymous with the rise of a distinctive interpretation of Luther" . . . "it might be said that the history of theology
in Sweden is a history of Luther research." [1] The Swedish historical
context is important: the unbroken continuity of the Swedish Church
with that of the mediaeval Church, and the close connection between
the Swedish Reformation and national Independence. Then, too, the
Scandinavian Churches escaped in large measure from the fierce inter-
necine struggles of the sixteenth century Germany regarding the legacy
of Luther and which resulted in the great Confessional documents of
German Lutheranism. Two Reformation doctrines have had special
importance: the idea of the "calling," of the place and duty of Christian
men within God's ordered creation: and that close association of
Church and State typified in a famous saying of Gustavus Adolphus,
"Sweden's Majesty and God's Church which reposes within it."

From this historical context it emerges that "the concept of revelation, the concept of the Church and the concept of the 'calling' may
be said to constitute the presuppositions of Swedish Luther research." [2]

The two great names associated with the beginning of the so-called
"Luther Renaissance" are those of Nathan Söderblom, and of Einar
Billing, and it is generally considered to date from the publication of
the latter's "Luthers Lära om Staaten" in 1900. The two great theologians of the next period are those of Anders Nygren and Gustav
Aulen, but with them must be associated a growing number of colleagues
and disciples. Billing lays down the lines for what was to become the
distinctive Scandinavian method of Luther study. In the first place,
the approach must be rigorously and exactly historical, paying attention
to Luther's technical vocabulary at the point where it emerges, and
comparing it with that of other theologians. On the other hand, it is
a concern with the historical Luther as a witness to and preacher of the
Christian Gospel. There is therefore an important systematic approach,
which has crystallized in the special characteristic of Scandinavian
Luther study, "motif research." E. M. Carlson, in a valuable critique
of this field, summarizes the Swedish pattern of Luther interpretation
in five points. 1. The method of motif-research. 2. The prominence
of the dualist background. 3. The dynamic-dramatic element in the
doctrine of the work of Christ. 4. The doctrine of the Church.
. 5. Agape as the "grundmotiv" of Christianity. [3]

"Motif research" is the search for the coherent theological centre

[1] E. M. Carlson. The Reinterpretation of Luther. Philadelphia, 1948, 29.28.
R. Bring. Einige Blätter aus der schwedischen Lutherforschung. Z. für syst. Theol.,
1931, 615-70. H. H. Schrey. Die Luther Renaissance in der neueren schwedischen
Theologie. Th. Lit. Z., 1949, Nr. 9, 514-27.
[2] Carlson, 35.   [3] Ibid. 165.

which underlies a given historical and philological context.[1] This
fundamental principle, the so-called "grundmotiv," has been defined
by Nygren as "the fundamental answer to a fundamental question."
Thus, in relation to Christianity, the fundamental question, the answer
to which differentiates it from other religions, is "How do men come
into fellowship with God?" Nygren, in his "Agape and Eros," answers
that there are three solutions to this problem. There is the "nomos"
motif of the Law, in Judaism, the "eros" motif of Hellenism and of
eudaemonistic religion, and the "agape" motif of Christianity. Whatever the limitations of this method, and its executants are well aware
of its dangers, it has certainly given rise to some of the most profound
theological discussions in modern theology, and can be studied by
English readers in the translations of two major works of Scandinavian
theology, Anders Nygren's "Agape and Eros" and Aulen's "Christus
Victor." [2] From the beginning Swedish theology has taken seriously
the element of dualism in the teaching of Luther. This arises from the
consideration of Luther's doctrine of sin. Arvid Runestam, Gustav
Ljunggren and Ragnar Bring have devoted special study to Luther's
anthropology of "the whole man" (totus homo) and of the use he makes
of the Pauline dichotomies, especially of "flesh" and "spirit." They
have emphasized the egocentric character of sin and the theocentric life
of the redeemed Christian. Though some theologians, like Runestam
and Bohlin, have emphasized the psychological aspects of this, and the
bearing of religious experience on Luther's theology, others have
treated this dualism in its systematic and theological aspect. Here
Ragnar Bring's "Dualismen hos Luther" (1929) is of pivotal importance.
Ragnar Bring treats the Devil as a serious element in Luther's thought
and will not explain him away in terms of superstition or pathology.
The Devil is for Luther, he insists, no mere metaphysical explanation
of the problem of evil. He stands for the whole cosmic field of conflict,
for that Kingdom of Evil which dominates sinful man in a fallen world,
but against which the Kingdom of God stands in inexorable and victorious battle. Both Bring and Hjalmar Lindroth stress the fact that
for Luther also the Law and Wrath belong to the tyrants who must be
overcome. Thus evil is not something negative, a mere defect of good,
but is actively, energetically at work in rebellious conflict with God.
Nor does Luther, in our modern error, divide evil sharply between

---

[1] Ibid. 36-44 : 166-71 : 216 ff. P. S. Watson (Translator's Introd. to A. Nygren,
Agape and Eros, pt. ii, vol. i. S.P.C.K., 1938, vii), says "the grundmotiv is that
factor in virtue of which a particular outlook or system possesses its own peculiar
character as distinct from all others."

[2] A. Nygren, Agape and Eros. 1932, 1939. G. Aulen, Christus Victor. S.P.C.K.,
1931.

moral evil in the world, and sin in the individual. The great battle line runs through the human conscience, and comes home to us in the "Anfechtung," where the Christian fights the good, supreme fight of faith, against the deadly tyrants, Sin, Death, the Devil, the Law and the Wrath. This is a real dualism. But Luther does not think of it as final or complete, and he will not snap the tension in the way of the Manichees. Nothing could be further from the thought of Luther than that of an eternal conflict where God and the Devil face each other across the chess-board of history, doomed to an everlasting stalemate. "A Word shall quickly slay him." The peculiarly strong Swedish emphasis on dualism is closely connected with their perception of the dynamic-dramatic element in the work of Christ.[1]

Aulen has made famous this "dramatic-dynamic" conception of the work of Christ. He has suggested it as an alternative to the "objective" doctrines of Atonement which derive from Anselm, and the "subjective" doctrines which are sometimes traced to Abelard.[2] He shows that there is another "classic" doctrine which goes back through Athanasius and Irenaeus to the New Testament, and which inspires the sometimes grotesque imagery of the Fathers. Others have joined in an intricate debate, carried on at a profound level. At the other extreme, von Engeström has emphasized those passages in which Luther seems to come near to Anselm (and to the emphasis of Lutheran orthodoxy). Perhaps one of the most important contributions, next to that of Aulen, is the "Försoningen" (1935) of Hjalmar Lindroth.[3] He suggests that Luther really breaks through the "aut poena aut satisfactio" dilemma of Anselm by his stress upon the obedience of Christ, and his acceptance of the consequences of human sin, by his use of the dramatic-dualist imagery of the Fathers, and above all by introducing the Law and the Wrath of God to the list of the tyrants overcome by the victory of Christ, and so bringing the doctrine of reconciliation into line with the whole Pauline teaching of the Law and Gospel. For Anselm, the Atonement is something finished, once for all, but in Luther there is a livelier sense of a tremendous victory of significance for a conflict still actively and frightfully engaged, a victory made manifest when God enters into fellowship with sinful men on the basis of forgiveness.

Here, too, is the culmination of Nygren's discussion of "Agape and Eros." He shows clearly how Luther grasped the meaning of "Agape" in the New Testament, as that spontaneous love of God, coming down to sinners, meeting them where they are, and creating worth in the

---

[1] Carlson, ch. 3, 48 ff.
[2] Ibid. 58.
[3] Ibid. 77 ff. ; Schrey, 517.

unworthy objects of His love, evoking in return that glad, spontaneous love of neighbour with that unconstrained willingness which is the characteristic stress in Luther's ethical teaching.

In another chapter we shall take note of Swedish theological discussion of Luther's doctrine of the Church, and of the place of the "Obrigkeit" and of Christian Vocation in the created order.[1] It has been said that Scandinavian Luther study is too ready to regard a question as solved when once it has been found and expounded in terms of Luther.[2] We wonder sometimes whether Luther always took his technical vocabulary as seriously as some of his modern disciples.[3] At times, listening to Törnvall or Wingren, we feel that this is very profound and very subtle, but we wonder if Luther was not even more profound because he was much more simple, and whether sometimes the questions asked are not our motifs rather than those of Luther and his age. But of the richness of the Swedish contribution there can be no doubt whatever, and for it all students of Luther must be deeply grateful. Among other Scandinavian contributions, the Danish theologian, Regin Prenter, has given us, in his "Spiritus Creator" (1946), one of the outstanding books in modern Luther study, while an exceptionally fine series of essays has come from the Finnish scholars, E. Sormunen, Y. E. Alanen and Lennart Pinomaa. It is greatly to be hoped that the debate will long continue, and that a close action and reaction of Scandinavian and German Luther scholarship will continue to fructify.

[1] G. Törnvall. Andligt och världsligt regemente hos Luther. Stockholm, 1940. G. Wingren. Luthers lära om kallelsen, 1942.
[2] Schrey, 526.
[3] Luther's acceptance of the many compromises agreed in discussion between Melanchthon and the English envoys in the Wittenberg Articles in 1536 must raise a doubt on this point.

Chapter

2

LUTHER IN ENGLAND

"Not by any means such a gentleman as the Apostle Paul, but
almost as great a genius."

S. T. COLERIDGE. "Table Talk."

THE story of Luther in English dress is of a few intermittent bursts of
translation. The rest is silence. Those periods of lively concern are
1520-40; 1560-80 in the sixteenth century, 1630-50 in the seventeenth,
the last part of the eighteenth and first part of the nineteenth centuries.

The story of the first infiltration of Luther's writings into England
has been often told in recent years.[1] Polydore Vergil refers to many
Lutheran books coming into England in 1520. Until Luther's drastic
revolutionary manifestoes appeared in the summer of that year, secular
and spiritual dignities in England had inclined to take the temporizing
attitude of Erasmus. But after Henry VIII had taken upon him publicly
to defend the orthodox doctrine of the seven sacraments, Luther was
openly proscribed as a heretic, and Luther's vigorous and blunt epithets
in reply were such as to make Henry his permanent antagonist. Luther
was accordingly proscribed, his books banned in December 1520 and
publicly burned at St. Paul's in the following May.[2] The official
condemnation of the arch-heretic was offset, however, by the pomp
and circumstance with which Cardinal Wolsey celebrated the occasion,
and the hostile gossip which filled London was more concerned with
Wolsey than with Luther. The contraband literature continued to
circulate and the mysterious Society of Christian Brethren, a kind of
"forbidden book of the month" club, continued to ply a precarious
trade between the ports, the great towns, the universities, and some of
the larger monasteries, like the notorious Reading and Bury. The
adventurous book agents passed from one centre to another, until they
were caught, recanted, or were imprisoned or burned, a highly dangerous trade of which relatively few survived to achieve respectability in

[1] H. E. Jacobs. Lutheran Movement in England, 1890. R. R. Williams. Religion and the English Vernacular, 1940. H. Maynard Smith. Henry VIII and the
Reformation, 1948. Part II. E. G. Rupp. Studies in the Making of the English
Protestant Tradition, 1947. Part I. P. Hughes. Reformation in England, I. London,
1951, 133 ff.
[2] H. M. Smith, op. cit. 253.

succeeding decades. The Steelyard Lutherans, who glower at us with devout covetousness from the canvases of Holbein, were arrested in 1525, and one of them, Hubert Bellendorpe, owned a copy of Luther's "De Libertate Christiana." The many lists of proscribed books issued by authority in the next years invariably contained books by Luther. Thus, in 1526, Cuthbert Tunstal not only prohibited works by Tyndale and the English exiles, but treatises by Luther. In 1529 Robert West, priest of St. Andrew Undershaft, was accused for having "commended Martin Luther, and thought he had done well in many things, as in having a wife and children, etc." [1] George Bull, draper of Much Hadham, dared to call Luther "a good man" to his cost. John Haymond, a millwright, possessed books by Luther and Tyndale. Robert Lamb, a harper, had gone about with a song in commendation of Luther. Thomas Patmore of Much Hadham was accused of having been to Wittenberg, and, it was alleged, had held converse with Luther and had read his books. Sigar Nicholson, the Cambridge stationer, was accused for circulating Lutheran writings, and Jeffery Lome, usher at St. Anthony's (Sir Thomas More's old school), was apprehended for dispersing abroad sundry books by Martin Luther, and for translating into the English tongue, " certain chapters of a certain book entitled 'Piae Predicationes,' wherein certain works of Martin Luther be comprehended." [2] It is known that William Tyndale translated some of Luther's writings. Those who wish to read Luther's celebrated "Preface to the Epistle to the Romans" would do well to read it in its fine sixteenth century English dress, in the beautiful 1938 edition of Tyndale's New Testament. This famous prologue was included in Matthew's Bible, patronized by the Government, by the Archbishop of Canterbury, and issued with royal permission. Thus in 1538, at a time when official English policy was soon to turn sharply away from the Continental Reformers, Luther was enabled to speak directly to an English audience. Nor is this mere conjecture. One Saturday, in April 1539, a priest of Our Lady's Church, Calais, entering from the choir after Evensong, found a soldier named Turner reading from St. Paul's epistle to the Romans and expounding it to an audience with the aid of the prologue. Botolph intervened with the remark that the layman should have told the audience when he was reading from St. Paul and when from the prologue. A heated argument followed. Finally, the priest Botolph read to the people himself from his own Testament of the "larger volume" and said, "Friends, I shall read unto you the same thing wherein he left, whereby ye shall, according to the translator's meaning, the better

---

[1] Foxe.   Acts and Monuments, iv. 582.
[2] Ibid. 586, v. 26.

understand the epistle to the Romans." He read from this for about
an hour (time enough to read the whole preface through).[1] This
Prologue, with the other prefaces, disappeared from the Great Bible.
The Cologne Fragment of Tyndale's New Testament had a preface
which incorporated much of Luther's "Preface to the New Testament,"
and this also appeared in English under the title "A Pathway into Holy
Scripture." Tyndale drew heavily on Luther for his exposition of the
Fifth, Sixth and Seventh Chapters of St. Matthew, while his "Wicked
Mammon" includes almost the whole of Luther's sermon on the
"Unjust Steward." [2] I think that Tyndale's "Prologue of the Prophet
Jonas" (1531?) shows signs that the author was acquainted with Luther's
exposition of that book.[3] John Frith, Tyndale's gifted comrade in arms,
translated Luther's "Appearance of Anti-Christ" under the name of
Richard Brightwell.

Of the Cambridge Reformers, it was Robert Barnes who came closest
in sympathy and opinions to Luther. Under the name Antonius
Anglus he lived for some time in Wittenberg, and his "Lives of the
Popes" (1535) represents one of the earliest excursions of the Reformers
into Church History. When he was burned in England in 1540 Luther
wrote him a handsome obituary notice in which he was called "St.
Robert." The good offices of Barnes had not been despised by the
Government in the years 1535-8, when Henry VIII was concerned,
above all, to prevent a coalition of foes against himself, and a council
of the Church at which he might be condemned. He toyed therefore
with the possibility of joining the league of Protestant princes, and
dangled before the German theologians the illusory prospect that
England might accept the Lutheran version of the Gospel. The
Wittenberg Articles of 1536, drawn up by the English envoys, Edward
Foxe, Nicholas Heath and Robert Barnes on the one hand, and Melanchthon, Luther and the Wittenberg doctors on the other, is interesting
as a revelation of the extent to which both sides were prepared to make
minor doctrinal concessions.[4]

John Rogers, one of the noblest of the English Reformers, literary
heir of Tyndale, and editor of Matthew's Bible, spent some time in
Wittenberg and is said to have held pastoral charge during his exile
in Germany. Miles Coverdale, pupil of Barnes, friend of Cromwell,
famous as a bishop and as the author of Coverdale's Bible, translated

[1] L. and P. Henry VIII, xiv. i. 1351. R. R. Williams (Religion and Eng. Vern., 76)
wrongly interprets this to mean that Botolph read in a different sense from Turner.
[2] J. F. Mozley. William Tyndale (1937), 127, 201. Rupp. Protestant Tradition,
51.
[3] Works, P.S. 1.447.
[4] Pruser. England und die Schmalkaldener, 1929. Rupp. Protestant Tradition,
89-128.

Luther's "23rd Psalm" into vigorous sixteenth century English, in which the Saxon pedigree is more pronounced than the Latin. There are some fine passages, as in the following description of the Church: "In the sight of God she is even as a pleasant, green meadow, which hath plenty of grass and fresh water: that is to say, she is the paradise and pleasant garden of God, garnished with all his gifts and hath his unoutspeakable treasure, the holy Sacraments, and that good word, wherewith he instructeth, guideth, refresheth and comforteth his flock."[1]

What might have been of greater moment in the story of English religion was the publication (at some time before 1539) of a collection of "Goostly Psalms and Spiritual Songs" by Miles Coverdale. These consist, almost, if not wholly, of translations from a German hymn book,[2] the most extensive English book of hymn translations until John Wesley made his first hymn book in Georgia in 1736. They include the most important German hymns of the first twenty years of the German Reformation. "Of 41 hymns," said Dr. Jacobs, "twenty-two are from Luther, two from Speratus, one each from Spengler, Dachs, Agricola, Justus Jonas, Decius and Greiser, four are well-known Lutheran hymns of uncertain origin, and seven we have not been able to identify, although their entire structure and spirit plainly show where they belong."[3]   Dr. Maynard Smith attributes the rhythm of Coverdale's version of the Psalms to his mastery of the Latin "cursus," but the sense of rhythm is no less remarkable in these translations which keep remarkably closely to the German.   Thus Luther's famous

> " Nun freut euch, lieben Christen gemein "

becomes a stirring:

> " Be glad now, all ye Christian men,
> And let us rejoice unfeignedly."

In his preface Coverdale expresses hopes which, could they have been realized, might have ushered in developments in English worship unfulfilled until the time of Isaac Watts.

"Would God that our minstrels had none other thing to play upon, neither our carters and ploughmen other thing to whistle upon save psalms, hymns and such godly songs as David is occupied withal. And if women sitting at their rocks (spinning) or spinning at the wheels had none other songs to pass their time withal, than such as Moses'

---

[1] Coverdale. Remains. PS. 312.
[2] Coverdale. Remains. PS. 536-88. The hymn book may have been Luther's second hymn book (1529). W.M.L. 6.280 ff. Otto Schliszke. Handbuch der Luther-lieder. Göttingen, 1948.
[3] Lutheran Movement. C. H. Herford. Literary Relations of England and Germany in the Sixteenth Century (1886), p. 8.

sister, Glehana's wife, Debora and Mary the mother of Christ have sung before them, they should be better occupied than with hey nony nony, hey troly loly and such like phantasies." [1]

It will be noted that, like Luther, Coverdale included hymns as well as Psalms, and might have continued for English Protestantism that healthy mediaeval tradition which included "Spiritual Songs" as well as the scriptural "Goostly Psalms" as fit vehicle for the praise of Christian men. Perhaps it was unfortunate that Coverdale, and Cranmer, unlike Luther, were not "singing men," but more likely they failed because the hymns do not fulfil their generally splendid opening lines,[2] and were perhaps in their rhythm and metre hardly suitable for congregational singing?

Some of Luther's "Betbüchlein" got into Marshall's Primer and filtered through into the Bishops' Book (1537). A long section of the splendid English Litany derived from Luther, and Luther's Baptismal service had some influence upon the English Prayer Book.[3] But after the death of Luther, and with the opening up of religious war on the Continent, the links with Wittenberg were fewer, and in the next decades it was to Peter Martyr, Martin Bucer and John a Lasco that the English Churchmen turned, while the Marian exiles at Frankfurt and at Zurich blended their own domestic liturgical and theological interest with those of the more radical reformers than those of Wittenberg. Nevertheless, a number of translations from Luther were made in the reign of Elizabeth. It was the golden age of translations, and though based on defective texts, their noble English is a sad contrast with modern translations of Luther, especially from beyond the Atlantic. In 1547 John Foxe translated "A Fruteful Sermon of the most Evangelicall writer Martin Luther made of the Angelles upon the 18th chapter Matthew" (H. Singleton, London). The little tract is dedicated to Foxe's friend, Henry Kuoche, with a preface in which he says of Luther:

"I will not say this author in all points to stand upright absolutely, as in the Sacraments, but what writer hath there ever been but some defects he hath left behind him?"

Foxe renders Luther on the ministry of angels, quaintly yet movingly:

"As we see in a bright day the sonne to shine more clear and lightsome than the blackness of the night time is dark. Thus doth God

---

[1] Coverdale. Remains. PS. 537.
[2] The same is true of a remarkable number among the thousands of hymns by Charles Wesley, so that we need not be too hard on Coverdale's forty and two.
[3] The Catechism which Cranmer caused to be translated was not Luther's Small Catechism, but the Nuremberg Brandenburg Catechism, which had been done into Latin by Justus Jonas and which consists of expository and catechetical sermons.

make us to see his benefits and good turns, which he bestoweth upon us through his angels." [1]

Foxe also edited his friend Henry Bull's translation of Luther's exposition of Fifteen Psalms, and in 1578 wrote a preface to W. Gace's collection of "Special and Chosen Sermons of Dr. Martin Luther collected out of his writings" (London, Thomas Vautrouillier, 1578)— this last a formidable volume of 481 pages.[2] Other translations of the period included "A prophesie out of Esaie of the Kingdom of Christ, by Dr. Martin Luther" (1578), James Bell's "Treatise touching the Liberty of a Christian (1579), "A right comfortable Treatise conteyning sundrye points of consolation" (Englished by W. Gace. Vautrouillier, London, 1580)—this Luther's famous "Fourteen of Consolation" (1520), a "Commentarie . . . upon the twoo Epistles Generall of Saint Peter and that of Sainct Jude gathered out of the Lectures and Preaching of . . . Martin Luther" (1581).

Then, in 1590, came a new translation of Luther's preface to the Romans made from the Latin of Justus Jonas, and published as "A Methodicall Preface prefixed before the Epistle to the Romans . . . made by Martin Luther, now newly translated out of Latin into English by W. W. student." [3] Most important of all was the translation of Luther's large commentary on Galatians (1531). This was published in 1575 by Thomas Vautrouillier, with a preface by Edwyn Sandys, Bishop of London.[4] The work, he tells us, was accomplished by an anonymous committee: "certain godly men have most sincerely translated into our language. Some began it according to such skill as they had. Others, godly affected not suffering so good a matter in handling to be marred, put to their helping hands for the better framing and furthering of so worthy a work. They refuse to be named . . . thinking it their happiness if by any means they may relieve afflicted minds."

The ensuing seventeenth century was to make large calls upon a Protestant moral theology, and no doubt this committee would have rejoiced to know that among the "afflicted minds" to whom their translation would bring consolation were two men of towering genius,

---

[1] J. F. Mozley. John Foxe and His Book (1940), 243. Two other early translations may be mentioned. " A Fruteful and godly exposition and declaration of the Kingdom of Christ . . . by Dr. Martin Luther " (W. Lynne, London, 1548) and a " Fruteful sermon of the great Blasphemy against God which the Papistes dayly do use " (1554 ?).

[2] Reprinted 1649, 1652, 1816, 1862.

[3] Reprinted 1632. Is it possible that " W. W." may be the redoubtable theologian William Whitaker (1548-95) ? He was a noted Latinist and translator and his writings show much deeper first-hand knowledge of Luther than most Elizabethan Divines. D.N.B. " Whitaker." P. S. Whitaker's Disputation on Scripture, 105, 140, 363, 541, 611.

[4] Reprinted 1616, 1649. Many of these translations, in their first editions, are in the British Museum.

John Bunyan and Charles Wesley. The preface is addressed to "afflicted consciences which grone for salvation and wrastle under the Cross for the Kingdom of Christ."

Modern Luther studies may have modified details, but they have seldom epitomized Luther's career as vigorously as here:

"Who being first a friar, in what blindness, superstition and darkness, in what dreams and dregs of monkish idolatry was he drowned, his history declareth, witness recordeth and this book also partly doth specify: whose religion was all in popish ceremonies, his zeal without knowledge, understanding no other justification but in works of the law and merits of his own making, only believing the history, as many do, of Christ's own death and resurrection, but not knowing the power and strength thereof. After he had thus continued a long space, more pharisaical and zealous in these monkish ways than the common sort of that order: at length it so pleased Almighty God to begin with this man."

In the ferment of the age which followed, Calvin's was the dominant voice, while the traditions of Zwingli and the Anabaptists, and of the older Lollards, found an English habitation and a name among the left wing of the Puritan movement.

In the 1620's and 1630's there was a revived interest in Germany. The English Princess Elizabeth, and her entourage in Heidelberg, might have brought the kind of communication which in a reverse direction had attended the marriage of Richard II with Anne of Bohemia in the fourteenth century. But the stern uproar of the Thirty Years War put an end to such peaceful penetration. The Calvinist Palatinate was not likely, in any case, to bring an especially Lutheran influence to birth. There was, perhaps, one result. It was at Heidelberg that Melchior Adamus delivered a series of lectures which were turned into biographies of some scores of leading Reformers, and the Life of Luther by Adamus found its way to England, was turned into English and printed in 1641.[1] By this time England had rung with the exploits of a Lutheran Prince, Gustavus Adolphus of Sweden. It was notable, therefore, that the work should have been dedicated to a former Ambassador to Germany, Sir Thomas Roe, last of the great Protestant Elizabethans, and a kind of Foreign minister in opposition as the Caroline court drew more and more towards the French, Austrian and Spanish cause.[2] It is also notable that the preface should mention Sir Thomas Roe's concern for Protestant unity and that it should couple with him the work of the Father of Ecumenicity, John Durie

---

[1] The Life and Death of Dr. Martin Luther. London, 1641.
[2] The Age of Charles I. D. Mathew (1951), 72 ff.

"first interested in the work by your honourable means and incourage-
ment . . . that the work is very well promoted and an hearty inclination
wrought towards a good correspondencie for Ecclesiasticall Peace."

That a Life of Luther might serve an eirenic purpose, and that
"Ecclesiasticall Peace" lay close at hand in the Europe of 1641 and
in England on the verge of ecclesiastical revolution, was perhaps too
hardy an optimism on the part of the editor and translator, Thomas
Hayne. Lest the preface seem lily-livered, however, two verses in
honour of Martin Luther were affixed, and Francis Quarles in one of
them makes it quite plain that the "good correspondencie for Ecclesiasticall Peace" stopped well short of the Church of Rome:

> "That Babels Whore,
> And all her bald pate panders may ev'n rore
> For very anguish, and then gnaw and bite
> Their tongue for malice, and their nailes for spite."

Luther's commentary on the Fifteen Psalms was reprinted in 1637,
and the 1578 volume of sermons re-issued in 1649 and 1652. In 1642
Edmund Ferrers published "An Abstract of a Commentary by Martin
Luther on the Galachians," supplemented by a number of theological
quotations of his own selection, a curious work which could hardly have
served a very useful purpose.[1]

In 1652 appeared the most interesting of all English versions of
Luther, the translation of Luther's Table Talk, "Colloquia Mensalia"
or "Divine Discourses," by Captain Henry Bell. We shall reserve this
work for separate and more detailed consideration. Here we may
observe that this would have been a remarkable feat, even had it not
been accomplished in prison, that it is the most solid work concerning
Luther to have been turned into English, and the vehicle whereby
the authentic flavour of Luther's work has been made available for
generations of English readers. In its composition, it achieved the
distinction, rare enough in the seventeenth century, of securing the
patronage of Archbishop Laud and of the Westminster Divines, and
its distinguished readers in later centuries included Lamb, Coleridge
and Carlyle.

In his "Grace Abounding" John Bunyan described how he got hold
of "a book of Martin Luther: it was his comment on the Galatians—
it was also so old that it was ready to fall piece from piece if I did but
turn it over. Now I was pleased that such an old book had fallen into

---

[1] In 1679 a tract appeared, " The Alcoran of the Franciscans, or a sink of lies and
blasphemies collected out of a blasphemous book belonging to that order called the
book of Conformities, with the epistles of Luther and Erasmus detecting the blasphemies of the Franciscans." E. Arber. The Term Catalogues, 1668-1709 (1903), 361.

my hands: the which when I had but a little way perused, I found my condition, in his experience, so largely and profoundly handled as if his book had been written out of my heart. This made me marvel." [1] The same commentary spoke to the condition of Charles Wesley at the beginning of the Evangelical Revival. On 17th May 1738, William Holland brought to Charles Wesley a copy of the book as a "very precious treasure," which Charles Wesley describes him as having "accidentally lit upon" but to which Holland felt himself to have been "providentially directed." Charles Wesley's Journal tells how they found the commentary "nobly full of faith," and henceforth there were frequent readings from this book within the societies. In June 1738 Charles Wesley records that "I read Luther, as usual, to a large company of our friends."

It seems that it was not this work, but Luther's preface to the Romans, which provided the occasion for the evangelical conversion of John Wesley. In the most famous of all extracts from his Journal, he tells of the fateful evening, 24th May 1738, and how,

"I went very unwillingly to a society in Aldersgate St. where one was reading Luther's preface to the Epistle to the Romans. About a quarter before nine, while he was describing the change which God works in the heart through faith in Christ, I felt my heart strangely warmed. I felt I did trust in Christ, Christ alone for salvation: and an assurance was given me that he had taken away my sins, even mine, and saved me from the law of sin and death."

It is all rather mysterious. There are no other references by the Wesleys to the preface to the Romans, and no information as to what edition, or in what language, the reading to which John Wesley listened was conducted. But for Wesley's explicit statement it would seem far more likely that the reading was taken from the preface to the Commentary on Galatians, from which Charles and Holland had derived such edification a few days before.[2]

Wesley had translated some of the great Lutheran hymns during his missionary labours in Georgia, and he retained a lifelong admiration for Luther as a "champion of the Lord of Hosts" (1738) and a "man highly favoured of God and a blessed instrument" (1749). The struggles and perils within the Methodist movement account in part for his criticism of Luther's "Galatians" in 1741. This "stillness" controversy cut at the nerve of the Methodist Gospel according to John Wesley, for whom this brand of quietism, a medley of Moravianism,

[1] J. Bunyan. Works. Ed. Offer (1862), 22.
[2] The discussions by J. A. Beet and T. F. Lockyer (Wesley Hist. Soc. Proc., vol. 8.2.61) add no material point to the evidence, except to call attention to the fact that there was a reprint of " W. W.'s " translation of the preface to the Romans in 1632.

pietism and Lutheranism infiltrated through Zinzendorf, seemed nothing less than "an enthusiastic doctrine of devils." At the height of the danger, Wesley took Luther's "Galatians" with him in his chaise on a journey from Markfield to London (15th-16th June 1741), and as the vehicle jolted and rumbled on its drowsy way John Wesley, who gutted books as skilful fishermen dispose of fish, reviewed its contents in his own mind, "the author makes nothing out . . . clears up not one considerable difficulty . . . quite shallow . . . muddy and confused . . . deeply tinctured with mysticism throughout." These are the kind of comments which, when we meet them in a modern review, tell us as much about the author as about the book under discussion. It was indeed a pity that Wesley only skimmed a few hundred pages of Luther: that there were not available for him those tracts in which Luther vehemently disposed of antinomians and mystical quietists in phrases more violent than had any place in John Wesley's genteel vocabulary. It was a pity that he never heard of those writings, like Luther's "De Servo Arbitrio" and "Concerning the Lord's Supper," in which his argumentation shows a use of reason more strictly logical, even scholastic, than Wesley's "Treatise of Original Sin" or "Appeal to Men of Reason and Religion." It was a pity that for John Wesley history, and especially church history, was always contemporary history and that he looked at the past, from Montanus to Luther, through the eyes of the Methodist Revival. It is true that there is more here than ignorance or misunderstanding. Wesley's theology has a different orientation from that of Luther, and between Luther's doctrine of the Law and Wesley's application of it (notably in relation to Believers), the Calvinist, Puritan and Anglican theologies had intervened.[1]

The Evangelical Revival brought an awakened interest in the theology of the Reformers, not least in the controversy between the Arminian and Calvinist wings of the movement.[2] Augustus Toplady died before he could finish a translation of Luther's "De Servo Arbitrio." In the first decade of the nineteenth century Erasmus Middleton brought forward a new edition of the 1575 translation of Luther's "Galatians,"

[1] Most of the citations needful to elucidate Wesley's views on Luther will be found in H. Carter, Methodist Heritage, 1951, App. 1.220. Also P. S. Watson. The Significance of Luther for Christians of other Communions (in the volume of essays presented to A. Nygren. "World Lutheranism Today" (1951)). F. Hildebrandt. From Luther to Wesley (1951).

[2] In 1765 a curious tract appeared in London entitled "A Short Historical view of the controversy concerning an intermediate State and the separate existence of the Soul between death and the Resurrection" (F. Blackburne. London, 1765. 2nd ed. 1772. This devoted an appendix to an "enquiry into the sentiments of Martin Luther concerning the Soul between death and the resurrection.") It is concerned to defend Luther against Perron's allegation that Luther had affirmed that the soul dies with the body, and quotes at length from Bayle, from Bell's edition of the Table Talk and from Luther's lectures on Genesis.

to which was prefixed a long historical sketch of Luther and his work, in which he quoted an older judgment of Cave that "Luther often gave a greater loose to his passions than he ought, and did not in his writings pay that deference to crowned heads which it is always necessary to pay." [1] Middleton's place in the Dictionary of National Biography is due to the fact that in 1768 he was one of the famous Oxford "Six" to be sent down for "Methodistical tenets." The charge against Middleton was that he "has officiated as Priest in a chapel of Ease belonging to the Parish Church of Chieveley in the County of Berks. and the Diocese of Salisbury, as appears by his own confession. He says, we must sit down and wait for the spirit for without it we can do nothing . . . that good works are unnecessary and no part of our justification but that we are saved by faith alone." Middleton effectively repudiated this caricature of his opinions, and later migrated to King's College, Cambridge, where he mysteriously acquired a B.D. [2]

The merits of the Rev. Henry Cole, D.D. (of Clare Hall, Cambridge), while not attaining, like Middleton, to the D.N.B. (not having been sent down from anywhere), deserve hearty commemoration of English students of Luther. His translations reveal the kind of Luther who appealed to English Evangelicals. He began to publish extracts from Luther as "an offering to the Church of God in the last days" and promised that "other works of the Beloved and Immortal Reformer will (with Divine Permission) appear in time." The volumes include sermons and expositions of Scripture, and, even more valuable, the fine "Operationes in Psalmos" (1518-21), the "De Servo Arbitrio," and the first five chapters of Luther's great Genesis commentary. Convinced that Catholic Emancipation meant a national calamity, he made a spirited translation of Luther's "Ambrosius Catherinus." His first translation seems to have been two anti-Papal scurrilities, the "Ass

---

[1] In 1845 a new version of Luther's " Galatians " appeared as " a new translation with notes," by the Rev. J. Owen, Curate of Thrussington, Leicestershire (author of " Lectures on Popery "). Owen claimed to have gone direct to the Jena edition of Luther's works (1611) and that the Elizabethan translation was no longer useful by reason of (i) an antiquated style, (ii) the meaning in some places was hardly intelligible, (iii) there are in it many omissions. Though Owen included useful and informative notes and an index, some of his translations are far from happy as when he renders Luther's technical word " larva " (i.e. veil, or mask) as " representative " (ibid. 95). The modern edition of Luther's Galatians, edited by J. P. Fallowes (Pembroke College, Cambridge), London (no date), is based on Middleton. A much more satisfactory edition is now promised from the publisher, James Clarke, with an introduction by the Rev. P. S. Watson, and we hope that at last an English edition will be available, the translation of which can be relied upon and which can be used as a tool.

[2] Pietas Oxoniensis, or a Full and Impartial Account of the expulsion of Six Students from St. Edmund's Hall, Oxford. London, 1768. Priestcraft defended, a sermon occasioned by the expulsion of Six Young Gentlemen from the University of Oxford, by The Shaver, 1768. Goliath Slain, being a reply to Dr. Nowell's Answer to Pietas Oxoniensis, 1768. D.N.B. Art. Middleton.

Pope" and the "Calf Monk," which, with appropriate cartoons, do not reflect the highest level of Luther's and Melanchthon's anti-Papalism.[1]

The Rev. Henry Cole was one of those who believed in the reconciliation between science and religion, on terms of unconditional surrender by science. He published a pamphlet against Sedgwick entitled "Popular Geology Subversive of Revelation" and delivered at Cambridge a University sermon on "The Bible as a Rule and Test of Religion and Science." When that noted Dissenter, Dr. Pye Smith, delivered a series of lectures on Geology and Revelation, at the Congregational Library, Blomfield St., Finsbury, the Rev. Henry Cole felt it his duty to attend, offensive to pious ears though these novelties might be. "Sir . . . your lecture of last evening on the Flood, and the demonstrations exhibited by the generality of your audience presented a scene of gratified irreverence, seldom perhaps surpassed by an assembly of infidels, congregated for the express purpose of enjoying an ingenious scoff at the records of the sacred Volume."

Dr. Cole issued a running commentary on these lectures in the shape of a series of letters to *The Times* on the theme "Evangelical Geology," and later published them ("A copy may be had gratis, by any clergyman of the Church of England") with the title "The Principles of Modern Dissentient Evangelism disclosed, and the Church of England proved to be the only conservatrix of the National Faith! The only safe instructrix of the Poor! and Indestructible but by her own hands!"

Carlyle hugely admired Luther and, including him in his "Heroes" under the heading "the Hero as Priest," sketched in characteristically forceful strokes a picture of moral greatness, "I will call this Luther a true great man: great in intellect, in courage, affection and integrity: one of our most lovable and precious men." If we feel that Carlyle's

---

[1] Nine volumes of translations from Luther appeared in the 1820's and 30's, which are often bound together and with which we may suppose Cole had some connection.
  Vol. 1, 1824. Select Works of Martin Luther. Tr. Cole. They include the Liberty of a Christian Man, the exposition of Psalm 51, extracts from commentaries and some sermons.
  Vol. 2, 1824. Select Works. Tr. Cole. They include the fine " Fourteen of Consolation," and " Of Good Works."
  Vols. 3 and 4, 1824. The Operationes in Psalmos. Bound with an exposition of Ps. 2 and (dated 1823) the Pope Ass, and the Calf Monk. Tr. Cole.
  Vol. 5, 1838. The " Galatians " (Elizabethan ed. reprinted).
  Vol. 6, 1838. Genesis 1-5. Tr. Cole.
  Vol. 7, 1819. Psalms of Degrees. Tr. Cole.
  Vol. 8, 1823. De Servo Arbitrio. Tr. Cole.
  Vol. 9, 1830. Sermons (reprint).
  Thus of these seven were the work of Cole. In addition Cole produced a Manual of the Psalms (translated from M. Luther) in 1837, and a small extract from the Genesis commentary (published posthumously, 1883), Gen. vi. 1-4, which he had obviously intended to carry further.

conception of history as moulded by the action of heroes comes near
to Luther's conception of the divinely inspired "Wundermann," we
might remember that what Carlyle meant by "Hero worship" comes
perilously close to what Luther means by Original Sin. But if we feel
that Carlyle, like J. A. Froude and S. T. Coleridge, too often admires
Luther for the wrong reasons, at least Carlyle achieved one of the few
really great hymn translations, in that rendering of "Eyn feste Burg"
which soars above the maimed and limping modern variants.[1]

Samuel Taylor Coleridge is a giant spirit of the nineteenth century
whose influence is still to be reckoned with, not least through its influence on the circle of F. D. Maurice and his friends. He made a close
study of Luther's Table Talk in the version by Captain Henry Bell.
To read Coleridge's marginal notes in his copy of that work is again
and again to be halted by some earnest ejaculation, some prayer, some
confession of a soul's struggle so intimate that the student almost
desists, as though intruding into confessions too private and personal
for academic survey. Then one remembers that this is simply the
Coleridge manner, the least satisfactory trait of his romanticism, that
in fact he was wont to treat the margins of all his books in this way,
even books from circulating libraries, even books borrowed from his
friends, not without half an eye to what they would make of it! In
fact, Coleridge's copy, with the marginal notes, of Luther's Table
Talk, preserved in the British Museum, is the copy borrowed without
leave from Charles Lamb, who described the friendly theft in a characteristic letter:

"Dear C.,

Why will you make your visits which should give pleasure a matter
of regret to your friends? You never come but you take away some
folio that is part of my existence. With a great deal of difficulty I
was made to comprehend the state of my loss. My maid Becky
brought me a dirty bit of paper, which contained her description
of some book which Mr. Coleridge had taken away. It was 'Lusters
Tables,' which for some time I could not make out. What! has
he carried away any of the tables, Becky? No, it wasn't any tables
but it was a book he called 'Lusters Tables.' I was obliged to search
personally among my shelves and a huge fissure suddenly disclosed
to me the true nature of the damage I had sustained. That book, C.,
you should not have taken away from me, for it is not mine: it is the
property of a friend who does not know its value: nor indeed have
I been very sedulous in explaining to him the estimate of it: but

[1] P. Smith. English Opinion of Luther. Harvard Theol. Rev., 1917, 129.

was rather contented in giving a sort of corroboration to a hint that he let fall, as to its being suspected to be not genuine,[1] so that in all probability it would have fallen to me as a deodand: not but I am sure it is Luther's as I am sure that Jack Bunyan wrote the 'Pilgrim's Progress' . . . so you see I have no right to lend you that book . . . I hope you will bring it with you." [2]

But Coleridge stuck to the borrowed copy, and with his marginal comments it has become the most precious of all volumes of Luther in English. The following characteristic comment shows that this volume was in fact the book which he took from Lamb's study.

"O for a Luther in the present age. Why, Charles, with the very handcuffs of his prejudices he would knock out the brains (nay, that is impossible), but he would split the skulls of our Christo-Galli, translate the word as you like: French Christians or coxcombs." [3]

It is no accident that it was from this circle, from the pen of Wm. Hazlitt, junior, that there came a new nineteenth century version of Captain Bell's Table Talk.

To turn from Coleridge, with his view of Luther as "the only fit commentator for St. Paul . . . not by any means such a gentleman as the Apostle, but almost as great a genius," to Julius Hare, that famous Fellow of Trinity, is to turn from a medley of profundity and misconception to the one Victorian Englishman who combined acute theological perception with accurate first-hand study of Luther. He had been taken as a child to Vienna and to Weimar, and had acquired a mastery of the German language early in life.

He was taken to the Wartburg at the age of ten and shown the mark on the wall where Luther had flung his ink-pot at the Devil. Hare developed accordingly an intense interest in Luther, and a considerable talent for flinging ink-pots on his own account, for his generous heart made him the defender of many desperate causes, not least that of Luther's reputation in England. His "Vindication of Luther" (1852), hardly more than a series of learned footnotes, defended Luther against such various nineteenth century calumniators as Möhler, Newman and

---

[1] I think this must refer to Middleton's remarks in his preface to the 1810 edition of Galatians. " It was a very great imprudence to publish such a collection as the Sermones Mensales or Colloquia Mensalia : for Luther's Table Talk is the subject of the book. It was published in 1571 . . . but Luther was not the author of that book the publication of which was the effect of an inconsiderate zeal." This in turn derives from a short-lived attempt on the part of some seventeenth century Lutherans to repudiate the Table Talk when it was made use of by Catholic polemic.

[2] E. V. Lucas. Letters of Charles and Mary Lamb, 1935. Vol. 2.284. The marginal notes by Coleridge, Ashley MSS. 4773. B.Mus. 227 show that this letter is wrongly dated (by Lucas) and must be earlier than 25th September 1819.

[3] Coleridge. Remains, iv. 64. His notes on Luther have also been reprinted in Notes, theological, political and miscellaneous. Ed. Rev. D. Coleridge, 1853.

Sir William Hamilton. It remains one of the most interesting volumes on Luther in the English language, and it is still to be read with profit. It is a very great pity that these rare gifts of understanding and interpretation were not concentrated, but were allowed to dissipate in a career where they could not be used to best advantage. "Mr. Hare," complained his bewildered Sussex parishioners, "he do come to us, and he do sit by the bed, and he do hold our hands, but he do say nowt." He left a superb collection of first editions of Luther's writings to Trinity College, Cambridge. His University sermons on "The Victory of Faith" were roused by the publication of Newman's "Lectures on Justification." Hare affirmed that this cardinal doctrine of Justification by Faith "had been acknowledged, at least implicitly by the greatest teachers of Christianity in the interval between St. Paul and Luther . . . only . . . they did not see . . . that unless the waters were kept ever flowing in freshness and might from the heavenly spring, a crust of weeds is sure to form over them. This Luther saw with a clearness which nothing could dim, with a certainty which nothing could shake." [1]

This circle of friends, Hare, Maurice and Kingsley, read and talked much of Luther, while over their interest hovered the friendly stimulus of the Chevalier Bunsen, who acted as a kind of Protestant Von Hügel to the religious and theological interests of the group. They particularly appreciated the translations by Miss Catherine Winkworth of the hymns of the Reformation. Julius Hare had been tutor to his brother-in-law, Frederick Denison Maurice, and it seems likely that from him Maurice gained an interest in Luther as well as an enthusiasm for Plato. The collection of books presented to Maurice on his enforced retirement from King's College, "The works of Origen, Athanasius, Chrysostom, Gregory Nazianzen, Luther and Calvin," is a significant selection which takes us far into Maurice's theology and the reason for its unexhausted significance for our day. The redoubtable Dr. James Rigg, the Methodist divine and theologian of the third quarter of the nineteenth century, delivered an all-out attack on the group in "Modern Anglican Theology" and charged them with perverting Evangelical truth with the cloudy corruption of Neo-Platonic mysticism.

Rigg's work is less an illumination of Maurice, Hare and Kingsley than of the extent to which the Evangelical Arminianism of the Wesleys had now conformed to the rigidities of nineteenth century Nonconformist Evangelicalism, and how badly a petrified Augustinian stood in need of refreshment from precisely those Greek Fathers whom

[1] D.N.B., Art. "Hare." J. H. Rigg. Modern Anglican Theology. J. Hare, "The Victory of Faith and other Sermons." Vindication of Luther, 1855.

Maurice found so fertile and congenial. The theology of Athanasius, Irenaeus and Origen provided for a more adequate solution of problems concerning the work of Christ than could be comprehended by the bitter strife of nineteenth century Protestants about the Atonement. Yet the diversity of these influences must not mislead us. The evidence supports Maurice's own vehement disclaimer of eclecticism. He found Luther to be a great Christian doctor, above all in his proclamation of faith as a living personal apprehension of Christ rather than a bundle of notions.[1] We can understand how a modern Scandinavian theologian has described Maurice as "an Anglican Lutheran," but we must not press this too hard: Maurice's references to Luther are warm, but not frequent enough or intimate enough to suggest that he was a dominant theological inspiration.

We cannot begin to summarize the modern spate of volumes on Luther, which are in proportion to the modern spate of volumes about everybody and everything. It may be said that from them all, however bad, there is always something profitable to be learned. The Victorian novel, "Chronicles of the Schönberg Cotta family," by Mrs. Rundle-Charles, which was read aloud in many a manse and rectory, while full of the simple pieties, sentimentalisms and platitudes of Victorian evangelicalism, moves about in realms of insight not realized by Denifle or Maritain.

American work on Luther has been uneven, and noticeably weak on the theological side. Preserved Smith and H. E. Jacobs wrote biographies of the Reformer and an edition of "Luther's Correspondence" which may still be used with profit and pleasure. Preserved Smith's more detailed review articles are always worth attention. More recently, Professor Roland Bainton has given us in "Here I Stand" a very fine popular study which rests on deep learning.[2] E. G. Schwiebert's "Luther and His Times," though better annotated, and though its author seems to have read most of the literature, is characterized by breadth rather than depth of learning.[3] But if neither the historical background nor the theological judgments are particularly profound, the work contains much useful information not readily available elsewhere.

Despite the sharp antagonism of the men of the Oxford Movement, Victorian England as a whole was sturdily Protestant enough to take

---

[1] Nörregaard. Z. für Syst. Theol (1938). "Frederick Denison Maurice." Life of F. D. Maurice, ii. 238.615. A. M. Ramsey. F. D. Maurice and the Conflicts of Modern Theology (1951). " Maurice (like Hare) is one of the few exceptions to the almost constant failure of Anglican theologians to understand Luther."

[2] R. Bainton. " Here I Stand." Abingdon Press, 1950.

[3] E. G. Schwiebert. "Luther and His Times." Concordia Press, 1950.

kindly to the memory of Luther. The Luther celebrations of 1883 were described by F. J. A. Hort from Cambridge.

"We had what was called a Conference here on Thursday at the Corn Exchange, when some interesting papers were read, and speeches made. The object, of course, was to honour a great and good man . . . he was sometimes violent and unwise, but those were exceptions only." [1]

In London the celebration took the practical form of the publication of an edition of Luther's Primary Works. This volume consisted of the two Catechisms, and the three great manifestoes of 1520, together with two essays by the learned editors, Dr. Wace and Professor Bucheim, of King's College, London. The work was of great practical value, but one result is that it provided the horizon for English acquaintance with Luther's theology for the next thirty years. Mackinnon's four volumes on Luther did signal service in summarizing the research of the first generation of the "Luther Renaissance." The chief criticism must be that he commits the one unforgivable sin of Luther study, which is to make Luther dull, and provokes the reflection that his brand of theological and historical liberalism singularly unfits him to interpret Luther's theology. Dr. J. P. Whitney kept a lively interest in Luther and was not blinded to his greatness by his greater enthusiasm for Erasmus, but he stopped short of Karl Holl in his encyclopaedic reading, and his judgments on Luther have to be received with caution. [2]

Boehmer's fine "Young Luther" and his "Luther in the Light of Modern Research" are among major works of German scholarship to be made available in English. [3] P. S. Watson's "Let God be God" [4] is the first full-scale exposition of Luther's theology in English and, among many great merits, it takes full account of Scandinavian as well as German Luther study. The works of the older English historians of the Reformation are by no means to be despised. When one has discounted the presuppositions of J. A. Froude and allowed for defective historical material available to Charles Beard and T. M. Lindsay, the modern student is abashed and rebuked to find how careful was their scholarship, and how much solid learning and genuine historical insight has gone into their work, and how much better written these are than most modern books on the Reformation.

French scholarship (P. A. Vignaux apart) has not added appreciably to the modern study of Luther. Funck Brentano's "Martin Luther" is an unfortunate work. L. Febvre's "Martin Luther: un destin" is an

---

[1] Life and Letters of F. J. A. Hort, A. F. Hort. 1896, ii. 306.
[2] A characteristically lucid and balanced study of Luther appeared in Miss C. V. Wedgwood's "Velvet Studies" (1946).
[3] Tr. Road to Reformation (1946) and Luther in the Light of Modern Research (1930).   [4] Epworth Press, 1947.

interesting psychological study but defective in theology and now outmoded in its scholarship. Henri Strohl's two volumes on Luther's
development, "L'Évolution Religieuse de Luther" (Strasbourg, 1922)
and "L'Épanouissement de la Pensée Religieuse de Luther" (Strasbourg, 1924) present an admirable survey of the state of critical discussion down to the time of their publication. In Holland, W. J.
Kooiman, in his "Maarten Luther," has produced a terse and skilful
popular Life which is a good handbook for teaching purposes. One of
the best modern Lives is the first volume of Miegge's "Lutero," and it
is greatly to be wished that the smallness of the Italian Protestant reading
public will not deter the writer from completing an admirable work
which combines thorough erudition with penetration.

There are signs of a quickening interest in Luther in England. The
revival of Continental theology, the growth of the Ecumenical Movement have stimulated interest in the theology of the different Protestant
confessions. The conversations about reunion and inter-communion
among the English Churches have made imperative a reassessment of
the various English traditions in the light of their historical origin and
development. But it still remains true that the only really ecumenical
movement is the theological conversation of the "learned world" of
scholarship, since here Roman Catholic and Protestant scholars share
a common task, and in matters of critical investigation a genuine
conversation.

Luther study is, and is likely to remain for a long time, a fruitful
field of critical investigation and theological interpretation. There is
still a dark side of the moon, in relation to Reformation studies. There
are three major problems singularly deficient in the scaffolding of monographs which is the prerequisite of interpretation. First, the theology
of late Scholasticism with special reference to Nominalism in Germany.
Second, the left-wing movements of the Reformation, in their relation
to late mediaeval heresy and mysticism: third, a much clearer appreciation of the sixteenth century humanists and, more especially of the
theological content of the "philosophia Christi." Luther study need
not wait on these problems, but it must be prepared to reconsider some
of its judgments in the light of them. In a sphere where a final word
can never be said, there is a real sense in which evaluations of Luther's
thought and influence must be interim judgments.

It is devoutly to be hoped that Luther studies will not be relinquished,
however, to those who have an ecclesiastical axe to grind, or a party
edge to whet, or to those who scour his writings in search of useful
"gobbets" for this or that polemical purpose. It is true that the English
student of Luther may be regarded askance by his fellows. They need

not be alarmed. There is not much danger that English Christians will take their Luther too seriously, or that "Luther says . . ." will be used to close, rather than open minds to new truth. The answer to them is simple. We read Luther because we find in one page of him more sparkling and refreshing draughts of truth than in scores by others, because there are few Christian writers of any age who can bring before us the heights and depths of the Christian gospel, or bring home so urgently the drama of the Christian warfare. Those who read Luther for their own soul's health will have no fears about what critical investigation may bring to light, and will not be deterred by ancient foes or modern prejudice.

There is a Luther about whom Germans have more right to speak than any of us: but Luther himself is bigger than the German Luther. There is a Luther about whom the Lutherans may speak with authority, out of a coherent living tradition, a rich pattern of confession and liturgy and life. But Luther himself is not to be identified with the Lutheran Luther, not of the German Lutheran Churches, the Scandinavian Lutherans, nor yet of the American Missouri Synod. There is a Catholic Luther, and there is a Protestant Luther, but he himself is bigger than any superimposed pattern. If his voice were allowed to break in, rough, disconcerting, but alive, on our English theological conversation, it might be that this would be yet another Luther whose authentic message, would men observingly distil it out, may be of power and force towards the mending of the Church and the healing of the nations.

Chapter

3

CAPTAIN HENRY BELL AND "MARTIN LUTHER'S DIVINE DISCOURSES"

"I must be forward to let my bell send such a peal that the same
shall ring and be heard throughout this kingdom and it may be
beyond."—HENRY BELL to Sir DUDLEY CARLETON.

1. THE NARRATIVE OF CAPTAIN HENRY BELL.

IN the year 1652 a folio volume appeared from the press of Wm.
Du Gard,[1] Suffolk Lane, London, entitled "Dris Martini Lutheri
Colloquia Mensalia or Dr. Martin Luther's Divine Discourses at his
Table, etc." It was the Lauterbach collection, "afterwards disposed
into Common places," by Dr. J. Aurifaber, and it had been translated
"out of the high Germane into the English tongue" by one, Captain
Henrie Bell. From the dedication by Thomas Thorowgood, addressed
to the Lord Mayor of London, John Kendrick, we learn that Captain
Bell had died before the publication of the book.

Imbedded among a number of prefatory documents is the intriguing
story entitled "Capt. Bell's Narrative, or relation of the miraculous
preserving of Dr. Martin Luther's Book."

This narrative was written and signed 3rd July 1650, by Henry Bell.
It begins solemnly, with a significance which the reader will better
understand when we have done. "I Captain Henrie Bell do hereby
declare both to the present age, and also to posterity. . . ." Henry Bell
relates how, while employed "beyond the seas in state affairs" under
James I and Charles I, he had heard that "above four-score thousand"
copies of Luther's "Divine Discourses" had been destroyed in persecution. He claims that the work had been circulated among the parish
Churches of Protestant Germany, "to be chained up for the common

---

[1] Wm. Du Gard (1605-62) studied at Sidney Sussex College, Cambridge, and was
thereafter usher at Oundle, Stamford and Colchester. He became Master of the
London Merchant Taylors' School in 1644. He ran a publishing house as a side-line
and got into trouble in 1649 for alleged Royalist sympathy. He was dismissed, his
press seized, and he was confined in Newgate for printing scandalous and seditious
pamphlets. He was soon reinstated and published Milton's great defence of the
English people against Salmasius. In 1653 he was again in trouble. The friendship
of Milton with Du Gard makes it probable that Milton knew Bell's edition of Luther's
Table Talk. Timperley. History of Printing, 531-2. S.P.Dom., 1650, vol. 5.500,
523.568. D.N.B:

people to read," but that Pope Gregory XIII and the Emperor Rudolph II banned the book throughout the empire, ordered its destruction and forbade it to be read, on pain of death.

Then, in 1626, "A German gentleman named Caspar Van Sparr," with whom Bell had become acquainted on his travels, found a copy of this book hidden among the foundations of the house "wherein his grandfather dwelt," and the book was "lying in a deep, obscure hole, being wrapped in a strong linen cloth, which was waxed all over with beeswax, within and without: whereby the book was preserved."

Van Sparr, realizing that the Emperor Ferdinand II was also liable to order the destruction of such a book, sent the work to England, with a covering letter about its discovery and begged that Bell would translate it. There followed a marvel: for Bell found the weeks slipping by, and he had been forced to neglect the task.

"Then about six weeks after I had received the said book, it fell out, that I beeing in bed with my wife, between twelv and one of the clock, she beeing asleep, but myself yet awake, there appeared unto me an antient man, standing at my bed's side, arraied all in white, having a long and broad white beard, hanging down to his girdle steed, who taking me by my right ear, spake the words following unto me: "Sirrah, will you not take time to translate that book which is sent unto you out of Germanie? I will shortly provide for you, both place and time to do it." And then hee vanisht away out of my sight.

"Being much thereby affrighted, I fell into an extreme sweat, insomuch that my wife awaking, and finding mee all over wet, asked me what I ailed? I told her what I had seen and heard, but I never did heed nor regard visions nor dreams. And so the same fell soon out of my mind."

Then followed events which were remembered with terrible clarity when Captain Bell recorded them, twenty years on.

"About a fortnight after I had seen the vision, on a Sundaie I went to White-hall [1] to hear the sermon, after which ended I returned to my lodging, which was then in King's Street at Westminster.[2] And

---

[1] Either in the open air, in the " Preaching Court," or in the Chapel Royal.

[2] King's Street was a narrow highway between the Palace of Whitehall and Westminster, and occupied the Westminster end of modern Whitehall, from above Downing Street, and across to the width of the Cenotaph. In the seventeenth century modern Whitehall was divided between Whitehall (the Palace and the Inigo Jones Banqueting House) : the Street (between the Holbein and the King's Street Gates) : and King's Street. King's Street was demolished in the nineteenth century. In Tudor and Stuart times its inhabitants included Lord Howard of Effingham, Edmund Spenser and (in 1647) Oliver Cromwell. A number of Knights and Captains in attendance on the Court lived in the street, which included a number of Inns (one of them, the Bell) and some less reputable establishments. G. S. Dugdale. Whitehall through the Centuries (1950), 147-9. J. E. Smith. Catalogue of Westminster Records (1900), 98-100. N. G. Brett-James. Growth of Stuart London (1935), 139.

sitting down to dinner with my wife, two messengers [1] were sent from the whole Council Board with a warrant to carrie mee to the keeper of the Gate Hous, Westminster, there to bee safely kept until further order from the Lords of the Council: which was don without showing mee any cause at all wherefore I was committed. Upon which said warrant I was kept there ten whole years close prisoner: where I spent five years thereof about the translating of the said book: insomuch as I found the words very true which the old man in the foresaid vision did saie unto mee, 'I will shortly provide for you both place and time to translate it.' "

When he had finished the translation, it came to the ears of Laud, who sent his chaplain, Dr. Bray, asking that the Archbishop might borrow both the original and the translation, and Bell, somewhat reluctantly, parted with the precious volumes. After two months Laud sent a message "to tell me that I had performed a work worthie of eternal memorie. And that he had never read a more excellent divine work: yet saying that some things therein were fitting to be left out." After this, Laud kept the work for another two years, but finally he returned it, with a gift of forty pounds, saying that he would tell the King, and "would procure order from his Majestie to have the said translation printed, and to be dispersed throughout the whole kingdom as it was in Germany." Then came Bell's release from prison, and the events which led to the fall of Laud.

The House of Commons, having heard of Bell's work, appointed a committee to examine it, sitting in the Treasury Chamber, presided over by Sir Edward Dearing,[2] and a distinguished refugee scholar beneficed in Essex, Paul Amiraut,[3] was asked to pronounce on the technical merits of the translation. "He found I had rightly and truly translated it according to the original." Two members of the Westminster Assembly, Charles Herle and Edward Corbet, were asked to report on it. Their judgment, given 10th November 1646, is printed in the "Divine Discourses," and says:

"Wee finde many excellent divine things are conteined in the book worthy the light and publick view. Amongst which Luther professeth that hee acknowledgeth his error which hee formerly held touching

---

[1] "Warrants for arrest issued by the council went for execution to Messengers of the King's Chamber, warrants to search for papers were issued separately to one of the clerks of the Council." J. R. Tanner. Constitutional Docs., James I. Cambridge, 1930, 131, n. 4.

[2] Sir Edward Dearing was the son of Frances Bell, d. of Sir Robert Bell of Beaupré Hall, Norfolk, and was probably a kinsman of Henry Bell. See A Genealogical account of the descendants of Sir Robt. Bell. J. H. Josselyn, 1896.

[3] Calamy. Nonconformists' Memorials (1803), iii. 7. Matthews. Calamy Revised, 10.

the real presence corporaliter in Coena Domini. But wee finde withall many impertinent things, som things which will require a grain or two of salt, and som things which will require a marginal note or a preface."

The 26th February 1646-7, the House of Commons gave order for the printing of the Book and directed that "the said Henry Bell shall have the sole disposal and benefit of printing the said book . . . for the space of fourteen years." This account, Bell concludes, he has written that the details may "prove a notable advantage of God's glory, and the good and edification of the whole Church, and an unspeakable consolation of every particular member of the same."

2. THE PRISONER IN THE GATEHOUSE.

In his valuable critical discussion of Luther's Table Talk the American historian, Preserved Smith, rejects the story of Captain Henry Bell out of hand. He calls it "such a tissue of mistakes and improbabilities that it is hardly worth serious criticism. It is clear from the absence of all other evidence, and the large number of early editions of Luther's Tischreden which have come down to us, that no such order was ever issued by Rudolphus as that which Bell describes."[1] He continues, "the ten years' arbitrary imprisonment is so improbable that it may be dismissed . . . the whole thing has the air of being invented to heighten the interest of the translation. Even the vision of the old man does not seem to be a genuine bit of self-deception."[2]

The learned American historian seems to have reserved his credulities for modern psycho-analytic theory, in his attempt to describe Luther in terms of an Oedipus complex. A very little trouble would have shown that he had been too brusque in his dismissal of Captain Bell. About the fate of Luther's Table Talk in Germany the honourable and gallant captain is speaking at second hand, and we do not even today expect a publisher's "blurb" to speak with scientific exactness: the bit about the copies being chained up (since Captain Bell had petitioned Parliament to put copies in every parish Church in England in this way) may be merely a corroborative detail. But all the facts about Gregory XIII and Rudolphus II suggest that they neglected no opportunity to ban and to destroy heretical literature.

[1] P. Smith. Luther's Table Talk (A Critical Study). Columbia Univ., 1907, 77. None the less, as Smith notes, Bell's edition is taken from a German edition corresponding exactly to no known edition that he had consulted.
[2] The seventeenth century, like the age of St. Augustine, had an ear for " mirabilia." Archbishop Laud's interest in dreams is notorious. Bell's story is no more extravagant than the celebrated vision by Pirckheimer in the sixteenth century (Willibald Pirckheimer's Briefwechsel. I. Bd. ed. Reicke, 1940, 128 ff.) or the vision of Colonel Gardiner in the eighteenth. (P. Doddridge. Passages in the Life of the Honourable Col. James Gardiner.)

F

But to doubt the arbitrary character of Bell's imprisonment is the unkindest cut of all. Since over several years he wrote a petition a fortnight, the State Papers of James I and Charles I are littered with traces of Captain Bell, and of an imprisonment which must have provided the clerks of the Council Chamber with one of the grimmest jokes in the history of the Civil Service. In fact, the "Narrative of Captain Henry Bell" does not tell half his story. The other half we shall attempt to tell for the first time, with the aid of impeccable documents.

ˏ It is a great pity that the whole story could not have been known to Charles Lamb and by S. T. Coleridge as they lovingly handled their copy of the "Divine Discourses." For it belongs to the romantic. It concerns a plot against the royal house: a dash across Europe by a young officer at the head of his company of musketeers, in an attempt to save the life of an English princess: of the diamond jewel which a grateful Princess bestowed upon him, and the autograph letter which her more canny Scottish sire allowed him to retain, after an interview at Theobald's while they walked in the garden, James I leaning on Buckingham. All these ingredients which would do for a novel by Dumas are recorded in documents preserved in our State Papers, as they were written in a darkened prison cell by an embittered remembrancer.

But was Captain Henry Bell an English d'Artagnan? May he not rather have been a forerunner of Titus Oates, a liar, a forger, an inventor of Popish plots? There was a time, be it admitted, when this melancholy alternative had the ear of no less creditable personages than the Lord Falkland and Archbishop Laud. It is our opinion, after many preliminary hesitations, that Captain Henry Bell was both gallant and honourable. But if he was an honest man, he suffered grievous wrong. And to tell the truth, if he had been a rogue, I think we could hardly ponder the pathetic yellowing documents of his experience, without some pity for his fate.

Thomas Thorowgood,[1] in his preface to the "Divine Discourses," speaks of "the noble captain (unknown to me yet), my countryman both by birth and education, of Norfolk and at Ely. His family is of great note and nobility in the former: his Father was Dean of Ely." [2] Henry

---

[1] Venn. Alumni, 4.235. A member of the Westminster Assembly. R. of Grimston, 1625 and of Gt. Cressington, 1661-9.

[2] If this be correct, John Bell must have been related to Sir Robert Bell, Speaker of the House of Commons under Elizabeth, of Beaupré Hall, Norfolk, whose manor lay in that tongue of Norfolk inserted into the Isle of Ely. His eldest son, Sir Edmund (d. 1605), had a third son, Henry Bell, who took orders. Blomefield, History of Norfolk, vol. vii. J. H. Josselyn. A Genealogical account of the descendants of Sir Robert Bell.

Bell, it seems from this, was son of John Bell, D.D., S.T.P., who had been Canon of Ely (1566-89) and Dean (1589-91). Dr. John Bell was associated with several Cambridge Colleges, Master of Jesus (1579-89) and Vice-Chancellor of the University during a memorable squabble about the University Press. Despite, or because of these academic connections, the Marprelate tracts dismiss him as a dunce. He died, 31st October 1591 at the age of sixty-one, and since Henry Bell was in the army in 1606, we may suspect that Henry was left fatherless as a child.[1]

Seventeenth century Europe offered scope for soldiers of fortune, and Henry Bell was one of a number of English and Scottish officers who plied this dangerous trade. He travelled far, and fought against the Turk in Austria and Transylvania. That he would put his services "against the common enemies of Christendom" in a list of his activities on behalf of the King of England is a reminder that the seventeenth century was closer to the Middle Ages than we sometimes think. He became skilled in the use of all arms, and "commanded continually before the face of the enemy, 500 men." [2] He served under German Princes, notably the Electors of Saxony and Brandenburg, and with the great Gustavus. In 1615 he was commended to the King of England by both Electors and the letter has survived in which John Sigismund, Elector of Brandenburg, commends "the bearer of these presents, Captain Henry Bell, who has lived among our soldiers for some time . . . whom we would fain have retained longer in our service . . . we beg that he may be given a place either at your court or in your army." [3]

Henry Bell's first diplomatic employment by James I was in an enterprise broached by our envoy, Sir James Moray,[4] by which the Elector of Brandenburg offered to sell James I a number of pine trees which would make excellent "great masts for his ships royall." This rare solicitude of a Prussian ruler for the development of the British

---

[1] Venn. Alumni, 1.128. Cooper. Athenae Cant., ii. 109. Strype. Whitgift, 131.171. He is said to have been scholar of Trinity, 1552. 1555, M. A. Peterhouse. University Preacher, 1567. Rector, Fulbourn St. Vigors, 1560-71. Rector of Fen Ditton, 1571. For his death, Willis, Cathedrals of England, ii. 369.

[2] The English ambassador's report on Bell, given to the Doge of Venice, says that he is used to " the drilling of new troops . . . skilled in the use of all sorts of weapons . . ." He could " not only undertake the captaincy of a company but the direction of artillery in which he was well versed." S.P. Ven., 1617-19, 34.39.49.56-8. 63.64.193.

[3] S.P. Foreign. (German.) James I, 16th May 1616. John Sigismund to James I. The letter is signed from the Prussian capital of Cologne on Spree (adjacent to the modern Berlin).

[4] David Mathew's statement, " there was no contact between England and the smaller German dynasties: no envoys : no traders " (Age of Charles I, 41), cannot apply to Brandenburg or Saxony.

navy was a strictly business affair, and Captain Bell informed the King when thirty great masts were ready for delivery, on terms of cash down.[1] In 1616 he was employed in the complicated claims and counter claims regarding the Mark, Cologne and Jülich.[2] Then, in an audience, John Sigismund told Bell (we quote Bell's narrative written to Charles I, twenty years later),[3] that he had "received very certain advertisement from Vienna of a dangerous Plot to be put in practice against His Majesty's (i.e. Charles I) very dear Sister, the Lady Elizabeth and the prince her son, under colour of a kind and loving invitation to meet the Empress at Ratisbon where the Imperial Diet would be held . . . it was concluded that she would never come back alive . . . and moreover a far greater mischief was to follow thereupon here in England." This was the kind of news which went to James I's head. The possibility that the whole thing was invented by Bell as a means of imposing on royal favour seems completely excluded by a number of autograph letters from the Elector to James I mentioning the Plot and commending Bell for his services. How real the plot was, and how much John Sigismund enlarged the rumour of it, is another question. The Elector told Bell that he would write the King about it, and showed him a letter next day, handing it to an officer of his court for instant despatch to England.[4] Bell was given safe conducts, signed by the Elector, that he might go to Vienna and enquire more closely. "I went accordingly to Vienna where I understood for certain that the Empress had written her letter to Princess Elizabeth, but in regard that the Imperial Diet was put off that year, the said letter was stayed."

Thence Bell went into Saxony "about His Majesty's affairs" and thereafter, "having disposed of the same I came speedily into England and gave His Majesty an account thereof. I related . . . the plot aforesaid and what I understood in Vienna concerning the same. Then His Majesty told me he had received a letter from the Prince of Brandenburg wherein mention was made" of the plot. "His Majesty commanded me to go back into Germany . . . to learn when the Empress should send the letter to his daughter and . . . to give His Majesty notice thereof." He commanded "letters of safe conduct in the Latin tongue and safe passage for myself and two servants."

[1] S.P.Dom. James I, 1620. S.P., 116.104.
[2] Wedgwood. Thirty Years War, 48.
[3] There are three main narratives by Henry Bell. (1) His statement of expenses in 1620. S.P., James I, 14.116.104. (2) His narrative to Lord Falkland, 1632. S.P., 16.218.61.1. (3) His narrative to the King, 1636-7. S.P., vol. 346.79.1. In addition there is his printed account in his " True Relation " (June 1646).
[4] This letter is preserved, S.P. (Foreign. German.) Jas. I, 81.14, May 1616. The other letters are Jas. I, 81.143-5, 24th May 1618, and 81.193, 6th Sept. 1618. It should be said that Bell's narratives, many years apart and which he could hardly have known to have survived, agree remarkably.

It seems that Captain Bell was back in England at the turn of the year, if he is the Henry Bell who married Sara Bubb in the Church of St. Martin-in-the-Fields, 12th January 1616-17.[1] That he was conceived to have rendered important service to the Crown is confirmed by another set of State Papers relating to the Venetian war, 1617-18.[2] A number of English soldiers were ruffling it in Venice, prominent among them the Earl of Oxford, making a nuisance of themselves with brawls and amours. Pressure was brought to bear from the English side that an English commander should be appointed over the Venetian forces, and the name of Captain Bell was seriously considered. No less a person than our ambassador, and no less an ambassador than Sir Henry Wotton,[3] could declare (we may discount for poetic licence) "Captain Bell is recommended by His Majesty as a man of great valour and experience in war . . . he has no equal in Christendom as a brave and experienced soldier." The Venetians were polite, but we suspect they had had enough of foreign mercenaries. "We should accept his offer," they said with Italian manners, "were it not for the difficulty of language, as we recognize his great merits." In vain did Sir Henry plead Bell's knowledge of Latin, and "considerable progress" in the vernacular. But whether the government left it too late (as Bell afterwards asserted) or Venetian policy had hardened, the brightest prospect of Bell's career was foiled. Instead of being Commander of an allied expeditionary force he had to come home sadly out of pocket. (He had had no *frais de représentation* for his travels in 1616, and, with permission from James I, had begun to raise troops in Venice in the haphazard seventeenth century way.) It was small consolation that the Council of Venice voted (Ayes 150: Noes 0: Neutral 6) that "Captain Bell be given . . . 200 crowns, and 100 to the Earl of Oxford for refreshments."

In 1618 Bell was sent again to the Elector of Brandenburg in his new capital in Prussia, at Königsberg (Regiomons).[4] The Elector told him that the Diet would be held that year, and that a letter of invitation had been sent to Elizabeth, and John Sigismund had written to James, at the same time commending "my diligent service." [5]

Captain Bell now departed to Vienna, and finding that a letter to the Princess had been already sent, he rode off to Heidelberg. In the hot summer he rode through the cool green trees up the winding road which enters the rose-red Castle, and opened his business to Sir Albert

---

[1] Register of St. Martin-in-the-Fields. Ed. Mason. Harleian Soc., 1898, 99.
[2] S.P. Venetian, 1617-19. 34.39.49.57.58.193.
[3] D.N.B. Bush. English Literature in the Earlier Seventeenth Century, 122.
[4] S.P. Charles I, vol. 346, 79.1. John Sigismund succeeded to E. Prussia in 1618, and the change of venue is a corroboration of Bell's narrative.
[5] S.P. (Foreign). James I, 24th May 1618.

Morton.[1] Bell had audience with the Princess Elizabeth, who took the invitation from her pocket and handed it to him, saying that she had intended to accept. The upshot was that Captain Bell took the letter to England, carrying at the same time a jewel containing eleven diamonds handed him by the grateful Princess. Arrived at Theobalds, the Duke of Buckingham took him out to where the King was seated in the garden. The King took him to his room and asked him to translate the invitation, word by word.[2]

James ordered Bell to return to Germany "with all speed" and wrote to Elizabeth to refuse the invitation, and also to the Elector of Brandenburg. The Elector told Bell that he had written again to the King.[3]

By now Henry Bell had invested all his own fortune in costly journeys across Europe and for the "safe management of the business" had hired squadrons of horse and musketeers. No doubt he had been extravagant. What we know of seventeenth century civil servants of far greater eminence than Captain Bell bids us not enquire too closely into the detailed arithmetic of his accounts. But the courts of Europe were too full of the alarms of plots and stratagems for us to blame Henry Bell for taking his mission very seriously, and very hopefully. At any rate, he once more returned home with nothing more than hopes and promises to tell his wife.

All in all, Captain Bell estimated that he had laid out over five thousand pounds in the service of the Crown, and this was much more than the government of James I was prepared to pay in good, hard

---

[1] In his printed " True Relation " Bell could appeal to a certificate given by Sir Albert Morton to the truth of this story.

[2] In her Life of Elizabeth (1938), Miss C. Oman makes the point (161-2) that such invitations were generally made in French or Latin and that it was unlikely that this would be given in " Dutch." But this is one of those unlikely things that may very well have happened, and there are so many other checks on Bell's story that the detail may be accepted.

[3] Bell rode back to London with Sir Thomas Wilson, who told him that among the Papers which it was his business to preserve were two letters from the Elector commending Bell. Bell asked if he might have them, but was told he could only see copies. " When I read them I found they were not rightly dated according to the originals, but were both dated at Cologne on the Spree in the year 1618, whereas the originals were dated, the one at Cologne on the Spree in the year 1616 and the other in Prussia (at least 500 miles from Cologne) in the year 1618 . . . he told me the dating of the extracts was mistaken, in regard he was forced to make great haste . . . to cause them to be written out of the original, and had already made.them up into a book, and was fain to cut them out again to take them to the King." This muddle proves an unexpected corroboration of Bell's good faith, for the originals of the letters, 16th May 1616 and 24th May 1618, are both signed as from Cologne on the Spree, as they well might be since the change of court to E. Prussia was so recent. Bell was right about the mistake of dates by Wilson but wrong about the place from which they were addressed. But his mistake was due to the fact that he had in fact seen the Elector at Regiomons, in E. Prussia. The third letter, 6th Sept. 1618, from the Elector, makes mention not only of Bell's services in regard to the abortive plot, but specially enumerates Bell's heavy expenses, " magnis sumptibus et impensis," no doubt at Bell's request.

cash, especially as every month that passed brought situations far more pressing in political significance than the story of a plot that had never come into fruition, and about which a good deal of scepticism might be pardoned. Bell claimed that he was to have been given a sum of five hundred pounds under the Great Seal, for thirty-one years. He was given a new office, a Patent under the Crown for surveying Lead, "to avoid falsifying thereof." We next hear of Henry Bell in the Peak District, where he expended what remained of his savings in trying to carry out the highly unpopular duties of a novel office. The result was that his Patent, which was to yield him twopence on every hundred-weight of lead, roused a fury of opposition from the miners. A Petition from the miners was presented to the Privy Council "that this patent was both unprofitable to His Majesty's Subjects . . . to the raising of the price of lead, more particularly to the poor miners." Finally, it seems that the Patent was taken away and given to Sir Robert Ayton.[1]

Then with a suddenness typical of the age, Captain Bell found himself a debtor in the Fleet, his last means running out, "he will be put into the dark dungeon and have to beg bread at the common gate." He sent a desperate petition to the Council asking that "he might have the nomination of two Irish barons" and that an order might be given to the Warden not to deal harshly with him.[2] Somehow, he seems to have emerged from these difficulties, though in 1625 his former ensign, James Moray ("brought up in the Queen of Bohemia's service"), was "arrested for debt by base fellows."[3] In 1625 Bell had obtained a licence for "measuring corn, coal and salt,"[4] and we find him writing to his "very dear friend," David Waterhouse (a soldier also confined in the Fleet), promising to use his influence to get him in the new foundation of Charterhouse, a happier asylum for soldiers of fortune whose fortunes had gone astray.[5] When, in the summer of 1624, there were troops sent to assist the Dutch, and in the autumn, to join the Count of Mansfeld's expedition, Bell had joined in the hubbub of touting for jobs and commissions. Bell wrote with the growing exasperation of his grudge upon him: the King had promised him a company, and relying on this Bell had talked about it to his friends. He could not bear the disgrace of not getting a company. He had been a soldier

[1] S.P.Dom. James I, 1619, vol. 109.164.165. July 1619, vol. 110.63. Sept. 17, vol. 111.73. 11th Dec., Acts of Privy Council, 1619-21, 140.41. Petition of Miners.
[2] S.P.Dom., 14.116.104, Sept. 1620. The financial difficulties of Aubrey of "Aubrey's Lives" illustrate the depth into which monetary difficulties might plunge people of good standing in society. It was easy to slip through the rungs of the social ladder, and once down, exceedingly difficult to climb up again.
[3] S.P. Charles I, 16.4.13.
[4] S.P. James I, 7th March 1625, 185.23.
[5] S.P. James I, 1623, 12th Dec., vol. 155.49.

for eighteen years, and three times sergeant-major,[1] and "had spent nine hundred pounds in His Majesty's service," but would quit his claim if he "may have a company or be made paymaster to the troops." [2]

His old Venetian acquaintance, the Earl of Oxford, wrote begging that Bell might have command of his company. But Conway evidently told him that all the best posts had already been disposed of.[3] In 1627 Bell was still touting for a post which might replenish his fortunes, and wrote asking that he might be allowed to escort the new levies to Denmark. He understands that Lord Conway had opposed the appointment, complains that ten years ago he had three thousand pounds, all of which had been exhausted. Is he now to be denied employment?

By now Captain Bell's case was simply a nuisance. Foreign policy had changed indeed from the days of Buckingham's ascendancy, from the public affection for the English princess and her German husband, for the glamorous Protestantism of the great Gustavus. What Bell called "the Austrian and Spanish" faction in high places at court and in the Council was not likely to be impressed by the story of an abortive plot by the Emperor striking indirectly at the Crown of England. This had long ceased to be a selling line, and indeed it was a story which the Government had good reasons for hushing up. Moreover, by this time, the financial embarrassments of the Crown were at their most acute, and it would be folly to pay thousands of pounds in hard cash, to wipe off this very bad debt. But Captain Bell's domestic situation was more urgent. There was an infant coming into the Bell family, and Bell had a final interview with the Lord Treasurer in which all his pent-up grievances flared out. He succeeded in arousing an equal and opposite but more dangerous hostility in return. "Stay yet longer," cried my Lord Treasurer, "and I will go to the Council and complain of you." [4]

It could not have escaped some members of the Council that there were loose ends about Bell's story. By now most of the key witnesses were dead or inaccessible. Suppose the whole story were a fabrication? Suppose Captain Bell had turned up suddenly before James I with the story of a plot, and with forged letters of safe conduct and a forged invitation to the Princess Elizabeth? Then Bell would be a rogue

---

[1] Sergeant-Major was the equivalent of a modern Brigadier.
[2] S.P. James I, 14.175.24.
[3] S.P., 14.167.45, 10th June 1624. E. of Oxford to Sec. Conway. It seems that Conway blocked the Venetian appointment, this commission and a further request in 1627. It is possible that his enmity was at work in the background to Bell's imprisonment.
[4] Bell's "True Relation," 1646. An Elizabeth, d. of Henry Bell, was baptized in St. Margaret's, July 1632.

indeed: but the Council would be free from an embarrassment and a possibly dangerous nuisance.

On 8th June 1631 the Privy Council gave warrant to its Clerk, Mr. (later Sir Wm.) Boswell, to search Bell's lodgings in King's Street, Westminster, and to remove all documents relating to his case. Bell knew now that trouble was impending, and that he might be arrested. But he did not keep quiet, and petitioned the Council. It is possible, though perhaps not probable, that his interview with the Lord Treasurer occurred after the search of his lodgings. In any case, it was with these threats hanging over him that he received the copy of Luther's "Divine Discourses" and had the vision of the old man who promised he would provide time and place for him to translate the book. The vision becomes psychologically explicable against this anxious background.

So, as we have heard, on 6th May 1632, a warrant, signed by the Lord Privy Seal, the Lord Chamberlain, Lord Falkland and Mr. Secretary Coke, was handed to the Messengers of the Council, with order to deliver Captain Henry Bell to the prison of the Gatehouse, Westminster, "there to remain until further order." [1] We may suppose that Captain Bell came quietly, leaving his wife at the door looking anxiously after him, her baby in arms and another child clinging to her skirt, rather like Christiana at the beginning of "Pilgrim's Progress," as her husband and his escort elbowed their way into the Sabbatic unsavoury bustle of King's Street. [2]

The Gatehouse was a grisly edifice between Dean's Yard and modern Tothill Street, Westminster, within a stone's throw of the Abbey; it had a long list of notable literary prisoners, who included Lovelace the Cavalier poet and Lilburne the Puritan. Gaol in the seventeenth century lacked some of the refined inhumanities of modern efficiency: much depended on the disposition of the gaoler and the means of the prisoner. But the Gatehouse was a speculation, let out to a Keeper and warders who lived on what they made. To be in the Gatehouse, without means, and with a wife and young children similarly destitute not half a mile away was a terrible disaster. [3] Bell wrote a petition as soon as he could, asking that he might at least have his maintenance granted him as a King's prisoner awaiting trial. Mrs. Bell had an

---

[1] Privy Council, 2.42.21.

[2] "On 5th Sept. 1628 all nuisances, obstructions, stalls, booths, etc. in King's Street were ordered to be cleared by the Privy Council, "tressels, boords, tubbs and other trash in the street," "stalls of all fishmongers and sellers of hearbes, rootes or any other things of that nature that stopp or hinder the passage" were to be removed. (Dugdale, 149.) But the road remained a notorious bottleneck until its demolition in the nineteenth century.

[3] E. C. Walcott. Memories of Westminster, 1851, p. 273. H. R. Wheatley. London Past and Present, 1891, vol. 2.88.

interview with my Lord Falkland which was, if anything, still more alarming. He told her "how foul his business appeared before the Council and that certain letters were conceived to be forged." [1] Bell wrote immediately to Lord Falkland with a long narrative of the whole story, affirming it to be the "plain and simple truth." [2] He sent another petition saying that he was "as falsely accused as Naboth was under King Ahab's government by wicked Jezebel's stubbornness" (a hit at the Queen and the Austrian-Spanish faction?). He was willing to divulge in writing an open publication of the proceedings of those sons of Belial, his false accusers.

In July it seems that the Council were willing that Bell might be released on bail. "The Council . . . having heard the report of Mr. Attorney-General touching the cause for which the said Captain Bell was committed, the examination whereof was referred unto him by the board: do hereby resolve that Mr. Attorney-General may discharge him from his present commitment upon bail." [3] It seems likely that if Captain Bell was allowed some liberty at this time it was to attend the funerals, at St. Margaret's, of his wife and daughter.[4] In all, three children died miserably during their father's troubles and we hear no more of Mrs. Bell after her interview with Falkland.

Henry Bell remained a prisoner. He now began the supreme literary occupation of his life, the bombardment of His Majesty's Government with over 210 petitions in nine years. From those which have survived, and from various minutes of the Privy Council, we can trace the ups and downs of his experiences. In 1633 he could write hopefully that "his case in Star Chamber being now ready for trial, he prays his writings may be restored to him, and that he may have counsel." [5] In 1634 he appealed to Archbishop Laud, saying that he was being "suffered to pine away by degrees and for want of food. If any one point be false" in his story "he will be content to undergo the most shameful death and horrible punishment that ever villain suffered." [6] The contact with Laud fits the story of how Laud heard of the Table Talk. It seemed in the autumn of 1634 that something might be done at last. 13th September, Bell complained that he had sent sixteen references

---

[1] S.P., 16.218, 16th June 1632.
[2] S.P. Charles I, 16.218, 61.2, 16th June 1632.
[3] Register of Privy Council, 20th July 1632.
[4] Register of St. Margaret's, Westminster, 1632. Burke. Memorials of St. Margaret's. The Register shows the death of Henry Bell (child), 2nd Jan. 1632. There are burials of two Sara Bells, 21st May 1632 and 7th August, and both are marked in the Register with the sign which denoted a child burial. In his " True Relation " (1646) Bell laid the death of his wife and three children at the Council's door. The third death, he claims, occurred in the period 1640-6.
[5] S.P. Charles I, 248.46, 1633.
[6] S.P. Charles I, 271, 1st July, 4th July.

to the Attorney-General, now deceased, who had sent him a message. "Commend me to Captain Bell and tell him that my hands are bound. I cannot bring his cause to a trial, nor do more than I have done: and as touching his imprisonment, I have no hand therein, he must petition the Lords for his liberty." [1]

For. the next months we turn to Bell's published account of ·his experiences in his "True Relation" (1646). At last a Bill had been put in against him . . . "most wickedly contrived . . . like thereunto was never heard of or known so long as this kingdom stood, devised by and upon their Lordships' meer conceits and pretended cogitations and weenings." According to Bell, Sir John Banks, Attorney-General, sent for him and said, "Captain Bell, the Lords of the Council have commanded me to send for you, and to tell you, that the Bill was not drawn against you with any intent to bring you to trial, but only to see what answer you would make thereunto . . . and their Lordships are now satisfied, they have ordered the Bill to be dismissed." The Attorney-General told him that the real reason for his imprisonment was his importunity, "such a continual clamouring for your money" when "there was not yet money to pay you." If Bell would be bound under a security of two thousand pounds, he might be released on bail. Bell claims that he sent the security within two days to Sir John Banks' Chambers at Gray's Inn. But he was not released, so that "my security was forced to neglect all their own affairs in trading and attend to petitions." Evidently somebody in authority had decided that Bell would never be quiet, and that it were safer to keep him confined, despite the order of the Privy Council to the Keeper of the Gatehouse (November 1634) that "Capt. Bell . . . having entered into bond with security, is to be set at full liberty." [2]

Now began a period of terrible hardship, and the gaolers vented their displeasure against one whom the King's Council delighted not to honour. Two years later Bell could write that "Since November 1634" he had " had nothing save bare bread and drink." He had taken the dangerous step of complaining about the keeper whose "wickedness, craft, subtlety, hypocrisy, oppression and deceitful usage . . . is beyond compare . . . it is a case most lamentable . . . not desiring so much favour as may be shown a dead dog, but my pressing for a just and legal trial, should be kept in prison." [3] In another, he tells how he is "constrained to sell his beer to the other prisoners for a little money to pay for the

[1] S.P. Charles I, 274.20, 13th Sept.
[2] There are other cases of an order for release from the Privy Council being ignored. A similar decision against a preacher, despite an order from Sir Dudley Carleton, was brought against Laud at his trial.
[3] S.P. Charles I, 328.9, 2nd July 1636.

washing of his linen to prevent him being devoured by vermin."[1] "He that is now the writer's black angel ... set to be his keeper, Richard Redding ... is encouraged daily to torment him ... is strictly cooped up in that cave of murder."[2] During five years he had sent 104 petitions and at last, in February 1636-7, he wrote another full narrative, hoping it might come into the King's hands.[3] He brought some influence to bear from the outside through some Scottish friends, so that Sir William Beecher at last condescended to look at the documents. Beecher, however, was not impressed by what he saw of the Elector's alleged safe conducts and sent an angry message to Bell. "That the Elector of Brandenburg's safe conduct makes quite against the petitioner and shows that he is rather guilty than otherwise: and that as a knave he has cheated the Lords and shall rot in prison: let him take heed lest he come to a public shame if he succeed not in his suit." But Bell had an answer. "The letters of safe conduct were despatched in an extraordinary manner. Very seldom, except such as carried business of great weight, were any such letters signed by the Prince Elector himself, but only his name subscribed by his secretary. These were subscribed by the Prince and in particular sort. M.P., viz. manu propria, a certain denotation of all states in Germany."[4] "Sir William Beecher says that I am a knave. I answer that I am as honest as the skin between Sir William's brow, which I will make good with His Majesty's permission with my sword, as befits a soldier." Nor has he cheated the Lords, but spent over five thousand pounds for lack of which "my wife and young infants miserably were destroyed. If I am guilty I will not refuse to lie and rot in prison."[5]

We find him reporting some alleged treasonable gossip in a vain attempt to catch the ear of authority. For by this time Bell's petitions must have become a joke. Finally, however, a supercilious note from Sir Dudley Carleton evoked one of Bell's most eloquent efforts. He has heard that orders are to be given to receive no more petitions (he has sent 216 in eight years). But "I must be forward to let my bell send such a peal that the same shall ring and be heard throughout this kingdom and it may be beyond. I have in this matter been handled contrary to God's Word and directly opposite to the law of this kingdom, of nations and of the whole world ... I may justly say that I would rather live among the Turks than here if Parliament be not held. I am in this just cause handled according to that tyranny which usurps the very consent of all people, 'sic volo, sic jubeo, sit pro ratione voluntas.'"

---

[1] S.P. Charles I, 1636, 329.46, 26th July.
[2] S.P. Charles I, 1636-7, 10th Feb., vol. 346.79.
[3] S.P. Charles I, 1637-8, 28th Nov., vol. 402.70.1.
[4] S.P. Charles I, 1637-8, vol. 402.70.2.   [5] Ibid.

He craves no favour, but justice, "being one line in argument . . . which I intend to divulge concerning the abominable usages, oppressions, insinuations and tyranny . . . which relation will make the ears of some to tingle." [1]

The tone of Bell's letter suggests, not only that he may have been hobnobbing with rebel intellectuals in the Adullamite society of the Gatehouse, but that he had heard that Parliament might soon meet. Parliament met in the beginning of November 1640 and a pent-up flood of grievances and petitions began to reach Westminster, while a whole series of imprisonments came to an end. Henry Bell was set free, and on 2nd December his cause was heard at long last by the King. (His thunder, stolen perhaps, since on this day Prynne, Burton and Bastwick presented their petitions to Parliament.) The King handed Bell's precious documents—the letter from the Empress and a certificate (signed "at Holbery shortly before his death") from Sir Albert Morton —to Mr. Smith of the Council Chamber, and bade the Lords look to Bell's recompense.

But Henry Bell's nemesis was still upon him. The State moved fatally towards disruption, the dire collision between King and Parliament. Henry Bell was loosed into a bitter world, sadly emptied of wife and children. An England ripe indeed for his old trade. But he was ten years older, and impaired in health of mind and body. We have no document which could show us him, as Col. Underwood's diary showed him a century before, hobbling pale and gaunt about the London streets. We cannot tell whether, when they ranged the cannon across Whitehall, beside the Banqueting House and facing Charing Cross, he was there to survey the scene with a critical and practised eye. His former patrons were dead, or on the wrong side of the rapidly parting ice-floe. As the war developed the Parliamentary party were not likely to devote much attention to the old story of how, long ago, Captain Henry Bell had saved the life of the mother of Rupert of the Rhine! His deposition was taken against Archbishop Laud (the signature the feeblest scrawl in all his writings).[2]

In it Bell told how he had been committed on a warrant signed by Laud and other members of the Council, "committed to the Gatehouse and there detained in prison eight years and upwards without showing any cause . . . the deponent exhibited to the Archbishop of Canterbury and others of the Council Board, 214 petitions, thereby endeavouring his enlargement, but could not gain his liberty, until this Parliament

[1] S.P. Charles I, 1639, 3rd August, 427.7.54.66. In his "True Relation" Bell reckoned his total unrequited disbursements at £5268.
[2] S.P. Charles I, 16.500.6, 10th Jan.

gave him the same." [1] But the deposition does not seem to have been brought up at Laud's trial, probably because Laud was not in supreme authority at the time of Bell's arrest and had no more responsibility than the rest of the Council. In 1646 Bell published a "True Relation of the Abominable Injustice, Oppression and Tyranny which Captain Henry Bell suffered nine years together . . . before this Parliament began "and" also what misery he hath suffered six years together since the beginning of this parliament only by reason their Lordships have not yet taken his hearing which the King did refer and send unto their Lordships."

This leaflet included a brief narration of his troubles which tallies reasonably accurately with the earlier narratives penned during his imprisonment and now in the Public Record Office. It was prefaced by an appeal to the King and followed by a complaint to the House of Lords. The last document throws light on his sufferings since his release. By reason of the dilatoriness of Lords nothing has been done in his cause, despite the intervention on his behalf of the Scottish Commissioners some three years before. As a result another child has come "to an untimely end" and Bell himself plunged into a depth of misery, so that he is "nearly destitute of food, raiment and lodging." We know that Henry Bell was alive on 3rd July 1650, when he signed the Preface to the Table Talk. We know that he was dead when the book appeared in 1652.

In Somerset House there is the copy of an oral, soldier's will, made on the field of battle,[2] and proved in July 1652, concerning one Henry Bell who died "in the Wars of Scotland, two years since" and in favour of his comrade John Godfrey.[3] In the Public Record Office there are a number of unpublished documents, Muster Rolls of Cromwell's regiments, relating to grants of Crown land by which (1649-50) the Government tried to cope with arrears of pay. Among those lists, No. 21 in Captain Savage's troop in Colonel Whalley's regiment of horse, is the signature of Henry Bell, while No. 14 is the John Godfrey in whose favour the will was made. In the same list is the name of the trumpeter, Bartholomew Barnes, who is one of the two witnesses of the soldier's will.[4] Here then are a Porthos and an Aramis for our elderly D'Artagnan.

Comparison of signatures and handwriting make it probable (I dare not say more) that this is our Henry Bell. The 1646 tract falls into

---

[1] Ibid.
[2] On the abuse of this practice. C. H. Firth. Cromwell's Army, 1902, App. J, 407.
[3] Probate Acts of Canterbury. Ed. Mathews. Vol. 6.18. Admon. with Will (197, Bowyer), 16th July, to John Godfrey.
[4] Commonwealth Exchequer Papers. S.P., 28, No. 3, M. 58. Remembrancer Certifs. See also Berry, "A Cromwellian Major-General," 1938, 104-5. Firth and Davies. Regimental History of Cromwell's Army. Bell, Godfrey and Barnes appear in a printed manifesto signed by the regiment in 1649.

place if he were a disbanded and unpaid soldier, plunged again into destitution. It may seem a fantastically far cry from the gallant captain, sponsored by a British Ambassador, in a short list for the over-all allied command in Venice, to a trooper in a regiment of horse. But Bell was ageing and had suffered many things. And as Robert Greene spoke for that age "what is gentry if wealth be wanting but servile beggary."

But if this be our Henry Bell, we are in luck indeed. For it so happens that the MS. exists in which the details of each man's military service, and the grants of land near Hemel Hempstead are recorded, and that Colonel Whalley's is the only regiment of which such clear account has survived.[1] For his service (presumably in the first part of the Civil War) under the Earl of Manchester, Bell was owed thirty-one pounds five shillings, and during this time was trumpeter to Captain Timothy Smith's troop in Colonel Saunders' Regiment.[2] There are two debentures owing to Bell (amounting to fifty-nine pounds six shillings and sixpence) for service in Col. Copley's regiment (Col. Copley ran a lucrative black market in his soldier's horses until discovered and cashiered). This may sound mere chicken-feed compared with the thousands of pounds of Bell's earlier career, but at least this was convertible into good, hard land. Thus, in 1650 Henry Bell, trooper, was a member of Capt. Savage's troop in Col. Whalley's regiment. This troop had an exciting pedigree: it was the lineal descendant of that troop which, under Major Bethell, executed one of the most dashing cavalry charges in our military history: the "forlorne design" at Langport which involved fording a river, and a steep charge uphill in the face of Goring's men, and in which, although the gallant Major was killed, his men routed a foe ten times their number. It was this troop, under Captain Pitchford, which had Richard Baxter as Chaplain, and which catechized him publicly from the gallery of the Church at Chesham (an old Lollard stronghold) in a fantastic scene which surpasses Scott's fiction in the opening pages of "Woodstock."[3] It was Whalley's regiment which attended the person of the King from June to November 1647. Though we have Baxter's testimony to its heady Leveller ferment, it seems that the regiment held aloof from the famous Ware mutiny of November 1647.[4] Finally, it was this same troop

---

[1] Harl. MSS., 427.
[2] "Trumpeters ought to be witty and discreet, because they are frequently sent to an enemy . . . they should be cunning and careful . . ." (Sir James Turner, qu. Firth. Cromwell's Army, 44.)
[3] Baxter. Autobiography, 56. (Everyman Ed.)
[4] If Bell were in another regiment in 1647 he may have been involved in the Ware mutiny. There is a reference in Rushworth, vii. "There was also one Bell condemned to run the gauntlet twice for being active in that mutiny." We read of John Godfrey as among other troopers arrested. But there was a Thomas Bell in the same regiment. Gardiner. Civil War, iv. 142.145. Firth and Davies, 209.

which staged its own private mutiny in 1649, when, in a desperate effort to obtain arrears of pay, some of the troopers (Bell was not among them) seized the regimental standards and barricaded themselves in the Bull Inn, Bishopsgate.[1]

If Captain Henry Bell of our story be Trooper Bell of Cromwell's Army, he set his affairs in order, and signed the preface of his book on 3rd July 1650, and moved north with the regiment towards the Scottish border. The 30th July there was sharp fighting. On the eve of battle Henry Bell and his comrade, John Godfrey, made a soldier's will, a compact that whoever died first should leave his property to the survivor, and this agreement was witnessed by Bartholomew Barnes, the trumpeter, and another. At Musselburgh battle was joined. Part of Whalley's regiment received the full shock of the enemy charge, staggered and gave ground: but other troops came up and carried the fight up to the enemy lines, only to be beaten back again as the enemy threw in his reserves. The day was carried by another troop of Whalley's regiment which, under Captain Chillenden, "charged them and put them to the run." We do not know if Henry Bell lived to fight another day, if he survived to behold the smoking glory of the dawn at Dunbar. But it would be fitting if he fell, in the strict sense of the good old word, in harness, if somewhere in Scotland that grizzled head lay face down among the heather.[2]

3. CAPTAIN HENRY BELL'S TRANSLATION.

It is time to look again at Bell's edition of the Table Talk. The publication of his "True Relation" (1646) of his sufferings was no doubt intended to reinforce the favourable judgment of the committee of the House of Commons on his "Divine Discourses." But the second Civil War now intervened. In 1650 Henry Bell sent another petition to "the Most Honourable and Supreme Power of England's Commonwealth in Parliament assembled." The order of the House of Commons in 1646, concerning his book, had been sent to the Lords, "but by reason of other weighty affairs the House of Lords was dissolved before they could despatch the same: it resting now only in the power of the most honourable assembly in Parliament to confirm and accomplish the same. Your Petitioner having already made choice of and appointed an honest and able man to print the same translated book, named Wm. Du Gard."

By now Captain Bell's hopes for his book were ambitious. It was not enough that it be printed "Cum Privilegio," but that, as copies

---

[1] Firth and Davies, 219. "The Army's Martyr" and "Walwin's Wiles." B.Mus., 554.
[2] Firth and Davies. The mathematical probabilities are that he died of dysentery, but occasionally history does itself poetic justice.

had been chained in all the churches of Protestant Germany—"your petitioner humbly prayeth that this most honourable assembly will confirm your aforesaid order . . . and therein also to recommend his said work in each countie within England and Wales and to order that everie parish in all the said counties may have and receive into their churches one of the said printed books to be kept therein as was done in Germany."

If Henry Bell really supposed that the Puritan Commonwealth, already theologically far to the left of Zürich and Geneva, let alone Wittenberg, would elevate Luther's "Divine Discourses" to a dignity equal with that of the Bible, the Prayer Book, the Homilies and the Book of Martyrs, he was to be disillusioned. We had better take his daring request as a symptom of the desperate and ruined condition of his fortunes. "Your petitioner," he ended hopefully, "being content to leave it to the discretion of every parish what in their free and voluntary will they shall think fitting to give him for the said book which hath cost him five whole years to translate, whereby he may be the better enabled to defraie the great costs and charges for printing and publishing thereof: which otherwise he shall not be able to accomplish."

That same year a prospectus was issued, prefaced by a portrait of Luther. In this various commendations were printed, including those of the famous Puritan preacher, John Downame,[1] and the grandfather of all Ecumenical Movements, John Durie. It seems that Captain Bell never fingered the fine new copies of his great work, which had cost so much. No doubt somebody made money out of the book, but not Captain Henry Bell.

Bell's translation is taken from Aurifaber's edition of the "Tisch-reden," the first edition of which appeared at Eisleben in 1566.[2] The first edition contained eighty-two chapters, but two of these are accounted for by a printer's error, and Bell has, like the subsequent editions of Aurifaber, eighty chapters. Bell included the whole of Aurifaber's long preface and ended with a collection of "Prophesies of Martin Luther" which appeared only in a pirated edition of 1571, so that Bell's edition corresponds to no known edition of Aurifaber.

Henry Bell had indeed taught Luther "to speak English," vigorous, redolent of the rhythm and phrasing of the English Bible, and the ·English liturgy. We must envy him that he could write not of the "Devil," but of the "Divel," a far worthier recipient, we feel, of Luther's inkpot. Coleridge has pointed out some errors of translation, and that

---

[1] Haller. Rise of Puritanism (1938), 65.79.
[2] Preserved Smith. Table Talk, 80.121. I have examined the 1566 edition in the British Museum. Tischreden oder Colloquia Doct. Mart. Luthers. Eisleben, 1566.

Bell missed the point of one or two puns (we may excuse him; the Gatehouse did not sharpen a man's sense of the ridiculous). Wm. Hazlitt, junior, has some vaguely patronizing remarks about Bell's work. He might have spared himself, for when he came to edit the work, he removed nearly all the topical illusions, and with a few touches succeeded in making the Table Talk much duller than either Martin Luther or Henry Bell.

But the most interesting section is the drastic abridgment by Bell of the long section in the original on "Vom Sacrament des Waren Leibs und Blutes Christi," now translated as "Of the Sacrament of the Lord's Supper." It will have been noted that the Parliamentary committee which examined Bell's book specially noted that in it Luther had acknowledged "his error which he formerly held touching the real presence corporaliter in coena domini."

Luther, of course, never did anything of the kind, and as far as I know there is no German edition of the Table Talk in which he makes any such dramatic retractation. It is obvious that this was the price paid by Bell to get his book authorized and published. The two alterations will be found in Bell's edition of Luther's "Divine Discourses" (1652), p. 263:

"Of the cause of the Sacrament of the Altar. 'The operative cause ... of this Sacrament is the Word and Institution of Christ who ordained and erected it. The substance is bread and wine, the form is the true body and blood of Christ *which is spiritually received by faith.*'" [1]

That could conceivably hold the Lutheran interpretation. The next is more explicit:

"The Pope well permitteth the substance and essence of The Sacrament and Bible to remain: but yet he will compel and force us to use the same according as his will and pleasure is to describe it, and will constrain us to believe the falsely feigned and invented transubstantiation, *and the real presence corporaliter.*" [2]

I am not inclined to blame an army captain (albeit the son of a Dean

---

[1] TR. (1566). Dieses Sacraments, sprach Dr. Martinus Luther, Ursach ist Das Wort und Einsetzung Christi der es gestifftet und aufgerichtet hat. Die Materia ist Brot und Wein, die Form ist der Ware Leib und Blut Christi, die endliche ursach warumb es eingesetzt ist der Nutz und Frucht das wir unsern Glauben starcken. 232.

[2] TR. (1566). Was die Substanz und das Wesen belanget, so lasst der Bapst die Sacramente und Bibel bleiben, allein will er uns zwingen das wir derselben Brauch sollen wie er will und zuschreibet. 232.

The sentence about transubstantiation and the real presence has no place in the original.

Bell's Table Talk was reprinted in a new edition in 1791, with a long preface by John Gottlieb Burckhardt, Minister of the German congregation at the Savoy in London. He reprints Bell's Preface and the Order of the House of Commons, but drops the report in which mention is made of Luther's retractation. The two extracts given above are retained.

and a professor of Theology) for not grasping that to make a theological fudge is heinous. But who advised him to do it, and what did he intend to do? Was he simply making Luther readable by "the saints and people of God in this Nation," i.e. by Puritans, Presbyterians, Independents, Sectaries, who would have turned in disgust from any doctrine of a real and corporal presence? If a King of France could reckon Paris well worth a Mass, might not a broken-down captain consider the repair of his fortunes worth a hint of receptionism? Was it, to throw an apple of discord, conceivably Archbishop Laud who made the suggestion? For it was Laud who at his own trial defended the liturgy against this very doctrine. "They say the Corporal Presence of Christ's Body in the Sacrament is found in the Service Book. But they must pardon me: I know it is not there. I cannot myself be of a contrary judgment and yet suffer that to pass," and again, "if it be only 'fiant nobis,' that they may be to us the Body and Blood of Christ: it implies clearly that they . . . are not transubstantiated in themselves into the Body and Blood of Christ, nor that there is any corporal presence in or under the elements." [1]

We might naughtily comment, that if the doctrine expressed and intended by Bell's translation, and by his pointed omissions and his notable addition, is so ambiguous that we cannot say if it is Puritan or Laudian, then Bell had indeed succeeded in putting Luther among the Anglicans. We cannot tell how many were deceived, and how many thought more kindly of Martin Luther because of it. And if this were the price for getting the book published, at least in this way more of the authentic spirit of Luther got into English hands than any other volume in the period. But for it, there would be a notable gap in the story of Luther in England. We cannot say if it was known to Bunyan and to Milton: but we do know what it meant to Coleridge and to Carlyle. For an amateur, Henry Bell had done a great work. And if we remember Luther's tremendous phrase, "Not reading and speculating, but living, dying and being condemned make a real theologian," why, then, we may count Captain Henry Bell among the true, the evangelical professors.

[1] Laud. History of the Troubles and Trials of . . . Wm. Laud (1695), 121.

PART

II

"CORAM DEO"

Chapter

4

A CRISIS OF VOCABULARY

"In almost all . . . the qualities of a preacher of Christ, Luther
after Paul and John is the great master."
S. T. COLERIDGE on Luther's " Table Talk."

AMONG many other things, the Reformation was a crisis of Christian
vocabulary. R. G. Collingwood, in his "Idea of History," has suggested the deep inter-relation of human ideas, speech, behaviour.
These things are bound together in the bundle of life, acting and
reacting upon one another. The changing pressures of social and
political existence necessitate new adjustments of ideas and words,
and eventually, though the element of novelty is always less than
superficially appears, new ideas and new words, so that every age of
revolutionary ferment brings with it a crisis of vocabulary.

This is true of all the intellectual disciplines. It is specially true of
the Christian religion, for it is concerned with historical events which
are remembered, represented and proclaimed in the proclamation of
the Word, and in those sacraments which are "visible words" and
which have to be made intelligible to each succeeding generation. The
New Testament itself is evidence of one such crisis, when the words
of Judaism and the words of Greece and Rome were melted and re-
minted in terms of the Christian revelation. Another crisis was provoked by the re-entry into Christendom, through suspect and alien
sources, of the philosophy of Aristotle, the famous challenge notably
resolved by Albertus Magnus and the great Thomas.

In the sixteenth century a new crisis was provoked by the decline
of scholasticism as a tool, a method of critical enquiry and as a vehicle
of theological conversation. And this crisis was apart from the Reformation, with which this essay is concerned. The humanist reaction
was vehement in its reaction against scholasticism before Luther had
written a line. Humanism began as a technical affair, "an educated and
cultural programme based on the study of classical Greek and Latin
authors," [1] and turning to new methods of historical and philological
criticism, carried through in the Universities among teachers of

---

[1] E. Cassirer and P. O. Kristeller. The Renaissance Philosophy of Man. Chicago,
1948. P. O. Kristeller. " Humanism and Scholasticism in the Italian Renaissance."
Byzantion, XVII, 1944-5, 346-74.

grammar and rhetoric and by secretaries and chaplains of princely courts. There was the new wave of Platonist influence (Augustinian and Neo-Platonic) against late mediaeval Aristotelianism. There was the Ciceronian revival—a sinister symptom of an age, like our own, bedazzled with rhetoric? Nor must we forget—and this cuts through all facile generalizations, and a too sharp opposition between humanism and the schoolmen—that there was a humanist Aristotelianism which persisted throughout the Renaissance and was much more congenial to scholasticism, and which is typified in Pomponazzi and Zabarella.

Positively and Christianly, sixteenth century humanism was the attempt to return to the Bible and the Fathers and to disentangle the religion of wayfaring Christians from the elaborate subtleties of the later schoolmen. Herein lies the significance of the humanist groups which included St. Thomas More, Stephen Gardiner and Erasmus. The warning which Gregory IX had given the University of Paris of what might happen if the philosophers usurped the place of the theologians had gone unheeded. When M. Gilson says that "Christian philosophy died, primarily of its own dissensions . . . Albertists, Scotists, Occamists, all contributed to the ruin of mediaeval philosophy," [1] he is echoing what Luther had said four centuries before, "Nay, all the Thomists, Scotists and the 'moderni' gnash their teeth against one another, nor is there any kind or character of men that war against one another with more ferocity and hatred . . . than the sects of the theologians, for each wants to reign alone, and to see all other sects utterly consumed." [2]

But Luther never put the case against the scholastic theologians more strongly than did Erasmus: they were his one very perfect hatred and they repaid his scorn with a hostility which nearly brought his ruin. [3] This was a war in which the humanists had been engaged for a generation. Tyndale could even appeal to St. Thomas More as a comrade in arms in that campaign. [4]

"Remember ye not, how within this thirty years and far less . . . the old barking curs, Duns's disciples and like draff called Scotists . . . raged in every pulpit against Greek, Latin and Hebrew?"

To-day, the late Schoolmen are receiving more sympathetic attention. Their systems, those "cathedrals of the mind," are seen as profound and even magnificent: the gaunt simplifications of Ockham are as

[1] E. Gilson. Spirit of Mediaeval Philosophy (1936), 401.
[2] M. Luther. Against Ambrosius Catherinus (tr. Cole, 1836), 82. Also W.A. 3.319.11.
[3] Erasmus has some bitter passages in his dedicatory epistle (1518) to his " Enchiridion Militis Christiani " (D. Erasmus Roterodamus. Ausgewählte Werke. Ed. Holborn. Munich, 1933, 4, lines 4-15 ; 5, 14-29 ; but see also 14, 25-30.)
[4] Tyndale. Works. P.S., vol. 3.75.

impressive in their way as those elaborate speculations of the subtle
Doctor Scotus, which have something of the intricate beauty of fan
tracery in stone. It was not so much Ockham, Scotus and Biel who
were the butt of the New Learning, as the warring parties of their
disciples, inferior minds whose narrow deference to the party line
revealed that the mind, as well as the body of the Christian world was
sick. The attempt, like all attempts, to return to a "simple gospel"
could only partially succeed. The end of the sixteenth century witnessed an inevitable recurrence of a Protestant scholasticism side by
side with a renewal of Catholic philosophy.

Martin Luther was involved in a further crisis of vocabulary, different
and distinct from that of the humanist attempt to regain the "philosophy
of Christ." His theological development has a significance far greater
than the personal spiritual need and the individual theological enquiries
in which it originated. From Luther's intuitions and affirmations was
erected a new technical vocabulary, and new theological categories,
and a new relation of Christian doctrines to one another. He had
never any love for novelty: later he poked scornful fun at the fanatics
who loved to invent obscure jargon, and he rejected the temptation
to surrender to the vague transcendental obscurities of the mystics.
Perhaps no description of the development of Luther's thought can
be anything more than an interim judgment. The present state of
studies of late scholasticism does not permit anything more than
hesitant and tentative opinions upon the amount of continuity and discontinuity in Luther's theology. Regin Prenter has pointed to the correct
method, which is to concentrate not on the "Whence?" or "Whither?"
but upon the "What?", the content of Luther's theology.[1]

To trace the changes in Luther's thought, particularly in the years
1509-21, is difficult and hazardous. Too often the Catholic approaches
the subject with the question, "At what point did Luther begin to go
wrong?" while the Protestant asks, "Where does Luther begin to be
Protestant?"—and in each case the definition of later Catholic or
Protestant orthodoxy is made the criterion.

The tendency is to over-simplify: to ignore the real elements of
dogmatic confusion and uncertainty before the Council of Trent, and
to dogmatize about Nominalist doctrines beyond the resources so far
provided by modern technical scholarship.[2] Another temptation is to
read too much between the lines, and to treat Luther's obiter dicta as

---

[1] Spiritus Creator, p. 10.
[2] J. Lortz. Reformation in Deutschland, 1.137.205-210. See the remarks of
P. Vignaux, Dict. Théol. Cath. XI, " the lack of monographs even about the most
famous Nominalists." Since then there has been considerable improvement, but we
still await a full, critical edition of Biel in terms of recent scholarship.

representing his firm theological beliefs and as though they represent a ready-made system.

Only a fool would suggest that the Great Divide between Catholics and Protestants is a matter of misunderstanding. But it seems certain that there has been all along a genuine element of misunderstanding, rooted in the insistence of both orthodoxies in interpreting an opponent terminology in its own way. Erasmus protested against Eck and Cochlaeus and Emser, who insisted on reading Luther in this manner. If the Protestant conception of "Faith" is treated as an intellectual assent, or a sentiment of confidence, then the doctrine of salvation "by only faith" becomes as shocking as Tyndale's "feeling faith" seemed to Sir Thomas More, as abstract and remote from life as the Homily of Salvation seemed to Stephen Gardiner, and as blasphemous as the "sola fide" has seemed to some modern Anglicans. The great interest of the writings of Pighius and Gropper, the so-called "mediating theologians," is that their writings represent the last real conversation between Catholics and Protestants on this subject.

The Catholic may only too easily conceive Luther's theology as a broken torso of Catholic orthodoxy, a compound of theological Philistinism and Vandalism: as though to the injury which decapitated the "Winged Victory" of Samothrace there were added the insult of planting some crude plaster effigy upon those lovely shoulders; ungainly disproportionate and destructive to the wholeness of Christian truth. The Protestant needs always to remember that Luther is the least typical of all Lutherans, the least typical of Protestants, invariably more disconcerting and alive than the various schools of his traditional and modern interpreters.

To examine Luther's development from the angle of his vocabulary, adjusted to the changing historical context of his life, has certain advantages. For one thing, it is traceable in genuine documents. We have not to go beyond undisputed facts in search of some presumed psychological pattern. Nor must we interpret them in terms of some nineteenth century variety of religious experience, while we may remember that it is Calvin, not Luther, who speaks of a "sudden conversion." The truth is that there are great gaps in our knowledge of Luther's early life which, in all likelihood, will never be filled, and which warn off all those who put forward a psycho-analytical theory of his development.

The historian will not lack a decent deference towards the psychologist if he reminds him of the limits of historical evidence, and the precarious character of such reconstructions after four hundred years. In an evaluation of the career of Martin Luther the first word must lie with the historian, whose proper task is to discriminate between the varying levels of the evidence, and the relative worth of the authorities. In an evaluation of the thought of Martin Luther the first word must be with the theologian who must interpret his writings in the light of the history of Christian doctrine and in relation to systematic theology. At least no psychological interpretation may flagrantly maltreat the canons of these two disciplines, and it may fairly be said that there has been no psychological diagnosis so far put forward which has not fallen foul of the canons of the historian and the theologian.

Concerning the moods and depressions of Luther's mature years there is indeed abundant evidence. Most of this has been usefully arranged in the volumes of Dr. J. P. Reiter.[1] But for the critical earlier years, the reliable evidence fails.[2]

We simply do not know whether the home of Martin Luther was

[1] Dr. Med. J. P. Reiter. Martin Luthers Umwelt, Charakter und Psychose. i. Die Umwelt, 1937. ii. Luthers Persönlichkeit, Seelenleben und Krankheiten. Copenhagen, 1941. Volume ii. assembles the evidence. For useful criticism of Reiter's analysis see P. Bühler. Die Anfechtung bei Luther. Zurich, 1942, 31-2.

[2] Earlier attempts at a psychological evaluation of Luther were those of Bruno Schön (1874), who depicted him as a paranoiac, Denifle who saw him as a moral degenerate (1904), Preserved Smith (American J. Psych., 1918) as an example of an Oedipus complex. Dr. J. P. Reiter's interpretation on the whole is more reserved, and mild in its conclusions, and the value of his work lies in his assembly of evidence, especially concerning Luther's middle years, and the period of illness (1527-8). He notes the periods of exaltation and depression which he claims follow a recognized psychological pattern, but he acknowledges the tremendous mental output of Luther throughout these years. In Reiter's opinion Luther drank too much, but the evidence on which this opinion is based is strained and maltreated, while Dr. Reiter shows a singular and disastrous inability to comprehend, or make any sense of Luther's theology. Reiter is laudably reticent about the struggles of Luther's monastic career, realizing the precarious nature of the evidence, and is inclined, following Grisar, to speak of it as a " mysticism of despair." A more recent article turns attention to these early years, Martin Werner's " Psychologisches zum Klostererlebnis Martin Luthers " (Schweizerische Z. für Psychologie, vol. vii. No. 1, 1948, 1-18). Werner rightly tilts at the reluctance of many Protestant historians to face the facts of any abnormalities in Luther's make up " as though such facts meant any depreciation of the importance of his personality in history." But in fact almost all the psychological studies, as we have seen, are used, or have been made use of, in exactly this polemical way. Werner concentrates attention on the visit to the Augustinian convent which Father Luther made on the occasion of the celebration of Luther's First Mass. Luther's own account of this, written in 1521, tells of his father's disgruntled dismissal of his own account of his heavenly calling with " Let's hope it wasn't an illusion of the devil," and of the embarrassing rebuke administered at the festal table, " Have you not read ' Honour thy father and thy mother ' ? " Werner greatly exaggerates the importance of this incident and finds in it " the true key to the right understanding of the paradoxes of Luther's guilt conflicts " (8). He finds this conflict to be between Luther's long inculcated fear and reverent obedience to his father and his new reverence for church authority. If Father Luther were right, then Martin Luther had entered a life condemned by God. Hence arose conflicts, which, as Werner rightly recognizes, were far deeper than a case of monastic " scruples." He suggests that the conflict was resolved when Luther, following the theology of Tauler, came to a doctrine of " resignation." His doctrine of humility and " accusatio sui " (see below, p. 148) led finally to an act of will by which he was willing to accept even damnation, if that were the will of God. Then, and then alone, he found peace. We cannot here discuss the details of this interpretation, save to remark that Werner makes ingenious use of

like that of Sören Kierkegåard, or, say, that of John Wesley, though the sifted later gossip indicates that Hans Luther was more sturdily normal than Michael Kierkegaard or Samuel Wesley, while Margaret Luther was no Susannah Wesley. We may believe his upbringing to have been tough and rough, like that of most children in that age, but some historians have exaggerated this side of things, and there was no doubt sunshine and laughter and companionship to offset pain and fear. Nor despite the vast background provided by Otto Scheel, do we know very much about his schooldays, unless it be the revealing sentence in after life, "Who ever loved a schoolmaster?"

There is considerable confusion in the evidence, critically examined, about the events and the motives which led him, in the year 1505, to drop the study of law, to disappoint his father's ambitions that he would make "a respectable and wealthy marriage," to enter religion and become an Austin Friar.[1]

Important events which followed are far from clear. The circumstances of his call to Wittenberg from Erfurt, in 1508, and for his return to the older University: the date and occasion of his first personal contact with Staupitz: the inner story of the dispute between the Augustinian Conventuals and Observants which led to his journey to Rome on behalf of the dissidents: the date of the journey and the circumstances which led him to join the other party after his return. In almost all of these questions the decision remains among probabilities, and provides a most insecure basis for a case history.

As a consequence, there is a great temptation to forget the haphazard and accidental quality of historical evidence, and to suppose that

incidents regarded as apocryphal by all reputable modern historians (8-9) and to point out that Luther speaks of " resignatio " before he knew Tauler. Even Werner has to face the problem that Luther's characteristic doctrine of Justification by Faith involves not a desperate action of the human will, but its reverse, the action of saving grace in Jesus Christ. He has thus to posit a new series of psychological crises to account for that. Thus he fatally splits the development of Luther's theology (1507-21) in two completely disparate parts. Fr. R. Weijenborg (Rev. d'Hist. Eccl., 1950, 659 ff.) rejects Werner's theory as a whole and points out that there is no trace of Luther's teaching about " resignation " before 1513, and that it can hardly be brought into relation with a situation alleged to develop rapidly in 1507. But he makes use of Werner for his own hardly more plausible ends, similarly developing a theory of crisis, not in terms of Luther's reverent obedience to his father, but from a serious conflict with his father which came to a head in 1507. It should be noted that most of these psychological interpretations (Preserved Smith, Werner, Weijenborg) are not by practising and expert psychologists, but by theologians and historians making use of psychological theories for their own purposes. The following psychological studies have not been consulted, but details are given for the sake of bibliographical completeness. Österreich. Parapsychisches bei Luther ? Z. für Parapsychologie, 54. 1927, 56 ff. Berkhan. Die Nervösen Beschwerden des Dr. Martin Luther, Archiv für Psychiatrie. XI, 1881, 798-803. Theol. Bl., 1938, 212. Luther aus dem Fenster des psychiatrischen Hospitals gesehen. Theol. Bl., 1942, 108. Luthers Psychobiogramm und Neurose.

[1] W.A. 8.573.24.

because we seek to solve certain questions, what evidence there is must speak to their condition. There are, for example, two Latin sermons of Luther preserved in Erfurt. They may be the earliest sermons of Luther which have survived, and on internal grounds (there is little external evidence) have been variously dated between 1509-13. In a recent essay, Fr. Weijenborg appears to succumb to this temptation when he inserts the two sermons into critical moments in these years, and relates the first sermon to the moment when Luther had returned from Rome, and gone over to the opposite party. But, in fact, the sermons might have been delivered upon any of some hundreds of occasions, the context of which has entirely escaped us. That the purely accidental survival of two discourses should exactly plug two important and controverted gaps in the story reconstructed by modern research is to stretch coincidence very far.[1]

We have said that until studies of Nominalist theology have been further sifted at the technical level, the points of divergences and difference within the late mediaeval schools must remain confused. Yet there are some facts about Luther's relation to Ockhamism. He received his Arts and his theological training from Nominalist teachers, for Erfurt was a centre of the "via moderna," [2] and he studied under Jodocus Trutvetter and Bartholomew Arnoldi of Usingen. When he became a friar, his theological studies under Johann Paltz (who left

---

[1] Fr. R. Weijenborg. La charité dans la première théologie de Luther (Rev. d'Hist. Eccl. XLV, 1950, 666) quotes Luther's marginal comment on Peter Lombard, on the vexed question whether the Christian's duty towards his enemies is to refrain even from the signs of wrath (signa rancoris), whether he may be content with general prayer for his enemies and if it is enough to refrain from doing them positive harm. W.A. 9.93.9-12, "Signa rancoris non tenetur dimittere, i.e. beneficia spiritu- \ alia quae amicis exhibentur et conversatio non tenetur. Generalia autem tenetur ut sunt orationes generales." Fr. Weijenborg omits the important last phrase, " Ita ut nihil optet mali injuste inferre." (See on this point K. Holl. Ges. Aufs. Luther, 167, n. 1, 188). Fr. Weijenborg contrasts this attitude with that of Luther in Sermon 1 of the two Erfurt sermons, where Luther demands that the Christian perform positive good works towards his enemies. Fr. Weijenborg then accounts for the change, by the part Luther played in the domestic Augustinian quarrel between the Observants and the Conventuals. " If Luther wanted to play a public rôle in his order he was forced to intervene in these conflicts " (p. 666, the imputation of a base motive will be noticed). Thus, on this view, Luther's marginal note which minimizes the duty towards one's enemies was written before Luther went to Rome, and shows him playing to the Observant gallery. Sermon 1 shows him playing to the opposite side after he had returned from Rome and " gone over " to the party of Staupitz. Thi argument is then made the basis for dating Sermon 1 at this juncture ! Even if it were true, it would not explain why Luther retained this view long afterwards, and its agreement with his developed doctrine of love, as evidenced by his later explicit references to this very point. W.A. 1.479.25 and 481.15. "Signa rancoris si sun rancoris, prorsus sunt omittenda."

[2] G. Ritter. Studien zur Spätscholastik. I. Marsilius von Inghen und die Ock-hamistische Schule in Deutschland, 1921. II. Via antiqua und via moderna auf den deutschen Universitäten des XV. Jarhunderts. Heidelberg, 1922. "Almost nothing is known about the theologians of the Erfurt Augustinians, Luther's immediate teachers." Ibid., 1.165.

Erfurt in 1507) and Johann Nathin (sometime pupil of Gabriel Biel) involved close acquaintance with the leading doctrines of Ockham and his successors, together with the doctrines of Scotus, who in these parts of Christendom provided the great rival system to that of the Venerable Inceptor.[1] We know that the text-book which Luther read for ordination was Gabriel Biel's treatise on the Canon of the Mass. Nominalism, therefore, was the one form of scholastic theology which Luther knew intimately.

This relationship finds confirmation in many of the Reformer's later utterances.[2] It does not seem that Luther read any of the anti-papal writings of Ockham until many years later,[3] and it must be noted that Gabriel Biel, the more immediate influence upon him, did not share in Ockham's anti-papalism.

Luther owed much to the stern discipline of logical, critical enquiry which he learned in the schools, and his best and most sustained pieces of theological argument, his "Contra Latomum" (1521), his "De Servo Arbitrio" (1525) and "Of the Lord's Supper" (1528), marshal theological and logical resources imbibed in earlier days and never needing to be repudiated. P. Vignaux has noted the continuity between Luther's first and last enunciated doctrine of the Trinity.[4] Luther avowed that in the great controversy about the reality of Universals he had been on the Ockhamist side.[5]

At least modern Ockhamist studies have imposed caution upon hasty generalization.[6] We can no longer be content to remark on the

---

[1] L. Meier, O.F.M. Ein neutrales Zeugnis für den Gegensatz von Scotismus und Ockhamismus im spätmittelalterlichen Erfurt. Franz. Stud. 26 (1939), 167-82 : 258-287.

[2] "Occam, magister meus, summus fuit dialecticus." TR. 2.516.6. "Ockham, my dear master." W.A. 30.ii.300.9. TR. 6.600.10. "Sum enim Occanicae factionis qui respectus contemnunt, omnia autem absoluta habent" is ironical comment. Luther greatly respected Ockham's intellectual power. Thus his marginal comment (W.A. 9.33.30), "satis ingeniose concordat et exponit verba B. Augustini" is echoed many years later in the Table Talk. "Occam, quamvis ingenio vicerat omnes." TR. 4.679.24. Many other references to Ockham are listed in W.A. 58.i.259-61.

[3] TR. 5.683.10 ; TR. 2.64.18.

[4] P. Vignaux. Luther Commentateur des Sentences. Paris, 1935, 25.29.

[5] TR. 4.679.9. "Terministen hiess man eine Secte in der hohen schule unter welchen ich auch gewesen." TR. 5.653.1.

[6] L. Baudry. Guillaume d'Occam. I. Paris, 1950. G. de Lagarde. Naissance de l'esprit laïque au déclin du moyen âge. Vols. iv-vi., 1942-6. Dict. Théol. Cath. arts. "Nominalisme," "Occam." Vol. xi. Pt. 1, 717-784, 876-889 (P. A. Vignaux). P. A. Vignaux. Justification et Prédestination au xivme siècle. Paris, 1934. Luther Commentateur des Sentences. Paris, 1935. E. Gilson. La Philosophie au Moyen Age. Paris, 1930, ch xi. Ph. Böhner. The Tractatus de Predestinatione . . . of Wm. of Ockham. New York, 1945. E. Guelluy. Philosophie et Théologie chez Ockham. Paris, 1947. E. A. Moody. The Logic of Wm. of Ockham. London, 1935. Wilhelm Ockham. Aufsätze zu seiner Philosophie und Theologie. 1950 (Franziskanische Studien). M. H. Carré. Phases of thought in England, 1949. G. Ritter. Studien zur Spätscholastik, I and II. Heidelberg, 1921-2.

"Voluntarism" of the Ockhamist emphasis upon God as arbitrary and sovereign will, and see his primary theological emphasis as a sharp division between reason and revelation. Rather is there a concern for the liberty of God, and an attempt (as against Peter of Auriol and Gregory of Rimini on the one hand, and the elaborate systematizing of Scotus on the other) to prevent God from being entangled in his universe, or in some theological system. The well-known scholastic dialectic of the "potestas absoluta"—what God is able to do in his own liberty, and the "potestas ordinata"—what God has in fact decided to do in revealed history and religion, is powerfully employed by Ockham to safeguard, first, the Liberty of God, but, second, also his Liberality and mercy, in addition, perhaps, to affording a supple means of extending the scope of theological speculation.

The Ockhamist stress upon the immediacy of knowledge, the drastic simplification and rejection of secondary causes of the famous dictum "quidquid Deus potest facere mediante secunda causa in genere causae efficientis vel finis, potest immediate per se" and the similar "frustra fit per plura quod potest fieri per pauciora"—reveal his thought as austerely critical, a radical simplification sharply opposed to the fascinating and impressive synthesis of Duns Scotus.[1] Over against Ockham's stress on the simplicity of God stands the attempt of Scotus to probe into the psychology of the divine Being.[2]

This is important for Luther's case, since he was trained within this theological tension, and as his marginal comments reveal, was more sharply critical of Scotus than of Ockham. To lump Scotists and Ockhamists together, as some historians have done, is to over-simplify.[3]

That this scholastic discipline influenced Luther's methods and technique is beyond question: all his days he recurred to the syllogistic form of argument and to illustrations from logic and from grammar. That there were deeper theological influences upon him and continuity as well as discontinuity in Luther's thought is very likely, though it will only be detected by patient and sympathetic appreciation of undertones, and not by superficial verbal resemblances.[4]

---

[1] "The Nominalism of William of Ockham, in its specific elements, is directly opposed to Duns Scotus" (quoted from E. Longpré in Dict. Théol. Cath., 877).

[2] "Duns Scotus has a psychology of God : for Occam there can be no such thing : Deity repels such analysis." Ibid., 881.

[3] The reference to Scotus as Luther's "scholastic master" by J. Burnaby, Amor Dei, 1938, 275, seems to rest on this misconception, even though there was one important area of theology where Scotists and Ockhamists agreed. "In moralibus Scotus et Occam idem sunt." TR. 1.135.11.

[4] P. A. Vignaux. "Sur Luther et Ockham" (Wilhelm Ockham, 1950, 30) says "The theme ' Luther and Ockham ' is not unfruitful if one prefers attention to the texts to seductive reconstruction." On the difference between Luther and Ockham's view of the relation between reason and authority. R. Josefson. Den Naturliga Teologins Problem hos Luther. Uppsala, 1943, 13-14.

The wrong way to account for Luther's relation to Ockhamism may be illustrated from two views which have been put forward concerning the origin of Luther's teaching about Justification, in relation to the "non-imputation" of sin. M. de Lagarde in his discussion of Ockham's moral teaching shows how Ockham employs the dialectic of "potentia absoluta" to show why original sin may be imputed, and why God is enabled not to impute sin when he forgives us.[1]

This is hailed as the preparation for Luther's doctrine of imputation and non-imputation. But, in the first place, the word "imputation" is not scholastic but Biblical and Luther's use of it stems from the time of his Biblical, rather than from his scholastic period. Second, as M. Lagarde has to admit (p. 89), Ockham is not here concerned with the positive imputation of the Righteousness of Christ but with the non-imputation of sin by the fiat of God's free and sovereign will. Third, Luther's doctrine is christologically conditioned and moves within the orbit of the redemptive work of Christ. Fourth, Ockham's teaching here is influenced by his Nominalist philosophy, so that what he has to say about non-imputation takes a negative view of sin: on the other hand, when Luther begins to expound this doctrine of imputation and non-imputation it is in breaking completely with the scholastic anthropology and stressing the egocentric character of concupiscence. Thus M. de Lagarde and others have simply been led astray by the Biblical word "imputation" and assume a pedigree which does not exist and which cannot be demonstrated from the documents.

C. Feckes made a similar attempt to derive Luther's teaching from Ockham by developing the scholastic use of the "potentia absoluta" and the "potentia ordinata." Both Scotus and Ockham affirm that "de potentia absoluta" God can justify and accept the sinner without demanding from him merits, good works, or the "habitus" of created grace or infused charity.[2] It is suggested that in this conception Luther found the root of his alleged affirmation that God may justify sinners

---

[1] Naissance de l'esprit laïque, vol. vi. 86 ff. He quotes Ockham Quodlib. III, qu. 9, "Dico quod potest fieri de potentia Dei absoluta, quod peccatum originale nullius diceret carentia, nec habitus naturalis, nec supernaturalis, nec debitum habendi aliquid, sed solum quod aliquis propter demeritum praecedens in aliquo sit indignus vita aeterna." In Sent. III, qu. 5, N ; IV, qu. 9, J. " Dico quod peccatum deleri non est aliquam rem absolutam vel relativam a peccatore amoveri vel separari, sed est actum commissionis vel omissionis ad poenam non imputari." See below, p. 174.

[2] Scotus, Ox. 1, d. XVII, qu. III, n. 29. "Deus de potentia absoluta bene potuisset acceptare naturam beatificabilem . . . existentem in puris naturalibus . . . sed non creditur ita disposuisse . . . non est necessarium ponere habitum supernaturalem gratificantem loquendo de necessitate respiciente potentiam Dei absolutam, licet sit necessarium loquendo de necessitate quae respicit potentiam Dei ordinatam." Ockham, " hoc dico quoniam Deus de potentia absoluta posset quemcumque acceptare sine tali habitu licet non de potentia ordinata." III, Sent. qu. V.E. Vignaux. Justification, 9.99.

without regard for their moral dispositions and supernatural qualities. But Luther's early writings, from the marginal notes of 1509 to the all-out attack on Nominalist theology in his theses of 1517, show a firm rejection of this very dialectic between the "absolute power" and the "ordained power" of God, and an emphatic concentration instead on what in fact God has done.[1]

Thus (1509), "It is to be observed that Charity (whatever may be possible) is in fact always given with the Holy Spirit."[2]

And (1517) in theses 56-7, "Against the Scholastic Theology":

56. "Nor can God by his 'absolute power' (potentia absoluta) bring it about that an act of friendship to God may exist and yet the grace of God be not present."

57. "Nor can God accept a man without justifying grace."[3]

It is a merit of the recent essay of R. Weijenborg to recognize that Luther did not derive his doctrines out of this particular dialectic. "Luther in his early writings accentuates the rôle of created charity rather than that of uncreated, i.e. the right to heaven."[4] Luther's own later distinction between "Deus Absconditus" and "Deus Revelatus" might seem at first sight to recall the scholastic dichotomy of divine power, "absoluta" and "ordinata," but it rather confirms the fact that such speculation is foreign from Luther's approach to salvation. He does not use the thought of the "Deus Absconditus" to open the door to elaborate speculation, but to shut it firmly, and to prevent men from worrying about matters which do not concern them, since God has reserved such themes for himself, and to bring home the great divine imperative that man should concentrate upon God as revealed to men in Jesus Christ.

The older Catholic view, championed by Denifle, was that Luther was a man of very mediocre theological talent, who muddled the scholastic teaching because, in addition to being a liar, he was rather a fool. But it is no proof of Luther's bad faith or ignorance to cite against him scholastic writings he could never have read, or even to contrast St. Thomas Aquinas with Luther's account of scholastic teaching, when we consider the overwhelming bias of his teachers towards the systems of Ockham and Scotus, and the new theological

---

[1] On this see the clear analysis of P. A. Vignaux. "Sur Luther et Ockham" (Wilhelm Ockham, 1950, 27). P. A. Vignaux shows that the Nominalist dialectic of the "absolute" and "ordained" power of God is not only concerned with the Liberty of God, but involves a conception of created human nature which has kept its integrity and is different from that of Luther. "Man, according to Luther, poses a more difficult problem relative to 'gratia justificans' than man according to Ockhamism" (ibid., 27).

[2] W.A. 9.42.36-7.

[3] Works. Clemen. 5.324.

[4] R. Weijenborg, La charité dans la première théologie de Luther, 627.

H

problems raised (e.g. by Peter of Auriol and Gregory of Rimini) in the fourteenth and fifteenth centuries.[1]

The earliest theological material of Luther to survive consists of his marginal notes on the Sentences of Peter Lombard. This was the great theological text-book of the later Middle Ages, and a work upon which almost all the great theologians wrote commentaries. Luther, as Sententiarius, was required to lecture upon it at Erfurt. For the Master of the Sentences Luther had a great and lifelong respect as a "great man."[2] And perhaps it is significant that Peter Lombard represents the twelfth century conflation of Scriptures and Fathers before the great infiltration of Aristotle in the next century. These marginal comments are scattered and occasional, and since he often argues "per contra" and for purposes of discussion too much can easily be read into them. In addition to these notes, there have survived his similar comments on the volumes of St. Augustine which he read at this time with an enthusiasm to which the marginal comments bear eloquent witness.[3]

There are many tokens that this new passion for Augustine was of decisive importance in Luther's theological development.[4] These marginal notes reveal that Luther's Ockhamist training had come into collision with a new stress of theological influence, and one far more congenial to his own spiritual needs and profoundest intuitions. In the background a third influence is to be observed, Luther's growing acquaintance with the Bible and his direct appeal to Biblical testimony.[5]

What no reader of the marginal notes can fail to remark, and a matter on which all commentators seem agreed, is the boldness and acidity of Luther's attack on the invasion of theology by philosophy, and the sharpness with which he turns on the philosophers, on Gabriel Biel, on Scotus and on Ockham. Thus he refers to the "rancid rules of the logicians," to "those grubs, the philosophers," to

[1] P. Vignaux remarks on the accuracy with which Luther summarizes Biel. " Justi-fication," p. 2.
[2] TR. 1.85.17. TR. 2.515.30. TR. 3.543.1. Also TR. 2.515.27: 517.10. W.A. 50.543.13.
[3] W.A. 9.31.6. " Lege id caput. Et aurea est disputatio et egregia de beata vita."
[4] Melanchthon noted the importance of this period and affirmed that Luther often read and memorized Augustine's works. (C.R. 6.159.) Despite Melanchthon, and despite two citations (W.A. 9.59.34, 60.26), Luther does not appear, at this time, to have read " Of the Spirit and the Letter " and the anti-Pelagian treatises. See also W.A.Br. 1.70.20 (Oct. 1516), " Before I fell in with his books I had very little room for him," and TR. 1.140.5, " In the beginning I devoured Augustine."
[5] W.A. 9.46.16, "Ego autem, licet multi inclyti doctores sic sentiant, tamen quia non habent pro se scripturam, sed solum humanas rationes et ego in ista opinione habeo scripturam, quod anima sit imago dei, ideo dico cum Apostolo ' Si angelus de coelo,' i.e. doctor in ecclesia, ' aliud docuerit, anathema sit '."

the "dregs of philosophy" and to "that rancid philosopher, Aristotle." [1]

These remarkable criticisms are much more than passing observations. They are a studied protest against the aggressions of late mediaeval philosophy into theology, and if their sharpened edge lies towards Scotus, it is also laid against Ockham and Biel. This is the attempt, aptly described by P. Vignaux as the detachment of theology from the "envelope" of philosophy. It is a programme, as radical in its simplification as the humanist return to the "philosophy of Christ." If we are content to define "humanism" in this immediate connection as a climate of opinion rather than any particular group of scholars, it is possible that Luther's first critical awareness came from the stimulus of humanism. Nevertheless, he developed that criticism in his own way, and the attempt, visible in the marginal notes, to strike back through Peter Lombard to Augustine and "the old fathers" was to lead to a more drastic result than theirs. There is evidence of this new discrimination in the letter written by Luther to John Braun (1509), when Luther was trying to fit his private theological studies within the cramping programme of a lecturer in philosophy:

"The study takes it out of me, especially in philosophy which from the beginning I would gladly have exchanged for theology, I mean that theology which searches out the nut from the shell, the grain from the husk, the marrow from the bone." [2]

We must not exaggerate. There are still matters on which Luther can gratefully quote the Ockhamists.[3] Yet perhaps the typical and revealing observation at this stage of his career is that with which he attempts to resolve a point which had baffled the Master of the Sentences,

---

[1] On the philosophers : W.A. 9.29.6, "numquam satis laudato Augustino, ut tamquam suspecta habere videatur quaecunque a philosophis sunt anxie explorata, sed nondum nota. Et certe nimis dedite in illis vepribus involucris et quae nugis meris sunt proxima versari." 24.24, "Stoicae igitur reliquiae sunt hodie maxima pars philosophorum. Nam in nudis verborum novitatibus et aequivocationibus certant." 47.6, "Sicut rancidae logicorum regulae somniant." 47.26, "Nunc tanta est philosophorum subtilitas ut etiam si verum esset, falsum esset." 31.32, "distinctio nominis deus personaliter et essentialiter est frivola et inutilis philosophiae confictio."
On Gabriel Biel, 74.8. "Hoc quod Magister hic dicit . . . negat Gabriel cum aliis . . . ego consentio Magistrum dimissis larvis philosophorum."
On Scotus, 43.21, "ex isto patet error et heresi proxima sententia Scoti." 54.19, "Excipiuntur ab hac tua sententia soli Scotistae et theologi nostro tempore: illi enim quaerunt et intelligunt." 29.25, "Quomodo credent haec nostri subtiles magis quam illustres ? "
On Aristotle, 27.22, " Sed multo mirior nostratium qui Aristotelem non dissonare catholicae veritati impudentissime garriunt." 23.7, " Melius hic Augustinus et verius de felicitate disputat quam fabulator Aristoteles cum suis frivolis defensoribus." 43.4, "commentum de habitibus opinionem habet ex verbis Aristotelis rancidi philosophi."
[2] W.A.Br. 1.17.4. We are not to suppose, as some have deduced from this sentence, that Luther had already come to his new understanding of " Justitia Dei."
[3] On Ockham, W.A. 9.33.30. On Biel, W.A. 9.40.36.

"To this difficulty, without rashness or prejudice—I say—resting on the foundation of St. Augustine . . ." [1]

In a cogent essay, P. Vignaux [2] has marked this discrimination of Luther in relation to the famous mediaeval dilemma raised by St. Peter Lombard in Dist. XVII of Book 1 of the Sentences, where he identifies the Holy Spirit with love (caritas) whereby man loves God, and God loves man. The later schoolmen had to deal with problems left unresolved by St. Augustine, and had to balance the notions of created and uncreated grace. They spoke of an indwelling "habitus" within the soul, and in explaining the statement of Peter Lombard they had to prevent the entanglement of the Holy Spirit, the transcendant cause of salvation, with any created virtue.

P. Vignaux suggests that Luther approached the problem directly, leaving the commentators to one side. Luther says:

"And it seems that the Master did not speak altogether absurdly when he says that this 'habitus' is the Holy Spirit. For this notion of 'habitus' has acquired a certain authority from the words of Aristotle, that rancid philosopher. Otherwise, it could well be said that the Holy Spirit is charity, which by itself co-operates with the will to produce the act of love." [3]

The difficulty for Luther lay in the conception of "habitus." If Peter Lombard had identified the Holy Spirit with the created "form" of the human soul, then he must have spoken "altogether absurdly." The problem arises when the Aristotelian notion of "habitus" is introduced. Take that away, and against the older background of Augustinian and Biblical vocabulary,[4] the statement becomes useful and intelligible.[5]

A more elaborate and less happy attempt to trace Luther's development by beginning with the doctrine of Charity in Gabriel Biel, has

---

[1] W.A. 9.52.33.
[2] Luther Commentateur des Sentences. Paris, 1935, 91-3.
[3] W.A. 9.43.2-8.
[4] W.A. 9.44.4, habitus adhuc est spiritus sanctus.
[5] R. Weijenborg does not upset this argument when he points out that for Biel "uncreated Grace" is simply a juridical entity, i.e. the right to heaven (625). But we are not concerned with what Biel thought to be the meaning of uncreated grace, but with what Luther thought. It is not P. Vignaux but R. Weijenborg who wrongly interposes Biel at this point. It is not certain that Luther had any direct knowledge of Biel's "Commentary on the Sentences" at this time. In the edition of Luther's marginal comments on the 1514 ed. of Biel, which was published in 1933 as a supplement to the Weimar ed., H. Degering gives it as his view that "Luther did not have the 1501 edition of Biel before him, but knew it only through notes taken from Trutvetter or Usingen" (viii.-ix.) ; and in any case Luther, W.A. 9.42.7 (on P.L., Bk. 1, Dist. 17, c. 3, and Aug. De Trin., Bk. 8, c. 8), makes plain that uncreated grace is much more than "a juridical entity." Luther's critical remarks about "almost all the commentaries on the Sentences" (W.A. 9.52.12) suggest that he was far from attentive to Biel in this matter. The one book which is the constant background to Luther's comments on Book 1 of the Master is Augustine's "De Trinitate."

been made in a recent essay by R. Weijenborg. The essay [1] falls into two parts. First, a theological examination of Luther's early teaching, in the marginal notes, in two early Sermons, and in Luther's "Dictata super Psalterium." The second part (659 ff.) discusses "Non-theological factors in the evolution of Luther's theology."

The author admits that this adventure into psychology is "temerarious" and "hypothetical" and we shall see no reason to grudge him either adjective. But since this interpretation underlies the first part of the essay, it will be convenient to summarize it first. The author offers a revised version of the theory put forward in 1948 by M. Werner, according to which Luther's theological development could be interpreted in terms of conflict with his father, Hans Luther.

The author begins with two letters which Luther sent to friends whom he invited to the celebrations concerning his First Mass.[2] In these letters Luther emphatically disclaimed any ulterior motive in inviting these guests, and makes it plain that he was not simply touting for the present customarily bestowed on such occasions. It is startling to find this friendly and wholly conventional disclaimer interpreted by Fr. Weijenborg, "already, in 1507, Luther could think of no real love, save disinterested love." (!) Every day, hundreds of invitations circulate among friends, and every day it is a safe guess that a proportion of them make plain that "we are inviting you for your own sake, and not for any present." The notion that such a phrase contains evidence of some austere ethical rigorism is quite superfluous. As well explain the traditional letter home of Tommy Atkins to his wife, "Hoping you are well as it leaves me at present," as evidence that the British soldier is trained in Augustinian theology, and notably the doctrine of proper self-love.

There follows a sketch of Luther's early career in terms of growing conflict between son and father. At first, a struggle within Luther's own mind between "admiration" for his hard-working father and "contempt" for his narrow bourgeois spirit. Luther, as a student, had risen in the social scale, and while the father had to keep account of every penny, the son "dispensed money without counting it." The crisis came when Luther had to choose a career, and when he detested

---

[1] La charité dans la première théologie de Luther. 1509-15. Rev. d'Hist. Eccl. 1950, vol. xlv. no. 3-4, 617-669. The Rev. Fr. may well have posed the right question, even if his solution and methods are unsatisfactory. P. A. Vignaux asks (Wilhelm Ockham, 28) " would not a study of the relation of Luther to Ockham and his school take as its starting point the analysis of ' caritas de facto' ? " We await with eagerness the examination of this question hinted at by P. A. Vignaux, 22, n. 5, for of all Catholic writers on Luther he shows the qualities of learning, accuracy and objectivity.

[2] Almost certainly not, as Fr. Weijenborg states, his ordination, which was separated from his First Mass by several weeks.

the narrow, sordid ambitions of his father on his behalf. The thunder-storm, the lightning flash which precipitated his desperate vow to enter religion offered Luther, on second thoughts, a providential escape. "The religious life would offer him supernatural, scientific and social (!) perspectives which he could never have attained in the world." [1]

But now there was deepened conflict in Luther's soul. "In order to forget his father, he felt obliged to shine among his companions." The famous lines in which, in 1521, Luther dedicated his "Concerning Monastic Vows" to his father, are then pressed into service.[2]

Hans Luther accepted the invitation to attend the celebration of his son's First Mass. "Foreseeing the battle," he "organized his defence" —dissuaded his wife from coming with him [3]—made a handsome gift of twenty florins and attended with a cavalcade of twenty friends. Luther, "preparing for his side of the battle," had made two unfortunate omissions; first, he had forgotten to secure the support of God, and underwent a nervous crisis during the sacramental celebration, and second, "thinking his father had already surrendered," he failed to count on the moral support which his father had derived from twenty florins and twenty horsemen!

How much more natural, and how much less strain on the evidence to suppose that the father, disappointed and disgruntled, had relented as thousands of parents before and since, and to show his forgiveness had decided to do the boy well. How natural that on this, the first occasion he met his father, Luther should get him in a corner and try to explain the imperious nature of his call, thus provoking the public utterance, "Have you never heard the words 'Honour thy father and thy mother'?" But it is not for nothing that Fr. Weijenborg uses the metaphor of conflict—ammunition, battle, surrender, because it is his thesis that Luther projected his inner conflict upon the universe, which he conceived as the arena of a dualistic conflict.

Luther made his declaration to his father "not without perfidy . . . wishing to provoke the admiration of his companions by insisting on the brilliant career he had abandoned." (The only "brilliant career" mentioned is that described by Fr. Weijenborg on his previous page— that "social perspective" *for* which Luther abandoned the world, and entered the monastery!) After his father's outburst, Luther knew that his father regarded him as a hypocrite, and this guilty knowledge set up scruples and mental conflict.

---

[1] It would be interesting to know why, on this view, out of the many religious orders in Erfurt, Luther should choose a mendicant order, the immediate " social perspective " of which would be to send him begging round the streets within view of his former fellow-undergraduates.
[2] W.A. 8.573-4.   [3] There is no evidence whatever of this.

It is for the psychological expert (which Fr. Weijenborg disclaims to be) to pronounce on psychological data. But it is for the historian to point out where evidence begins and where illegitimate imputation of motive begins. The constant imputation of base motive by Fr. Weijenborg does not derive from any new evidence, and indeed can be traced back to Cochlaeus in the sixteenth century, whose use of mediaeval demonology to bespatter Luther has certain affinities with the twentieth century psychological counterpart. "If one reads between the lines," exclaims the Rev. Father (p. 667). If one does, indeed, one has little difficulty in ranging oneself with Cochlaeus, Denifle and Fr. Weijenborg. The lines themselves, however, yield less exciting but more trustworthy conclusions.

The author concludes this sketch with the disarming comment that "the theories on which Luther leans, arising from his conflict with his father, and which seem to find their origin in this conflict, bear striking resemblance with the results of his theological revolution" (p. 605). But there is really nothing striking about it, or rather the "striking resemblance" in Fr. Weijenborg's exposition of Luther's theology derives from the fact that there is a similar heightening of tension, and an exaggeration of Luther's language.

The first part of the essay deserves more consideration. The author draws attention to Luther's emphasis in the notes on Peter Lombard (still, as he admits, within the orbit of orthodoxy) [1] on Christ as the object of faith, and on the importance of faith itself.

---

[1] P. 632. An attempt is made to demonstrate (with particular reference to W.A. 9.52.25-30) that Luther's doctrine of the Trinity is " not quite orthodox " and denies the infinity and actuality of God. The author hails R. Otto as having recognized the " naïvely heretical " character of Luther's views on this point. (But Otto refers, not to this passage, but to W.A. 9.38.28, where he misunderstands Luther, a point which R. Prenter (Spiritus Creator, 183 n.) has sufficiently answered.) He accuses Luther of introducing the Aristotelian concept of " potertiality " and " act " into the internal life of the Trinity. The evidence is said to be W.A. 9.52.25-30. " I would say, indeed, that ' to love ' is the same thing as ' to be,' but not of him who loves only, but of the lover, the beloved, and the love, in such wise that he who loves, and his ' being ' are not two things (aliud et aliud), nor the beloved and being two things, nay, rather, the same being : nor is the love another being." The context of this passage is that it occurs in the midst of a running commentary on problems (arising out of St. Augustine's " De Trinitate ") which are discussed and elucidated by Peter Lombard in Bk. 1, Dist. XVII. and Dist. XXXII. of the Sentences. If the Spirit is peculiarly called the Divine Love, the question arises, put by the Master at the head of Dist. XXXII., " Whether the Father or the Son loves by the Holy Spirit, since in God ' to love ' is the same as ' to be.' " The question is whether the Father and the Son love solely by reason of the Holy Spirit, or from their own being, just as the similar question arises whether the Father finds His Wisdom in the Son alone. To say that the Holy Spirit is the love wherewith the Father loves the Son, and the Son the Father, might easily suggest that the Father and the Son derive from the Spirit, since in God to love and to be are the same (Dist. XXXII. c. 8). This leads to a dilemma, for such a doctrine would be a denial of the doctrines of generation and of procession, and c. 9, Peter Lombard refuses to attempt its resolution. Luther inclines to the view that the Father and the Son find their love only in the Holy Spirit (" et nihil aliud "), and that

When Luther comes to treat of Grace, Sin and Free Will, however, it is claimed that he confuses the calculated structure of the anthropology of Biel (636). It is beyond dispute indeed that Luther came to break decisively with the Nominalist doctrine of man, and a glance at his "Theses against the Scholastic Theology" (1517) shows that this was the spear-point of his attack. What is in question is whether the repudiation emerges here. In this connection Fr. Weijenborg finds great significance in Luther's lengthy comments (W.A. 9.70-2) on Peter Lombard (Book II (Dist. XXIV-XXVI)).

To the query of the Master (Dist. XXIV) whether man might have remained in the state of primitive innocence, Luther adds "per contra" a quotation from St. Bernard that "not to stand is to go backward," but he adds that St. Bernard is speaking not of the state of the innocent or of the blessed, but of "our state, if indeed it be a state and not rather a flux" (W.A. 9.70.1-4). Fr. Weijenborg then glosses this with Luther's comment (W.A. 9.71.38) on Dist. XXVI, that those who are damned are not condemned because they have had no chance of accepting grace, but because they reject it when offered and so retrogress, and go backward.[1] Fr. Weijenborg draws the startling conclusion, "the sense of Bernard's words comes to this, then, that not to progress is sin!" This alleged ethical rigorism of Luther is then contrasted with Biel, who says that it is not necessarily culpable if the soul refuses to respond to the

---

it is illegitimate to attempt to conceive the Father or the Son in abstraction from the whole life of the Blessed Trinity. He puts his view forward hesitantly and relying " on the foundation of St. Augustine " (W.A. 9.52.32 : 53.14 : 53.29—the thrice repeated reference to Augustine in a few lines is notable). In this context W.A. 9.52.25-30 becomes intelligible. Rather than an importation of Aristotelianism, it is the Ockhamist protest against the elaborate metaphysic of the Scotists which underlies Luther's whole treatment. Luther's emphasis on the mutual life of the Three Persons leads him to think of the Divine love as that of " lover, beloved and love." For a lucid account of Luther's marginal notes, related to the context, see P. Vignaux (Luther Commentateur, 31-44). Fr. Weijenborg bolsters his assertion with reference to a sermon of Luther's commonly dated 1514-15, but which he assures us he has "decisive reasons " (none are given, and they must be entirely subjective) for dating in 1509. Here Luther follows the Augustinian analogies of mens, memoria, voluntas, and mens, notitia, amor (W.A. 1.28) with the more original illustration from the Aristotelian concept of res, motus and quies. According to Fr. Weijenborg this implies that the Holy Spirit is the actualization of the Father and the Son. Even if it were legitimate to gloss the passage in the marginal notes with a sermon illustration (possibly five years apart), in the one case Luther calls the Divine Love the " actuality " of which the Holy Spirit is a potential, and in the other, the Holy Spirit is the actuality—this even on Fr. Weijenborg's showing ! In any case a sermon which has as its closing sentence (W.A. 1.29) " Quare Deus Actus " can hardly be said to show that Luther has compromised the doctrine that God is pure Act.

[1] This quotation from St. Bernard was indeed important for Luther, but not as Fr. Weijenborg interprets it. See also W.A. 56.173.13 : 239.23. " When we begin not to want to become better, we cease to be good," as St. Bernard says. Thus the alleged " ethical rigorism " is St. Bernard's as well as Luther's. Also W.A. 56.486.6. " To stand still in the way of God, that is to go backwards, and to progress, that is always beginning afresh (semper a novo incipere)."

prompting of grace. The reader must not be deceived. It is not Luther who is confusing Biel's anthropology, but Fr. Weijenborg who has confused the issue by contrasting what Luther has to say about the damned, with what Biel has to say about backsliders. Luther, on p. 71 of the marginal notes, has a careful discussion of the relation of Free Will and Grace within the framework of Peter Lombard and Augustine. He says that in the case of the two ultimate extremes of the "Beati" and the "Miseri" we may speak of necessity." The "Beati" necessarily choose the good, and the "Miseri" find good impossible (23-24). The "Beati" are in servitude to righteousness, and the "Miseri" to sin. Nevertheless, Luther adds, this "servitus" is a "libertas." Here is simply the thoroughly Augustinian notion that the final state of the blessed is that they are unable to sin in the presence of that God whose service is perfect freedom. But, Luther continues, the wayfaring Christian is in neither extreme but somewhere in the middle [1] (quasi medio). And he finds "the good is difficult, but not impossible" and that "evil is easy, but not necessary." It is noticeable how in describing this passage Fr. Weijenborg heightens the terminology, rendering "Miseri" by "demons, damned, non-justified . . . totally carnal," apocalyptic language of which there is no hint in Luther but which is congenial to Fr. Weijenborg's dualistic interpretation of Luther's theology of conflict. This dualism he finds expressed clearly in W.A. 9.70.13:

"The same man insofar as he does the things which are of the spirit alone and which are done internally is called Spirit, Spiritual.

"The same man insofar as he thinks the things which are of the senses and which are external is called Flesh, Sensual."

It is interesting to observe that this passage which Fr. Weijenborg selects to show Luther's dualism, is the very passage cited by Karl Holl [2] to show that Luther has reached in the marginal notes his later doctrine of the "totus homo," the conception of man, body and soul, inwardly and outwardly as one moral personality. At least Holl could claim that there are other passages in the marginal notes to support this stress (W.A. 9.83.30, est tamen una eademque anima. Also 76.20. 85.10). We may more modestly assert that Luther at this point remains within the categories of Augustinian thought and has not yet approximated to the more truly Biblical dichotomy of "flesh" and "spirit."

Fr. Weijenborg draws the conclusion that "Free Will has lost all

---

[1] See Luther on Rom. 12^2 (1515-16). W.A. 56.442.24. "This life is a road to heaven and hell. None is so good that he may not become better, none so bad that he may not become worse until at last we reach the extremity."

[2] K. Holl. Luther, 189 and n. 4.

significance in this scheme and man is determined by charity on the one hand and by concupiscence on the other. Here below the just man is a mixture of 'spirit' and 'flesh': he carries within him a saint and a demon who dispute for his being" (638). The reason for this is said to be that for Luther "Charity becomes a new entity existing side by side with Free Will and influencing it only from without," whereas for Biel "Charity is a supernatural quality of the Will."

This seems a disastrous over-simplification of Luther's thought at this stage, and makes nonsense of his repeated references in this section to prevenient and created grace and to the infusion of faith, hope and charity. It is true that Luther rejected the notion of an "habitus" (W.A. 9.43.4) and, unlike Peter d'Ailly and a good many other theologians, could therefore accept Peter Lombard's equation of "Charity" with the Holy Spirit. But because Luther rejected this Aristotelian conception of "habitus" which was far from clearly defined among the theologians, it is not to be deduced that at this time he rejected the Augustinian conception of Grace, or that he thought of it as purely external.[1]

Fr. Weijenborg has rendered service by calling attention to four major theological preoccupations of Luther in the marginal notes: with Christ and Faith on the one hand, and with Sin and Concupiscence [2] on the other.

By separating the first two, and by ignoring "Christ," and "Faith," in his psychological diagnosis, Fr. Weijenborg misinterprets the significance of the marginal notes in Luther's theological development. That development needs no psychological myth to account for it, straining and bursting the historical evidence. No doubt there are important psychological factors to be taken account of in the case of Luther, as in the case of St. Cyril of Alexandria or St. Thomas Aquinas. But it is an elementary fallacy to suppose that the psychology disposes

---

[1] It is notable that Luther never uses the word "charity" in the section under discussion, and that on p. 72 there are frequent references to grace, prevenient grace and merit (a purely external reference to grace would make the conception of merit heretically Pelagian, and Fr. Weijenborg has admitted that "Luther in his early writings emphasizes the rôle of created charity" (627)).

[2] Fr. Weijenborg says of Luther's discussion of "Concupiscence" (75.12 ff.) that Luther has not yet developed the opinion that concupiscence is essentially sin." But Luther does say that, before baptism, concupiscence is accompanied by evil, and this, he alleges, would make the conversion of the unbaptized unintelligible, since their conversion would demand a miracle, in order to release them from the prison of the flesh. But the answer to Fr. Weijenborg's objection lies in the very sentence of Peter Lombard to which Luther's note is addressed, viz. "The concupiscence of the flesh is dismissed in baptism." The remedy of the unbaptized sinner is to seek baptism. That he should turn to God is indeed a miracle, but this is wholly explicable within the Augustinian categories of Grace. I would not deny that at one point (75.30-35) Luther has an exceptionally vehement picture of the violence of concupiscence— "sed per justitiam regeretur."

of the theology, that it somehow discredits it, or that it absolves students from the discipline of treating the theology on its merits. It is an even more clumsy polemic which refuses to evaluate a doctrine, not in terms of highly disputable and controverted origins, but of mature and defined enunciation.

Here, then, in the marginal notes is the double motive, Christ and Faith on the one hand, and Sin and Concupiscence on the other, which can be traced through the succeeding lectures of Luther on the Psalms and on the Epistles to the Romans, Galatians and Hebrews. It is a motif which can be summarized in a phrase which recurs many hundreds of times in those lectures: ["Coram Deo." A doctrine which treats seriously the depth and tragedy of the human predicament because it considers man and his world in the presence of the Living God.]

There is a further truth to be observingly distilled from Fr. Weijenborg's ingenious and learned devices. If, as P. Vignaux says, Luther had made a fateful discrimination between theology and the philosophic "envelope," [1] then, against the background of his intense Augustinian and Biblical studies the categories and notions into which he had been trained must have begun to strain to bursting point.

Rejecting the notion of an "habitus," holding a doctrine of merit, of infused virtues, and not yet able to achieve what Regin Prenter calls the "Biblical realism" of personal encounter between God and man: sensible of the power of sin, and more and more aware of it as a subtle and all-pervading egoism within the very citadel of the soul, Luther evokes the problem posed correctly by Fr. Weijenborg—what, on this showing, is the power of Free Will? Here Luther could get no final help from St. Augustine, for about these questions the great African Doctor left riddles about which his greatest modern interpreters are divided. Now, in the sixteenth century Luther rejected the post-Augustinian structure of theology with its delicate and precarious balance of philosophy and theology, reason and revelation, created and uncreated grace, divine transcendant cause and infused habitus. Thus the pressure of theology and the need of his own soul moved him towards the crisis of a "novum et mirum vocabulum."

[1] It is a merit of P. Vignaux's exposition that he accounts squarely for Luther's objections to the philosophers, but that Fr. Weijenborg cannot fit these things into his psychological diagnosis.

Chapter

5

THE BRUISED CONSCIENCE

"He doth most gravely debate ... of the rise of these temptations,
namely blasphemy, desperation and the like, showing that the Law
of Moses as well as the Devil, death and hell hath a very great
hand therein, the which at first was very strange to me: but considering and watching, I found it so indeed."
JOHN BUNYAN. " Grace Abounding."

"ONE thing is more and more clear from recent research: the inner,
personal experience of Luther, and his scholarly, theological and,
above all, exegetical discoveries cannot be separated." There are
explicit statements of Luther himself which support this judgment of
Heinrich Bornkamm.[1] "I did not learn my theology all at once, but
I had to search deeper for it, where my temptations took me."[2] Luther's
autobiographical fragment (1545) concludes, "This I tell you, reader,
that you may remember that I am one of those who . . . have learned
by writing and by teaching."[3]

That Luther underwent acute spiritual conflict as a monk, is a fact
more solidly attested in his writings than any other single fact of his
career.[4] It is true that the integrity and accuracy of Luther's account
was impugned by Denifle, who declared it to be a cunning and lying
fabrication which Luther dared only to ventilate when living witnesses
had passed from the scene.

The more sober judgment of the Catholic historian, Lortz, is that
Luther's behaviour as a monk was "correct" and he regards the moral
depravity theory of Denifle as discredited and untenable.[5]

When we discount for rhetoric, and for that heightening of language
so characteristic of the mediaeval preacher, there is a solid core of
testimony to be drawn at various dates from Luther's lectures, sermons,
letters and Table Talk. Luther took seriously his vows, and the

---

[1] H. Boehmer. Junge Luther (ed. Bornkamm), 362.
[2] TR. 1.146.12, " Vivendo, immo moriendo et damnando fit theologus, non intelli-
gendo, legendo aut speculando." W.A. 5.163.28, " Living, nay, rather dying and being
damned make a theologian, not understanding, reading or speculation."
[3] W.A. 54.186.
[4] There are scores of passages cited, W.A. 58.1.6-32.
[5] There is the testimony of Matthew Flacius Illyricus in 1543 that a former companion of Luther, who had remained a Catholic, testified that Luther " lived a holy
life among them, kept the Rule most exactly and studied diligently." Scheel. Luther,
ii.10. Miegge, 68.

goal of evangelical perfection. When, in 1521, he declared that he had not entered religion "covetously or to gratify my belly" [1] (he quotes Hugh of St. Victor), the disclaimer was not superfluous since there were those among Luther's contemporaries who lacked any genuine vocation, and not a few who did pursue carnal objectives within the religious frame. But Luther sought to keep his Rule with whole-hearted diligence. "I had no other thought, but how I might keep my Rule." [2]

When Luther came to attack the Observants within the Augustinian Order, it was not, as Grisar suggested, because of his moral laxity, but on the very ground of fidelity to holy obedience. He attacks the Observants together with all who seek "exemptions," and all who claim special treatment on the ground of some imaginary "singularity" —ostensibly on the ground of strictness, but in fact dissolving the whole bond of monastic discipline. Luther's was by no means the only voice raised against the evil of exemptions. [3]

Not only did Luther observe the Rule, but he exercised himself beyond the ordinary.

"It's true. I was a good monk, and kept my order so strictly that I could say that if ever a monk could get to heaven through monastic discipline, I should have entered in. All my companions in the monastery, who knew me, would bear me out in this. For if it had gone on much longer, I would have martyred myself to death, what with vigils, prayers, readings and other works." [4]

He read the "Vitae Patrum" and longed to imitate one of the old Desert Fathers "who would live in the desert, and abstain from food and drink, and live on a few vegetables and roots and cold water." [5]

At first, the business and novelty of the monastic life left no time for sad preoccupation. "I know from my own experience, and that of many others, how peaceful and quiet Satan is wont to be in one's first years as a monk or priest." [6] Then Luther found himself carried out

---

[1] W.A. 8. 574. TR. 4.303.16.
[2] W.A. 47.92.10 : 8.633.4.11.
[3] Luther was sent to Rome (1510) on behalf of seven Observant Houses who withstood the project of their Vicar-General, Staupitz, to amalgamate them with the Conventuals. The appeal failed, and on his return Luther " went over " to the side of Staupitz. The reason is not, as Cochlaeus suggested, vulgar ambition on Luther's part, but that fidelity to the claims of obedience which remained a lifelong trait. The appeal to Rome had failed, and further opposition to the Vicar-General could only mean the undermining of the discipline of the order. Holl (Luther, 199) discusses Luther's references to the Observants. Luther's lectures on the Psalms and Romans (1513-15) contain frequent stress on the duty of obedience and the evils of " exemption " and " singularity." W.A. 3.444.21. W.A. 56.192.28. Strohl. Évolution, 129 ff. Miegge, 60.
[4] W.A. 38.143.25 : 40.ii.574.8.
[5] W.A. 40.ii.103.12.
[6] W.A. 8.660.31.

of his depth by swift and alarming spiritual currents. Despite the careful and unremitting use of discipline, of the means of grace and offices of consolation, he found a growing spiritual uncertainty, hopelessness and frustration.

"I tried to live according to the Rule with all diligence, and I used to be contrite, to confess and number off my sins, and often repeated my confession, and sedulously performed my allotted penance. And yet my conscience could never give me certainty, but I always doubted and said, "You did not perform that correctly. You were not contrite enough. You left that out of your confession. The more I tried to remedy an uncertain, weak and afflicted conscience with the traditions of men, the more each day found it more uncertain, weaker, more troubled." [1]

"For I hoped I might find peace of conscience with fasts, prayer, vigils, with which I miserably afflicted my body, but the more I sweated it out like this, the less peace and tranquillity I knew." [2]

"The more holy, the more uncertain I became." [3]

"For I used to ask myself, who knows whether such consolations are to be believed?" [4]

The Nominalist theology, with its dialectic of possibilities and its recurring "perhaps," was ill calculated to support trembling spirits. Despite its apparent optimism, the common-sense stress on "doing what in one lies" and the careful balance of grace and merit, it remained a system which threw a practical emphasis on the human will.[5] And although, as Fr. Weijenborg has shown, the doctrine of charity in Biel allows a firmer stress on the necessity of supernatural grace than is commonly suggested, there were, as he admits, two alarming

---

[1] W.A. 40.ii.15.15.   [2] W.A. 44.819.10.
[3] W.A. 26.12.12.   [4] W.A. 40.ii.411.14.
[5] " The doctrine of Biel is a doctrine of merit " (P. A. Vignaux. Luther Commentateur, 47), " Free Will is more essential to merit than the infused virtue of charity " (P. A. Vignaux. Dict. Théol. Cath. XI, 771-2). See the remarkable sentences in " Gabrielis Biel Quaestiones de Justificatione," ed. Feckes, 1929, which include the following :
Liberum arbitrium hominum ex suis naturalibus sine gratia elicere potest actum moraliter bonum (p. 50).
Liberum arbitrium ex suis naturalibus sine dono gratiae potest quodlibet peccatum mortale novum cavere (ibid.).
Homo per liberum arbitrium ex suis naturalibus potest divina precepta quoad actus substantiam implere. Sed non ad intentionem precipientis que est consecutio salutis nostre (p. 51).
Viatoris voluntas humana ex suis naturalibus potest diligere Deum super omnia (p. 58).
Actus amoris Dei amicitie super omnia non potest stare in viatore de potentia Dei ordinata sine gratia et caritate infusa (p. 60).
Stante lege nullus homo per pura naturalia potest implere preceptum de dilectione Dei super omnia (p. 62). See P. A. Vignaux, " Sur Luther et Ockham." (Wilhelm Ockham, 1950, p. 23).

and critical points of uncertainty. In order to be saved, a man must possess the indwelling habitus of charity, but there was no certain means of telling whether this habitus really was within the soul. A man must love God above all things, but there was no sure criterion with which to distinguish this genuine love from a false and feigned love, from that hypocrisy which even Biel noted as a deadly peril to the just.[1]

But whatever the cause, there is no doubt of Luther's uncertainty, and that this scepticism undermined for him all outward consolation proffered to him by authority.

"After vigils, fasts, prayers and other exercises of the toughest kind, with which as a monk I afflicted myself almost to death, yet the doubt was left in my mind, and I thought 'Who knows whether these things are pleasing to God?'" [2]

If we want an English name for his case, we may employ John Bunyan's tremendous phrase "the bruised conscience." [3] Luther's own more objective word was "Anfechtung"—temptation. What "Anfechtung" meant for Luther is only apparent in his maturity, in the light of the lonely decisions of his "terrible revolutionary vocation" [4] (1517-21). But "Anfechtung" belongs to no special period of his career. Certainly it was not some kind of spiritual growing pains to be ended in some conversion experience, and then over and done with. "Anfechtung" is that unremitting spiritual conflict which never ends until death, the final "Anfechtung" for which all previous temptation is a preparation. This battle comes home to the Christian in his conscience, in that ultimate and inescapable separateness of each human soul. There are as many forms of temptation as there are Christians, but one way and another temptation always touches the supreme issue of faith. "So every Christian has his temptations. He who would believe, let him reconcile himself to the fact that his faith will not stay untempted. The Devil will do all he can to quench the spark of faith before it comes to a flame." [5]

Luther's early spiritual struggles belong to "Anfechtung," and if we remember to examine the date of our quotations and if we beware of

---

[1] R. Weijenborg, 622, n. 11, 630.
[2] W.A. 40.ii.414.15.
[3] That John Bunyan should find his own spiritual pilgrimage mirrored in Luther's Galatians is testimony to the autonomy of Protestant moral theology. Conversely Bunyan's "Grace Abounding" and "Jerusalem Sinner" illuminate Luther's teaching about "Anfechtung." But behind Bunyan there is a whole casuistry of faith, and Bunyan's writings are the genial survival of a whole literature of Protestant moral theology.
[4] Miegge, 65.
[5] W.A. 29.63.9. W.A. 9.588.11. "There is no Christian man on earth without temptation" (1519-21). W.A. 50.660.1 (1539).

spiritual temptations

reading too much into the earlier experiences, it will be profitable to discuss something of the meaning for Luther of "Anfechtung" at this point.[1] In the first place, it is striking that Luther chooses the word "Anfechtung" with its suggestion of combat rather than "Versuchung" for "temptation."[2]

For "Anfechtung," says Vogelsang, "is a conception drawn from life, not doctrine. ' Anfechtung ' lies on the frontier where life separates itself from doctrine."[3] We might call it an existential word since it concerns man as he grapples with himself and the universe. But we must not be misled into supposing that this is mere subjectivism. The whole meaning of "Anfechtung" for Luther lies in the thought that man has his existence "Coram Deo," and that he is less the active intelligence imposing itself on the stuff of the universe around him, than the subject of an initiative and action from God who employs the whole of man's existence as a means of bringing men to awareness of their need and peril. "It is God's eternity, holiness and power which thus endlessly threaten man at every moment in his whole existence, in his life and action, in the intention and decision of the moral life in the faith and hope of his religion. God's ever present judgment it is which holds a man in the loneliness of his conscience, and in absolute responsibility and which with his every breath consigns him to the Almighty and Holy One to prosper or destroy."[4]

Luther strongly criticized the moral theologians of the Middle Ages for their preoccupation with "carnal temptations."

The attempt to explain his spiritual struggles in terms of an aberrant sexuality has been a grotesque failure.[5] His often casual references to these such temptations betray no such obsessive concern. He is unable to understand why St. Jerome should have been so exercised about such things.[6] He dismisses with scorn the suggestion that St. Paul's thorn in the flesh was his affection for Thecla. Luther went to

---

[1] Among many modern essays, the following are of special interest. G. Jacob. Der Gewissensbegriff in der Theologie Luthers. Tübingen, 1929. E. Vogelsang. Der Angefochtene Christus bei Luther. Berlin, 1932. Y. J. E. Alanen. Das Gewissen bei Luther. Helsinki, 1934. L. Pinomaa. Der Zorn Gottes in der Theologie Luthers. Helsinki, 1938. P. Bühler. Die Anfechtung bei Martin Luther. Zurich, 1942.

[2] Pinomaa. Zorn Gottes, 155. Bühler. Anfechtung, 79.83 n. Bühler has a useful summary of Luther's vocabulary concerning temptation, in relation to his German Bible.

[3] Vogelsang. Angefochtene Christus, 4. Prenter. Spiritus Creator, 34.

[4] Vogelsang. Ibid., 18. See the famous utterance in the Table Talk. (TR. 4.4777), " If I were to live long enough I would write a book about Anfechtung without which nobody can understand the scriptures or know the fear and love of God, nay, he cannot know what the Spirit is."

[5] " Gründlich verfehlt " (J. Lortz. Ref. in Deutschland (1940), i. xi. Miegge, 71.76-8). TR. 1.121 (1531), " Non sensi multam libidinem. Pollutiones habui ex necessitate corporali, mulierculas ne aspexi quidem cum confiterentur."

[6] TR. 4.5097. TR. 5.6305. TR. 5.6317. TR. 3.3777.

confession, he said, "not about women, but about the really knotty problems," [1] and he says that the "desire of the flesh" (concupiscentia carnis) is more easily overcome than spiritual temptations.[2]

In effect, the sharpness of Luther's criticism of the moral theologians at this point is the measure of his own desperation when he found that the doctors stopped short of the really knotty problems of "spiritual temptations, temptations about faith and hope, temptations of un-worthiness and temptations about predestination." [3] These temptations all concern a man's standing "Coram Deo." It does not seem probable that at the first period of Luther's monastic struggles, he was exercised about predestination. For him the agony came from the fact that he felt himself "in the presence of God to be a sinner with a most unquiet conscience."

What it means to feel guilty and condemned, under the Wrath of God, is an experience sufficiently remote from modern sophistication, but it is an experience described by Luther again and again with a recurring exactness and a poignant realism which makes such passages stand out, often with sombre and solemn beauty.

To be under the Wrath of God means a terrible reversal of St. Paul's exultant cry in Romans 8. If God be against a man, what can be on his side? [4]

"When this battle is joined, and a man sees nothing but hell, no escape is before his eyes. He believes that what is happening to him must be endless, for it is not the wrath of a mortal man, which must have a limit, but the Wrath of the eternal God which can never have an end." [5]

To such a man who has offended God, all things work together for ill.

"When he is tormented in 'Anfechtung' it seems to him that he is alone: God is angry only with him, and irreconcilably angry against him: then he alone is a sinner and all the others are in the right, and they work against him at God's orders. There is nothing left for him but this unspeakable sighing through which, without knowing it, he is supported by the Spirit and cries, 'Why does God pick on me alone?'" [6]

"Then remorse comes, and terrifies the conscience. Then all's well with the world and he alone is a sinner. God is gracious to all the world save to him alone. Nobody has to meet the Wrath of God

---

[1] TR. 1.518.
[2] TR. 1.240.12. TR. 1.47.15. W.A. 3.486.24. " prius est concupiscentia carnis vincenda et facilius est."
[3] Vogelsang. Angefochtene Christus, 17. Pinomaa. Exist. Charakter, 102.
[4] W.A. 5. 78.38, also W.A. 56.84.28.   [5] W.A. 5.210.13.
[6] W.A. 5.79.14.

I

save he alone, and he feels there is no wrath anywhere than that which he feels and he finds himself the most miserable of men. So it was with Adam and Eve when they sinned. Had God not come when the cool of the day arrived, they would never have noticed their sin. But when he came, they crawled away. . . ." [1]

In the presence of the Wrath of God, a man feels his shame exposed for all to behold.

"He is put to sin and shame before God . . . this shame is now a thousand times greater, that a man must blush in the presence of God. For this means that there is no corner or hole in the whole of creation into which a man might creep, not even in hell, but he must let himself be exposed to the gaze of the whole creation, and stand in the open with all his shame, as a bad conscience feels when it is really struck. . . . God takes all honour and comfort away and leaves only shame there, and this is his misery." [2]

To such a man, not only the hand of every man, but the universe itself seems actively hostile.

"For he who is an enemy to God has the whole creation against him." [3]

"For the whole creation seems at enmity with such a man." [4]

"Here God appears terrifyingly angry, and with him the whole creation." [5]

Thus there is nothing which cannot become the vehicle of the Wrath of God.

"God can make a wisp of straw as heavy as a hundred hundred-weight of corn, so do not despise those who have only small temptations." [6]

This thought Luther again and again expresses in terms of a favourite Biblical illustration, the panic-stricken flight of an army at the sound of a "driven leaf" (Lev. 26[36]).

"For where sin is, there is no good conscience, but only insecurity and incessant fear of death and hell, with which no joy or pleasure can abide in the bottom of the heart, but as Leviticus says, such a heart is terrified at a rustling leaf." [7]

"For there is nothing more trivial and insignificant than a dry leaf which lies on the ground, so that the very insects crawl over it . . . yet when its 'hour' comes, then steed, man, spear, armour, King, Prince, the whole might of an army shall flee at its rustling—whom otherwise

---

[1] W.A. 19.210.14 (1526).
[2] W.A. 19.216.27.   [3] W.A. 16.455.15.
[4] W.A. 3.168.14 (1514). Pinomaa. Zorn Gottes, 83, n. 4, for an important note on " all creation " in Luther's thought.
[5] W.A. 1.557.38 (1518).   [6] W.A. 45.397.2.   [7] W.A. 10.1.ii.27.14.

neither Hell nor the Wrath of God nor Judgment was able to terrify, but indeed only made them harder and prouder. What fine fellows we are! We are not going to be afraid for any Wrath of God, and we stand upright and then we are in panic and we run away from a power-less dry leaf! At such a rustling a leaf becomes the Wrath of God, and the whole world on which a moment before we strutted in our pride, becomes too narrow for us." [1]

Thus the sinner is hemmed in with anxiety and fear, and his con-science is a prison to him.[2] Cramped, cabined and confined in a kind of spiritual claustrophobia, the experience passes over into its opposite, the restless desire to flee to the ends of the earth, under the desperate certainty that there can be no escape from God.

"For this is the nature of a guilty conscience, to fly and to be terrified, even when all is safe and prosperous, to convert all into peril and death." [3]

"For so it is that conscience fears all creatures." [4]

"There is no flight, no comfort, within or without but all things accuse." [5]

"So long as all goes well with him, and stays so, he is proud and superior to God and all that God is, and is so hardened and tough that never was adamant so hard. But when he begins to sink and be cast down, then there is nothing so timid and downcast in heaven and earth, so that he would like to creep into a mouse-hole and the whole wide world becomes too narrow for him, and then he is ready to seek and take help from friend and foe, whether respected or despised." [6]

Of exceptional interest, because so early in date, is a passage from that sermon of Luther on John 3[16], which may well be one of the two earliest sermons preached by him, and which certainly belonged to the early years of his monastic career. After describing the fate of those who abuse the gifts of God Luther comes to the bad conscience (mala conscientia):

"And this is the worst of all these ills, that the conscience cannot run away from itself, but it is always present to itself and knows all the terrors of the creature which such things bring even in this present life because the ungodly man is like a raging sea. The third and greatest of all these horrors and the worst of all ills is to have a judge." [7]

---

[1] W.A. 19.226.16.
[2] W.A. 40.1.520.1. "Carcer theologicus meus infernus est." See Pinomaa. Existen-tielle Charakter der Theologie Luthers. Helsinki, 1940, 128. Jacob. Gewissens-begriff, 24.
[3] W.A. 44.504.   [4] TR. 2.581.   [5] W.A. 1.557.39.
[6] W.A. 19.209.9 : W.A. 3.231.18. "Non enim potest fugere a conscientia sua propria." This thought is expressed by Augustine. "For, O man, whatsoever thou wilt, thou canst flee except thy conscience." Ps. xxi. Exp. 11. Serm. 1 (Eng. tr., 244).
[7] W.A. 4.602.7 (1509-12).

A note at the end of the discourse adds: "His conscience will be his greatest pain, because the soul cannot escape from itself, and yet it cannot avoid falling into horror." [1]

The fact that such anguish can be experienced in this present life colours Luther's ideas of purgatory and of hell. The most poignant description of this agony was written in 1518, and though he expressly ascribes it to "a man I knew," its vividness has led many to suppose that behind it lies his own personal experience.

"I knew a man, who said that he had often suffered these pains (infernal torments) in the shortest possible compass of time, so great and infernal that 'nor tongue nor pen can show' nor can those believe who have not experienced, so that if they were completed, or lasted half an hour, or even the tenth part of an hour, he would utterly perish, and his bones be reduced to ashes. Then God appears horrifyingly angry and with him, the whole creation. There can be no flight, no consolation, neither within nor without, but all is accusation. Then he laments, 'I am cast away from thy face: Lord, accuse me not in thy Wrath.' In this moment, marvellous to relate, the soul cannot believe it can ever be redeemed, but believes that it is suffering a punishment not yet complete, . . . and left only with the naked longing for help, and terrifying trembling, but it knows not whence help can come. This is the soul stretched out with Christ, so that all his bones can be numbered, nor is there any corner not filled with the most bitter bitterness, horror, fear, dolour, and all these things seem eternal. And to use an illustration, it is as though a sphere should pass over a straight line, so that the point of the line which is touched supports the whole sphere, yet does not embrace the whole sphere. So the soul at this point, when it is touched with this passing eternal inundation, feels and drinks nothing less than eternal punishment, but it does not last, for it passes on." [2]

But the sting of hell is the guilty conscience:

"Therefore we consider that this hell is a bad conscience." [3]

"If the Devil had not a bad conscience, he would be in heaven . . . the Devil would not be afraid of burning rocks or external torments: it is from within that his tortures come, in his heart." [4]

"I find indeed in the Scriptures that Christ, Abraham, Jacob, Moses, Job, David, Ezekiel and many more have experienced hell in this life." [5]

---

[1] W.A. 4.604.28. W.A. 56.410.25: 411.20. Luther finds support for this theme in Prov. 28[1], Isa. 57[20], Isa. 48[22], Ps. 1[4], Lev. 26[36], Isa. 30[17].

[2] W.A. 1.558.7.33. Also W.A. 5.208.13-21.

[3] W.A. 10.iii.192.15 (1522). W.A. 4.445.12. W.A. 4.274.13.

[4] W.A. 44.617.30. "Nostri duo diaboli, peccatum et conscientia." W.A. 40.1.73.2. W.A. 40.1.661.11. W.A. 1.514.23.

[5] W.A. 7.450.14. Other refs., Vogelsang. Angefochtene Christus, 35 n. Pinomaa. Exist. Charakter, 73.

The result is that the soul begins to murmur against God, and even to hate the supreme majesty, in the sin of blasphemy: "he goes on to destruction in desperation, blasphemy, hatred of God and he will hate the law and from day to day will turn more and more against God, and his hatred of God grows, the more his fearful conscience persists." [1]

How could the soul make acts of love to God while within there raged this torment of secret rebellion, and in this case were not those very actions that deadly hypocrisy condemned by Biel, and so yet one more instrument of condemnation? Luther said of himself, in 1545, "I did not love, rather I hated this just God who punishes sinners, and if not with silent blasphemy, at least with huge murmuring I was indignant against God." [2] In 1526 Luther recalled how "I myself have more than once been offended almost to the very depth and abyss of despair so that I wished I had never been created a man." [3]

"Before the Law came, we were living at ease, secure, thinking nothing was wrong, but afterwards the law entered in, and showed us what kind of people we were, and commanded those things which, even if we had wished, we could not have performed. Then I simply was driven to despair, so that I began to hate and blaspheme God, who seemed to deal so unfairly with me." [4]

We must return to the theme of "Anfechtung" in the light of Luther's developed doctrine of the remedy and relief afforded by the Gospel. There are two specially fine expositions of the subject. First, his exposition of the Book of Jonah (1526), and second, his sermons on the story of the Canaanite Woman (Matthew 15[21-8]). There could be no better Biblical narrative for Luther's conception of "Anfechtung" than Jonah.[5] The story of a prophet who disobeys the command of God, and who attempts to run away from his divine vocation, the theme of judgment and repentance, preached to a great pagan city, the heathen sailors, the storm, the sleeping prophet awakening to disaster, his shame and penitence, his dreadful peril, desperate anguish, and miraculous deliverance: Luther makes the most of it, and it is a superb example of his preaching. We have already quoted from it, to illustrate the plight of the guilty conscience. But in this exposition, the dark shadows are hidden within the light of the gospel. Jonah's plight begins to be alleviated from the moment that he acknowledges his sin.

"For the heavy burden of sin in the heart and conscience becomes a

---

[1] W.A. 40.1.500.2. [2] W.A. 54.185.
[3] W.A. 18.719.8. [4] W.A. 39.1.558.2 (1538).
[5] H. Bornkamm. Luther und das Alte Testament. Tübingen, 1948, 27. Alanen. Das Gewissen bei Luther, chapter 3. Abraham's attempted sacrifice of Isaac also illustrated this truth. W.A. 5.225.5-25.

little lighter through the confession of sin. And so, very weakly, faith begins to burn. For he confesses the true God, maker of heaven and earth, which is no small beginning of faith and blessedness. For a heart completely cast down and in despair cannot open its mouth so wide, but it is dumb, or it slanders God and cannot think, believe or speak of God other than as a fearful tyrant, or as of the Devil, and only wants to flee and get away from him. Yes, it would that God were not God, so that he might not suffer such things from him, and so he forgets to confess and does not acknowledge his sin. He is so far sunk and hardened in anxiety (Angst) that he sees and feels nothing but anxiety and thinks only of getting free from it, and yet cannot be free because he is yet in his sins. So he stays for ever in sin and death. So let us learn from this the real art and trick of coming out of all need and anxiety (Not und Angst), namely, to take knowledge of sin before all else, to come straight out with them and confess them freely." [1]

The terrible feature of this predicament is that the sinner cannot turn to God.

"Hell is no more hell, if you can cry to God. . . . But nobody would ever believe how hard that is, to cry unto the Lord. Weeping and wailing, trembling and doubting, we know all about them. But to cry unto the Lord, that is beyond us. For our bad conscience and our sin press down on us, and lie so about our necks, so badly that we feel the Wrath of God: and the whole world could not be so heavy as that burden. In short, for our nature alone, or for the ungodly it is impossible to stand up against such things and cry out to God himself, who is there in his anger and punishment and not go elsewhere." [2]

Thus "When Jonah had come so far as to cry to God, he had won." [3]

The story of the Canaanite woman, and of the bantering dialogue with which Our Lord tested her, is, like Jonah, admirably fitted to the theme of "Anfechtung." Here is a humble woman ("but she is no simpleton in matters of faith; she is rather a Knight of Faith who wins the victory over God himself") [4] who clings to the will of Jesus of Nazareth to save, even though he refuses to answer, even though his replies to her entreaties sound baffling and hostile.

"See what a serious game the Lord plays with her faith . . . his heart is friendly towards her, and he intends to do good to her, but . . . he shows himself hostile to her, and hides his love and favour behind a mountain."

---

[1] W.A. 19.214.16.21.   [2] W.A. 19.222.25.
[3] W.A. 19.223.17.
[4] W.A. 20.280.17. D. M. Luthers Evangelien Auslegung. Göttingen, 1939, 503 ff. Also W.A. 5.201.21.26. " Ita haec tentatio eorum proprie est quorum magna est fides."

"Compare that with your own faith," says Luther, "and see if you could stand up to this first little temptation."[1]

But this temptation conceals God's merciful intentions towards us.

"God behaves as though he is going to deal with us in a different way from his promises, but he really does it so that the Old Adam may be killed and our faith proved."

"To think in one's heart that God is not good and kind, but will deal with us as a Judge, that is against the Gospel, and it is to slander God. Very few experience this. The saints do, and God has patience with them."

As in the exposition of Jonah, Luther stresses the difficulty of prayer in such distress. If we could only pray:

"Lord, this man is tempted in his conscience, and if it be pleasing to you, and for your honour, help him!—ah, that is easily said, but in the time of 'Anfechtung' we know nothing of this."

And when the soul emerges safely and triumphantly this does not mean in any wise that the will of Christ has changed.

"For Christ does nothing against the Gospel, he does not make a bad conscience, but he redeems it. Bad consciences are the fault of our nature and free Will."

In another sermon, in 1525, on the same theme, Luther intensified the trial of faith.

"See what a hard blow it is when God shows himself so seriously angry, and when he hides his grace so high and deep. They know that only too well who experience this in their heart, and who feel and think that God will not keep to what he has promised and will let his word be falsified."

But, in fact, the story of the Canaanite woman is written for our comfort, "that we may know how deep God hides his grace, and that we are not to think of him according to our feeling and thinking, but simply and only in terms of his Word."

"Christ shows himself here, as the heart feels. It sounds as though he had answered a plain 'No' and yet this is not so. Therefore the heart has to turn away from its feeling, and with firm faith it must grasp the deep, secret 'Yes!' which is under and above the 'No,' and so we must accept God's verdict upon us: then we have won and caught him in his own words."[2]

We may put beside this profound intuition a similar striking passage from the "Jonah":

[1] Also W.A. 15.453-7.
[2] W.A. 17.ii.200-204. M. L., Ev. Ausl., 507-10.

"Notice what a sharp vision the heart must have, to be surrounded by sheer wrath and punishment from God, and yet to see and feel, not punishment and wrath, but grace and goodness. That is, to refuse to see and feel them, though feeling and seeing them in the very highest degree, and to see and feel the grace and the goodness, though they are most deeply hidden. See what a great thing it is to come to God, that a man must break through to him through his wrath, through his punishment and displeasure, as though it were all sheer thorns, nay, pikes and swords." [1]

Thus the doctrine of "Anfechtung" is the clue to Luther's conception of Faith, for nobody who has taken seriously these passages can possibly suppose that Luther regarded faith merely as an intellectual assent, or an emotion of confidence.

"And so faith is no sleeping thing, as the monks have preached. They laugh at us, as though we knew how to preach no other faith than is preached among the Turks. Such is their blindness, that they think faith is a light thing, and so they consider something else must come along, which is greater than faith alone. But we say, faith is a splendid, honest and busy thing, for it takes the field. You must fight against your own nature, and against all and everything, Poverty, Pestilence, War and Famine which rises against you, and drives you to believe that God has forgotten you." [2]

Not only is "Anfechtung" the clue to his doctrine of Faith, but it is vital to the dialectic between Law and Gospel, so important for his doctrine of Justification. But we have already anticipated too much, by quoting from Luther's writing at a time when he had found an answer to his problems. In returning to the period of his spiritual distress as a monk, we might heed some of his words about Jonah.

"For you must not regard him here as he will be when he is rescued and restored to honour, but as he sticks in shame and cannot see how he can ever get out of it. For if a heart knew or saw this, then shame and conscience could not hurt so much. But God removes all the honour and comfort from his eyes, and leaves only the shame there, that is the rub." [3]

He was well aware that such temptations and struggles did not come the way of all men.

"Not many men suffer this trouble and anxiety, in fact, very few, and these not without intermission . . . and under the advice of the doctors they put it down to the complexion, or to melancholy, or

---

[1] W.A. 19.224.16-24.
[2] W.A. 29.63.66.   D. M. L., Ev. Ausleg., 512.
[3] W.A. 19.216.33.

the influence of the heavenly planets, or they find some natural cause." [1]

On the other hand, he believed that a false security of conscience was one of the great evils of the age.[2] His case against the penitential system of the late mediaeval Church, in the light of Nominalist theology, and as expressed in Indulgences was not that it failed to solace, but that it succeeded too well. The complaint against "false peace and security," which is the climax of his famous Ninety-five Theses, echoes a constantly recurring complaint of his earlier lectures on the Psalms.[3]

"Ah! (they say) what are you worrying about? It isn't necessary: you have only to be humble and patient. Do you think God requires such strict conduct from you? He knows all your imaginings, and he is good. One groan will please him. Do you think nobody can be saved unless he behaves so strictly? Where would all the others be, then, in whom you see no such violence? Perish the thought that they should all be lost. It really is necessary to observe 'discretion,' etc. And so gradually the unhappy soul forgets the fear of the Lord, and that the Kingdom of heaven suffers violence." [4]

Luther calls this "tentatio cogitationum de securitate" the greatest and final temptation. He is fond of quoting St. Bernard that "the greatest temptation is to have no temptation."

Many among Luther's advisers must have thought he was suffering from the well-known spiritual disease called "Scruples." [5] This condition of the distressed soul was treated in works of moral theology by Cassian, William of Paris, John Nider, Gerson and Gabriel Biel. Luther may have known the book of Nider, "For the consolation of timid consciences," which outlines the stages "Knowledge, faith, opinion, doubt, scruples" which might lead to the disease.[6]

We know also that he read treatises by Gerson, whom he praised as the "Doctor Consolatorius," [7] and he may have read his "Concerning

---

[1] W.A. 10.1.ii.101.20.

[2] W.A. 3.447.21. "The greatest vice of our age is security and lukewarmness." W.A. 3.423.40, "'Securitas' is worse and more terrible than all adversity." 433.24 : 444.11 : W.A. 56.281.5-25, "This security is the mother of hypocrites and the cause of hypocrisy."

[3] Luther had seen this security vanish in the presence of imminent death, and knew the terrors it could bring. It is this which underlies the vehemence of his attack on Indulgences, that they lull souls into false security. See W.A. 5.206. H. Bornkamm. Luthers Geistige Welt, 39.

[4] W.A. 3.447.30.

[5] From the Latin "scrupulus," a tiny pebble in the shoe which causes annoyance out of all proportion to its size. For a modern Catholic treatment of the subject, see "The Nature and Treatment of Scruples." D. Casey, S.J. Dublin, 1948.

[6] Scheel. Luther, ii.232.237.

[7] TR. 1.496. "Solus Gerson scripsit de tentatione spiritus. Omnes alii tantum corporales senserunt."

the Remedies of Weakness of Spirit" and "Of the Consolation of
Theology" and "Against the Foul Temptation of Blasphemy."[1] It
is evident that Luther's anxiety led him to an extreme scrupulosity,
and there are many references to it in his writings.

"When I was a monk I was so anxious in my conscience that I
would not dare to possess a pen without consulting the prior. . . . Such
a web did we spin from our fancies."[2]

"Whatever you did, the scruple (scrupulus) remained whether it did
really please God, or whether something more was required."[3]

"He confessed all that he had done wrong from his youth up, until
at last his preceptor in the monastery punished him."[4]

"My conscience could never give me certainty, but I always doubted
and said, 'You did not perform that correctly. You were not contrite
enough. You left that out of your confession.'"[5]

Quite obviously scrupulosity was a symptom of Luther's spiritual ill,
and we need not deny some dangerous and morbid elements in his
condition. But it is significant that although he knew all about
"scruples," since he has some acid comments on "scrupulants" in his
lectures, he never diagnoses his own troubles in those terms. There are
similarities, but there are great differences between the exact scrupulosity of a tender conscience, and the "scruples" which are the result,
not of religious insight, but a neurotic confusion. There is the world
of difference between the scrupulosity of the saints, and a self-centred
scrupulosity which denotes moral obtuseness.[6] In Luther's case, too,
it seems that the differences between his troubles and "scruples" are
more important than the common symptoms. Those who, like A. V.
Müller, have attempted to dispose of his problems as an extreme case
of scrupulosity have lamentably failed to account for the development
of his theology.[7]

The use of the Sacrament of Penance, the advice of spiritual directors
were among the remedies for afflicted souls, and we know that Luther

---

[1] Miegge. Lutero, 116. Vogelsang (Angefochtene Christus, 15) says that Gerson's
doctrine differs from Luther's. 1. The temptations are simply scruples of the soul.
2. They are not the dealing of God with man, but a subjective condition. 3. They
are not seriously concerned with the Wrath of God. 4. They have predominantly
natural causes. 5. They are to be overcome by cheerful advice and the restoration
of a sense of proportion. 6. To overcome them is to gain merit. Also E. Wolf.
Staupitz und Luther, 147 ff. K. Holl. Luther, 235 ff.
[2] W.A. 49.629.1.
[3] W.A. 18.783.26.
[4] TR. 1.200.30.   [5] W.A. 40.ii.15.15.
[6] See Casey, " Nature and Treatment of Scruples," 10.
[7] Miegge. Lutero, 84.86 n. On the devil as the cause of uncertainty. W.A.
5.248.29, " Nam ipse est proprie diabolus, id est calumniator, qui nos accusat et
conscientiam etiam in his confundit, quae recte gessimus . . . tum quae male egimus
supra modum magnificat." See also W.A. 5.158.10.

availed himself of these to his comfort. For many, such troubles were easily resolved, but there were others, and Luther knew some among his contemporaries, for whom the distress deepened into mental illness. Luther found help in books, in St. Bonaventura, pseudo-Dionysius, Gerson,[1] and later, from Tauler. In after years he recalled advice from some of his directors, as it still echoed in the memory. "My Son, God is not angry with you, but you are angry with him." . . . "My son, has not God himself commanded us to hope?"

But the greatest help came to him from the Vicar-General, Johann von Staupitz. Long afterwards, when Staupitz, who remained a Catholic, lay dying, he wrote of his affection for Luther "passing the love of women," and he maintained a beneficent interest in Luther from the time of their first meeting.[2]

Staupitz it was who, perhaps alarmed by Luther's abnormal introspection, and impressed by his outstanding gifts, induced Luther to closer Biblical study, and to proceed to his Doctorate in Theology, and the public career of teaching and preaching which it would entail. Later, when Luther was tilting at the mystical devotions of many religious, he said, "These are mere Satanic illusions, among which I would have been imprisoned as a monk, had not Staupitz recalled me to the public profession of Theology."[3]

Staupitz came of noble family, and he studied at Cologne, Leipzig and Tübingen, taking his Doctorate in 1500. It has been suggested that in theology he leaned to the via antiqua, between the Thomists and the great Augustinian doctor Aegidius Romanus, while he was influenced by the exponents of the "devotio moderna." As a professor, he seems to have been more successful in his friendships than his lectures. At any rate, he told a story against himself of how he tried to give a course of lectures on the Book of Job, but that he soon found that he was tormenting Job with an affliction worse than that of boils, and that he gave up after the eleventh chapter, to the great relief of the audience, of himself, but, above all, of Job![4]

But he was an able administrator, and his common sense, tenderness and sense of humour made him a fine director of souls. Luther paid repeated tribute to him, and perhaps the acknowledgments are an unconscious tribute to that mediaeval religion to which he owed more than he ever knew. "If I didn't praise Staupitz I should be a damned, ungrateful, papistical ass, for he was my very first father in this teaching,

[1] On Gerson. TR. 2.1351 : TR. 2.1492 : TR. 2.2457 : TR. 5.5711. P. Bühler. Anfechtung bei Luther, 155-160.
[2] The problems of Luther's relations with Staupitz are treated at length in the standard work, E. Wolf, Staupitz und Luther, 1927.
[3] Scheel. Dok., 472.   [4] Scheel. Luther, ii.367. TR. 5.98.21.

and he bore me in Christ." [1] "I cannot forget or be ungrateful, for it was through you that the light of the Gospel began first to shine out of the darkness of my heart." [2] "If Dr. Staupitz had not helped me out . . . I should have been swallowed up and left in hell." [3] When Luther went to him with the cry "My sins! my sins! my sins!" he found wisdom and comfort at hand.[4] When he disclosed to him his horrifying doubts, Staupitz it was who said, "You don't know, Martin, how useful this temptation is to you, for God is teaching you not to be afraid," [5] and he added that such temptations were as meat and drink to Luther.

There seems little doubt that Staupitz brought to Luther a wholesome corrective to the Nominalist theology. He brought the Thomist and Augustinian emphasis on grace at work within the soul: he brought also an acknowledgment of the importance of humility, and may have brought to Luther's notice the startling and, for him, important Latin rendering of Prov. 18[17]. "Justus in principio est accusator sui." With this there was the emphasis of the modern devotion on conformity with Christ in tribulation and in suffering, on a love of God ready, if need be, to be resigned to hell. But there were differences, too, between the theology of Staupitz and that of his pupil. Staupitz remains within the bounds of received teaching, and the doctrine of merit underlies his conception of Christian faith and behaviour, while the thought of conformity with Christ remains an imitation through discipline and spiritual exercises. "Staupitz is not, in the strict sense of the word, a forerunner of the Reformation. But it is easy to see how much comfort Luther could have received in his difficulties, concerning piety and theology, from his superior." [6]

But it was concerning the Sacrament of Penance that Luther derived his most comfortable word from Staupitz. Luther described the incident in a letter in 1518:

"I remember, reverend Father, how once, among those most pleasant and helpful talks of yours, with which the Lord Jesus often gives me wondrous comfort, that on one occasion this word 'poenitentia' was mentioned. We were moved with pity for many consciences and those tormentors who teach with rules innumerable and unbearable what they call 'a Method of Confession.' Then we heard you say, like a voice out of heaven, that there is no true 'poenitentia,' unless it begins with a love of righteousness (justitiae) and love of God. And this is rather

---

[1] Scheel. Dok., 512.   [2] Ibid. Dok., 74.
[3] Ibid. 461.
[4] T.R. 6.106.33.
[5] Other refs., W.A. 58.1.290.
[6] Miegge. Lutero, 110. E. Wolf. Staupitz und Luther, 87-122.

to be considered the beginning of 'penitence' which is by those others considered the end and consummation.

"This your word stuck in me like some sharp and mighty arrow (Ps. 120, v. 4) and I began from that time onward to look up what the Scriptures teach about penitence. And then, what a game began. The words came up to me on every side jostling one another and smiling in agreement, so that, where before there was hardly any word in the whole of scripture more bitter to me than 'poenitentia' (which I sought to feign in the presence of God (coram Deo) and tried to express with a fictitious and forced love), now nothing sounds sweeter or more graciously to me, than 'poenitentia.' For thus the precepts of God become sweet to us when we understand them, not only by reading books, but in the wounds of the most sweet Saviour." [1]

Luther goes on to say that when he learned Greek and Hebrew he found that their interpretation confirmed this use of the word. It is not altogether clear just what it was that Staupitz said to Luther, but Ernst Wolf, who has made a detailed examination of this passage against the background of the writings of Staupitz, concludes that it touches two important matters.[2]

"1. The primary meaning of 'poenitentia' is a change of mind made possible through Grace alone, and this means a displacement of the rules of the 'Method of Confession' and the over-emphasis on works of penance.

"2. The Love of Righteousness and of God is the motive and beginning of repentance."

The first corresponds to the translation of "poenitentia" by the English Reformers, as "repent" rather than the traditional "do penance." The second meant that the penitent turns from the contemplation of his own sin, and the assessment of his acts of satisfaction, to the love of God and of Righteousness.[3] That Staupitz directed him toward the "wounds of Jesus" meant that Luther was turned towards the most tender theme of mediaeval devotion, and along the road which would lead to his own "Theology of the Cross."

Thus, by word and by deed Staupitz brought relief and consolation to Luther. But there came a point when he could go no further, when he had to realize that here was something other than "scruples," when he stood, like a good general practitioner faced with something not in

---

[1] W.A. 1.525.   [2] Staupitz und Luther, 240.
[3] W.A. 5.163.30: 164.38 (1519) for a remarkable passage on the relation of hope and "poenitentia." "At quomodo poenitebit, nisi speret misericordiam Dei ? An dicendum est morituro peccatori : Absit a te, noli sperare, non habes merita, ex quibus tibi spes possit provenire ? Hoc iam esset non theologisare, sed diabologissare ! " W.A. 5.164.14.

the text-books, and where he could recommend no specialist. There is a poignant sentence of Luther about the moment when Staupitz said to him, "I don't understand you, that is beyond my ken." "Then thought I," said Luther, "nobody experiences this but you, and then—I felt like a dead body."

Chapter

6

THE RIGHTEOUSNESS OF GOD

"How dearly Martin Luther loved St. Paul. How dearly would
St. Paul have loved Martin Luther! And how impossible that
either should not have done so."
S. T. COLERIDGE on Luther's "Table Talk."

WE do not know when Luther began to study the Bible, though he
must have begun his novitiate by learning portions of scripture which
he would recite in the divine offices. It is certain that it became for
him an all-important and absorbing study, until his mind was impregnated with the words and themes of the Bible, and he could handle the
Biblical material with a facility which was the envy of his enemies, and
with a frequent penetration into the exactness of Biblical vocabulary
which modern Biblical scholarship has confirmed. But if the Bible
was soon to become paramount with him, beyond Augustine and the
Fathers, it was initially the meeting-place of all his problems, concentrated in one word. Here is his testimony, in the autobiographical
preface which he wrote, at the end of his life (1545), before the Wittenberg edition of his Latin works. After rehearsing his career down to
the year 1519, he pauses, and there follows this statement:
"Meanwhile then, in that year (1519), I turned once more to interpret
the Psalms, relying on the fact that I was the more expert after I had
handled in the schools the letter of St. Paul to the Romans and the
Galatians, and that which is to the Hebrews. Certainly I had been
seized with a greater ardour to understand Paul in the Epistle to the
Romans (captus fueram cognoscendi), but as Virgil says, it was not
'coldness of the blood' which held me up until now, but one word
(unicum vocabulum) that is, chapter 1. 'The Justice of God is revealed
in it' (Justitia Dei). For I hated this word (vocabulum istud) 'Justitia
Dei' which by the use and consent of all doctors I was taught (usu et
consuetudine omnium doctorum doctus eram) to understand philo-
sophically of that formal or active justice (as they call it) with which
God is just, and punishes unjust sinners.
"For, however irreproachably I lived as a monk, I felt myself in
the presence of God (coram Deo) to be a sinner with a most unquiet

conscience nor could I trust that I had pleased him with my satis-faction. I did not love, nay, rather I hated this just God who punished sinners and if not with 'open blasphemy' certainly with huge murmur-ing I was angry with God, saying: 'As though it really were not enough that miserable sinners should be eternally damned with original sin, and have all kinds of calamities laid upon them by the law of the ten commandments, God must go and add sorrow upon sorrow and even through the Gospel itself bring his Justice and his Wrath to bear!' I raged in this way with a fierce and disturbed conscience, and yet I knocked importunately at Paul in this place, thirsting most ardently to know what St. Paul meant.

"At last, God being merciful, as I meditated day and night on the connection of the words, namely, 'the Justice of God is revealed in it, as it is written, "the Just shall live by Faith,"' there I began to under-stand the Justice of God as that by which the just lives by the gift of God, namely by faith, and this sentence, 'the Justice of God is revealed in the gospel,' to be that passive justice, with which the merciful God justifies us, by faith, as it is written 'The just lives by faith.'

"This straightway made me feel as though reborn, and as though I had entered through open gates into paradise itself. From then on, the whole face of scripture appeared different. I ran through the scriptures then, as memory served, and found the same analogy in other words, as the Work of God (opus) that which God works in us, Power of God (virtus Dei) with which he makes us strong, wisdom of God (sapientia Dei) with which he makes us wise, fortitude of God, salvation of God, glory of God.

"And now, as much as I had hated this word 'Justice of God' before, so much the more sweetly I extolled this word to myself now, so that this place in Paul was to me as a real gate of paradise. Afterwards, I read Augustine, 'On the Spirit and the Letter,' where beyond hope I found that he also similarly interpreted the Justice of God: that with which God endues us, when he justifies us. And although this were said imperfectly, and he does not clearly explain about 'imputation,' yet it pleased that he should teach a Justice of God with which we are justified.

"Armed with these cogitations I began to interpret the Psalms again." [1]

The narrative is in the main straightforward, and most of it can be checked against quotations already cited in these pages. But there are certain problems which must be faced. In the first place, to what period of his career does Luther refer when he speaks of his discovery

[1] W.A. 54.179-87.

about "Justitia Dei"? A superficial reading might suggest that he refers to the year (1519), when "armed with these cogitations" he began the second course of lectures on the Psalms. But it can be demonstrated that Luther had developed his teaching on this subject in these terms, at least by the time of his lectures on Romans (1515-16). The notion of a dislocation of the text, that refuge of desperate scholars, put forward by A. V. Müller, has no documentary evidence to support it, and as K. Holl pointed out, would make Luther commit grammatical solecisms.[1] The suggestion that Luther in his old age made a slip of memory and confused his first and second lectures on the Psalms is hardly more convincing.[2] Stracke has made a careful examination of the whole of this autobiographical fragment, and Luther emerges surprisingly well from the test.[3] After thirty years, he is not unnaturally a month or two out here and there, gets a detail misplaced now and again, but when we remember that famous edition of the letters of Erasmus, which had more than half the dates wrong, and some of them years out, we can count this preface yet another disproof of the legend of Luther's anecdotage.

In fact, as Stracke pointed out, Luther's use of the phrase "captus fueram" makes perfectly tenable the interpretation that Luther has gone back in his reflection to an earlier period. Before attempting to identify this date more precisely, we must discuss the authenticity of the statement as a whole.

To impugn this was intended as a crowning demonstration of Denifle's "Luther und Luthertum." Denifle brought forward, in an appendix, a catena of 360 pages, giving the exposition of Rom. 1^{17} by sixty doctors of the Western Church, which, he said, demonstrated beyond a doubt "not a single writer from the time of Ambrosiaster to the time of Luther understood this passage (Rom. 1^{17}) in the sense of the justice of God which punishes, of an angry God. All, on the contrary, have understood it of the God who justifies, the justice obtained by faith."[4] Here, then, is the dilemma. Either Luther was a fool, or he was a liar. Either he was a bragging incompetent, boasting in his senility, or he was adding the last untruth to a long series of lying inventions. For Denifle, the two conclusions were not mutually exclusive.

Denifle included in the demonstration passages from the recently

---

[1] K. Holl. Luther, 194-6.   [2] K. Holl. Ges. Aufs. III, Westen, 187, n. 2.
[3] Luthers grosses Selbstzeugnis. Leipzig, 1926. H. Bornkamm. Archiv für Ref., 1940, 120.
[4] Quellenbelege zu Denifles Luther und Luthertum. 2. Aufl. 1.2. Abt. Die abendländischen Schriftausleger bis Luther über Justitia Dei (Rom. 1^{17}) und Justificatio. H. Denifle. Mainz, 1905. Strohl. L'Évolution religieuse de Luther. Strasbourg, 1922, 149 ff.

K

rediscovered lectures of Luther on Romans. This was intended as proof that Luther himself had used the supposed newly discovered meaning at a time anterior to 1515.

That part of his argument falls to the ground if we suppose Luther in fact to have spoken of a period before 1515. We may, therefore, re-sharpen Denifle's usefulness as an advocatus diaboli at this point, and present polemic with an argument here which, as far as we know, has been little noticed. In the Sentences of Peter Lombard, on which Luther lectured in 1509, and in the famous Dist. XVII of Book 1, to which, as we have seen, Luther paid special attention, there is imbedded a quotation from St. Augustine's "Spirit and Letter" which gives the so-called "passive" interpretation of "Justitia Dei":

"The love of God is said to be shed abroad in our hearts, not because he loves us, but because he makes us his lovers: just as the justice of God (Justitia Dei) is that by which we are made just by his gift (justi ejus munere efficimur): and 'salvation of the Lord' by which he saves us: and 'faith of Jesus Christ' that which makes us believers (fideles)." [1]

The words are glossed by the Master of the Sentences, "And this is called the Justice of God, not with which he is just, but because with it he makes us just." At any rate, it seems clear that although in 1509 Luther had not read Augustine's "Spirit and the Letter," he had read an extract concerning this interpretation of the "Justitia Dei" during his study of Peter Lombard. [2]

Denifle's *tour de force* was impressive, and like most polemic of this kind, got a good start of its pursuers. [3] Among many replies the most notable were the essays by Karl Holl and Emmanuel Hirsch. [4]

In the first place, it was pointed out that Luther in speaking of the "use and consent of all doctors" was referring not to Rom. 1[17], but to the "unicum vocabulum" of "Justitia Dei." The distinction is important, for, if granted, it means that the doctors in question were not the exegetes but the systematic theologians, and their views are to be found, not in the commentaries on the Epistles of St. Paul, but in those

---

[1] Peter Lombard. Migne. P.L., 192.568.

[2] Though it does not occur at exactly this point, it is possible that Luther's comment (W.A. 9.43.1), " Sicut Christus est fides, justitia, gratia nostra et sanctificatio nostra," refers to this passage.

[3] Professor J. P. Whitney was impressed by Denifle's arguments, though he had not read Holl and Hirsch in reply. He concluded " Intentional untruth on Luther's part might be supposed, but a preferable explanation is defective memory, and the difficulty of correctly describing one's past and one's development over a distance of changing years " (Hist. Ref., 1940, 506). In the light of Stracke's examination, this does not seem a possible solution.

[4] K. Holl. Ges. Aufs. III. Westen, 171-88. Die " Justitia Dei " in der vor-lutherischen Bibelauslegung des Abendlandes, 1921. E. Hirsch. Initium Theologiae Lutheri. Festschrift für Julius Kaftan, 1920. H. Bornkamm. Justitia Dei in der Scholastik und bei Luther. Archiv für Ref. 39, 1942.

passages which concerned the conception of divine justice in Commentaries on the Sentences, and the like. Denifle's enormous collection of documents attested a wrong indictment.

Denifle, it is true, could appeal to a passage in Luther's lectures on Genesis, in which he referred to "hunc locum," i.e. Rom. 1[17], as the centre of his difficulties.[1] But these lectures were not published until after Luther's death, and then only in the form in which they were reported. If there is glossing to be done, the 1545 fragment is primary, and Denifle, in his argument, showed some embarrassment at this point. As Holl was not slow to point out, nobody could say how many of Denifle's sixty doctors of the West could have been known, at first- or second-hand, to Luther, or whether he had studied the exegesis concerning Rom. 1[17]. Holl proceeded thoroughly to analyse Denifle's authorities and disentangled two main streams of mediaeval exegesis, going back to Ambrosiaster and to Augustine. He showed that Ambrosiaster keeps in mind the problem of the Divine integrity, how the just God can receive sinners, and that while stressing the merciful promises of God, he keeps also the conception of retributive justice. Augustine is less concerned with justice as a divine property than with that bestowed righteousness, the work of grace infused within the human soul, on the ground of which sinners are made just in the presence of God. But Holl pointed out that neither of these expositions, nor all the permutations and combinations of them made thereafter, really met Luther's problem. "That from the time of St. Augustine the Western Church spoke of justifying grace, and that the later schoolmen strengthened this conception by their teaching about an "habitus" is something known to all, and it is quite certain that Luther was not unaware of it." [2] Emmanuel Hirsch dealt with a notable and fundamental omission from Denifle's authorities, namely, the Nominalist doctors whom Luther knew, and whom he had in mind when he said, "I was taught." He showed that Gabriel Biel, though admitting, even stressing the need for grace, and for the divine "Misericordia," normally preferred to reserve "Justitia" for the retributive justice of God which punishes sinners.[3] This interpretation, which Hirsch based on Biel's

---

[1] " Anxie et sedulo laborandam de illa sententia intelligenda. Rom. 1. Justitia Dei revelatur in evangelio. Ibi diu querebam et pulsabam. Obstabat enim vocabulum illud : justitia Dei quod usitate sic exponebatur : justitia Dei est virtus qua ipse Deus est formaliter justus et damnat peccatores. Sic omnes doctores hunc locum interpretati fuerant, excepto Augustino : Justitia Dei, i.e. ira Dei." W.A. 43.537.13.

[2] K. Holl. Ibid., 172.

[3] " Pronior est ad largiendum de sua misericordia et bonitate quam ad puniendum de sua justitia." Biel. Collect. II. Dist. XXVII, q. 1, a. 2, concl. K. (ed. Feckes, 32). " Divinam justitiam dampnantem reprobos et ad divinam misericordiam salvantem electos. . . si ergo avertat suum arbitrium ab actu peccati considerando divinam justitiam dampnanten reprobos et convertat ipsum " (ibid., 33.1.22-6).

commentary on the Sentences, seems confirmed by an examination of some scores of sermons by Biel upon the feasts of the Christian year.

Even more important than these arguments is the abundant testimony of Luther's good faith in this matter which is yielded by writings of other years, many of which, since they had never been published, might well have been completely forgotten by Luther. It is quite certain that, whatever the truth about his statement, it was no later invention, made up at the end of his life. Thus, in 1515:

"Wherefore, if I may speak personally, the word 'Justitia' so nauseated me to hear, that I would hardly have been sorry if somebody had made away with me." [1]

In 1531 (published 1538):

"For thus the Holy Fathers who wrote about the Psalms were wont to expound the 'justus deus' as that in which he vindicates and punishes, not as that which justifies. So it happened to me as a young man, and even today I am as though terrified when I hear God called 'the just.' [2]

"Justice, i.e. grace. This word I learned with much sweat. They used to expound justice as the truth of God which punishes the damned, mercy as that which saves believers. A dangerous opinion which arouses a secret hatred of the heart against God, so that it is terrified when he is so much as named. Justice is that which the Father does when he favours us, with which he justifies, or the gift with which he takes away our sin." [3]

There are three passages in the Table Talk which must embody some core of truth. These suggest that Luther met his difficulty, before he came to the Epistle to the Romans, and in the interpretation of Psalm 31[1]. "In justitia tua libera me." But the difficulty, "Justitia Dei" understood as retributive justice, is the same.[4]

Two facts seem clear. First, that in his early career Luther found the conception of the "Justitia Dei" a stumbling block. Second, that this rock of offence did become for him the very corner-stone of his theology. The doctrine of Justification by Faith came to hold, in consequence, for him and for subsequent Protestant theology an altogether more important place than in the Catholic and mediaeval framework. In the sixteenth century men like Sir Thomas More and Stephen Gardiner found it hard to understand what all the Protestant fuss was about, and some striking parallels might be cited among modern Anglican scholars. Thus, even if we had not Luther's explicit testi-

---

[1] Scheel. Dok., 12.
[2] Ibid. 237.   [3] Ibid. 245.
[4] TR. 4.4007 : TR. 5.5247 : TR. 5.5553.

mony in the fragment under consideration, it would be necessary to invent something very like it to account for the remarkable and fundamental transformation in his thought. Denifle's demonstration may be held to have failed in so far as he attempted to show that Luther had wittingly perverted mediaeval teaching, and to have failed, too, in the more fundamental charge that Luther had in fact made no theological discoveries at all.

Thus in his narrative Luther explains simply and clearly why Rom. 1[17] was the climax of his difficulties. Luther already knew and believed that God condemned sinners through the Law. Now, in Rom. 1[17], he found that through the Gospel also [1] was revealed the "Justitia Dei," which he took to mean the strict, retributive justice of God.

If the reader, having absorbed the academic roughage of this critical discussion, will turn back to the autobiographical fragment, he will find it tolerably plain. We can understand how, in the presence of a God who weighted everything against the sinner, Luther was filled with that "huge murmuring" which he elsewhere often and eloquently described, but which a man dared hardly admit to himself, so closely did it approximate to "open blasphemy." This inward ferment added to the outward practices of devotion and penitence an element of strain and unreality, an enforced hypocrisy which in turn aggravated the spiritual conflict. This was not merely an academic affair, though we need not shrink from admitting the theological enquiry of a theological professor into such a category. What he learned and taught about the Justice of God became for him a "carnifex theologistria," however, by reason of the unquiet conscience within. It was this fifth column, within the citadel of the soul, which betrayed him. Miegge's judgment is valid: "In the case of Luther, the religious crisis and the theological crisis are not to be separated."

But if the difficulties congealed for him at Rom. 1[17] the answer lay close at hand in the reassuring words, "the just shall live by faith." As Holl suggests, Luther's problem lay, not in how to combine the divine justice with the mercy (misericordia) or the goodness (bonitas) of God, but in the conception of justice itself. Luther's mental clarification came when he saw this to be not simply a divine attribute, but a divine gift to men. "Because he trembled before God's punishing Justice, felt himself crushed by it, and yet recognized its verdict honestly as true, he was enabled to apprehend its final meaning. God does not send his Grace alongside his justice . . . but he sends it through his justice . . . God is nothing but sheer goodness, which is always giving

---

[1] See below, p. 163.

itself. This was more than a new exposition of Rom. 1[17], this was the fountain of a new doctrine of God." [1]

To this statement the history of four centuries of Protestant church-manship bear witness: the Institutes of Calvin, the Anglican Homily of Salvation, the sermons of John Wesley, the hymns of Gerhardt, Watts, and of Charles Wesley attest the richness and many-sidedness of the spiritual tradition which stems from this moment. This is not at all to assert that Luther's mental illumination at this point was some intricate theological matter. It was perhaps rather simple, and perhaps one of the reasons why Luther towers above so many other Christian teachers is that he was, after all, a rather simple person. He never claimed for this particular moment of insight that it was of universal novelty. "Nevertheless," says Joseph Lortz, and a Catholic testimony at this point is helpful, "it was new for him." [2]

It was of moment, too, that within this conception of Justitia, there lay the tension between two mighty spiritual traditions, the Hellenic conception of Justice, and the Biblical theme of the Righteousness of God. Moreover, the conception of the "Justitia Dei" points to the heart of the fundamental mystery of the Christian religion, that which in the end destroys all smooth and rounded theodicies, the proclama-tion that the Holy God receives sinners, and that the Eternal has dealings with men in time. In the following pages we shall see some implications of Luther's discovery. Here we are content to remark that it seems to have occurred and to have been of importance in his development. There is every reason to believe him when he speaks of the relief and easement which it brought to him, though if we remember that he speaks in similar high terms about his discovery concerning "poenitentia" and that he was always hypersensitive to the impact of words, we shall not exaggerate the significance of what is sometimes called the "Turmerlebnis." [3] To think of it in terms, say, of the evangelical conversion of John Wesley, is to beg questions for which the evidence fails.

Modern scholarship has moved away from Denifle's misfired salvoes.[4]

---

[1] Holl. Ibid., 188. Bornkamm. Justitia dei. 30-32.
[2] Reformation in Deutschland, 1.183.
[3] Or " Tower experience " from the tower in the monastery in which, traditionally, Luther made his discovery about the " Justice of God."
[4] The evidence concerning the place where Luther studied is confusing, and subsequent alterations in the structure of the Black Monastery at Wittenberg make it almost impossible to identify it. In the Table Talk Cordatus and Lauterbach speak of the " hypocaustum," a warm room in the tower. Schlaginhaufen says " Dise Kunst hatt mir d SS auf diss Cl. eingeben "—" this art, the Holy Spirit gave me in this Cl." The suggestion that Cl. means " cloaca " is the guess made by certain later editors, and in the first edition of his Luther Grisar declared (Eng. tr., i.396) " It is clear that the secret chamber was simply the closet or privy." In an appendix

It has moved from consideration of the fact to an enquiry concerning the time of the discovery.

The terminus a quo seems reasonably fixed by the words of Luther, "When I became a doctor, I did not yet know that we cannot expiate our sins." [1] For, although a better case can be made out for 1509 than is commonly supposed, it seems much more likely that the change occurred after his public profession of Biblical Theology. On the other hand, it seems to have preceded the lectures on the Epistle to the Romans (1515-16), by which time his teaching about Justification by Faith is plainly developed.

It has been suggested that Luther's first course of lectures were upon the book of Genesis. In a rather vague paragraph in "On the Councils and the Churches" (1539) Luther is claiming to have studied the Fathers "before I set myself so stiffly against the Pope," and he says, "I took up Hebrews with St. Chrysostom's glosses, Titus and Galatians with the help of St. Jerome, Genesis with the help of St. Ambrose and St. Augustine, the Psalter with all the writers that were to be had." [2] It is suggested that the only date into which such lectures could be fitted is the period 1512-13. But the evidence is very far from satisfactory, and no manuscripts have survived.

It seems preferable to begin therefore with the fact that Luther became a Doctor in Theology in October 1512. We know from the Journal of John Oldecop that Luther was lecturing on the Psalms in

to the sixth volume (504) he refrained from so definite a claim, but was careful to cite all the evidence in its favour. Other interpretations of the mysterious Cl. which have been suggested are " cella " and " capitulum." Most scholars now believe it to have been a warmed room in which Luther studied. This controversy is of little moment, but it provoked from Preserved Smith probably the oddest paragraph which has ever been written about Luther.

" It is certain and yet strange that this revelation was vouchsafed to him in the privy of the Black Cloister, situated in the little tower overlooking the town walls. One is tempted to connect the fact with the monk's neurosis, referring to parallel cases of obsession driving people to go through certain ceremonies at stated times, often ceremonies of a quasi-religious nature at times least natural for them. It is simpler, however, to recollect only that Luther was a busy man, with little leisure for private meditation and that the Rule enjoined spiritual reflection at these times. In telling the story of the monk who prayed while sitting on the stool and had a controversy with the Devil about the propriety of doing so, Luther probably referred to his own practice. It must naturally have seemed odd to him at the time, however, that such a revelation should come on such an occasion and, thinking over the reason, he symbolized it. The greatest triumphs of the spirit are in the vile substance of the flesh, which is regarded by the spiritual man and is stated literally to be in a manner, a latrina and cloaca. Conversely therefore the cloaca might stand for the flesh in which the message of the spirit was revealed " (Harvard Theol. Rev., vol. 6, 1913, 420-1).

If there is an evident point where psychoanalytic theory stops being an austere and scientific mental discipline and becomes a mesmeric witchcraft which befuddles the historical judgment, this would seem to be it.

[1] W.A. 45.86.18. Strohl. Évolution, 145.

[2] W.M.L. 5.142. H. Boehmer. Luthers erste Vorlesung. Leipzig, 1924, 4. Schwiebert. Luther and His Times, 282.

1513.[1] On the 8th July in that year, there appeared from the press of John Grünenberg, in Wittenberg, an edition of the Psalter with wide margins appropriate for interlinear and marginal notes, and this was the edition which Luther caused to be printed for his own use, and for his students. Boehmer suggests that Luther began the course on 16th August 1513, on a Tuesday at 6 a.m., that he lectured twice a week, and that he finished with the Psalms on 20th October 1515.[2]

Luther adopted the division into Glossae, the brief, exegetical and critical comments, and the Scholiae, the longer theological expositions. Two incomplete but invaluable manuscripts of these have survived. The first, the so-called Wolfenbüttler Psalter, is Luther's own copy, with the interlinear and marginal glosses. All of this, save two leaves, has survived. The glosses include very many critical comments gleaned from Augustine, the Glossa Ordinaria, Nicholas of Lyra, Faber Stapulensis, and others, including Cassiodorus, Paulus Burgensis, John de Turrecremata and Reuchlin.[3]

Much more important, but in far less satisfactory preservation, is the Dresdner Psalter, which consists of Luther's Scholiae, and of this between a third and a quarter is missing. The binding and pagination are of a later date, and have problems of interpretation which are complex enough. A third manuscript consists of Luther's copy of the Psalterium Quintuplex of Faber Stapulensis (Paris, 1509).[4] This was the latest critical instrument available for Luther and he used it as a model for his text, and for the summaries of the Psalms which he inserted at the head of each. He seems to have made some marginal notes while awaiting his own Psalter from the printer, but as the work also contains many other comments made at a much later date, it is almost impossible to date these comments with accuracy and the work is to be used with caution.

This is but the beginning of critical difficulties. At some time between 1515 and 1516, Luther began to revise his material with a view to publication.[5] Some of it has been worked over, and in the first four Psalms, while some of the material can be safely dated in 1513, there is much which must be allotted to 1516.[6] Nor can it be said how the

---

[1] " Tho düsser sülven Tidt hoff ann M. Luther den Psalter Davidt tho lesende, und was dar flittich by und hadde vele thohörers." W.A. 3.1.
[2] Boehmer, erste Vorlesung, 5.   Luthers Werke.   Cl.   Vol. 5.40 (Vogelsang).
[3] Luthers Werke (Vogelsang), 5.39.   [4] Ibid. 40. W.A. 4.463.1.
[5] W.A.Br. 1.53 ff. Authorities are not agreed whether the letter should be dated 9th September (Boehmer, Clemen), or 25th December (so Preserved Smith. Luther's Correspondence, 48).
[6] It seems that W.A. 3.27.7-31.38 (Leaves 15-16 MS.) may be dated 1513: W. A. 3.15.13-26.18 (Leaves 2-5) and W.A. 3.39.21-60.7 (Leaves 18-25), Ps. 1 and 4, respectively, date from 1516. These conclusions result from examination of ink, paper and internal evidence, and were originally made by Boehmer (Erste Vorlesung) and are accepted by Wendorf.

Glossae should be related to the Scholiae, for though it seems fairly certain that he worked well ahead with the Glossae, the critical foundation for his interpretations, it is impossible to relate most of them accurately. The practice of the editors of the Weimar edition (Vols. 3 and 4) in printing the Glossae and Scholiae together to make a commentary, gives an entirely misleading picture of the real state of the manuscript evidence, and has always to be borne in mind when using these volumes. Moreover, as Wendorf has shown, Luther was in the habit of leaving plenty of space at the end of his Psalms for afterthoughts, and for references back at a later stage.[1] No doubt many of his notes were in fact added in this way. Dating the extracts is therefore a matter of delicacy and confusion.

The handwriting which covers the pages is neat. As Boehmer says, it could hardly be smaller, so that the crowded pages, with underlinings, crossings out and the innumerable customary abbreviations present problems more intricate than the critical apparatus of the Weimar edition suggests. Dr. K. A. Meissinger claims to have found some thousands of more than trivial misreadings. When, finally, we remember that these documents are not Luther's lectures, but simply the collection of lecture material, on the basis of which he dictated or lectured, it can be seen how precarious it is to ask the questions whether and at what point Luther's discovery about the justice of God emerged. In any case, such a discovery might not immediately intrude into such documents.

Early one summer morning in 1513, then, the young Professor of Biblical Theology entered the lecture-room of the Augustinian house in Wittenberg. The Dresdner Psalter contains the careful notes of what may represent his inaugural lecture, "Good sirs, fathers and brethren, you have come, as I see, with great and benevolent spirit, to do honour to the famous prophet David." The professor disclaimed the intention of making an eloquent encomium of David "lest I seem to be speaking above what is seemly." "For I feel very surely the weight upon my neck of this task, which for a long time I was reluctant to undertake (all in vain) and to which I yield only when compelled to do so by order (coactus preceptis). For I confess plainly that to this day there are some Psalms I cannot understand, and unless the Lord enlighten me with your merits, as I hope, I cannot interpret them."[2]

Luther's statement that he had been reluctant to lecture, and had, in fact, done so under instruction can be linked with his later statement

[1] H. Wendorf. Der Durchbruch der neuen Erkenntnis Luthers im Lichte der handschriftlichen Ueberlieferungen. Hist. Vierteljahrschrift, 1932, 124.285, p. 142.
[2] W.A. 3.13-14.

in 1516, that he had been ordered to prepare these lectures for publication. The facts suggest the watchful and kindly prompting of Staupitz in the background. He it was who had induced a reluctant Luther to proceed to his doctorate, and to the career of public teaching which this must involve.[1] Here is a further hint that Staupitz selected the Psalms as a theme for Luther, as best fitted to the state of his studies, and perhaps also with an eye to Luther's own spiritual difficulties.

In many ways the Psalms were fitted for a tyro. Their text was common knowledge to lecturer and audience, who had the Psalms by heart and who made them, in the Divine Offices, the framework of their devotion. In the Psalms, as in hardly any other Biblical book, the height and depth of the Christian warfare is expressed, but never without the assurance of the divine promises, and the hope of victory. It would be difficult to exaggerate what the Psalms came to mean to Luther throughout his life, and not least because he found in them all the comfort of the true "communio sanctorum" of Christian solidarity.[2]

"For a man's heart is like a ship tossed on a wild sea, driven by stormy winds from the four corners of the world. Here it is buffeted by fear, and care about coming disaster: there grief and sadness come along in present evil. Here comes a breeze of hope and expectation of coming happiness: there blows security and joy in present blessings. Such tempests teach us to speak with earnestness, they open up the heart and reveal what is at the bottom of it. For whoso is caught fast in fear and need speaks about misfortune very differently from the man who floats on joy: and the man who floats on joy speaks and sings about joy very differently from him who is caught fast in fear. When a sad man laughs or a happy man weeps, it doesn't come from the heart, we say; that is, the depths of the heart are not opened and what is in them is not shaken out.

"What is the greatest thing about the Psalms, but this earnest speaking amid these tempests of every kind? Where does one find such words of joy as in the psalms of praise and thanksgiving? There you see into the hearts of all the saints, as into lovely and pleasant gardens, yes, as into heaven itself, and see what fine and gay' flowers of the heart spring up out of fair and happy thoughts towards God because of his benefits. On the other hand, where do you find deeper,

---

[1] " I, Doctor Martin, was called and constrained to take my doctorate, with no thanks to myself, but out of sheer obedience." W.A. 30.iii.386.30. Also W.A. 43.667.33. TR. 5.99.24.

[2] Held says that the lecture material consists of a " living mixture of exegesis, dogmatics, preaching and personal confession." St. u. Kr., 1930, 7. It includes at least one sermon (on the Martyrs) by Luther. W.A. 3.342-6.

more sorrowful, more pitiful words of sadness than in the psalms of lamentations? There again you look into the hearts of all saints, as into death, nay, as into hell. How gloomy and dark it is there, where there is manifold and distressed contemplation of the Wrath of God. So, too, when they speak of fear and hope, they use such words that surpass the art of a painter to depict fear and hope, and such as no Cicero, no orator could so express." [1]

On the other hand, as Luther frankly admitted, obscurities and difficulties abounded. Textual difficulties, the transitions from Hebrew to Latin, problems of exegesis arose which were insoluble in an age lacking modern critical and historical instruments. Here Luther found immense relief in the traditional and many-sided exegesis of the later mediaeval theology. Just as the allegorical method enabled the early Church to evade certain problems which were dangerously insoluble in default of critical method and historical apparatus, so the more elaborate schemes which developed after the time of Augustine enabled exegetes to develop a many-sided interpretation of Scripture, often wooden and arid, leading sometimes to the most extravagantly subjective interpretations of Scripture, but at least suggesting what Origen had sensed, what the later doctors of the Church had never forgotten, the richness and mystery of the Biblical world, as it seemed to them like some vast unexplored ocean of truth, or like the whisperings of a mighty forest.[2]

Later, Luther not only abandoned, but vehemently attacked this method of exegesis. But he employed it throughout his lectures on the Psalms,[3] and it provided a young doctor with a bunch of exegetical keys. If one would not do, then another might serve to unlock some mysterious and closed door into revealed truth.

He was critical of the literal interpretation employed by Nicholas of Lyra, whom he condemned in similar terms to the complaints of the Fathers about the way the Rabbis misinterpreted the Old Testament.[4] But we must remember that Luther was concerned immediately with the Psalms, and that a literal interpretation of the Psalms would leave many of them baffling indeed, so that even Lyra himself made frequent use of tropology. Not only the theology, but the devotion of the Church demanded that the Psalms should be Christologically interpreted, and this is the ground of Luther's exegesis, as

---

[1] Vorrede auf den Psalter. M. L. Vorreden zur Heiligen Schrift. Munich, 1934, 20-21. W.M.L. 6.386-7.
[2] J. Daniélou. Origène. Paris, 1948, 174.
[3] Hamel, p. 35. G. Ebeling. Die Anfänge von Luthers Hermeneutik. Z. für Theol. u. K. 48. 1951, 162-230.
[4] W.A. 3.335.33. "Istum autem Psalmum Lyra suum Rabbi Salom. secutus lacerat potius quam exponit."

it may well be the reason why Staupitz commended them to his study and interpretation.

Luther states his convictions in the preface to the Wolfenbüttler Psalter. "All those who have a carnal understanding of the Psalms, as the Jews have, apply them always to the old stories outside Christ (extra Christum). But Christ opens . . . minds that they may understand the Scriptures." [1] The fourfold scheme consists of the historical, allegorical, tropological and anagogical explanations.[2] The historical interpretation is fundamental, and this in the "literal prophetic" sense Luther referred to Christ. "All prophecies and all the prophets ought to be understood of Christ Our Lord, unless it appears by plain words that they treat of something else." [3] The allegorical reference is to the Church, the whole People of God. Tropologically the application is to the individual Christian (de quolibet spirituali et interiore homine).[4]

This is a more adequate framework than might at first sight be supposed. The literal prophetic sense laid the foundation of devotion and interpretation, in the Mighty Acts of God in His Son Jesus Christ, that historical revelation, once for all, which is the centre of the Christian proclamation and the Biblical and Apostolic testimony. The tropological sense, like many of the collects in the Liturgy, links what God has done "for us" with his saving activity "in us." This interpretation is saved from the perils of atomism, subjectivism and false mysticism by the allegorical interpretation which insists, in Bernard Manning's phrase, that all religious experience is ecclesiastical experience, that God addresses man within the solidarity of creation, of humanity and of the People of God. Finally, not less necessary, the anagogical interpretation insists that all problems and solutions are broken and partial in time, since they relate to "homo viator," and point to strangers and pilgrims beyond the horizon. This is, no doubt, to dress up mediaeval exegesis in the jargon of modern ecumenical theology, but the framework is there, and it is a richly suggestive one.

The fourfold method was not rigidly applied, for in fact there were many variations, many schemes of mediaeval exegesis.[5] But it was of undoubted service to Luther in dealing with the Psalms, and at this stage of his development. We must be thankful that he soon abandoned it, but we have reason to be glad that he began by using it. For, of the four tools, two came to be of catastrophic importance. The christo-

[1] W.A. 3.11.14.   [2] W.A. 3.11.33.
[3] W.A. 3.13.7, also 225.37 : W.A. 4.379.35 : 305.6 : 349.13.
[4] W.A. 3.13.16.
[5] B. Smalley. Bible in the Middle Ages. E. Vogelsang. Die Anfänge von Luthers Christologie nach der ersten Psalmenvorlesung, 1929, 16-31. H. Bornkamm. Luther und das Alte Testament. Tübingen, 1948, 74. F. Hahn. Die Heilige Schrift als Problem der Auslegung bei Luther. Ev. Theol. March, 1951.

logical groundwork involved constant preoccupation in study and interpretation, with the person and the work of Christ, that meditation on the "Wounds of Jesus" which had been the wholesome direction pointed out by Staupitz to his anguished pupil.[1] Second, an emphasis which does not appear at the beginning of the lectures, a growing awareness of the importance of the tropological reference, which relates the divine action in Christ to the work of God in the soul.[2]

In his important essay, Erich Vogelsang drew attention to this combination of christological and tropological interpretation, and suggested that here is the key to Luther's discovery about "Justitia Dei." He suggests that Luther's illumination came when he applied this concept of divine justice, first to the work of Christ, and then to the application of this to the soul, on the ground of faith. Vogelsang suggests that though there are signs of movement and tension early in Luther's lectures, "The real wrestling begins from Ps. 30-31 onwards, but the solution and the goal are not yet attained."[3] He finds clear evidence of a transformation of Luther's thought in Ps. 70-71, and a conception of divine justice as that with which God makes us just, which recalls Luther's language in the autobiographical fragment of 1545.

"Ps. 70. The Justice of God is all this: to abase oneself to the uttermost (sese in profundum humiliare) and this properly Christ expresses here. For he is the power and justice of God through his uttermost and deepest humility.[4]"

"Ps. 71. The 'judicium Dei' considered tropologically, for so it is most frequently taken in Scripture . . . for this is called the 'judicium Dei': as the justice (justitia) or the strength or the wisdom of God: that is, with which he makes us wise, just and humble or by which we are judged."[5]

"Wherefore, whoever wants to understand the Scriptures wisely needs to understand all these things tropologically: truth, wisdom, salvation, justice (justitia), namely with which he makes us strong, saved, just, wise. So also the works of God and the way of God, all of which things, Christ is in the literal sense, and morally all these things are faith in him (fides ejus)."[6]

There is here, indeed, a striking resemblance to the words, written

---

[1] W.A. 4.379.38. "Sicut Christus caput est Ecclesiae ita Scriptura quoque in capite id est ante omnes de ipso loquitur : igitur sit principium, caput, id est principalis sensus verborum tuorum, veritas " (3.63.1). " Crux enim Christi ubique in Scripturis occurrit " (4.87.35).

[2] W.A. 3.335.21. " Tropologicus sensus est ultimatus et principaliter intentus in scriptura " (3.458.8). " Qui apostolum et alias scripturas vult sapide intelligere oportet ista omnia tropologice intelligere " (3.531.33 : 3.532.12).

[3] Vogelsang. Anfänge, 43.

[4] W.A. 3.458.4-7.   [5] W.A. 3.465.1.33.

[6] W.A. 3.458.8-12.

by Luther in 1545 "from this point, the whole face of the Scriptures was altered. I ran through the Scriptures as memory served and found the same analogy in other words as 'work of God' (opus Dei) that which God works in us, strength of God (virtus) that with which God empowers us (sapientia), wisdom of God, with which he makes us wise, 'fortitudo Dei,' 'salus Dei,' 'gloria Dei.'"

Vogelsang's whole treatment of the subject is suggestive and important, and almost convincing. Without committing ourselves to Ps. 70 and 71 as the exact point of Luther's illumination, we may accept the view as probable that Luther did come to a new understanding of the "Justice of God" at some time during his lectures on the Psalms (1514). A later review of the subject was made by Wendorf in 1933, on the ground of detailed examination of the manuscripts in question. He is highly critical of Vogelsang's handling of these documents, and gives many proofs that Boehmer was a far more reliable historian in this respect.[1]

Wendorf pointed out that scholars had too easily assumed that nothing could be based upon Luther's expositions of Ps. 1-4 on account of the confusion of the MS. With great care and ingenuity he disentangled the true state of the MS. and succeeded in showing clearly that there are some passages which with reasonable confidence could be dated in 1513.[2] In these early paragraphs he found a treatment of "judicium" and a conception of forgiveness which he suggested must be subsequent to Luther's change of mind about the justice of God. He drew especial attention to Luther's comment:

"'The just man falls seven times and rises again, but the impious are turned unto evil' . . . because he does not excuse his sins, but soon confesses them and accuses himself: and when this is done they are soon remitted and he rises again." [3]

He concludes that "When Luther wrote down these pages for his Collecta, the decisive hour must already have lain behind him." [4] "In the Scholia to Psalm 1 as the first place where his re-orientation becomes plain, the point becomes visible at which the revolution of his thought world began." [5]

On the whole, this seems far less convincing than the argument of Vogelsang. Granted that the strictures on Vogelsang's handling of

---

[1] H. Wendorf. Der Durchbruch der neuen Erkenntnis Luthers im Lichte der handschriftlichen Überlieferungen. Hist. Vierteljahrschrift, 1932, 124.285. Bornkamm. Justitia Dei, 39.

[2] Of the Dresdner Scholiae he says MS. 14b is to be excluded since it is simply Luther's preface to the whole Psalms : Leaves 2-5 date from 1516, 12a dates from 1513, as do leaves 15 and 16. Durchbruch, 302.

[3] W.A. 3.29.17. Durchbruch, 316.

[4] Ibid. 317.   [5] Ibid. 325.

MSS. are justified, granted that Wendorf has performed excellent service in calling attention to the MS. of Psalm 1, and in clearing up difficulties avoided by earlier scholars, has he not fallen before an obvious but subtle temptation? Having cleared away the later accretions and laid bare the foundation, has he not been tempted to find in this what he has been looking for, and been too predisposed to suppose that because he has so skilfully answered one question, the clue to the more intricate problem of Luther's discovery must emerge at this point? There is here a genuine emphasis on the need for confession, on the "accusatio sui" as the true meaning of acts of penitence, but there does not seem any great movement away from what Luther had already said in his marginal comments on Peter Lombard, and the evidence about "Justitia Dei" fails almost completely. There is certainly nothing which recalls, as do Ps. 70 and 71, the autobiographical fragment of 1545.

We conclude, therefore, that, as Vogelsang suggests, the new orientation of thought seems likely to have occurred in the course of the lectures on the Psalms, 1514.[1] It is hardly likely that any closer date will be arrived at. We must beware of certain conclusions where such material is concerned, and we must not succumb to the perennial temptation to all historians, of propounding certain judgments where in truth the evidence is insufficient.

[1] Vogelsang.   Anfänge, 57, n. 2.

LUTHER'S "DICTATA SUPER PSALTERIUM"

(1513-15)

"He who would understand Luther rightly must keep fast hold
on the idea that Faith, according to his view, by an inherent, irre-
pressible necessity must produce good works."
JULIUS HARE. "Vindication of Luther."

LUTHER'S lectures on the Psalms show us the tension and movement
of his thought at a critical stage in its development. We have seen
something of the complexity of the critical problems involved in the
use of his lecture materials. We have found reason to believe that it
was during this period that Luther came to a new understanding of
the meaning of the "Justitia Dei," and have indicated some of the
evidence that the mental clarification is reflected in the lectures
themselves.

The view that in these lectures Luther stands entirely on Catholic
ground was devastated by Karl Holl. He showed that Denifle and
Grisar put forward this view because they had vested mental interests
in maintaining it, and he justly deplored that superficial skimming
of the surface which "has no feeling for accents." [1]

On the contrary, Holl affirmed that "it would be more just to say
that the whole later Luther is already present in the Lectures on the
Psalms." [2] The interpretation of movement of thought and a changing
content of vocabulary is a delicate and intricate matter. Luther continues to use traditional words and categories, long after he has ceased
to use them in their former sense, and after the background of his
thought has changed their meaning. Thus he uses the Nominalist
formula "facienti quod in se est," and the conceptions of "condign"
and "congruous" merit throughout these lectures, although his growing stress on the unmerited gift of grace has obviously altered their
content for him. [3] He has, as we shall see, a characteristic of giving old

[1] Holl. Luther, 157. [2] Holl. Luther, 111, n. 1.
[3] Holl. Luther, 156: W.A. 4.262.4: 4.329.33: Vogelsang. Anfänge, 72, gives
an analysis of the references to "merit" in these lectures and distinguishes:
1. Passages with a positive Catholic interpretation. W.A. 3.85.35: 91.12: 126.22:
129.9: 149.13.

technical terms a new meaning. We cannot easily tell, therefore, whether some words remain on the surface of his thought, like unmelted blocks of ice drifting for a time upon the warmer waters into which they disappear, or if they have for him a stubbornly traditional meaning.

Nor is it enough to consider isolated words, apart from their coherence. Yet this inner coherence, in the nature of things, is hard to detect in a mass of uneven lecture material relating to themes as diverse as those treated in the Book of Psalms, and as we always have to bear in mind the changing subject matter of his exegesis in considering the development of Luther's vocabulary.

The period between Luther's Marginal Notes on Peter Lombard (1509) and the Lectures on the Psalms is a time of his intense preoccupation with Biblical study. It is also the period when St. Augustine most influenced his mind.

The older view was that Luther represents a return to Augustinianism. Catholic historians declared it to be a one-sided Augustinianism which marked classic Protestantism, or which produced the movements of Bajus and Jansen within the Roman Church. The older Protestant view was to place Luther within a so-called "evangelical succession" of St. Paul, St. Augustine, Luther and Wesley. The recent trend has been in another direction. The massive scholarship of Karl Holl and Anders Nygren have so damaged the older view that the doctrine of the "evangelical succession" can no longer be stated in the former clear-cut way. They drew attention to some of the disparate elements in Augustine's thought which Luther came strongly to repudiate, and showed that despite the resemblances the orientation of Luther's doctrine of sin, grace and salvation profoundly differs from that of the great Doctor of the West.

But this, too, is a subject on which the last word is far from having been said, and we may not ignore a massive Biblical and Christian substance in St. Augustine to which all post-Augustinian theologies of salvation, including Luther's, have been indebted.

2. From Ps. 50 onwards passages critical of the doctrine. W.A. 3.284.8.11.16 : 285.27 : 287.12 : 291.9, but intermingled with some in the traditional sense. W.A. 3.337.31.38 : 343.29 : 360.25.
3. From Ps. 84 onwards an attack on the notion of merit. W.A. 4.13.20 : 15.31 : 17.20 : 39.12 : 41.16.
4. A clear exposition of the unmerited nature of salvation. W.A. 4.258.30 : 263.12 : •278.8.
5. An explicit reference to " condign " and "congruous " merit appears (at the request of his hearers ?). W.A. 4.312.39 (344.4).
6. The repudiation of merited salvation. W.A. 4.361.13.24.27 : 375.24 : 390.22 : 393.2 : 422.13 : 426.8. But Hamel, 1.186, and Ebeling, 180, doubt Vogelsang's interpretation here.

L

The suggestion which A. V. Müller offered as the clue to Luther's development, that there was a revival of Augustinianism in the milieu in which Luther was trained, has never got beyond the stage of an interesting hypothesis. Augustine was always a main ingredient in mediaeval theology. The Bible and the Fathers, Augustine, Aristotle, were the main elements. You might add a double dose of Augustine to the pre-existing mixture of Peter Lombard and Aristotle, but the result would be a Gregory of Rimini, or a Bradwardine, a recognizably mediaeval Augustinianism worlds apart from Luther's theology as it developed in these formative years.

Nor was this a mere dialogue between Luther and Augustine. Hamel, whose scholarly comparison of Luther with Augustine [1] in these years is of great value, reminds us that "between Luther and Augustine stands Peter Lombard and, above all, 'Occamism'" and expressed a provocative judgment by adding that "Augustine did not make Luther a Neo-Platonist, but Luther turned Augustine into a 'modernus.'"

Luther quotes from many works of Augustine in the course of these Lectures, but his major source is the "Enarrationes in Psalmos Davidis" [2] and his quotations from this work exceed all his other quotations from other sources put together. As in his notes on Peter Lombard there are frequent laudatory references to Augustine.[3] Many of his illustrations are taken from him, and at least two of his constant and favourite figures of the work of Christ, the thought of the Saviour as the hen, under whose covering wings the chicks gather together, and the thought of Christ as the Good Samaritan. The admiration is not uncritical, and there are occasions when he accuses Augustine of doing violence to the text.[4] Above all, it is perhaps Augustine's constant insistence on a christological [5] reference of the Psalms which is the congenial bond between the two commentaries.

There is a good deal to be said for Miegge's comment that Luther and Augustine met, not on the ground of philosophy, but of religion and piety.[6] It was as an example that St. Augustine appealed to Luther, as an emblem of veritable humility, of that "accusatio sui," which at this time he regarded as the true disposition for grace, and Luther

---

[1] A. Hamel. Der Junge Luther und Augustin. 2 vols. Gütersloh, 1934, vol. 1.15.
[2] F. Held. Augustins Enarrationes in Psalmos als exegetische Vorlage für Luthers erste Psalmenvorlesung. St. u. Kr., 1930. There are 270 explicit refs. to St. Augustine, and all save twenty cite the Enarrationes.
[3] W.A. 3.397.23 : 475.24 : 188.8.
[4] W.A. 3.132.40, "aliter Augustinus." 3.254.37, "violento ductu opus est."
[5] Held. Ibid., 16. Held suggests that part of the attraction o f the Enarrationes for Luther lay in the fact that, in the main, they were sermons expounded for the people.
[6] Miegge. Lutero, 126. Also Hamel, i.224.

repeatedly refers to the story of Augustine's conversion in Book 8 of the "Confessions." [1]

Of the debt and the dependence there can be no doubt. But not less interesting are the silences and the differences. Hamel points out that Luther quotes hardly at all from the many passages in the Enarrationes where Augustine treats of Grace, and though Luther can still speak of gratia gratificans, gratia gratis data, and prima gratia,[2] it may well be that he was already restive about the Augustinian view of the relation between grace in and after baptism. We shall see how faith has for Luther a more markedly christological orientation than in Augustine, and that he goes beyond him in the daring extremity with which he envisages Christ's humiliation on behalf of sinners.

Although Augustine repudiated a selfish egoism which is a root of sin, he recognized a proper measure of self-love, which is indeed an integral part of his doctrine of salvation. Luther came to find the heart of sin in a restless egoism which moves in the secret, hidden depths of the personality, masking itself under innumerable splendid disguises, but which is wholly to be repudiated in face of the judgment and the justice of God. Hamel suggests that while suffering and tribulation are regarded by Augustine as ills which posit a problem of theodicy, for Luther they are signs of grace which attest that the Christ really shares the "via passionis." And although during this period Luther's doctrine of grace is far from being clarified, his new thought of "Justitia" brings implications which move away from the Augustinian conception of grace infused within the soul.

The view has been put forward, by Hunzinger a generation ago, more recently by Erich Seeberg, that Luther at this time betrays the strong influence of a Neo-Platonism derived partly from St. Augustine, and partly from that mystical tradition which found classical expression in the writings of pseudo-Dionysius.

Luther's clearest reference to this "negative" theology occurs in the Scholiae on Ps. 65[1]. "To thee, the praise of silence." The reference to Dionysius at this point he derived from Faber Stapulensis. Luther

---

[1] Hamel, 40. See the remarkable passage, W.A. 3.549.26. " If you want an example for this exposition, take the conversion of St. Augustine, Conf. Bk. 8 . . . see there what it is to be in a turmoil and not to speak . . . so that he who has not experienced (non est expertus) this ' compunction ' and meditation cannot find any words with which to teach this Psalm. Thus it is difficult for me, too, who am outside the experience of ' compunction ' and yet talk about compunction. For nobody speaks fitly or really hears any scripture unless his feelings are conformed to it, so that he feels inwardly what he hears and speaks without, and he says, ' Ah, yes, that's it.' Therefore because I cannot speak practically out of ' compunction ' I will set forth the example and practice of Blessed Augustine." On the significance of this passage for Luther's own religious development, see E. Wolf, Staupitz und Luther, 145.
[2] Holl, 156, and refs. ad loc.

contrasts silence before the Divine Majesty with the eager chattering of "our theologians who are so bold with their disputations and assertions about divine things." Luther says that this affirmative theology is to the "negative" as milk is to wine, "and this is to be treated, not in disputation and much speaking, but in the greatest silence and quietness of the mind, as in a rapture or ecstasy. And this makes the true theologian. But no university gives him his diploma, but only the Holy Spirit." [1]

Luther here reverts to his long-standing attack on the scholastics, and especially the Scotists with their elaboration of a Divine psychology. His view is that classically expressed by Hooker, "Dangerous it were for the feeble brain of man to wade far into the doings of the Most High: whom although to know be life, and joy to make mention of his name: yet our soundest knowledge is to know that we know him not as indeed he is, neither can know him: and our safest eloquence concerning him is our silence, when we confess without confession that his glory is inexplicable, his greatness above our capacity and reach. He is above and we upon earth: therefore it behoveth our words to be wary and few." [2]

As Luther still uses the Nominalist language about merit, so he uses the language of the mystical tradition. It would be strange indeed if a devout monk, of intense piety, giving so much of his time to worship, prayer and contemplation, used any other language, or that he should not contrast the comparative merits of the contemplatives with the noisy theological skirmishes which had aroused an impressive chorus of contemporary disrelish. Thus he speaks of the contemplatives as the "wings of God since he flies in them and dwells in the affections of enraptured minds." [3] On the words "the hiding place of God is darkness"—he comments "first, because he dwells in the riddle of faith, and in the dark. Second, because he dwells in light unapproachable . . . therefore B. Dionysius teaches how to ascend by entering into anagogical darknesses and through negations. Because God is thus hidden and inaccessible." [4]

Later, Luther was strongly to repudiate this "theology of glory,"

---

[1] W.A. 3.372.20. Vogelsang. Anfänge, 160, n. 1. In the Lectures on Romans (1515-16) Luther cites this Psalm with a new reference, viz. no longer concerning the negative theology, but the emptiness of human righteousness. W.A. 56.247.26. "To thee is the silence of our righteousness." (Tibi debetur silentium de nostra Justitia, quod ipsum est tibi laus de Justitia tua.)
[2] Laws of Eccl. Polity, Bk. 1.
[3] W.A. 3.112.1.
[4] W.A. 3.124.29. The thought expounded is Biblical and in the classical theological tradition. "How oft amidst thick clouds and dark doth Heaven's all-ruling Sire choose to reside, his glory unobscur'd, and with the majesty of darkness round, covers his throne." (Milton, "Paradise Lost," Bk. II.)

but even at this stage it is possible to distinguish a novel insistence on the importance of faith. This is apparent in Luther's use of the technical expressions of the mystic theologians, of purgation and illumination of the mind, and above all in the conception of "ecstasy" or "excessus mentis" which passed from Platonism into Augustine, Dionysius and St. Bernard.

The expression is treated by St. Augustine at two main points in the "Enarrationes in Psalmos." First, the ascription of Psalm 31 to David, "in an ecstasy" which he defines as "a transport of the mind which is produced either by panic or by some revelation." [1] The second is the phrase in Ps. 116[11], "I said in my haste, All men are liars," which the Latin rendered "ego autem dixi in ecstasi mea, omnis homo mendax." This Augustine interprets as "panic when persecutors threaten and when the sufferings of torture threaten or death impends, and human weakness suffereth . . . for in this Psalm the voice of the martyrs is heard. But ecstasy can be used in another sense also when the mind is not beside itself with fear, but is possessed by some inspiration of revelation." [2]

The enigmatic phrase, Ps. 116[11], evidently fascinated Luther, for he returns to it. He takes account of St. Augustine's comments and reproduces his definition,[3] but with one difference. "Excessus mentis," he says, means "either the alienation of mind, or panic of mind in persecution," or "the rapture of the mind into the clear knowledge of faith," and this is really what is meant by "ecstasis." [4] This conjunction of "ecstasis" with "faith" is important: it is not made by Augustine even though his discussion of this Psalm begins as Ps. 116[11] demands with the theme of faith. A further comment of Luther on this verse says, "For as long as I am or was a man, I did not see that all men are liars. But now because I believed and am "in excessu mentis" and have become a spiritual man by faith, judging all things and judged by none, I see that he who is not in the same "excessus" and does not believe, is a liar." [5] Later, he adds, "a man would not stand alone . . . but would become a liar unless he remained truthful in the confession of faith." [6] His final comment on the verse is "this

---

[1] Augustine on the Psalms (Library of the Fathers), vol. 1.231, "vel pavore, vel aliqua revelatione." M.P.L., 36.226, ed. Lyons, 1564, "aut pavor, aut intentio ad superna." M.P.L., 36.230. R. Jolivet. Saint Augustin et le Néo-Platonisme chrétien, 1932, 112.
[2] Ibid., 5.299, ed. Lyons, "nam et alio modo dicitur ecstasis cum mens non pavore alienatur sed aliqua inspiratione revelationis assumitur." M.P.L., 36.1492.
[3] Held notes the remarkable extent to which Luther takes his definitions of words from St. Augustine, 19.
[4] W.A. 4.265.32.
[5] W.A. 4.267.16. The reference to 1 Cor. 4[3] is not to be ignored.
[6] W.A. 4. 267.29.

is that ecstasy in which by faith (per fidem) a man is raised above him
self that he may behold good things in the future." [1]

Even in the last quotation Luther's thought is Biblical, for he has in
mind the example of Jeremiah brooding in solitariness among the ruins
of Jerusalem, which he has noted in an earlier lecture. "And so this
prayer is made 'in excessu mentis' and like Jeremiah (Lam. 3[28]) who
shall sit solitary and be raised above himself." [2] The conjunction of
"excessus mentis," Jeremiah, and Ps. 116[11], is made explicitly in Luther's
marginal comment at this point, in his copy of Faber's Psalter. "This
is 'excessus' when a man is lifted out of himself like Jeremiah and thus,
illuminated (illuminatus—another technical expression of the mystics),
sees what it is to be nothing (quam sit nihil) and as though from above
gazes down at himself in his clouds and darkness, as though seated on
a mountain and looking down. See Ps. 30 at the end." [3]

This reference in Luther's copy of Faber's Psalter at Ps. 116[11] to
"Ps. 30 at the end," shows that, where we might least expect it, Luther's
thought is christological, for here the theme of the "excessus mentis"
is applied to Christ and it is referred to "that ecstasy in which, placed
in the highest exultation of suffering, he cried 'Why hast thou forsaken
me?' and this it is to be cast forth from God. Tropologically, however,
it means that everyone who so casts himself forth and humbles himself
before God (coram Deo) is the more heard. But this nobody does
except in an ecstasy of mind (in extasi mentis), that is, in the most
pure illumination of mind. . . ." [4]

Here is an excellent illustration of Luther's use of tradition. He
begins by taking a definition from Augustine, and expounding it in
close reliance on Augustine's commentary, and he does not hesitate
to use the technical vocabulary of mystical theology. But he brings
these within the orbit of Biblical Faith,[5] and of Christology. The twin
interpretations of "excessus" as "fear" and as "rapture" can both
be interpreted "coram Deo," as "fear and trembling" in the presence
of the Living God, as well as by the apprehension of faith.[6] Thus in

---

[1] W.A. 4.273.14. See also W.A. 5.107.16.   [2] W.A. 4.150.25.
[3] W.A. 4.519.20.26, also W.A. 3.114.17.
[4] W.A. 3.171.19, also W.A. 3.166.24, "in excessu mentis meae—raptu meo in
cruce."
[5] But is not faith here a Platonized conception, the understanding of the invisible
world? It is true that Luther found deep meaning in the definition of faith in
Hebrews 11[1], "the proving of things not seen." But it had significance for him precisely because it was a Biblical definition, and it came to mean for him that man is
cut off from the dimension of sight by sin, and thus the hearing of faith is the only
way to apprehend God. Here is no Platonizing of faith, but the germ of his magisterial doctrine of the Word. W.A. 4.95.1, "In sacris et divinis prius oportet audire
quam vïdere, prius credere quam intelligere, prius comprehendi quam comprehendere,
prius captivari quam captivare."
[6] See W.A. 5.208.24 : 213.33 : 214.10 : 217.35 (Ps. 116[11]).

his exegesis at the end of Ps. 30 he relates the conception in this way to the profound humiliation of Christ, and our humiliation before God.

We have seen that Augustine and Luther concurred in stressing the christological interpretation of the Psalms.[1] There is abundant evidence that, just as the thought of the "Justitia Dei" conveyed to him the thought of retributive justice, so, before his discovery, Christ himself appeared as a judge. Thus, at different levels of his writings we find:

"I knew Christ as none other than a stern judge, from whose face I wanted to flee, and yet could not." [2]

"Christ was for me, not a mediator, but a judge." [3]

"I used to turn pale, when I heard the name Christ." [4]

"I have often been terrified by the name of Christ, and when I saw him on his Cross, it was like a lightning stroke to me." [5]

Now, however, the passive interpretation of "Justitia Dei" applied christologically brought him to a new sense of the work of Christ [6] as the hinge of salvation.

And it is this work of God in Christ, which took place in history, which is reproduced when Christ lives in us. But this birth and dwelling of Christ in us is not conceived of in the language of mysticism, but is related to the Word, to Faith and to the conscience.[7]

No less striking is the concentration upon the Cross as the crown and climax of Christ's identification with us. "For the Cross of Christ runs through the whole of Scripture." [8] "You see, therefore, the passion and Cross of Christ is everywhere depicted, so that we can very well say with St. Paul, 'We will know nothing save Christ, and him crucified.'" [9]

Luther speaks boldly of the extreme humiliation of Christ, and will not soften or blur the realism of the Gospel picture by attributing the

---

[1] W.A. 4. 281.35 : 329.13 : 344.7 : 443.23.
[2] W.A. 38.148.12, also 45.482.16 : 46.46.5.
[3] W.A. 40.1.326.1.
[4] W.A. 40.1.298.9.
[5] W.A. 47.590.1 : 41.653.41.
[6] W.A. 3.542.9, " Opus autem singulariter Dei est Christus in sua tota vita." W.A. 4.61.22, " Christus est opus Dei et gloria ejus." W.A. 4.16.20, " Sic nunc justitia nostra Christus est et pax nostra quam Deus nobis dedit." W.A. 4.18.31, " Justus fuit ante omne opus quod ageret, sc. ab initio conceptionis."
[7] W.A. 3.365.17, "Accedet Christus sc. ad nos per fidem et ad Deum per seipsum." W.A. 3.504.11, " Ita Christus per fidem requiescit in sinu cordis in memoria et conscientia quieta." W.A. 3.148.1, " Dominus Jesus protector qui regnat et presens est super me." Also W.A. 3.593.28 : 3.447.15, " Perseveres in spe et fide et gratia et unione Christi." 3.553.28, Cant. 1, " Osculetur me osculo oris sui i.e. filius per spiritum patris sui uniat me sibi."
[8] W.A. 3.63.1, " Crux enim Christi ubique in Scripturis occurrit." 3.167.20.
[9] W.A. 4.87.35.

cry of dereliction to a prayer of Christ on behalf of the Church. Closely linked with this christological concentration is the tropological reference to the humiliations and passions of Christians.[1] "This Psalm is to be believed, that the Lord wept very often, and especially at night, even though it is not written in the Gospels."[2] He gives to the thought of the descent to hell a spiritual significance which coloured his conception of the pains of hell and purgatory in these years, a conception which he found confirmed in Tauler and the "Theologia Germanica" at a later date, but which did not originate then, as the references in these lectures reveal.[3]

Thus Christ fulfils the righteousness of God.[4] What he has done and suffered is on our behalf.[5] "And it is true that he was cursed by the Lord: because the father made him a curse for us and he truly died on account of sin."[6] He is content to use the traditional classic metaphors of ransom,[7] and redemption,[8] though it is striking that nowhere in these lectures does Luther use the phrases "reconciliatio Dei" or "reconciliari Deo."[9] At one point Luther uses the figure which he was to develop strikingly, the thought, derived from Isaiah 28, of "Christ's strange work"—the "opus alienum dei." "For what is more strange for a saviour, than to destroy? And yet Christ behaves in this way with his own."[10] Here is the thought which we have found in the conception of "Anfechtung" and which will become important in Luther's dialectic of Law and Gospel, the apparent contradiction

---

[1] W.A. 3.202.23 : 427.26 : 437.29 : W.A. 4.330.30.

[2] W.A. 3.70.30. See also 71.3, "Totus Psalmus est questus et vox hujus galline nostre affectuosissime et vox dulcis dulces lachrymas provocans nisi lapides essemus et duritia duriores. Est ille totus psalmus velut impetuosus ignis et impatientissimus zelus ex corde Christi erumpens." 3.121.32 : 3.463.17, "Et hoc judicium est in cruce Christi nobis ostensum."

[3] W.A. 3.452.29, "Quia tentatio et dejectio est spiritualis descensus ad inferos." See Vogelsang. Angefochtene Christus, 40. Prenter. Spiritus Creator, 31-.3 Also W.A. 3.431.30 : W.A. 4.76.15. For the association with the conception of purgatory, W.A. 3.426.8 ff. : 3.433.3, "Si ergo triduo in inferno fueris : signum est quod tecum Christus et tu cum Christo sis."

[4] W.A. 3.463.26, "Quare Evangelium impletum est judicium et justitia et opus Dei, via Dei etc. sicut ad literam Christus hec omnia est in persona sua." Luther uses the Biblical phrase "reputare" (Rom. 4³ and Ps. 106³¹), but seldom (W.A. 3.479.5 : 438.21) and without any special significance. The phrase "imputare Justitiam Christi" is not found at all in these lectures. W.A. 4.19.26.27 are not used in the sense of the imputed "Righteousness of Christ." When Luther (Ps. 31²) refers to "non-imputation" it is simply in terms of the text, and of Augustine's comments upon it. There is something to be said for Vogelsang's view, that in the Psalms, Luther's tropological interpretation foreshadows the later description of imputation, which is in any case distinct from the formal Melanchthonian doctrinal scheme. Anfänge, 85-7.

[5] W.A. 3.211.16.

[6] W.A. 3.426.28 : 3.548.23.

[7] W.A. 3.69.27 : 418.24 : 494.32 : 585.18.

[8] W.A. 3.147.15 : 401.2 : 367.28 : 621.3 : 494.35.

[9] Vogelsang. Anfänge, 110, n. 1.   [10] W.A. 3.246.19 ff.

in the nature of God, as he speaks to us through the voice of condemnation, and in the act of salvation.

The christological concentration carries over into Luther's conception of faith. All things are given to us in faith in Christ.[1] "Semper oritur et germinat pax et justitia Christi."[2] "For in Christ all those things are given to us which were promised aforetime."[3] Hence Luther is at pains to show that faith for him means more than an intellectual notion.[4] "The place of faith is in the conscience."[5] This faith is no human achievement, but is God's good gift.[6]

Thus against this christological background, and with the clear perception of faith, not as a human work, but as a divine gift, we may observe, in these Lectures, the stress on "only faith."[7]

We saw how, in the marginal notes on Peter Lombard, Luther reveals a fourfold preoccupation: with Christ and faith on the one hand, and with sin and concupiscence on the other, and we suggested that it was the heightened awareness of the mercy of God in Christ which deepened his conception of the sinfulness of the human heart. What Luther has to say about Christ and Faith in the Lectures on the Psalms has a similar implication for his doctrine of sin. And in this connection we must observe the part played in this period by the conception of "Humility."[8]

The virtue of humility was cardinal to the conception of the monastic vocation. The Rule of St. Benedict devotes long and beautiful attention to this virtue and its degrees, and it is treated by almost all the great doctors, not least in the writings of St. Bernard. Luther also treats of humility as one virtue among others, but in the Lectures on the Psalms we can trace a development which was to find its completion in the Lectures on Romans in the following year.

Here, again, Luther leans on Augustine, and he cites the personal example of Augustine as the emblem of true humility. With Augustine,

---

[1] W.A. 4.127.19 : 4.215.24 : 3.649.15 : 4.414.14 : 4.61.22. "Christ is the work and glory of God. And he himself through faith and grace appears among his own." 4.16.20 : 3.350.30. Vogelsang. Anfänge, 79-80.
[2] W.A. 3.459.32.
[3] W.A. 4.127.19.
[4] W.A. 3.176.12, "Totum hoc est in fide et non in sensu atque ratione." 4.107.33 : 4.356.13, "Affectum, non intellectum requirit fides . . . fides non intellectum illuminat immo excecat, sed affectum : hunc enim ducit quo salvetur, et hoc per auditum verbi."
[5] W.A. 3.603.11 : 651.2, "Fides est 'locus' animae quia domus conscientiae nostrae."
[6] W.A. 4.266.27. "This faith, in which all good things are contained, is the gift of God." 3.649.17.
[7] W.A. 4.438.4, "Fides sola justificat." 4.247.21, "Sola enim fides rectificat." 4.241.25, "Justitia quae in nobis est ex deo per fidem." Also 3.320.20 : 4.380.20.
[8] Hamel, 52 ff. R. Josefson. Ödmjukhet och Tro. Stockholm, 1939, 11-101. W. von Loewenich. Luthers Theologia Crucis. Munich, 1933, 174 ff. L. Pinomaa. Existentielle Charakter, 19-37. L. Pinomaa. Zorn Gottes, 165, n. 1.

L

too, he reckons the contrasting and capital vice to this virtue to be pride, "superbia." [1]

We have seen that Luther found special significance in the sentence in Prov. 18[17]. "Justus in principio accusator sui est," a line often quoted by the doctors, including Gerson and Biel.[2] This thought of humility less as a virtue of humble obedience than as the acknowledgment of sin is a conception which acquires increasing emphasis throughout these lectures and Josefson calls this "accusatio sui," "Luther's decisive definition of Christian humility." [3]

With this thought of "humilitas" as consisting of recognition of sin is allied the conception of "judicium." It has been observed that Luther does not use the conception of "poenitentia" throughout these lectures, but that he does develop frequently and at length the conception of "judicium" which covers the notion of "acts of penitence." "Judicium," we may say, is repentance "coram Deo," and is a theocentric expression.[4]

It is the essence of "superbia" that a man will not acknowledge his sin.[5] It is the essence of "humilitas" to accuse oneself.[6] That such recognition is the work of the Holy Spirit is hinted at in these lectures and becomes explicit in the Lectures on Romans.[7]

It is this pride which characterizes the Jews, the heretics and those "Observants," those who claim "exemption" from discipline on the ground of "singularity," and all whose bitter truculence betrays the

---

[1] Holl. Ges. Aufs. Luther, 289.4, claims that Luther's use of " superbia " has a different inflection from that of Augustine. The thought in Augustine is of the overbearing egoism which leads to sin, whereas for Luther it is manifested in the denial of sin, and the attempt to justify oneself in the presence of God. W.A. 3.15.35, " All sin is superbia." W.A. 3.568.20 : 215.27 : 259.29 ff.

[2] Miegge, 116. Loofs. St. u. Kr., 1917.415.

[3] Josefson, 42. W.A. 3.30.3 : 31.10 : 51.6 : 81.14 : 191.5 : 284.2.33 : 345.30 : 353.2 : 378.10 : 420.18 : 429.2 : 433.24 : 455.25 : 462.30 : W.A. 4.87.23 : 90.36 : 172.35 : 198.8 : 204.33 : 241.25 : 242.24 : 370.25 : 376.35 : 383.7 : 488.27 : 519.23.

[4] For judicium as " accusatio sui." W.A. 3.179.3 : 203.6 : 208.5.33, " Humilitas enim ipsa est judicium." 289.15, " et hoc est judicium . . . sc. seipsum accusare et judicare." 462.23 : 464-5, a long note of two pages on "judicium." W.A. 4.132.27: 204.33 : 245.34. " Judicium autem est omnis damnatio et crucifixio veteris hominis." 354.39. W.A. 3.463.18, "Et hoc judicium est in cruce Christi nobis ostensum."

[5] " Impius et superbus primo est excusator sui ac defensor, justificator et salvator." W.A. 3.288.32 : 284.32. Cf. Milton's climax to the story of the Fall. " Paradise Lost," Bk. IX, " Thus they in mutual accusation spent the fruitless hours, but neither self condemning."

[6] " Omne studium nostrum id esse debet, magnificare et aggravare peccata nostra et sic semper magis ac magis accusare et assidue judicare, condemnare. Quanto enim quis se profundius damnaverit et peccata sua magnificaverit tanto aptior est ad misericordiam et gratiam Dei." 3.429.7 ff. 3.458.4 : 3.26.22. Holl. Luther, 290. Pinomaa, 22. Hamel, 54.

[7] W.A. 3.290.31 : 466.9 : W.A. 4.355.8 : W.A. 56.360.2. Prenter. Spiritus Creator, 25.

opposite temper from humility.[1] There are passages where Luther seems to conceive of humility as a kind of predisposition for grace, a human achievement which makes a man "apt" for salvation. "For the more deeply a man shall condemn his own sin and magnify them, so much the more apt (aptior) is he for mercy." [2]

There is truth therefore in Sormunen's comment on Luther's use of "humilitas" at this stage. "As Luther had begun by striving to attain perfection, so now he strove to be a thorough sinner. Luther's conception of Christian humility as the disposition for grace stands in organic relation with the influence of the mystics in deepening the apprehension of sin on the one hand, and on the other in the renewing of the Augustinian thought of ' humilitas—humiliatio.' " [3]

According to Pinomaa, Luther's use of "humilitas" begins as an anthropocentric conception, as a human work, but became changed for him into a theocentric word, as that apperception of one's own sinfulness which is only possible existentially, "coram Deo." [4] Hamel suggests that Luther found "humiliatio" to be a more drastic and dynamic word than "humilitas," and that this usage marks the movement in his thought, a closer alliance with the notions of tribulation and temptation.[5]

The tension within Luther's use of "humilitas" continues in his Lectures on Romans. At one point he exclaims "For what does the whole of Scripture teach, except humility?" [6] There, too, "humilitas" is the genuine accusation of self.[7] There, too, is the thought that humility is a pre-requisite of grace.[8] As in the Psalms, it is a mark of the humble that they are ready to hear the Word of God.[9] Humility is finally replaced by faith, not in the sense that the word drops out of

[1] For the Jews. W.A. 3.154.14.32. Heretics. 3.202.36,334.15.445.8. Observants. 3.155.8 : 332.17. W.A. 4.313.7. For all three groups, W.A. 3.172.33. " Such are the Jews, such are the heretics, such are all those who are superstitious in their ' singularity,' who put aside obedience and faith and establish their own righteousness . . . for the death of Christ only profits the humble, and every proud man is a denier of Christ." 3.203.4 : 331.29 : 355.4. W.A. 4.136.29. Holl. Luther, 198 ff.
[2] W.A. 3.429.9. Also 3.442.33 : 433.30 : 429.34.
[3] Quoted Pinomaa. Existentielle Charakter, 21.
[4] Von Loewenich, 174-5. W.A. 3.345.29, " Nemo per fidem justificatur nisi prius per humilitatem se injustum confiteatur. Haec autem est humilitas." 3.285.6, " Sed veritatem justitiae tuae quae est humilitas et confessio peccati, accusatio sui." 3.465.2, Luther can even write " Humilitas sola salvet." W.A. 4.473.17, also 3.301.30.
[5] " Judicium autem est omnis damnatio et crucifixio veteris hominis . . . et est humiliatio et exaltatio." W.A. 4.245.34 : 357.14 : 265.18 : Hamel, i.66. Pinomaa, 27, " Hoc nostra translatio clarius exprimit, quia nolle audire verbum Dei est non humiliare, sed superbe ex sensu proprio cui fit verbum stultitia, refutare." 4.339.16 : 351.4 : 378.29.   [6] Josefson, ch. 1. W.A. 56.199.30.
[7] " Perfecta enim cognitio sui ipsius humilitas est, perfecta autem humilitas perfecta sapientia est, perfecta sapientia perfecta spiritualitas est." Romans, ed. Ficker, ii.175.23.
[8] " Et ista humilitas et compunctio in bonis operibus facit ea esse grata." W.A. 56.370.20. W.A. 56.252.26.
[9] W.A. 56.218.7.

Luther's vocabulary, or ceases to have meaning for him as a Christian virtue, but that the conception of man's passive waiting upon God is taken up into the word "Faith," as the means whereby man abandons his own self-righteousness and apprehends the righteousness of God.[1] Ficker noted that from the eleventh chapter of Romans onwards, Luther speaks of "humilitas" but sparingly, and that the conception of faith has taken its place.[2]

Even more striking evidence of the movement of Luther's thought, and of his growing recognition of the depth and intensity of human sinfulness, is provided by his use of the scholastic conception of the "synteresis." [3]

The "synteresis" is defined by St. Jerome as that "spark of conscience (scintilla conscientiae) which is not extinguished in Adam even as a sinner, after he was ejected from Paradise . . . and by which we know that we are sinning (qua . . . nos peccare sentimus)." [4]

The synteresis is differently conceived by different schools of mediaeval thought, and the emphasis varies from a "spark of conscience" to a faculty of the will, or a function of the practical reason.[5] It has been said that St. Thomas conceives it as "the habitual knowledge of the primary principles of moral action; that faculty of his reason which enables him to know unerringly and directly the first moral principles." [6] But if it is a "habitus" it is "not one that is obtained

---

[1] W.A. 56.471.17. Pinomaa, 33. von Loewenich, 177.

[2] Some allowance ought to be made here for the changing subject-matter of the Epistle to the Romans, from ch. 12 onwards.

[3] von Loewenich. Luthers Theologia Crucis, 56 ff. L. Pinomaa. Zorn Gottes, 66, n. 1. Existentielle Charakter, 37-54. Köstlin. Luther's theology, i.148.54. Hans Meyer. Philosophy of St. Thomas Aquinas (St. Louis, 1945), 197. Braun. Concupiscenz, 297.

[4] The term comes from St. Jerome, Commentary on Ezekiel, bk. 1, ch. 1, where a spiritual interpretation of the four faces of Ezekiel's vision is given, and the fourth, that of the eagle, is given by Jerome as " synteresis." It is suggested that this is a scribal error for " syneidesis." But whatever the origin, it became a useful scholastic term.

[5] Alexander of Hales and St. Bonaventura make it a habit of the will, and for them the knowledge of first principles is a habit of the intellect, conscience. St. Albert thought that practical reason was the subject of synteresis and that it is a faculty distinct from will and reason. Duns Scotus seems to have thought of it also as a function of the intellect. (See G. Stratenwerth. Die Naturrechtslehre des Johannes Duns Scotus, 1951, 40 ff.)

[6] St. Thomas, "Synderesis autem non se habet ad opposita sed ad bonum tantum inclinat : ergo synderesis non est potentia." (Summa Theologica, 1.79.12.) " Synderesis dicitur lex intellectus nostri inquantum est habitus continens praecepta legis naturalis quae sunt prima principia operum humanorum." 2.1. qu. 94, art 1. " Habitus autem ex quibus conscientia informatur, etsi multi sunt, omnes tamen efficaciam habent ab uno primo principio sc. ab habitu primorum principiorum, qui dicitur synderesis." 1, qu. 79.13. "Unde specialiter hic habitus interdum conscientia nominatur." According to Biel, the synteresis is no "actus vel habitus in voluntate " but ".aliquid necessario dirigens saltem in universali ad operationem justam et rectam." II, dist. 39, qu. 7, art. 2, concl. 1, it is an inextinguishable spark (scintilla inextinguibilis).

by repeated actions, but a primitive original power innate in our minds."

On the one hand, the conception is linked with conscience, and with the remnant of the divine image in fallen man: on the other, it provided a connecting point with the mystical tradition, with its partiality for a spark of the divine within the soul (Seelengrund, acies mentis, scintilla mentis).

Luther cites the synteresis in his marginal notes on Tauler, and points to the writings of Gerson as his authority for his definition.[1] "See Gerson in mystical theology." But he had already made frequent citation of it in his Lectures on the Psalms. "And there is such a natural desire in human nature indeed, because the synteresis and desire of good is inextinguishable in man, though it is hindered in many." [2]

On three occasions Luther uses it in connection with the murmuring of conscience. "For there is nobody so bad who does not feel the murmuring of reason and the synteresis." [3] "For the remnant (that is, reason and the synteresis) which go on murmuring, always cry to the Lord, even if, forced by sin, the will should sin." [4] Here the synteresis is in close association with conscience, and in a further passage he speaks of the feeling of the synteresis.[5]

Luther's fullest exposition of the subject is in his Sermon (26th December 1514?).[6] He says that fallen man has a desire to be saved and to live well. This desire is like sparks under ashes, or seed hidden in the ground, or "materia" awaiting a "forma." The verse in Isa. 1^9, "Had not the Lord left us a seed, we should have been as Sodom," is interpreted moralistically as "unless the synteresis and remnants of nature had been kept, all must have perished." [7]

Here, then, is a traditional conception which Luther seems to expound in traditional terms. The rare occasions on which he employs it do not yield an exhaustive definition, and it is hard to see how and whether he distinguished it from "conscientia," though it is clear that for him it relates to man's knowledge of, and desire for good. As Luther came to a more radical interpretation of the human dilemma, and the complete inability of sinful men to sustain their own righteousness in the presence of God, the validity of this notion was bound to come in question. It is in the Lectures on the Epistle to the Romans that he breaks with the traditional use of the conception.

[1] W.A. 9.99.36.   [2] W.A. 3.238.11. Holl, 178.
[3] W.A. 3.94.17.   [4] W.A. 3.535.36, also 4.253.23.
[5] " Quod in affectu remansit syntheresico a domino suscipiatur et possideatur." W.A. 3.603.31.
[6] W.A. 1.30-37. von Loewenich, 60.
[7] W.A. 1.32.10.

In Rom. 1[20] he discusses the pagan knowledge of God which he ascribes to a "syntheresis theologica," and which, he says, is "inobscurable in all." The error of the heathen is not that they had no "syntheresis theologica," but that they made the wrong use of it. They have erred in the minor, not in the major of this practical syllogism.[1]

The second citation is Rom. 3[10]. "For we are not wholly inclined to evil, since a portion is left to us, which is affected towards good things, as is evident in the syntheresis."[2] Nevertheless, this occurs in a passage which stresses that men cannot help loving themselves above all things—"which is the sum of all the vices." This tension becomes clearer in the remarkable reference at Rom. 4[7].[3] It is the climax of an attack by Luther on the Nominalist doctrine that a "man can love God above all things by his own powers, and can fulfil the commands of God according to the substance of the deed, but not according to the divine intention, because apart from grace. O Fools, O Sowtheologians." Luther then attacks these sacrilegious views in a paragraph which centres in the thought of "Concupiscence."[4]

Luther says that these Nominalists stress the fact that the will has a "synteresis" which, though but weakly, is inclined to good. "And this tiny motion towards God (parvulum motum in Deum) which a man can perform by nature, they dream to be an act of loving God above all things. But behold, the whole man is full of concupiscences (notwithstanding this tiny movement)."[5]

By now Luther has come to think more radically of the damage done by sin, not only as the "loss of original righteousness but of the strength of all his powers, of mind and body, and of the outward and inward man."[6] Concupiscence has become a fermenting, restless egoism at work in every part of the personality. The conception of synteresis has become useless and dangerous, and Luther abandons it.[7]

Luther has reached his anthropology of the "whole man" which

---

[1] W.A. 56.177.14. This is the only place where Luther uses " synteresis " of the knowledge of God, and it is noticeable that he calls this by the special term " syntheresis theologica." " Hec Major syllogismi practici, hec syntheresis theologica est inobscurabilis in omnibus. Sed in minore errabant dicendo et statuendo. Hic autem i.e. Jupiter vel alius huic simulacro similis est hujusmodi etc. Hic error incepit et fecit idolatriam, dum quisque studio suo subsumere voluit."

[2] W.A. 56.237.6.   [3] W.A. 56.275.18.

[4] The word " Concupiscentia " and derivatives occur seven times in almost as many lines.

[5] W.A. 56.275.20, also 280.12.   [6] W.A. 56.312.8.

[7] W.A. 56.355.28. The last reference is implicit. " It is said that human nature has a general notion of knowing and willing good. But it goes wrong in particulars. It would be better to say that it knows and wills the good in particular things, but in general neither knows nor wills the good." This does not mean that Luther denied the " syntheresis theologica " by which all men know that there is a God, or that he denied that there was that in man which made him capable of hearing the Gospel. Holl, 246.

leaves no part of him exempt from the divine condemnation. The repudiation of the Nominalist use of synteresis becomes clear in his second course of Lectures on the Psalms (1518-19), where he contradicts the view of the synteresis as an innate knowledge of "first principles" by the affirmation, "This is false. Faith is the first principle of Good Works." As in the case of "Humilitas," so now with "synteresis." Faith as a great master conception takes over the truth in the earlier vocabulary.[1]

Luther has no lengthy discussion of Original Sin and of "Concupiscentia" in the Lectures on Psalms, as he has in the marginal notes on Peter Lombard,[2] and as he was to develop these notions during the Lectures on Romans, and this may be a reminder to us of the occasional nature of these theological comments, which were evoked by the Biblical material on which he was commenting. "Luther's doctrine of Sin was in a transition stage," says Hamel of these Lectures, and "remnants of Ockhamist teaching and Augustinian notions are mingled together."[3]

In his marginal notes on Peter Lombard, Luther had denied the persistence of Original Sin after Baptism, believing it to be a denial of the virtues of that Sacrament to maintain such persistence, and he had ventured to contradict the Master of the Sentences at this point. Now, however, he can quote Peter Lombard with approval in this matter.[4]

The guilt of original sin may have been remitted in baptism, but the "misery of infirmity" remains, as a "weakness in the memory, a blindness in intellect, or a disorder in the will,"[5] and as a "dolour of conscience,"[6] which are only gradually healed by grace, in the inn where Christ, the Good Samaritan, has placed us.[7]

---

[1] W.A. 5.119.12 ff.   [2] W.A. 9.75.   [3] Hamel, i.129.
[4] W.A. 4.207.25. "Unde Magister et Doctor circa secundum Sententiarum recte legem membrorum vocant ' tyrannum ' ' morbum nature ' ' languor nature ' etc. quia animam incipientem vivere graviter captivat." Contrast W.A. 9.75.26, " Sententia igitur Magistri non est tenenda sc. quod peccatum originale sit fomes, languor naturae, tyrannus etc."
[5] W.A. 3.453.7. "Quia dimissa culpa adhuc multa nobis restant de peccato inflicta sc. infirmitas in memoria, coecitas in intellectu, concupiscentia sive inordinatio in voluntate. Ex quibus tribus omne peccatum originaliter descendit. Ipsa autem sunt relique peccati originalis etiam dimissi in baptismo." Also W.A. 3.187.36 : 285.13. W.A. 4.206.27. The glosses 206-7 are of great interest, cf. 207.32. " Sic enim intelligit homo se esse infirmum et nihil, quando incipit agere velle que novit, que presumpsit facere mox cum novisset. Sic enim passio ire, superbie, luxurie, cum absens est facilis, presumitur victu ab inexpertis. Cum presens est, sentitur difficillima immo insuperabilis, ut experientia docet." W.A. 4.211.10 : 214.25 : 153.7.
[6] W.A. 3.231.13.
[7] W.A. 4.211.10. " Iste tres vires anime intellectus, voluntas, memoria etiam in baptisatis manent in infirmitate sua et stabulo, ubi semper habent necesse curari." W.A. 3.231.37, " Semper enim in stabulo nos habet Samaritanus in quo dolorem oleo gratie mitigat et infirmitatem cura stabularii sensim medetur."

We cannot enumerate the hundreds of occasions when Luther uses the phrase "coram Deo," either by itself, or in contrast to "coram hominibus." Luther knew that he was returning to the Biblical dimension here. "For this word is frequent in the Scriptures, 'In the sight of God,' 'In the presence of God,' 'with God,' 'before God.'" [1]

The conception of "Judicium" is important in this connection, for it is almost more prominent in these lectures than its great complementary word "Justitia."

We have seen that Luther uses it in preference to "poenitentia," to cover the "acts of penitence," and to denote that "humilitas" and "accusatio sui" which a man must find in the presence of God. [2]

Thus what Luther has said about "Justitia Dei" and its christological and tropological reference, is set within this theocentric context. The righteousness which is given to man on the ground of faith, the righteousness of a man's own works which must be renounced, are righteousness "coram Deo." [3]

Although the justified man is covered by the Righteousness of Christ, as the chicken by the wings of its mother, and although the Good Samaritan has taken him in charge, his cure is a gradual thing, and is not accomplished all at once. "For we who are justified are always in movement, always being justified, for so it comes about that all righteousness in the present instant is sin with respect to what will be added at the next instant." [4] "For we are always having to return to the beginning and start over again." [5]

Two other themes deserve comment before leaving Luther's Lectures on the Psalms, his exposition of the relation between Law and Gospel, and his treatment of the Wrath of God. Runestam has pointed out that in these lectures Luther has not yet arrived at the dialectic of Law and Gospel which was to become the normative element in his exposition of the Gospel, as in the famous 1531 Commentary on Galatians. That is not to say that it is not important for Luther at this time. He makes a clear distinction between the Law and Gospel, "For in this

[1] W.A. 3.479.8: 77.2: 79.23: 112.24: 129.21: 171.29: 174.17: 203.20: 283.15: 284.17: 285.1: 287.32: 288.6: 459.16: 525.18: 541.39.

[2] Other refs. to Judicium. W.A. 3.90.24: 203.6: W.A. 4.132.18.37: 133.34: 198.9: 204.32: 281.22: 282.18: 284.16: 289.1: 294.21: 299.21: 357.10: 378.4: 379.4.11: 520.15: 521.34.

[3] W.A. 3.43.30: 66.6: 111.10: 173.25: 179.2: 323.31: 369.4: 462.4: 463.1: 532.13: W.A. 4.38.19: 80.9: 114.3: 114.16: 127.14: 165.16: 236.14: 246.20: 247.25: 248.2: 300.12: 388.33: 425.9: 438.9: 443.10.

[4] W.A. 4.364.14, also 362.32.

[5] W.A. 3.47.7: 47.2, qui enim justus est, justificetur adhuc. W.A. 3.512.24 ff. Holl. Luther, 290.

the difference between the Gospel and the Law is indicated. The Law is the word of Moses to us, the Gospel, on the other hand, is the word of God in us. For the one stays outside, speaks in figures and in the shadows of what will one day become visible. The other, however, comes inwardly and speaks of inward, spiritual and true things." [1]

Luther stresses that the law of God is good and that it is immutable, and that God required that it be performed from the heart. He will not abate the rigour of the law by the Nominalist distinctions: to perform the law "according to the substance of the deed" avails nothing "coram Deo," if the intention of the heart be wrong.[2] Moreover, he emphasizes even more than Biel and Peter Lombard the fact that genuine obedience to God must spring freely and spontaneously and gladly from the heart. It is this stress indeed which was to mark his developed theme of "the Liberty of a Christian Man" and which Sormunen has declared to be the characteristic stress of Luther's ethical teaching.[3]

Pinomaa says that Luther's Lectures on the Psalms are "almost drenched" with the theme of the Wrath of God. Here the nature of his commentary must be remembered, for the words "odium," "ira" and "furor" occur hundreds of times throughout the Psalms, through which a strong dualistic tension may be observed, for there are few Biblical books where the contrast between the poor, the righteous, the godly and the proud, impious and ungodly is more marked. In consequence St. Augustine's "Enarrationes in Psalmos" return frequently to this theme, and Luther follows Augustine very closely in many of his distinctions and his expositions of this subject.[4]

In the first place, and following Augustine, Luther is concerned to safeguard this conception from anthropomorphic association,[5] "For his wrath is not as he is in himself." [6] "For the punitive effects of God

[1] W.A. 4.9.28. Holl, 176, 291. Runestam. Den Kristliga Friheten hos Luther och Melanchthon. Stockholm, 1917, 44.
[2] W.A. 4.323.20. W.A. 3.129.22 : 430.1 : 451.24.
[3] Eino Sormunen. Die Eigenart der Lutherischen Ethik. A.A.S.F., vol. 29. Helsinki, 1934, 33. W.A. 3.649.2, " Qui in fide et spiritu est, ipse ex corde et libertate et hilaritate Deo servit et vias ejus ambulat, quia in corde, i.e. in affectu sunt, in voluntate placent semite ei et amat illas quia ex amore et radice cordis illas ambulat." W.A. 3.17.1. W.A. 3.300.10.
[4] L. Pinomaa. Der Zorn Gottes in der Theologie Luthers. Helsinki, 1938, 19. Two Appendices (206-211) in this essay set out the relation between Luther's expositions, and his citations from Augustine and from the Vulgate.
[5] Pinomaa. Zorn Gottes, 80.
[6] W.A. 3.35.13. " Non enim ira sic est sua, quia in ipso sit. Sed quia creatura in qua est ira, est ejus et ipsius nutu et imperio affligit impios, ipse autem in se manens quietissimus et tranquillus, immo summe bonus et non turbatus. Nam tam est bonus Deus, ut quicquid ipse immediate agit, non sit nisi summum gaudium et delectatio et non affligit, sed magis reficit. Sed in impiis ipse se subtrahens et in summa manens bonitate applicat creaturas quarum una alteram affligit."

M

are his wrath. Not as he himself is in himself." [1] God is sheer goodness, and by his own actions can do nothing but good. But he "withdraws himself" from the ungodly and "applies the creatures" to work wrath.

A second distinction taken from Augustine, is of importance, the difference between the "Ira misericordiae Dei," the merciful wrath of God, and the "Ira severitatis," the wrath of His severity.[2]

God's merciful wrath is that which is shown to the saints, and it brings them to penitence and to trust in him, and with this wrath he chastens them for their sins in this present life, instead of abandoning them to the wrath of His severity in eternal punishment. That the impious are punished is intended also as a warning and comfort to the godly.[3]

"For in this life God punishes the ungodly (impios) that the rest of the ungodly may be terrified and that it may be shown that they will not go unpunished. And that by showing this, the godly may be comforted, since, as the ungodly will not go unpunished, so the godly will not go uncrowned. And thus the godly are comforted that they may behave with perseverance and strength. For if God did not punish the bad, they would have the best of the argument against the good, since they would have been just in vain, and suffered so many things vainly for the sake of righteousness. And this would shake the just exceedingly! But now, so that he may comfort and console them, he smites the ungodly that they may have an argument that it is not for nothing that a man is bad or good." [4]

The chastening wrath of God may be displayed through many agents, including the temporal ills of plague, pestilence, sword and famine.[5] But when the wrath of his severity is poured out on the ungodly, there is no mercy to be found, and this is no mere temporary chastening through outward misfortune, but it is the eternal punishment which afflicts the soul, the punishment of hell itself.[6]

But there is a final form of the wrath of God's severity, a conception which Luther took from Augustine and from St. Bernard, the wrath

---

[1] W.A. 3.591.34.

[2] Pinomaa, 73. Luther saw this distinction in Ps. 6[1]. "Domine, ne in furore tuo arguas me, neque in ira tua corripias me." W.A. 3.68.37, "Difficillimum est credere Deum esse pium et mitem in percussione et corruptione sua, sed omnis patiens trepidat et timet, ne ira et furor Dei sit super eum .. quia alia est ira misericordie, alia severitatis." Also W.A. 5.203.37 (1519-20), "Hoc versu manifeste duplicam virgam Dei docet : aliam misericordie aliam irae." Also Vogelsang. Angefochtene Christus, 33.

[3] On the difference between the godly and ungodly here. W.A. 3.170.10 : 208.40. See also W.A. 5. 217-8 : 367.11.

[4] W.A. 3.322.26 ff.   [5] W.A. 4.343.17.

[6] W.A. 3.72.21, "In ira et furore corripiunt qui solum puniunt solum vinum infundunt, sine fructu et emenda castigant, sc. ad vindictam explendam, secant vulnus et non emplastrant. Hoc est diabolicum." W.A. 3.488.34.

of God which is manifest not by Divine action, but by Divine inaction, not by his angry words, but from his silence. This is the terrible "aversio Dei."[1] Luther's distinction between a wrath of mercy and a wrath of severity seems to belong chiefly to the years before 1517, and it is replaced by the dialectic of Love and Wrath, and Grace and Judgment. But he never abandoned the thought of the Wrath of God, and his joyful discovery of the "Justitia Dei" did not mean that the idea of the divine anger against sin could be abandoned. Long ago Theodosius Harnack showed, as against Ritschl, that Luther's idea of the Wrath of God is that it is far from being a mere fiction, something imagined and conjured by the fearful conscience.[2] But, as in the Bible and in many classic theological systems, there is a tension but not a complete dualism. It is, Pinomaa suggests, in the Cross of Christ that Luther unifies his doctrine of God.[3] "Here God's Wrath is united with his Love. In the conception of God there is no room for dualism, but Love overcomes Wrath. God himself prepares the atonement for sinners. God himself is the subject of the suffering of the Cross. Deeper than this, human thought cannot penetrate" (Sormunen). Karl Holl suggests that the theme of the Wrath of God served to deepen and to sharpen Luther's conception of the divine love and mercy.[4]

[1] Pinomaa, 77. W.A. 3.330.10. "Tunc magis irascitur Deus, quando nihil irascitur et dimittit in desideriis suis ire impios crescere et proficere et non destruit eos." Also 3.35.20 : 433.4 : 420.18 : 4.52.34.
[2] That the conscience does sometimes misapprehend God in this way is an element in Luther's teaching. W.A. 5.166.25.
[3] Pinomaa. Zorn Gottes, 191.
[4] Holl. Luther, 42. Theod. Harnack. Luthers Theologie, Pt. 1, 307-362. 1927. W. Koehler. Dogmengeschichte. Vol. I, Reformation. Zurich, 1951, 238 ff.

Chapter

8

LUTHER'S LECTURES ON THE EPISTLE TO THE ROMANS (1515-16)

> "It was because he felt through all the depths of his heart and soul
> and mind that God and Christ and Salvation and Justification and
> Grace and Holiness are not words and shadows but realities . . .
> that as one shadow after another revealed its hollowness to him,
> he bade it avaunt and vanish."
> JULIUS HARE. " Vindication of Luther."

THE discovery and publication of Luther's lectures on the Epistle to
the Romans form the greatest single achievement of the Luther "renaissance." These lectures are the one work of magisterial significance
to be added to the great corpus of Luther's writings already known and
studied for four centuries. His lectures on the Psalms contain profound
intuitions, memorable aphorisms, but the material is too complex and
unwieldy to have more than a specialist significance, and most students
will be content with gleanings in the footnotes of Karl Holl and other
secondary studies.

It is otherwise with the Epistle to the Romans. Here is a coherent,
manageable theme treated by Luther at the exact and proper climacteric
of his own spiritual development, as we may believe soon after his
mental clarification concerning "Justitia Dei" had opened the way into
the Pauline exposition of the Christian gospel. These lectures are
indispensable to an evaluation of Luther's development even though
in them Luther's thought is still in movement (it never ceased), still
immature.

In 1899, Dr. J. Ficker of Strasbourg began to edit a copy of the
Lectures which had been made by Aurifaber and others, 1555-60, and
which was in the Vatican Library.[1] This was the material which
Denifle flourished with éclat in the faces of Protestant scholars, and
which he utilized in his formidable collection of mediaeval exegesis
of Rom. 1^{17}. Then, by a freak of scholarship, Luther's own original
copy was found to be lying in a show-case in the Royal Library in Berlin.
It had long been known, catalogued and exhibited during the Luther

[1] H. Strohl. L'Évolution Religieuse, 12.19.

celebrations of 1846, but thereafter neglected. Denifle was moved to high flights of sarcasm [1] and affected an exasperated incredulity which no doubt masked disappointment that his secret weapon had now been offset by a more valuable document. The Berlin original included the Glossae as well as the Scholiae, and despite certain obliterations in binding, presents a text which, conflated with other sources, is in the main intact and reliable.[2] The critical Weimar edition (vol. 56), by Dr. Ficker, is in admirable contrast to the edition of the Psalms, a generation before, and is the measure of the progress of critical Luther research in the intervening period.[3]

Thus the material is more coherent, the manuscripts are in better shape, the critical problems infinitely simpler, and the edition much superior to the lectures on the Psalms. As with the earlier lectures, Luther had Grünenberg print an edition of the Biblical text, leaving ample room for marginal and interlinear comments for his own and his students' use. He proceeded to cram his copy with commentary fluent, tidy, minute. His lectures occupied the period between 3rd November 1515 and 7th September 1516.[4] Certain paragraph signs indicate how the lecture material was broken up in the lectures.[5] They remind us that what we have is no mere written commentary, but that they were expounded with ardent (and sometimes drowsy) eloquence in the early morning, as the days and months rolled on, from the dim chilly hours of winter to the warm drenching sunshine of the summer, to an audience which, like all academic audiences in all times and all places, rendered attention fitfully, always eager to be distracted by a gust of wind or a vagrant butterfly.

What Luther has to say to us is refracted through the Bible. The

---

[1] H. Denifle. Die abendländischen Schriftausleger bis Luther über Justitia Dei. Mainz, 1905, 307, n. 1.

[2] W.A. 56, XVIII.

[3] The two chief MSS. are Berlin, Staatsbibl. 64, theol. qu. 21, and Rom. Pal. Lat. 1826 (P). W.A. 57 contains student notes on the lectures which reveal that Luther often departed freely and widely from the text of his material. A German translation of the Lectures by E. Ellwein appeared in the Munich edition of Luther's works, 1935.

[4] Boehmer. Luthers erste Vorlesung, 6, n. 4. Road to Reformation, 121. V. Schubert and K. Meissinger. Luther's Vorlesungstätigkeit (1920). John Oldecop reports, " Im jare 1515 des mandages na dem witten sondage, is Quasimodogeniti kam ik to Wyttenberge . . . und umme de tit hof an Doctor Martinus Luther epistolas Pauli ad Romanos lesende. Der Doctor hadde darup bi Johan Grunenberg den bok-drucker bestellet, dat de epistula Pauli de rige ein wiet von der andern gedrucket wart umme gloserens willen." Ficker, W.A. 56.XIII, cites Luther's words to Spalatin, 9th Sept. 1516, " absoluta professione lectionis Paulinae," to confirm that the course ended early in September.

[5] The text appears to have been a combination of the 1509 Basel text of Frobenius with that of Faber's edition of the Vulgate, with emendations from Luther. On Luther's growing critical independence, see Boehmer, Road to Reformation, 126, and for his references to the original Greek and Hebrew, W.A. 56.LV. From Rom. 9 onwards Luther made use of the N.T. of Erasmus.

Weimar edition indicates at least sixteen hundred direct citations from the Bible, apart from the Epistle itself, an indication of the extent to which his mind was saturated in the Biblical material. Luther was fully aware that this meant for him, and would mean for his contemporaries, a radical displacement among the hierarchy of studies. "For I believe I owe this duty to the Lord, of crying out against philosophy and turning men to Holy Scripture. For perhaps if anybody else were to do it . . . he would be scared or would not be believed. But I who have already wasted many years in such things, and have experienced and hear of many like myself, see that it is a vain study doomed to perdition . . . it is high time to be transferred from other studies and to learn Christ and 'him crucified.'" [1] Not that the Bible had been neglected: Denifle's massive catena is proof that nearly all the doctors of the Middle Ages had turned their attention to the exegesis of this epistle. But just as a Michelangelo and a Rafael display their genius in their very handling of subjects treated by hundreds of artists before them, and just as their artistry is moulded and determined by the stubborn nature of the material they handle, so Luther is most Luther when he is most Paul. [2]

Next to the Bible, St. Augustine is his major authority (there are upwards of one hundred and twenty direct citations). Luther had studied Augustine's comments "On certain propositions from the Epistle to the Romans." More important, in the interval since his Lectures on the Psalms, he had come to know the anti-Pelagian treatises, and notably "Of the Spirit and the Letter." The differences between Luther's theology and that of the African doctor are important, and we must reckon with them before we are done, but we must not underestimate the extent to which at this time these Augustinian writings were congenial and illuminating. Hamel, in his careful and valuable comparison between Luther and Augustine, remarks on Luther's debt to the Augustinian perceptions of the radical nature of sin, and of that human solidarity to which the doctrine of Original Sin bears witness. [3]

Luther makes plain at the outset what he understands to be the theme of the Epistle to the Romans.

"The chief end of the Apostle in this letter is to destroy all Righteousness (Justitiam) and wisdom of our own, and that the sins and unwisdom which were not (i.e. were not considered as such by us, on account of such Righteousness) should on the other hand be established, increased and magnified (i.e. should make them be acknowledged as still existing,

[1] W.A. 56.371.17.26. See also W.A.Br. 1.88.24.
[2] On the relation of Luther to St. Paul, especially in relation to Rom. 7, P. Althaus, Paulus und Luther über den Menschen. Rev. ed. 1951.
[3] A. Hamel. Der junge Luther and Augustin, vol. 2, 1935, 35 ff.

and to be many and great) and thus, that Christ and his Righteousness are necessary for us, for their genuine extermination. And he does this until chapter 12, yet from this point to the end, he teaches the quantity and quality of the good works we ought to do, on the ground of Christ's own Righteousness received (ex ipsa Justitia Christi accepta). For "coram Deo," it is not the case that a man becomes just by doing just works (as the foolish Jews, Gentiles and self justifiers arrogantly trust) but by being just, he does just deeds." [1]

The antithesis "coram Deo"—"coram nobis" (or coram hominibus) is fundamental to the understanding of Luther's exposition of the Gospel and not least to the appreciation of his anthropology. This Biblical and Augustinian phrase reveals the dimension within which Luther discusses "Righteousness": the concern is not, in the first place, with man's behaviour in relation to his fellows, or his place within the hierarchy of creation, but with man as he stands in the presence of the Holy and the Living God, who is of purer eyes than to behold iniquity, yet who of His pure mercy receives sinners in His Son Jesus Christ. [2]

It is revelation, and not man's own insight, wisdom, or religious experience, which shows man his real predicament, and which reveals him to be "coram Deo" a sinner, unrighteous in all his acts, under condemnation. A man can only face this truth about himself in the presence of another righteousness, which God has given to men in Jesus Christ, and which men can never deserve or achieve, but which can only be accepted.

"For God wills to save us, not by our own (domesticam) righteousness and wisdom, but from without (extraneam), not one which comes and is born from within ourselves, but which comes into us from without, not growing in our own soil, but which comes from heaven. Thus it is by all means necessary to learn this external and other (aliena) righteousness. For this reason must our own and inward righteousness be first removed." [3]

---

[1] W.A. 56.3.6. So also the beginning of the Scholia. " The sum of this epistle is to pull down, and pluck up and to destroy all the wisdom and righteousness of the flesh (i.e. however great it may be in the sight of men, even coram nobis), and however sincere and from the heart, and to implant, establish and magnify sin (however much it may not be, or its existence be unrecognized). W.A. 56.157.2.
[2] Among many other references, W.A. 56.3.13 : 10.5 : 10.21 : 12.27 : 14.7 : 26.3 : 27.8 : 33.24 : 34.5 : 41.3 : 41.12.13 : 42.1 : 46.22 : 76.3 : 122.5 : 135.22 : •157.3 : 159.11 : 159.23 : 171.9.27 : 173.31 : 174.1 : 201.15 : 204.9 : 205.6 : 206.8 : 208.24 : 215.6 : 216.23 : 217.16 : 221.29 : 229.13 (six times in a few lines !) : 233.24 : 234.25 : 235.33 : 236.6 : 246.28 : 247.6 : 247.13 : 260.19 : 261.5 : 268.32 : 283.17 : 285.22 : 289.25 : 290.26 : 303.8 : 309.18 : 327.27 : 395.8 : 418.30 : 422.6 : 436.15 : 443.18 : 448.6 : 449.20 : 500.7.
[3] W.A. 56.158.10. Also W.A. 56.279.22, " Therefore I have rightly said, all our good is outside us (extrinsecum nobis) and that is Christ, as the Apostle says, " He is made unto us Wisdom and Righteousness and Sanctification and Redemption."

To know this is only possible in Faith, that good fight [1] which has to be maintained against our own judgments, feelings and experience. The opposition to "fides" of "sensus" [2] (sense) is an important technical usage of Luther in this connection, and it denotes the "wisdom of the flesh" upon which Luther insists that the heretics and the arrogant rely, the ground of their self-confidence and trust in their own righteousness.

Sin is not only evident in the depraved activities of wicked men, though Luther pays due attention to these things as he expounds St. Paul's terrible indictment of the pagan world. He insists that human ingratitude is the beginning of the human disaster, that this led the creature to vanity, from vanity to blindness, from blindness to error, "the worst of all and the cause of idolatries." [3] He refuses to weaken the force of the statement that God handed these pagans over (Rom. 1[24]) to their vile passions and to a reprobate mind. "God wills sin, not because of sin itself, nay, rather he himself does not will sin because he hates it because it is sin, but he wills it because of the punishment and the ill it brings, that he may have regard to the punishment rather than the sin." [4]

This raises an objection. "But at this they growl," then they are damned without fault, for they are forced to do what they cannot fulfil, and "are obliged to the impossible." [5] Luther here refers to a piece of scholastic jargon, used by d'Ailly and others, which at Rom. 4[7] he makes the text of an illuminating digression.

"Inept and foolish is the saying, 'God obliged us to have grace,' and therefore to what is impossible. I excuse the most pious God. He is innocent of such imposture. He did not do this, he did not oblige us to have grace, but he obliged us to fulfil the law, that when we had been humbled he might then give his grace to those who beseech it. But these people make grace a cause of indignation and imagine what is abominable. For what else is it to say 'God obliged us to have grace, nor does he wish to accept the fulfilment of the law "according to the substance of the deed" if it is not fulfilled "according to the intention of the lawgiver," than to say—"Lo, are we then to fulfil the law without Grace? Is it not enough that God has laid on us the burden of the law, without adding his demand that we should have grace, as a new exaction?" O arrogance. O ignorance of sin, ignor-

---

[1] " The life of the ' new law ' is a fight and a warfare." W.A. 56.128.16.
[2] W.A. 56.249.25 :   250.3.5 :   250.23 :   253.19 :   256.1.12 :   275.4 : and especially 446.12.30. Prenter. Spiritus Creator, 93 n.
[3] W.A. 56.178-88.
[4] W.A. 56.180.32.
[5] W.A. 56.182.29.

ance of God, ignorance of the Law! Thus when God offers grace to the lowly, because he sees that we cannot fulfil his law, that we may fulfil it from grace, these people are not yet humbled, they still do not understand that the law cannot be fulfilled 'according to the substance of the deed' (as they themselves say), unless they take 'the substance of the deed' to be a purely external operation. This assuredly they do not, but it is thus far internal, that it is a work performed for God's sake, and from the heart, and by an act chosen naturally and voluntarily, all of which things contribute to 'the substance of the deed.' These foolish people do not see, that the will, even if it were permitted, would never do what the law commands. For it is slow to good, prompt to evil. Which they themselves assuredly know in their own experience, and yet they speak so impiously and sacrilegiously. For as long as it is reluctant towards the law, it is turned away from it and thus does not fulfil it. So it is the work of grace, to make it willing and cheerful (libentem ac hilarem) towards the law. So I rightly said that all our good is outside us (extrinsecum nobis)—that is, Christ." [1]

This thought that the obligation to have grace makes a "new exaction" on the part of God recalls Luther's autobiographical fragment:

"I was angry with God, saying, 'As though it really were not enough that miserable sinners should be eternally damned by original sin, and have all kinds of calamities laid on them by the law of the ten commandments, God must add sorrow on sorrow, and even through the Gospel bring his Justice and his wrath to bear.'"

It may well be that this misconception helped to aggravate Luther's difficulty with regard to Rom. 1[17]. Luther shows here that the Nominalist argument turns grace itself into part of the law, though he admits also that their doctrine of the "substance of the deed" should not be thought of in terms of the purely external act. But he presses the psychological distinctions to the point where they break down, before the fact of the paralysis of the human will through sin. It is an Augustinian and mediaeval truth that Christian obedience must be free and willing, but Luther's stress on this cheerful and spontaneous quality as indispensable, is characteristic and constant.[2] It is not enough for men to obey the law outwardly "unless they do it with a cheerful and pure will." [3] "They can never fulfil the law, while they do not obey from the heart." [4] The unregenerate "do good works wholly from fear, or from love of reward . . . not with a cheerful will." [5] "Those who seek God do it freely and cheerfully for God's own sake and not

---

[1] W.A. 56.278.25.
[2] See E. Sormunen. Die Eigenart der Lutherischen Ethik. A.A.S.F., 1934, 33 ff.
[3] W.A. 56.205.22.   [4] W.A. 56.205.36 : 264.31.   [5] W.A. 56.235.6.

on account of any creaturely possession, whether bodily or spiritual," [1] and this "is not the work of nature, but of the grace of God." "Grace is therefore to be sought, that a man, changed in the spirit, may desire and perform all things with a cheerful and willing heart, not from servile fear, or puerile cupidity, but with a free and virile mind. This the Spirit alone works." [2] "This is to be understood of the whole heart, which acts, not from servile fear, or out of the puerile advantage of cupidity, but which freely performs or omits to act, out of love of God, and this is impossible without that love diffused by the Holy Ghost." [3]

It is because all obedience to God, apart from grace, lacks this quality of free, spontaneous, happy service that Luther asserts the bondage of the sinful will. Thus, at Rom. 8^3:

"Where is 'Free Will' now? Where are those who try to make out that, from our own natural strength we can make an act of love to God above all things . . . it is no use to say that we can fulfil the law 'according to the substance of the deed, but not according to the intention of the law giver,' as though from ourselves there was a capacity for will and action, but not in the way in which God desires, i.e. in grace, and thus grace has a certain use, but is not necessary, nor have we met with a vitiated nature through Adam's sin, but we stand in the integrity of our natural powers. Thus philosophy stinks in our nostrils, as though reason always seeks the best things, and we chatter about the Law of Nature." [4]

The weakness of the human will, however, is a symptom of the radical evil wrought by sin in the human personality. The human solidarity in the sin of Adam does not remove individual responsibility, for each human being has joined himself by his own deeds to the mass of sin.[5] At Rom. 5^{14} Luther raises explicitly the question, "What, then, is Original Sin?" He repudiates the scholastic definition deriving from Anselm which thought of it as the "absence of Original Justice" or as a mere predicate of quality. He asserts that it is "not only the privation of light in the intellect and of strength in the memory," but "the loss of all uprightness and powers of all our faculties, whether of the body or the soul, of the whole of the inward and the outer man." [6]

"It is ready for evil, nauseated by good, a disgust at light and wisdom, a delight in error and in darkness, a running away from, and abomina-

[1] W.A. 56.241.22.   Also 264.31.   [2] W.A. 56.336.14.
[3] W.A. 56.337.13.   Also 502.2.25.
[4] W.A. 56.355.2.   Also 385.15.   " Free Will as constituted outside grace has simply no capacity for righteousness, but is necessarily in its sins. That is why the blessed Augustine himself says in ' Contra Julianum,' I would rather call it a will in bondage, than free will (servum potius quam liberum arbitrium)."
[5] W.A. 56.286-7 : 316-7.   [6] W.A. 56.312.6.

tion of good works, a running towards evil. . . . For God not only hates this privation and imputes it . . . but also all this Concupiscence . . . and so the old Fathers rightly said that 'Original Sin is the tinder, the law of the flesh, the law of our members, the weakness of nature, a tyrant, our original disease. For man is like a sick man, whose mortal sickness is not simply to have lost the health of one member, but in addition to losing the health of all the members has suffered the weakening of all the senses and powers, and in addition is nauseated by the things that are good for him, and desires the things which can only do him harm.'"[1]

Concupiscence here is, as we have already seen, much more than the temptation to fleshly lusts: it is the orientation of the whole human person in its egoism, its self-seeking and its rebellion against God. It is a distinction between Luther and Augustine that while Augustine speaks of the sinner as bent, or crooked (curvatus), and so bowed down to the earth, and to earthly good things, Luther regards this curvature as a perversion to egoism.[2]

"For that is called 'the old man' which is born from Adam, not according to nature, but according to the vitiated nature . . . and it is not only called the 'old man' because it does the works of the flesh, but even more when it does righteous acts and treats of wisdom, and exercises itself in spiritual goods, nay, even when it loves and cleaves to God. The reason is that in all these things it enjoys (fruitur) the gifts of God and makes use of God (utitur) . . . so profound is this iniquity . . . and this is figured in the woman in the gospels who was bowed down."[3]

"For Scripture describes man as bowed down to himself (incurvatum in se) so that not only bodily goods, but spiritual goods also he turns to himself, and seeks himself in all things."[4]

"For the prudence of the flesh always loves itself above all else, even more than God."[5]

"For man makes himself the final and ultimate object and idol . . . this crookedness and depravity and iniquity is described many times in Scripture under the name of fornication and idolatry . . . and is in the hidden depths of our nature, nay, rather is nature itself, wounded and in ferment through the whole so that not only is it impossible to remedy without grace, but it is impossible fully to recognize it."[6]

---

[1] W.A. 56.312.10.
[2] This has been pointed out by A. S. Wood (S.J.T., 1950, 7) following A. Nygren, Agape and Eros, ii.267, n. 3. On the other hand, Luther uses the Augustinian distinction between " frui " and " uti," our enjoyment of God for his own sake, and our making use of God for our own ends, in the Augustinian manner, especially when discussing our love towards God.
[3] W.A. 56.325.2.
[4] W.A. 56.356.4.
[5] W.A. 56.359.9.
[6] W.A. 56.361.15.

Luther then gives a list of earthly, bodily and spiritual goods, and affirms that the "prudence of the flesh" clings to them all. "Man, I say, turns all these to himself, seeks his own good in them all, and horribly makes an idol out of them."[1]

"For grace sets before itself no other object than God, to whom it is moved and directs itself: it sees him alone, and it moves towards him in all things, and all those other things which it sees to be in the way, it passes through as though it did not see them, and simply turns to God. . . . Nature, on the other hand, sets before itself no other object than the self, to which it is moved and directs itself, and all those other things, even God himself, it by-passes as though it did not see them, and turns to itself . . . thus nature sets itself in the place of everything, and even in the place of God, seeks only its own things, and not those of God. Thus it is to itself the first and greatest of idols. Then it turns even God into an idol for itself, and the truth of God into a lie, and at length all God's creation and all his gifts."[2]

What has been called Luther's anthropology of the "whole man" shows most clearly when he expounds St. Paul in Rom. 7. Here is the thought of man as a single responsible person. There are two orientations, but these are the Biblical dichotomy of "flesh" (sarx) and "spirit" (pneuma), not the Platonic dualism of "body" and "soul."[3]

"For the same person is 'spirit' and 'flesh': thus what the flesh does the whole man is said to do. And yet what resists is not the whole man but is rightly called a part of him."[4]

"The same man (idem homo) is at the same time 'flesh' and 'spirit'."[5]

"But because the flesh for the spirit make up one total man, contrary things can be attributed to the whole man, which derive from his contrary parts. Thus there is a kind of communicatio idiomatum, since the same man is spiritual and carnal, just and a sinner, bad and good."[6]

This division and tension is not found in the carnal man.

"For there the whole man is flesh, for the spirit of God does not abide in him."[7]

"Without the spirit, the whole man is the 'old man' and the 'outward man.'"[8]

And, at Rom. 7[25]:

"See how one and the same man, at the same time, serves the law

[1] W.A. 56.362.15.					[2] W.A. 56.356.22.
[3] Pinomaa. Existentielle Charakter, 52. Prenter. Spiritus Creator, 25.93. Holl, 141. Hamel, ii.68. J. Iwand. Glaubensgerechtigkeit nach Luthers Lehre, 21. On the Biblical usage concerning "sarx" and "pneuma." R. Bultmann. Theologie des Neuen Testaments. Tübingen, 1948, 228 ff. P. Althaus. Paulus und Luther, 1950. H. Stomps. Die Anthropologie Martin Luther, 1935.
[4] At Rom. 7[20]. W.A. 56.342.34.			[5] W.A. 56.350.27.
[6] W.A. 56.343.16.			[7] Ibid., 24.			[8] W.A. 56.345.31. Also 416.8.

of God and the law of sin, is at the same time just and sins. For he does not say 'my mind serves the law of God' nor 'my flesh serves the law of sin,' but he says 'I, the whole man, the same person, I serve both servitudes." [1]

Luther's most striking affirmation of this truth is to be found, not in the commentaries, but in one of his sermons in 1522:

"'The flesh' is the whole man, with body and soul, reason and will. And every man has fleshly senses, moods, affections and will who is not born of the spirit. For the soul is so imbedded in the flesh, which seeks to guard and protect it, that it is indeed more 'flesh' than the flesh itself." [2]

What we have quoted of the "whole man" in relation to sin must be balanced with what Luther says about "the whole man" in relation to the grace of God. We must not make Luther too modern, and caution has to be used in speaking of "personal relationships" or "human personality." On the other hand, Luther is nearer to the Biblical view of man on the one hand, and the modern analysis of personality on the other, than the psychological distinctions of late Aristotelian scholasticism.[3] His profound intuitions of the infinite subtleties of human egoism,[4] and the dark ferment always at work in the hidden depths of the human soul, anticipate truths which modern psychological science has analytically established.

Nevertheless, we repeat, Luther's is an anthropology "coram Deo." This truth about man is revealed by God, and only partly realized by man himself.

"For the Judgment of God is infinite in subtlety. And there is nothing so refined, but it is gross in his presence, nothing so just that it is not unjust, nothing so true that it is not found a lie, nothing so pure and holy that it is not polluted and profane in his presence (coram Deo)." [5]

Luther takes up the theme of his lectures on the Psalms, of that "accusatio sui," that humility which accepts the judgment of God, and out of which the humiliated soul cries for divine mercy. Thus the

---

[1] W.A. 56.347.2. Also W.A. 8.119.14.   [2] W.A. 10.1.ii.301.27.
[3] That Luther himself believed this, is clear from W.A. 56.354.14 ff., where he says the "recentiores doctores" speak with little authority because "they speak without the testimony of Scripture." Their subtle psychological distinctions have brought it about that the true difference of "flesh" and "spirit" has ceased to be understood.
[4] The conception of egoism as the core of "Concupiscentia" may be, as Sormunen asserts ("Eigenart," 36) "the great gift of the German mystics to the religious genius of Germany," but Luther found in Tauler and the "Theologica Germanica" congenial and confirming evidence of conceptions already developed in his earliest writings.
[5] W.A. 56.246.27.

whole work of Justification becomes dynamic. It is not a mechanical process, for what is at stake is a movement of the whole man towards God. Luther's use of "humility" in these lectures is interesting, for it is obvious that the conception is moving towards the point when the word "faith" will more adequately convey what Luther means: the emptying of the soul of all pride and self-righteousness and its cleaving to God in his promises, in his Word, in Jesus Christ. "For what else does the whole Scripture teach save Humility?" [1]

"For this is the whole business of the Apostle and his Lord that he should humble the proud, and bring them to a knowledge of this thing, and teach them to need grace, that he may break down their own righteousness, so that when they are made humble they may seek Christ, and confess themselves to be sinners, and thus perceive grace and be saved." [2]

"Humility is the universal Justice" [3] in the distributive, Aristotelian sense of the word, since in its sight all are equal. Thus humility is more and more closely joined in Luther's mind with faith. "This is the work of humility and faith." [4]

The movement, "accusatio sui"—"humilitas"—"humiliatio"— "fides" explains why Luther will have nothing to do with the idea of a "fides informis." At Rom. 1^{17} he rejects Lyra's exposition of "from faith to faith" as the change from "fides informis" to "fides formata."

"The sense seems to be that the Righteousness of God is wholly from faith (ex fide), in such a way that progress does not lead to sight, but always into a clearer faith, as 2 Cor. 4 . . . always believing more and more, so that 'He that is just, is justified hitherto,' lest anybody should forthwith consider himself to have apprehended, and thus cease to progress, i.e. begin to backslide." [5]

Thus faith is a special kind of understanding (intellectus). "This understanding is faith itself, a knowledge of things invisible and to be believed. It is a hidden understanding, for it is of those things which a man cannot know of himself." [6] As we have seen, Luther constantly brings the judgment of faith into contrast with the judgment of "sensus."

"For whenever God gives a new degree of grace, he gives it in this way, so that it comes against all our understanding (sensus) and counsel . . . thus this transformation of our own "sensus" is the most useful

[1] W.A. 56.199.30. R. Josefson. Ödmjukhet och Tro, 10 ff.
[2] W.A. 56.207.7. Also 252.17, " in immensum nos oportet humiliari."
[3] W.A. 56.449.9.
[4] W.A. 56.218.13: 276.32, " in humble faith ": 34, "on account of the humble sighing of faith ": 282.12, " on account of the humility of faith ": 428.12, " only the works of humility are good works."
[5] W.A. 56.173.7. " Fides informis is simply not faith," 172.21.   [6] W.A.56.238.27.

of all knowledge for Christ's faithful people. And the clinging to our own 'sensus' is the most hurtful resistance to the Holy Spirit. For example—When Abraham was commanded to go out, not knowing whither he went, that was against his 'sensus.' And when he was commanded to offer his son, this was the most tremendous transformation of 'sensus,' as Rom. 4 proves. And sharp, displeasing and desperate, did the will of God appear about Isaac. And yet it afterwards proved to be the best, most benevolent and most perfect thing to have happened. David and the Virgin Mary are other examples." [1]

Luther will not split faith into certain truths to be accepted by the mind, and faith as a personal relationship. We cannot drive a wedge between faith in Christ's person, and belief in His words, or in His Word which is the Gospel. "Faith is indivisible." [2]

But faith cannot be separated from the object of faith, which is Christ as he comes to us in the words and promises of the gospel. "Faith and the promises are related to one another." [3] "Thus faith ratifies the promise, and the promise requires faith." [4] Thus God "is justified in his words, i.e. when he is believed in the gospel concerning the fulfilment of his promise." [5]

"For inwardly the words of God are as true and just as God Himself. But they are not yet like this in us until our wisdom yields to them, and by believing gives place to them and receives them." [6]

In this connection Luther employs a striking permutation of the familiar mediaeval and Augustinian figure of the sick patient and the doctor.

"He is like a sick man who believes the doctor who promises him most certain health, and who obeys his precepts in the meanwhile in hope of that promise of health, and abstains from the things which are forbidden him, lest he hinder that promised cure and aggravate the disease, until at last the doctor fulfils what he promised." [7]

It is when we assent to God's words and recognize his judgments as true that we are justified.

"For that passive Justification of God with which he is justified by

[1] W.A. 56.446.11. Also 233.2 : 423.19 : 425.4 : and 447.23. " Thus the Christian man ought most chiefly to rejoice when things go exactly contrary to his sense (sensum)."
[2] W.A. 56.249.20. Although Luther here (as Holl points out, 120) uses the traditional argument of the Roman Church against heretics, the quotation will bear this wider implication. It is important to note, with Prenter, that without the presence of the Holy Ghost, faith in the words and promises of God would simply be the " fides historica " which Luther refuses to call faith.
[3] W.A. 56.45.15.   [4] W.A. 56.46.15.
[5] W.A. 56.225.15 : 226.18 : 251.12. " The faith in Christ, by which we are justified, is not only to believe in Christ, or the person of Christ, but to believe in all the things that belong to Christ."
[6] W.A. 56.226.14.   [7] W.A. 56.272.3. Prenter, 90.

us is itself our active justification by God. For he counts as justice, that faith which regards his words as just, for 'the just lives by faith' . . . for he is justified and conquers in his words when he makes us such as his word is, that is, just, true, wise, etc. And thus we are turned into his word, not his word into us. For he makes us such when we believe that this is his word, i.e. truth and righteousness." [1]

"For to know ourselves as sinners is by faith alone (sola fide), for it is not manifest to us, nay, rather we are more often not conscious of the fact. Thus we must hold to the judgment of God and believe his words, with which he has declared us unjust, for he himself cannot lie. And thus this is necessary even though not evident, 'For faith is the evidence of things not seen' and is content with the words of God alone." [2]

But Luther cannot speak of faith on the one hand and, on the other, of the Righteousness of God, without the theme of Jesus Christ. It is this christocentric emphasis which separates his treatment of justification from that of the Nominalists, with their discussion of a divine "acceptance" and their persistent recourse to the dialectic of the "potestas ordinata" and the "potestas absoluta." [3]

Luther's most outspoken utterance in this connection is at Rom. 5^2.

"He speaks against those presumptuous persons who think they can come to God apart from Christ, as though it were sufficient for them to have believed, and thus 'sola fide' not through Christ (per Christum) but alongside Christ (juxta Christum) or beyond Christ, not needing him having once accepted the grace of justification . . . but it is necessary to have Christ always, hitherto and to eternity as mediator of such faith . . . it must be 'through faith' 'through Christ' in order that all that we do or are able or suffer may be through faith in Christ, and yet in all these things we acknowledge ourselves to be unprofitable servants, and by Christ alone (per Christum solum) do we consider ourselves able to have access to God. For so it is in all the works of faith, that we are made worthy in the refuge and protection of Christ and His Righteousness. 'Therefore we are justified by faith' and our sins are remitted 'but it is per Jesum Christum Dominum nostrum.'" [4]

---

[1] W.A. 56.226.24. H. Iwand. Glaubensgerechtigkeit nach Luthers Lehre, 11.
[2] W.A. 56.231.9 : 428.17. "For they are invisible things announced (in the Gospel) and only perceptible by hearing and by faith."
[3] Those who compare Luther's Romans with the evidence assembled in P. A. Vignaux's study, "Justification et Prédestination au XIVe siècle," will appreciate this point.
[4] W.A. 56.298.22. See also 252.31, "Ac per hoc soli Christo Justitia relinquatur, soli ipsi opera gratiae et spiritus. Nos autem semper in operibus legis, semper injusti, semper peccatores." 318.20, "' The Grace of God ' (with which we are justified, nay, rather, which is in Christ in the beginning as the sin of man in Adam) and the ' gift,' viz. which Christ sheds abroad from the Father in those who believe in him." 252.5, To believe in Christ is to turn to him with all our hearts, and to subordinate all things to him (in ipsum ordinare).

Luther follows this with a sharp assault on those mystical theologians who imagine they can contemplate the uncreated Word apart from the image of the passion of Christ. This is no formal orthodoxy, but the very nerve of the fight of faith, that "militia Christi" [1] which runs through the human conscience.

"Whence, then, is our defence? Nowhere save from Christ and in Christ. For if there shall come some reproach against the heart which believes in Christ, testifying against him concerning some evil deed, then it turns itself away, and turns to Christ (ad Christum!) and says— 'But he made satisfaction. He is the Righteous One,' this is my defence. He died for me, he made his Righteousness to be mine, and made my sin his own, and if he made my sin his own, then I can have it now no longer, and I am free. And if he has made his Righteousness mine, I am righteous with the same Righteousness as his. But my sin cannot swallow him up, but it is swallowed up in the infinite abyss of his Righteousness, since he is God, blessed for ever. And so, God is greater than our own heart. Greater, infinitely greater, is the counsel for the defence than the counsel for the prosecution. God is the defender, the heart is the accuser. What, is that the proportion? Thus, thus, even thus it is. 'Who shall lay anything to the charge of God's elect? Nobody. Why? Because it is God who justifies. Who is it that shall condemn? Nobody. Why? It is Jesus Christ (who is very God) who died, nay, rather, who is risen again. If God be for us, then, who can be against us?'" [2]

It is one of the many merits of Prenter's "Spiritus Creator" to show how rich is Luther's doctrine of the work of the Holy Spirit, and its place in the doctrine of justification, in preventing faith from becoming a mere "fides historica," and in preventing faith in Christ becoming a mere dogmatic scheme, since the presence of the Holy Ghost makes justification the work of the living, personal God.[3] That a man should perform the commands of God willingly and freely "is impossible without the love shed abroad by the Holy Ghost." [4]

"For those are not the best Christians who are the most learned and read many things and possess the most books. For all their books and all the understanding of them is 'the letter' and the death of the soul. But those are the best Christians who perform those things which they read in books and teach others to do them, with the most free will.

---

[1] W.A. 56.350.17 : also 128.16.
[2] W.A. 56.204.14. Pinomaa. Existentielle Charakter, 109. " In this passage the 'existential' significance of the Law breaks through." See also W.A. 56.37.26, " God does not give grace freely in the sense that he will demand no satisfaction, but he gave Christ to be a satisfaction for us."
[3] R. Prenter. Spiritus Creator, 73 ff.
[4] W.A. 56.337.15.

N

But they cannot do these things with such a free will unless they have the Holy Spirit. And it is to be feared that in our day men become learned with the multiplication of books, but most unlearned Christians." [1]

"To be 'led by the Spirit of God' means freely, promptly, cheerfully to mortify the flesh, i.e. the old man, i.e. to condemn and renounce whatever is not God, even themselves, . . . freely to abandon the good things, and to embrace the ills that come. And this is not the achievement of nature, but of the Spirit of God in us." [2]

"Nevertheless he is not a 'spirit,' i.e. the inward man, unless he has the Holy Spirit: thus it can properly be admitted that by these "fruits of the spirit" are to be understood the fruits of the Holy Spirit. Yet 'spirit' is more aptly taken as the inward man, as a good tree bears good fruit and 'flesh' a bad tree bearing bad fruit." [3]

"The Holy Spirit makes new men by his indwelling (inhabitatione)." [4]

"For nobody can have the right mind about God (recte sentire) unless the Spirit of God is in him." [5]

"I think that 'the law written in the hearts of men' is that 'love shed abroad in our hearts by the Holy Ghost' which is properly the law of Christ and the fullness of the law of Moses, nay, rather, is law without law, without measure or end, knowing no limit, but spread out over all things, which the law commands or can command." [6]

"For true it is that those who are Christ's have the spirit of Christ and walk rightly even though they do not understand . . . for they perform before they shall understand, nay, rather, they draw their understanding rather from life than from doctrine." [7]

"See how the Apostle joins the fountain with the stream. 'Love,' he says, 'through the Holy Ghost which is given to us.' For it is not enough to have the gift unless the giver also be present, as Moses begged in Exodus 33. If thou go not up before us, carry us not up from hence." [8]

"To the elect who are loved by God and who love God, the Spirit works all things together for good." [9]

Prenter has drawn special attention to the significance here, of Luther's comments on Rom. 8[26] and the intercession of the Spirit. "The Spirit helpeth our infirmities" because "without the help of the Spirit it would be impossible to bear this work of God, with which he hears us and does what we ask." [10]

"For it is necessary for the work of God to be hidden and not understood when he does it." [11]

"For it is concealed under a species contrary to our thoughts and

[1] W.A. 56.338.5.　　[2] W.A. 56.366.14.　　[3] W.A. 56.76.18.
[4] W.A. 56.76.16.　　[5] W.A. 56.186.1.　　[6] W.A. 56.203.8.
[7] W.A. 56.276.16.　　[8] W.A. 56.308.26.　　[9] W.A. 56.381.15.
[10] W.A. 56.376.4.　　[11] W.A. 56.376.31.

cogitations. Whence Gabriel said to the Virgin, 'The Holy Ghost shall come upon you (superveniet), i.e. above the things you can conceive' . . . for we do not understand the work of God until it is performed . . . yes, yes, we do not know how to pray as we ought. Therefore the Spirit is necessary for us, who helps our infirmities." [1]

Prenter points out that the Holy Spirit here is much more than the abstract and transcendent cause of salvation, the uncreated mover of created grace, for he is the living personal God at work in the human heart.

We can turn now to the positive evaluation of Justification itself. We remember first that what is in question is our standing "coram Deo"—"In the presence of God there is none who is just." [2]

We saw in Luther's summary of the epistle that in order to our Justification, our confidence in all human righteousness must be taken away, that by the Law and the Gospel we must be brought to that accusation of self which admits the truth of the verdict of God, and to that humility which no longer boasts of its own goodness, but simply cries out for the forgiving righteousness of God.

"For it cannot be that a soul filled with its own righteousness can be replenished with the Righteousness of God, who fulfils only those who hunger and are thirsty. Therefore he who is full of his own truth and wisdom is not capable of the truth and wisdom of God, which cannot be received save by those who are empty and foolish. Therefore let us say to God, 'O how willingly will we be empty that thou mayest be full in us. Freely I will be weak, that thy strength may dwell in me: freely a sinner that thou mayest be justified in me, freely a fool that thou mayest be my wisdom: freely unjust that thou mayest be my Righteousness!' Lo, this is what it means to say 'Against thee have I sinned that thou mightest be justified in thy words.' " [3]

In his initial summary of the Epistle Luther had said, "For 'coram Deo' it is not by doing just works that one becomes just, but being made just, one does just deeds," and this theme is recurrent through his commentary. [4]

---

[1] W.A. 56.377-8. The passage contains a tribute to Tauler, " who has treated this patience and sufferance of God and brought it to light better than any other in the German language," 13.14.   [2] W.A. 56.449.20.   [3] W.A. 56.219.3.
[4] W.A. 56.3.13 : 22.24. " For it is the same thing to be just 'apud Deum' before God, and to be justified before God (apud Deum). For he is not considered just by God because he is just, but because he is considered just by God, therefore he is just. For none is considered just unless he fulfils the law in deed. But none fulfils the law save he who believes in Christ. And thus the apostle means to conclude that out of Christ (extra Christum) none is just, none fulfils the law." 255.18, " For not by doing just works are we made just, but being just we do just deeds. Therefore Righteousness is by grace alone " (" Non enim justa operando justi efficimur, sed justi essendo justa operamur. Ergo sola gratia justificat ").

As Luther would later record in his autobiographical fragment, here he quotes with approval the Augustinian view that the Righteousness of God is not simply an abstract quality of the divine nature, but God's own saving action, and His gift to us.[1] "He describes what and what manner this Justice of God is, not with which He himself is just, nor with which anyone else can be just, but which nobody can have except by faith." [2]

"Only in the Gospel (solo evangelio) is the Righteousness of God revealed (who may be and how he may become just before God), by faith alone (per solam fidem) with which the Word of God is believed . . . for the cause of salvation is the Righteousness of God. And this 'Righteousness of God,' again, ought not to be understood as that by which God is just in himself, but that whereby we are justified by him, which he performs through faith in the Gospel." [3]

This conception of "Justitia Dei" Luther affirmed in his autobiographical fragment to have been confirmed by St. Augustine's "On the Spirit and the Letter," but he thought that Augustine had not the right notion about "imputation." The long and important section of Luther's lectures at Rom. 4[7] is therefore of exceptional interest. We shall let Luther speak for himself, for it is only too easy to read back into Luther the later categories of Protestant theology. There is certainly nothing here of the elaborate Protestant doctrine of a scheme of imputed merits. Luther simply expounds Rom. 4[7], where he meets the Biblical phrases, in the Latin—"reputare ad justitiam," and the quotation from Psalm 32, "Beatus vir cui non imputabit Dominus peccatum"—"Blessed is the man to whom the Lord will not impute sin." Luther includes at this point a full exposition of this section of Psalm 32, and it is when we compare what he has to say here with what he said in his Lectures on the Psalms at this point, that we grasp the movement and direction of his thought. Luther's thought is no more concerned with the forensic associations of these phrases than is St. Paul. He is concerned with the persistence of sin in the believer, not as a mere tinder (fomes peccati), but as that ferment of egoism for which man is accountable since his whole personal existence is involved in it, but which in the redeemed is restrained by God, until it is finally driven out by grace, a work growingly fulfilled but never perfectly achieved in this present life.

Anybody who will turn to what William of Ockham has to say about concupiscence and original sin, and about the non-imputation of sin,

---

[1] He cites Augustine, " On the Spirit and the Letter," at W.A. 56.36.11 : 172.5.
[2] W.A. 56.37.18.
[3] W.A. 56.171.28.

will see that it is based on very different principles from those of Luther. Luther's whole conception of the depth of concupiscence and of the paralysis of the human will, as well as his christocentric orientation is contrary to Ockham's stress on human liberty and merit, to the Nominalist view of the nature of evil and to its use of the dialectic of the twofold power of God. To say that Ockham's teaching prepared the way for Luther here is a most superficial misreading of the situation.[1] Luther's exegesis at this point in his lectures on the Psalms and those on Romans, betrays a wholly different origin.

"The just man, then, is the man 'to whom the Lord does not impute sin,'" [2]

"The saints are inwardly always sinners and thus outwardly they are always justified. The hypocrites inwardly are always just, and thus outwardly they are always sinners. By inwardly, I mean, as we are in ourselves, in our own eyes, in our own estimation. But outwardly, what we are in the sight of God, and in his sight (reputatione). Therefore we are outwardly just when we are just, not of ourselves or of our works, but only by the reputation of God." [3]

"Since therefore the saints always have their sin in view and implore Righteousness from God according to his mercy, by this fact they are always reckoned just by God . . . on account of this confession of sin. For they really are sinners, but they are just by the merciful reputation of God (reputatione miserentis Dei). Ignorantly they are just, they know themselves as unjust: sinners in deed, they are none the less just in hope." [4]

"So every saint is a sinner and prays for his sins as 'Justus in principio est accusator sui.' '. . . therefore this is the wonderful and most sweet mercy of God who has us at the same time sinners and not sinners. At the same time sin remains and does not remain.'" [5]

It is most important to observe that Luther is concerned here with what John Wesley calls "Sin in Believers," with the continuance of concupiscence in the redeemed, which scholasticism did not regard as sin, but only as the material of sin. We have seen that for Luther this was a superficial assessment. The sin referred to in Rom. 4[7] is, "not only of sins in deed, word and thought, but of that tinder, the desires, affections, and inclinations towards sin . . . which he says bring forth death as their fruit. Therefore what theologians call actual sin is

[1] So G. de Lagarde. Naissance de l'esprit laïque, vi. 86-8, and the quotation there from Garvens. "That Ockham with his views prepared the way for the imputation doctrine of Luther, in view of the similarities of both teachers, hardly needs proof by quotation"! The only similarity, in fact, is in the phrase "non-imputation," which both found in the Bible.
[2] W.A. 56.268.19.   [3] W.A. 56.268.27.   [4] W.A. 56.269.25.
[5] W.A. 56.270.6.9.

rather the work and fruit of sin, sin itself is that 'fomes' (tinder) and concupiscence, or readiness to evil and difficulty towards the good." [1]

"For this evil really is sin, which God remits by his non-imputation by mercy (non-imputationem ex misericordia) to all, who acknowledge it and confess it and hate it and seek to be healed from it." [2]

"It is an error to suppose that this evil can be healed by works, as experience testifies . . . but it is in the mercy of God that this remains and is not imputed for sin to those who call upon him, and sigh for his liberation." [3]

"Thus, then, we are sinners in ourselves and yet by God's reputation we are just through faith." [4]

There follows the illustration (see above, p. 169) of the sick man who believes the "most certain promise" that the doctor will heal him, and the familiar Augustinian picture of Christ as the good Samaritan.

"In the same way our Good Samaritan Christ took the half dead invalid into the inn and undertook to cure him of his sickness, and began to heal him with the promise of most perfect health in the future life, and not imputing sin (i.e. concupiscence) to death, but in the meanwhile in hope of the promise of the cure forbidding him to do or not to do those things which would hinder that cure and increase sin, i.e. concupiscence. Is he not therefore perfectly just? No, but at the same time he is a just man and a sinner (simul peccator et justus), a sinner in very deed, but just by the sure promise and reckoning (reputatione) of God that he would free him from it, until he is made perfectly whole. And in this way he is perfectly whole in hope, but in fact is a sinner, yet he has the beginning of Righteousness, in that he always seeks more, and always knows himself to be unjust." [5]

Luther goes on to say that while he had accepted the scholastic definition of original sin (as lack of original justice) [6] he thought of it as something which could be entirely removed. He could not understand how, when he had made his confession, he was still a sinner.

"I thought that all my sins were taken away and removed, even the inward sin . . . thus I fought with myself, not knowing that the remission was indeed a fact, but that there was no taking away save in hope, i.e. that it is to be taken away by grace given, which it begins to take away, and that it is not from now on imputed as sin. That is why those are mere ravings which say that a man by his own powers can love God above all things, and do the works prescribed, 'according to the sub-

---

[1] W.A. 56.271.1.
[2] Ibid. 20.   [3] Ibid. 24.
[4] Ibid. 30.   On " reputare " see W.A. 56.42.17.
[5] W.A. 56.272.11.
[6] I.e. the doctrine on which Ockham's exposition is based.

stance of the deed, but not according to the intention of the lawgiver, because not done in grace.' O Fools, O Sowtheologians!" [1]

Let those who proclaim this doctrine prove it in their own lives. "If you are without concupiscence, we will believe you." [2]

"But this concupiscence is always with us, and therefore the love of God is never in us, but it has only begun by grace, and by healing the remainder of concupiscence thus far, so that we do not yet 'love God with all our heart,' but through his mercy this is not imputed for sin, until the whole is removed, and the perfect love of God is given to believers, and to those who go on seeking and persevering right to the end." [3]

Luther rejects more firmly than ever the doctrine of the synteresis, this "tiny movement of the soul" [4] (see above, p. 150).

"So this life is the life of cure from sin, not without sin . . . the Church is an inn and a hospital for the sick and for those being cured." [5]

Luther then expounds the important verses of Ps. 32 which are quoted in Rom. 4[7]. We have noted that he hardly ever mentions the words "reputare" or "imputare" without adding the words "misericordia Dei"; if we want a characteristic formula we should quote "sola reputatione Dei miserentis per fidem." His conclusion of the matter is that all our good is to be sought in Christ.

"For if the confessions of the saints are only to be understood of past sins, and they are pure in the present, why are not only past but even present things confessed, except that they know that there is sin in them, but that it is covered and not imputed on account of Christ, that they may plead that all their good is outside themselves, in Christ, who is none the less in them by faith." [6]

This Righteousness of Christ, the last phrase in the quotation reminds us, is never something merely legally external, but is Christ's personal presence in the believer through faith, and by the Holy Spirit.

Luther's conception is dynamic, and worlds apart from the caricature put forward by Denifle and others, of an antinomian who sins behind the covering and external merits of Christ, or even the milder, but not less perverted view which considers that Luther would encourage the Christian to slack or let up in the moral struggle.

"For all this life is a time of wanting righteousness, but never having it perfectly, for that is for the future life. But to want it is to show with all our strength, our studies, prayers, works, sufferings, that we desire Righteousness but that we have not attained it perfectly." [7]

[1] W.A. 56.274.5. [2] W.A. 56.275.7. [3] Ibid. 11.
[4] W.A. 56.275.21. [5] Ibid. 25. [6] W.A. 56.279.32.
[7] W.A. 56.280.17.

Luther sees a godly fear as a necessary element in the Christian life, since without it the nerve of faith is cut, and the Christian falls into the evil ways of security ("the mother of hypocrites") or despair.[1]

"For God leaves us thus in this sin, in this tinder, in concupiscence, that he may keep us in his fear and in humility that we may always keep running to his grace, with fear (semper pavidi) lest we sin, i.e. always praying that it be not imputed to us and sin begin to dominate."[2]

The last line is important, for it shows that Luther's thought of "imputation" is not to be divorced from his doctrine of the "whole man" and of the personal work of Christ, active and present in the believer. When God imputes sin, then it is free to exercise its powers and to dominate; when he does not impute it, then this ferment is held in restraint, while grace is able to do its healing work, before which in the end the concupiscence must vanish away.

Thus "non-imputation" is the active mercy of God at work, in response to the humble soul, conscious of its own need, and stripped, in the presence of God, of its own righteousness.

"For by this alone does sin become venial, and not imputed, because we groan on account of it, lest God should damn us for it, lest he impute it to us, and seeking his mercy, we implore him to take it away by grace, and thus confess ourselves sinners, and hold ourselves to be sinners by weeping, penitence, grieving and tears. But if this fear and solicitude stop then soon (mox) comes security, and when security comes, then (mox) God imputes it again for sin."[3]

This, on account of "the humility of faith in fear, consists in hope and in the non-imputation of God. They have the ferment, but they are grieved on account of it, and call for grace."[4]

"Therefore the royal way and the way of peace in the spirit is to know one's sin and to hate it and thus to fall into the fear of God lest he impute it and permit it to dominate, and at the same time to pray for his mercy, that he would free us from it and not impute it."[5]

"For righteousness and unrighteousness are taken in Scripture very differently from the way in which the philosophers and lawyers interpret them. For they assert it to be a quality of the soul, but in the Scriptures righteousness consists rather in the imputation of God than the essence of the thing itself. He is a possessor of righteousness, not who only has a certain quality, nay rather, he is altogether a sinner and unjust, but whom God on account of the confession of his unrighteousness and his imploring mercifully reputes the righteousness of God

[1] Ibid. 281.4.   [2] Ibid. 281.5.   [3] Ibid. 281.11.
[4] Ibid. 282.11.   [5] Ibid. 283.7.

and wills to regard as just in his presence. Thus we are all born and die in iniquity, i.e. unrighteousness. We are just by the sole reputation of the merciful God by faith (sola autem reputatione miserentis Dei per fidem verbi ejus justi sumus).[1]

Luther's doctrine of justification in these lectures is summarized in his famous phrase, "always a sinner, always just" (semper peccator, semper justus).[2] This does indeed draw attention to his doctrine of the "whole man": the whole person is at the same time, in judgment to condemnation by virtue of his own intrinsic character, and yet, through the Righteousness of God embraced by faith in Christ, in a right relation with God.

But if we would do justice to the richness of Luther's thought we must turn to an expansion of this formula, "always a sinner, always a penitent, always just" ("semper peccator, semper penitens, semper justus").[3] There is an important group of passages which stress the dynamic character of justification.

There is a progress in the Christian life, but it is a progress in faith. "Progress is not by sight, but always into a clearer faith . . . 'from faith to faith,' always by believing more and more so that 'he that is just, is justified hitherto.'"[4]

The last phrase, "qui justus est, justificetur adhuc," is a quotation from Rev. 22[11] which has special significance for Luther, and he makes recurrent use of it.[5] Another sentence to which he keeps returning is the saying of St. Bernard that when we begin not to want to be better, we cease to be good.[6]

"For only Christ is just and has righteousness, but we are always being justified so far (adhuc) and we are in justification."[7]

Thus Luther speaks of our being justified "more and more" (magis et magis),[8] and he affirms the continual progress of the Church.

"Wherefore the whole life of the new people, the faithful people, the spiritual people is nothing else . . . than to seek and ask to be justified even unto the point of death, never to rest, never to have apprehended

---

[1] W.A. 56.287.16.
[2] The phrase is the motto of Strohl's " Évolution de Luther," 4.
[3] W.A. 56.442.17.   [4] W.A. 56.173.9.
[5] W.A. 56.259.14. " All just works are preparatory, if done in grace, to the following progress of justification, according to the saying ' Qui justus est, justificetur adhuc '."
[6] W.A. 56.239.14. " For this life is passed in a state, not of possessing, but of seeking God, always seeking and always looking for him, i.e. seeking again and again . . . for not the man who begins to seek, but he who perseveres and seeks ' until the end,' shall be saved. . . . For he who does not progress in the way of God, goes backwards. . . . And when we begin not to want to be better, we cease to be good, as St. Bernard has it."
[7] W.A. 56.49.22.
[8] W.A. 56.254.29 and 443.6 : 446.5.

. . but always to expect a righteousness dwelling outside themselves thus far (adhuc) always themselves thus far living and being in sins." [1]

But the most striking passage is that at Rom. 12². "Be ye transformed."

"This is said about progress. For it is said to those who now begin to be Christians, whose life is not static (in quiescere) but in movement, from good to better, as a sick man moves from sickness into health, as the Lord shows in the half-dead man taken into the care of the Good Samaritan." [2]

This is immediately followed by a further citation of the St. Bernard quotation, and the words:

"For it is no use for a tree to be living, to blossom, unless fruit comes from the blossom." [3]

He then takes the Aristotelian gradation of "not being," becoming, being, action, passion, and of matter, form, operation, passion and applies this to man and to his justification.

"Man is always in not being, in becoming, in being, always in privation, in potency, in act, always in sin, in justification, in righteousness, i.e. always a sinner, always penitent, always just (semper peccator, semper penitens, semper justus)." [4]

"For because he repents, he becomes just from being unjust. Therefore repentance is a medium between unrighteousness and righteousness. And thus he is in sin as a 'terminus a quo' and in righteousness as a 'terminus ad quem.' If therefore we are always repenting, we are always sinners, and yet at the same time we are just and are justified, partly sinners, partly just, i.e. nothing save penitents ('partim peccatores, partim justi, i.e. nihil nisi penitentes')." [5]

With these passages may be compared earlier citations in which we showed how Luther makes use of the Augustinian figure of Christ as the Good Samaritan,[6] and the mediaeval figure of the Christian as a sick man, and a convalescent who is gradually healed.[7]

At Rom. 3[7] Luther uses a more original comparison. He says that the Righteousness of God is to be shown in three ways. First, when he punishes the unjust, and thus human injustice proclaims his own ineffable Righteousness. Second, when our injustice is placed beside

---

[1] W.A. 56.264.15 : also 259.18.   [2] W.A. 56.441.14.
[3] Ibid. 22.   [4] W.A. 56.442.15.
[5] W.A. 56.442.17. The expression "partim . . . partim" does not contradict Luther's conception of the "whole man."
[6] Hamel says that, although Luther employs this Augustinian figure, the emphasis is different in Luther. Luther's emphasis is much more on Christ as the Good Samaritan, Augustine concentrates on the Christian as the sick and wounded man.
[7] W.A. 56.70.23. "Deus in Christo regenerat hominem generatum sanatque vitiatum a reatu statim, ab infirmitate paulatim." Also 235.37 : 272.12.

his righteousness and his appears beautiful in comparison with our ugliness. Third, when he justifies us.[1]

Luther likens God in this matter to some skilled master craftsman of the Middle Ages. He can demonstrate his skill in these three ways. First, when he points out the defects in the work of his own bungling apprentices and chides them with irrefutable arguments. Second, when his own superb workmanship is set beside theirs, and it becomes apparent by the comparison that his is the work of a master, and theirs but botched and clumsy. But the third, and the best way in which the master can demonstrate his skill, is when he gives it away, when he imparts his own skilled mysteries, the tricks of the trade, to his own workmen, so that they themselves possess the perfection of his craft. And this, says Luther, is best of all, for it shows his "benevolence and humanity." "And so the just God is effectively laudable in us, because he makes us like himself." [2]

These passages represent an integral part of Luther's arguments. They are in no wise to be discounted as a mere remnant of orthodoxy, which Luther would soon abandon, or was in process of abandoning for a purely external and antinomian doctrine of imputation, with no real belief in sanctification. The thought of the transformation of the Christian life through the power of faith, and of the Holy Ghost lay deep in Luther's Biblical material, and in Augustine, and indeed in all his authorities. But we have seen that Luther develops this theme, expounds and illustrates it with figures of speech which are his own. Moreover, we must set beside them other passages in which he speaks of the disciplined ardour of the Christian life.

"And so sin is left in the spiritual man, for the exercise of grace, for the humiliation of pride, and for the repression of presumption, which if a man does not sedulously study to expel, without doubt he has now, even if he commit no further sins, that for which he may be condemned. For we are not called to a life of ease (non enim ad ocium vocati sumus), but to labour against passions which would not be without guilt (for they are truly sins and damnable indeed) unless the mercy of God did not impute them. But he does not impute them only to those who fight agressively against their vices, invoking the grace of God. Wherefore let him who comes to confession not suppose he can lay down his burdens and live quietly, but let him know that with the

---

[1] W.A. 56.221.15, " quando nos ex nobis justificari non possumus, et ipsum accedimus ut ipse nos justos faciat confitentes, quod peccatum exuperare non valeamus. Hoc facit quando verba ejus credimus : per tale enim credere nos justificat, i.e. justos reputat. Unde dicitur Justitia fidei et Justitia Dei effective."

[2] W.A. 56.220-2. Also W.A. 56.227.2, " Justificat . . . in verbo suo, dum nos tales facit."

burden laid down, God's warfare is on, and he takes on another burden for God against the Devil and his own domestic vices." [1]

Thus the initial movement of repentance, "accusatio sui," humility, faith is accompanied by a movement within justification, a growth and a progress in the Christian life which is never complete in this life, but is consummated at the resurrection. It is evident that we are not concerned with some doctrinaire plan of salvation, but with the turning of living men to the living God.

Karl Holl, in a fine and justly famous essay, showed that Luther's teaching in his "Romans" is not to be conceived along the lines of Melanchthonian orthodoxy, in terms of an exclusively forensic notion of Justification and "imputation." [2] He paid due attention to the passages we have been considering, but he drew from them the conclusion that for Luther justification involved not merely a "declaring righteous," but also a "making righteous." "To declare righteous and to make righteous (Rechtfertigung und Gerechtmachung) are inwardly connected as means and end. One and the same divine will embraces the whole of his action on men." [3]

Holl's strong ethical emphasis was perhaps a necessary reply to the attacks of Denifle and others who portrayed Luther as an antinomian who sought to undermine morality. His essay is a masterly survey of the material. He stresses throughout the divine initiative and activity in Luther's doctrine. "The whole new life from beginning to end is exclusively God's work." [4]

None the less, the conception of Luther's doctrine as involving a "making righteous" in Holl (and also in Seeberg) has been the subject of devastating criticism from modern German and Scandinavian theologians. "God," said Holl, "puts the sinner in a right relationship with Himself out of sheer mercy: that he does this, is a miracle . . . but he can do this without compromising His holiness. For exactly as he guarantees man fellowship with Himself, he creates the conditions whereby to raise him up, and to drive out his sinful nature." [5] "As the great artist sees the finished statue in the rough marble, so God sees already in the sinner, whom he justifies, the righteous man that he will make of him." [6]

---

[1] W.A. 56.350.5. Luther insists on the need for prayer, discipline and penitence. " Instanter orandum, instanter discendum, instanter operandum, castigandum, donec ista vetustas eradicetur et fiat novitas in voluntate. Non enim dabitur gratia sine ista agricultura suiipsius." W.A. 56.257.28.
[2] Holl. Luther, III. Die Rechtfertigungslehre in Luthers Vorlesung über den Römerbrief mit besonderer Rücksicht auf die Frage der Heilsgewissheit.
[3] Ibid. 123.   [4] Ibid. 119.
[5] Ibid. 128.
[6] Ibid. 125.

Thus for Holl, Justification is a proleptic, analytic judgment.[1] The weakness of this is that despite Holl's tribute to it, it seems to diminish the element of wonder and miracle, the paradox that the Holy God receives sinners, here and now, on the ground of the Righteousness declared in Jesus Christ.

A more formidable criticism is that this lets in the Catholic doctrine of justification as a "making righteous" by a back door, since the new life of the Christian is a growth into a real righteousness of his own, given to him by God, and this becomes the real continuing ground of his standing with God, not in the end different from the Augustinian notion that "God crowns his own gifts" and the Catholic doctrine of "Faith formed by love."

Prenter adds that the weakness of Holl and Seeberg's exposition is that it sets the doctrine in an idealist perspective.[2] If justification is a proleptic judgment, then the whole process of justification is set under the sign of the Law, and though Holl and Seeberg talk in Protestant terms, they seem to make a pietistic identification of the "new man" in Christ with the "converted man."

It is true that Luther speaks of growth, and of the sanctification of the sinner, but his growth from baptism to death in this world is "semper peccator, semper penitens, semper justus." On the one hand, he is a sinner, and his own righteousness is under condemnation: on the other hand, again and again he turns to the righteousness of Christ (justitia aliena). In this life he is "flesh"—"the old man," and "spirit"—"the new man," but there is progress in this Christian life for the old man is disappearing. But this progress is not growth into a righteousness of one's own on the ground of which man stands "coram Deo," but a progress in faith and hope and love, a dwelling in the Righteousness of Christ, through faith, in the power of the Holy Ghost.

It is of course undeniable that Luther speaks of the transformed life of the Christian. The images of the sick man, of the master craftsman, the fight against evil, the constant use of "proficere, non stare," and of Rev. 22[11], "qui justus est, justificetur adhuc," are reminders that the Christian progress is by faith in Christ which is the sole continuing ground of Christian existence. Luther's famous "Progress, that means always beginning afresh (semper a novo incipere)," means that the Christian man has continual recourse to the righteousness of the Living Christ.

"See now, what was said above, that at the same time the Saints, while they are just, are sinners. They are just because they believe in

---

[1] For A. Ritschl, justification is a synthetic judgment. See Holl, 125, n. 1.
[2] Prenter. Spiritus Creator, 110 ff.

Christ, whose righteousness covers them and is imputed to them, sinners, however, because they do not fulfil the law and they are not without concupiscence. But they are like sick people in the care of a doctor, who are really ill, but only begin to be healed or made whole in hope, i.e. becoming well, for whom the presumption that they were already well would be most harmful, for it would cause a relapse." [1]

There are two features in the doctrine of Justification itself which need to be noted. What we have called the dynamic quality of Luther's doctrine of Justification is not the description of a process only. It does justice to what modern Biblical theology describes as the eschatological element in this doctrine. Justification must involve, as Dr. Vincent Taylor has said, "An eschatological act brought into the present, which has meaning for a man, here and now." [2]

In some sense God's final verdict upon men has been given in his own saving intervention in Jesus Christ. This righteousness may be apprehended by a man here and now, by faith. As long as he persists in that dynamic relationship (Luther's "semper timendi"—"semper pavidi" against the assurance of a false security is to be remembered), he need not fear the final judgment, and he has the full, joyful assurance of faith. [3]

There is a further difficulty arising from the nature of man. Here on earth he is a stranger and a pilgrim (homo viator). And who is man? Is he the baby in the cradle, or the man who at the end of the day will pass from faith to sight and stand in the presence of God? And how does each moment of his changing existence relate to his beginning and his end? It is the necessity to apply eschatological concepts to "homo viator" which blurs the doctrine of the Church and sacraments, and also the doctrine of justification. Thus the doctrine of justification cannot be made smooth and tidy. The tendency of later orthodoxies, Catholic and Protestant, is to abandon eschatology and to map out the various moments of a process of salvation. It is not the least valuable feature of Luther's discussions of justification that he lived before the development of the Protestant "ordo salutis." [4]

This does not mean that Luther is consistent and coherent throughout these lectures. He can still speak in terms of the older technical theology of grace.

Thus he can speak of works preparatory to justification.

[1] W.A. 56.347.8 ff.
[2] " Forgiveness and Reconciliation," 1941, 36.
[3] On the doctrine of the assurance of faith, see Holl, above. And for a comparison with Augustinian and mediaeval teaching, G. Ljunggren, Zur Geschichte der christlichen Heilsgewissheit. Göttingen, 1920.
[4] It is perhaps .an unavoidable weakness of A. S. Wood's useful essays; S.J.T., 1950, 1 and 2, that he deals with justification and sanctification in successive phases.

"By the works of the law are not meant those things which are done preparatory to acquiring justification . . . for whoever by such things disposes himself towards justification, is already in some way just. For it is a great part of righteousness to will to be just . . . nay, unless all the just did such works that they might be justified more and more (justificentur magis et magis) none would be just. Therefore those works are good, because they do not trust in them, but by those things they prepare themselves for justification, in which alone they trust to find their future righteousness. But those who work like this are not under the law, for they desire grace and hate the fact that they are sinners." [1]

The passage ends "ergo sola gratia justificat." [2]

It is clear, however, that he has given the older terminology a new setting, and this is even more evident when he comes to speak of "first grace" and of "co-operating grace."

"For to our first grace as to glory we always are to hold ourselves passively as a woman to her conception. For we also are the betrothed of Christ. So before grace we pray and ask, yet when grace comes and the soul is impregnated with the spirit, it is needful that it should neither pray nor work, but only suffer. Which is certainly a hard thing to be performed and afflicts one severely. For the soul without the act of understanding and willing to be, is led into darkness, and is as though going to perdition and annihilation, which it vehemently flees." [3]

This passive attitude towards God's initiative is true not only of the beginning, but of the growth of the Christian life.

"For I call 'first grace' not that which is infused in the beginning of conversion, as in baptism, contrition, compunction, but all subsequent and new grace which we call a degree and increase of grace." [4]

We observed Luther's triumphant christological reference when treating Rom. 8, and we have noticed some striking observations at Rom. 12[2]. Between them lie the long discussions of Predestination and Free Will. Luther could not have avoided such discussion, for it lay immediately in his path. What he has to say about Free Will and Predestination at this point is, with one important qualification, what he will say, ten years later, in his famous controversy with Erasmus.

Luther stands midway between the long mediaeval discussion of these problems and the Protestant controversies which were to occupy the next century and a half. He owes much to St. Augustine, but he owes something, too, to the Nominalist tradition. With St. Augustine,

---

[1] W.A. 56.254.19. [2] Ibid. 255.19.
[3] W.A. 56. 379.1. [4] W.A. 56.379.10.

he stresses the grace and glory of God, and the bondage of the human will apart from grace, in the things pertaining to salvation. But with the later schoolmen he is concerned for the Divine Liberty, for the God who is "debtor to nobody" (a scholastic phrase twice quoted in this part of Luther's Romans), and he has the Ockhamist distrust of secondary causes. Above all, he is concerned for the immutability of God, for with this is bound up the faithfulness of the divine promises. Luther has a horror of contingency, where chance or the unpredictable spontaneity of the human will might mock the purposes of God. As we shall see, he believed this problem needed careful handling, for he knew in his own experience and in that of others, that speculation on such subjects might easily lead to terrible despair.

The mediaeval thinkers had built up a framework of elaborate distinctions, since they had to acknowledge the divine prescience and the divine sovereignty while leaving full scope for the doctrine of merits and of the freedom of the will inseparably bound with it. Luther brusquely rejects such subtleties.

"Whom he foreknew, them he also predestinated . . . not because he foresaw their merits." [1]

He rejects the familiar mediaeval distinction between "consequent necessity" and "necessity of the consequence."

"Our theologians indeed . . . say that the elect are necessarily saved but by necessity of the consequence, not consequent necessity. But these are only empty words, especially when by consequent contingency they wish to understand, or at all events, they give an occasion of understanding that salvation stands or falls with our will. For thus I once understood the matter. But this "consequent contingency" is irrelevant to the matter." [2]

"For there is no contingency with God 'simpliciter,' but only in our sight (coram nobis). Since even the leaf of a tree does not fall to the ground without the will of the Father. Thus therefore it is of the essence of things, that our times are in his hands." [3]

Luther, like St. Paul, begins with the positive side of this doctrine, the fact that our salvation is grounded in the unfailing purpose of God.

"All these things argue that predestination and the sureness of election and not the righteousness of the human will is the cause of salvation." [4]

"For now when he says, 'Who shall accuse? Who shall condemn? Who shall separate?' he shows that the elect are not saved contingently but necessarily." [5]

---

[1] W.A. 56.83.27.   [2] W.A. 56.382.21.   [3] W.A. 56.383.19.
[4] W.A. 56.89.15.   [5] W.A. 56.381.27.

"Not by our merits, but by sheer election and his unchangeable will . . . by his unchangeable love are we saved. And thus he proves through all these things, not our will, but his inflexible and sure will of predestination. For how would it be possible for a man to break through all these things, in which a thousand times he would despair, unless the eternal and fixed love of God led him through them, and the Spirit himself by his presence helped us and made intercession for us with groanings which cannot be uttered?" [1]

Luther undertakes to do three things, to produce scriptural proofs for his beliefs, to answer objections, and to console those who are frightened by them.

The scriptural examples are those of the calling of Isaac and of Ishmael, Esau and Jacob. Then John 10[28], 13[18], 6[44], Ps. 113, 2 Tim. 2[19], and the story of Pharaoh and the Exodus. The objections Luther declares to come from the wisdom of the flesh (prudentia carnis). There are, first, those who are always asking "Why?" and to those Luther must answer, with St. Paul, "O man, who art thou who repliest to God?"

There are those others who complain that man is given Free Will with which to merit, or not to merit, salvation.

"Free Will as constituted apart from Grace has simply no faculty for righteousness, but is necessarily in sins. Therefore Augustine rightly says in his book 'Contra Julianum,' 'it is a bound rather than a free will (servum potius quam liberum arbitrium).' For it is when it has received grace that it really becomes free, at all events in respect of salvation. For it has always a certain natural freedom but in respect of those things which are in its own power and which are below, but not in the things which are above, since it is held captive in sins, and then cannot choose the good according to God." [2]

But, second objection, does not God will all men to be saved? Again Luther turns to scripture.

"Christ did not die absolutely for all, for he said 'This is my blood which is shed for many'—he does not say, for all, 'to the remission of sins.'" [3]

But does not this mean that men sin by necessity? Luther distinguishes between the necessity which comes from being left in the consequences of sin, and the necessity of "coaction." Nobody is forced to sin, or sins against his will.

"For he who hates sin is outside sin, and one of the elect, but those whom God hardens, these are they to whom he gives voluntarily to

---

[1] W.A. 56.382.4. [2] W.A. 56.385.15.
[3] W.A. 56.385.29.

O

wish to be and stay in sin and to love iniquity. Such are necessarily in sin with a necessity of immutability, but not of coaction." [1]

Then is it God's fault that they are as they are? Again, Luther turns to St. Paul, "thus God wills and such willing is not unjust, for all things are his." [2] God "owes nobody anything" (nulli aliquid debet—an Ockhamist phrase).[3] Thus St. Paul, at the end of Rom. 11[35].

Luther says that to the "prudence of the flesh," this doctrine leads to blasphemies, but to the elect who have the "prudence of the spirit" it brings "delight with ineffable joy." But here Luther is aware of his third promise, to speak some consolation to those who find the doctrine of predestination a torment and a temptation. "Tentatio de predestinatione" is indeed for Luther to be numbered among the most serious of "Anfechtungen." Luther knows that this doctrine has special difficulty for those who begin to leave the "prudence of the flesh" and who are progressing in the "prudence of the spirit." This doctrine is full of comfort if it is rightly received, for it teaches men to despair of themselves, and this godly fear is a good sign.

"Thus if anyone is too much afraid that he is not one of the elect, or is tempted about his own election, let him give thanks for such fear, and rejoice to be afraid, knowing with confidence that God cannot lie who says 'the sacrifice of God is a broken, i.e. desperate, spirit.' " [4]

This brings Luther to an important part of his teaching on predestination, the thought of the "resignatio ad infernum." Luther believed that the soul is not finally humbled before God until it acknowledges God's righteous judgment, and is content with his will, even if this involves the soul's own condemnation to hell. Luther's teaching in his "Romans" about "resignation to hell" is yet another example of his habit of employing common technical terms and adapting their notions to his own uses. He had begun to study Tauler at this time, and the parallels have often been pointed out between what he has to say about "resignation" and Tauler's teaching. Yet the roots of Luther's teaching can be found in his "Psalms" before he knew Tauler at all. The development of his theology in the next years, as a "Theology of the Cross," was to have certain common traits with that of the German mystics, and to recede into the background of his mature theology. Yet even here the differences are important. Holl has

---

[1] W.A. 56.386.2.   [2] W.A. 56.386.9.
[3] On Luther's doctrine of Predestination here, and other mediaeval systems, see Rondet, Gratia Christi. Paris, 1946, ch. 8. Ph. Boehner. Wm. of Ockham's " Tractatus de Predestinatione." New York, 1945. E. Gilson. Introduction à l'étude de Saint Augustin. Paris, 1949, 185 ff. P. A. Vignaux. Justification et Prédestination. L. Baudry. La Querelle des Futurs Contingents. Paris, 1950. E. Wolf. Staupitz und Luther, 69 ff., 169 ff.
[4] W.A. 56.387.20.

shown that Luther is seriously concerned with the righteous judgment of God, and that for him "resignation" is a grim, desperate business, taken more seriously than by the mystics. In his fine essay on this theme, Vogelsang shows that for Luther the heart and climax of the doctrine is christological, the thought of the grim obedience of the Son of God on our behalf.[1]

But there are two features of this doctrine in Luther which have been less observed. First, the "resignation to hell" is the final and logical conclusion of the whole argument of this epistle, which was, as Luther said, to destroy and overthrow all human righteousness. The movement, sin—accusation of self—humiliation—humility finds its end when the sinner acknowledges the justice of his own condemnation; when he is prepared to accept this condemnation, then he has indeed been stripped of his own righteousness. Second, as we shall see, Luther regards this resignation as a supreme work of grace within the soul as a final, drastic surgery which God applies for the extirpation of our pride. We cannot but set this doctrine against that scholastic teaching which Luther repeatedly attacks in this commentary, the doctrine that a man may make an act of love to God, from his own natural powers. On the contrary, Luther shows a real love to God means the end of all self-love, and an act of such love it is when the soul is wholly resigned to the will of God, even though this should involve condemnation and pain. The "resignation to hell" shows Luther's teaching at the opposite pole from that of the Nominalists, from that deadly human self-righteousness, the extirpation of which is the theme of the Epistle to the Romans.

Luther expounds three degrees of signs of election. (i) Those who are content with the will of God, and do not murmur against it, but who trust they are among the elect, and do not wish to be damned. (ii) Better, those who are resigned and content, or at least desire to be content, even if God did not wish their salvation but put them among the reprobate. (iii) The most extreme, those who really resign themselves to hell for the sake of the will of God, as perhaps many do in the hour of death. These last are truly purged of the "prudence of the flesh."[2]

Thus "those who really love God with a filial love and a love of friendship (amicitiae) which does not come from nature, but only from

---

[1] Holl. Luther, 150 ff. W. von Loewenich. Luthers Theologia Crucis, 210 ff. Vogelsang. Angefochtene Christus, 68 ff. E. Wolf. Staupitz und Luther, 161, 203.
[2] It may be asked whether the whole movement of " accusatio sui " to " humilitas " and " resignatio " can be included, according to Nygren's theory under a doctrine of " agape " ? There seems point here to Carlson's criticism. Re-interpretation of Luther, 188.

the Holy Spirit . . . freely offer themselves to the will of God even for hell and for eternal death if God so will, so that his will may be fully done. Thus they seek no things of their own. And yet as they themselves so purely conform to the will of God it is impossible that they should remain in hell, for it is impossible that they should remain outside of God who have cast themselves so utterly upon his will. For he wills what God wills. Therefore he pleases God. If he please, then he is beloved. If he is beloved, then he is saved." [1]

But it is asked, whether in fact God ever asks such a thing, that a man should resign himself to hell and to damnation or to be anathema from Christ? Luther replies that in many people the love of concupiscence is so deep, that it needs to be extirpated.

"But it is not extirpated save by the infusion of superabundant grace through this most difficult resignation." [2]

"And it seems to me that this is the pain of purgatory that the soul in its imperfect love is horrified at this resignation until it makes it and is content to be anathema from God." [3]

And then comes the striking christological reference:

"For even Christ was damned and abandoned more than all the saints. And his sufferings were not, as some imagine, light and easy. For really and truly he offered himself to eternal damnation to God the Father for us. And in his human nature he behaved in no other way than as a man eternally damned to hell. On account of such love to God, God at once raised him from the dead and hell and thus devoured hell. Whence it behoves all the saints to imitate him, some more, some less." [4]

This leads Luther to an allied thought which he was to develop in the following years as an integral part of his "Theology of the Cross," the thought that the Christian shares the sufferings of Christ, and that therefore there is a hiddenness and contradiction about all his life on earth.

"For our good is hidden, and that so deeply that it is hidden under its contrary. Thus our life is hidden under death, our joy under our hatred, glory under shame, salvation under perdition, the kingdom under exile, heaven under hell, wisdom under foolishness, righteousness under sin, strength under infirmity." [5]

We may summarize Luther's use of this doctrine in four points. First, it is congruous with Luther's whole picture of the movement of justification, beginning with the recognition of sin and ending with

---

[1] W.A. 56.391.7. The change from the plural to the singular at the climax of this argument is striking.
[2] W.A. 56.391.22.   [3] W.A. 56.391.29.
[4] W.A. 56.392.7.   [5] W.A. 56.392.28.

acknowledgment of the will of God as a just condemnation, the recognition that salvation of such a sinner must indeed be "mercy all." Second, this is completely opposed to the Nominalist doctrine that a man may make an act of love to God from within his own natural spiritual resources. Luther knew very well the qualifications with which the Nominalists hedged this doctrine, but he knows that they are inconclusive since any real act of love to God must be free and unconstrained, and this is only possible when the will has been set free by grace. Third, Luther's exposition occurs within his exposition of Paul's discussion of predestination and reprobation in the 9th to 11th chapters of the Epistle to the Romans. But, fourth, this is intended as no mere academic discussion about the possibility of "disinterested Love." as later controversy would conceive it. Luther's interest is intensely practical, for he is concerned with the theme of Predestination as a very serious form of "Anfechtung." Thus his discussion comes to an end with a startling poignancy at Rom. 9^{16}.

"Here I must enter a warning, lest any whose minds have not been purged rush into these speculations and fall into an abyss of horror and despair. Let him first purge the eyes of his heart in meditating on the wounds of Jesus Christ. Nor would I talk about this, did not the order of the lectures and necessity compel me to do so. For this is the very strongest wine and the most perfect and solid food for the perfect. The most advanced theology! . . . But I am as a child who needs milk, not food. Let those who are as I am, do likewise. The wounds of Jesus are safe enough for us." [1]

[1] W.A. 56.400.1.

Chapter

9

LUTHER'S LECTURES ON THE EPISTLE TO THE GALATIANS (1516-17) AND ON THE EPISTLE TO THE HEBREWS (1517-18)

> "A proof worthy of the manly mind of Luther, and compared with which the pretended demonstrations . . . are mischievous underminings of the faith, pleadings fitter for an Old Bailey thieves' counsellor than for a Christian divine. The true evidence of the Bible is the Bible—of Christianity, the living fact of Christianity itself."
>
> S. T. COLERIDGE on Luther's " Table Talk."

THUS far we have concentrated on Luther's theology as reflected in the exclusively theological material of his lectures. It is well to remember that all this time the circle of his influence was widening. In May 1512 he had become sub-prior and regent of studies: from May 1515 he had been district overseer of eleven monasteries, "that is, eleven times prior," involved in an increasing momentum of business affairs, and disciplinary chores. More important, from 1511 he had been preaching, and from 1514 had the wider audience of the parish church. He had now embarked on a career of preaching which was to make him one of the great preachers of his age, or indeed of any time. Von Schubert has warned us against too sharply separating the professor and the preacher, and has pointed out that the class-room became Luther's pulpit and the pulpit the place of teaching.[1] We have seen how Luther's theological studies and religious enquiries went hand-in-hand, and that his exposition of Romans became a timely vehicle for his own hard-won convictions about the Christian life. His characteristic theology is reflected at this time in his correspondence, as two familiar extracts (1516) remind us:

"Therefore, my sweet brother, learn Christ and him crucified: learn to pray to him, despairing of yourself, saying: Thou Lord Jesus

---

[1] H. Von Schubert and K. A. Meissinger. Zu Luthers Vorlesungstätigkeit. (Sitzungsberichte der Heidelberger Akad. d. Wiss. Heidelberg, 1920.)

art my righteousness, but I am thy sin: thou hast taken on thyself what thou wast not, and hast given me what I was not. Beware of aspiring to such purity that you will not wish to seem to yourself, or to be a sinner. For Christ dwells only in sinners. For that reason he . . . descended from heaven that he might dwell among sinners." [1]

"The Cross of Christ is distributed through the whole world, to every one certainly comes his portion. Do you therefore not cast it aside, but rather take it up as a holy relic, kept not in a golden or silver case, but in a golden, that is a gentle and loving heart." [2]

The second extract betrays a growing insistence on the conformity of the Christian with Christ in suffering, and the contradiction of the Christian's existence on earth, the "hidden" character of its true nature. As his teaching on "resignation" in Romans has a common trait with that of Tauler, so this teaching on conformity with Christ in suffering has parallels with the imitation of Christ in the teaching of the "devotio moderna." If we ask how far Luther, at this time, was influenced by the mystics, we must, as Vogelsang says, distinguish between the mysticism of the Victorines which did not influence him, that of the type of St. Bernard which slightly influenced him, and that of the "devotio moderna" with which he had much in common, as he himself avowed in his tribute to Tauler and to the "Theologia Germanica." Their emphasis on "inward religion," and on the personal and egocentric character of sin was congenial to his thought. Yet the thought of a divine spark or seed on "ground of the soul," so dear to the mystics, and the basis of what has been called their "incurable optimism," [3] is a part of scholastic doctrine which in the form of the synteresis, Luther repudiated at this very time. Luther's teaching about conformity with Christ has differences, which are more important than the similarities to the mystics, and it becomes part of his developing theology of the Cross. There is no deep undercurrent of mystical thought expressed in Luther's terminology as there is in the writings of Thomas Müntzer and in some of the first Anabaptists. [4]

In our study of Luther's development we shall continue to concentrate upon his considered academic writings. But in turning to the next series of lectures, let us remember that we are at the watershed of Luther's career. This is the eve of the great, drastic upheaval of the Reformation. By 1517 Luther had made Wittenberg the citadel of a

---

[1] Preserved Smith. Luther's Correspondence, 34. To Spenlein. April 1516.
[2] Ibid. 35. To Leiffer. April 1516.
[3] J. M. Clark. The Great German Mystics. Oxford, 1949, 49.
[4] Miegge. Luetro, 118. H. Bornkamm. Eckhart und Luther. Stuttgart, 1936. Luther und Böhme, 1925. E. Seeberg, Luthers Theologie in ihren Grundzügen, 1950, 26. Thomas Müntzer. Politische Schriften, ed. Hinrichs, 1950.

new method of teaching, a radical simplification of theological studies, involving the displacement of scholasticism and the return to the Bible and the "old Fathers." In February 1517 he sent a series of propositions against the Aristotelians to his friends Trutvetter and Lang at Erfurt. In May he could write of Wittenberg, however, as of a victory already won.

"Our theology and that of St. Augustine are going ahead, and they reign in our University and it is the Lord's doing. Aristotle is gradually going down, perhaps into eternal ruin. It is wonderful how out of favour are the lectures on the Sentences. Nobody can hope for an audience unless he professes this theology, i.e. the Bible or St. Augustine or some doctor of real authority in the Church." [1]

Luther used the occasion of the promotion of his pupil, Franz Gunther, for an all-out attack, in ninety-seven theses, against the teachings of Scotus and Ockham, d'Ailly and Biel.[2] He sent copies to Erfurt and Nuremberg and offered to debate them in those cities. He waited anxiously and eagerly to see if the challenge would be taken up. Nothing came of it.

But when, a few weeks later, he put out ninety-five theses about the practical abuse of indulgences, he fired an explosive train which shook Christendom, and upheaved a world. Luther himself was caught up in a new momentum of events. We shall find evident traces of them in his theology, and in his lectures sandwiched between those fateful journeys and disputations and conferences of 1517-19. But for the moment, we return to the cooling mornings of late October and the familiar lecture-room in Wittenberg, and the normal academic grind of a new term, with its chastening admixture of old and new faces.

Luther lectured on the Epistle to the Galatians between 27th October 1516 and 3rd March 1517. As before, Grünenberg printed the texts, with the wide margins for the notes and comments. But Luther's own copy has not survived. All that remains of his first course of lectures

---

[1] W.A.Br. 1.99.8.
[2] These theses are important for Luther's relation to Nominalism, and show that Luther did not muddle and misunderstand the doctrines he attacked. In a short but valuable sketch, " Sur Luther et Ockham " (Wm. Ockham, 1950, 21 ff.), P. A. Vignaux links them with the fierce marginal notes which Luther made in the new edition of Biel's " Commentary on the Sentences " (1515-16). These notes were published (" Luthers Randbemerkungen zu Gabriel Biels Collectorium in quattuor libros Sententiarum und zu dessen Sacri canonis missio expositio. Lyon 1514," ed. Degering. Weimar, 1933) as a supplement to the Weimar edition in connection with the 450th anniversary of Luther's birth. P. A. Vignaux analyses the background of Luther's Theses, 57 and 94, and shows that what is in debate is not simply Luther's opposition to the Nominalist dialectic of the " potentia absoluta," but a conception of the integrity of nature apart from grace, and despite sin, which is the real fundament of Luther's opposition to the Ockhamist doctrine of man. (Vignaux, 26-7.)

on Galatians is a copy taken down by one of his students, possibly a young Augustinian from Cologne, Augustine Himmel.[1]

Fortunately, at one point, where he had perhaps cut a lecture and made up from a fellow's notes, a passage is repeated, so that there is a check upon his accuracy. The printed version of the lectures (1519), despite its pointed and practical digressions about the new Church struggle, is also some sort of check. On the whole, since Luther seems to have dictated some parts word for word, Dr. Meissinger believed we can come very close to what Luther said, though we lack the valuable additional mass of the preparatory material.

It will not be needful to recapitulate the main line of those doctrines, as we have noted them in lectures on the Psalms and on the Epistle to the Romans. Again, we remember that to some extent Luther's emphasis is conditioned by the material, and that he is perforce more occupied with the question of the Law and Gospel, and with the notion of Christian liberty, while the latter part of the epistle calls forth some explicit and remarkable comments on the nature of Christian love. It is clear, however, that faith is rapidly becoming a master word, which takes into itself the rich complex of associations which, in the "Romans," we traced in the movement, accusatio sui—humility, faith. But here, again, we must let Luther speak. The contradiction between the Righteousness of God, and the condemned righteousness of men, is reflected in the dialectic of Law and Gospel.

"For the Law and the Righteousness of the Law are the shadow and figure of the gospel, and of the righteousness of faith." [2]

Luther rejects the view that "Law" in the Pauline epistles is concerned only with the ceremonial law. It is his perception that, on the contrary, every imperative which stands over and against men as a commandment, including the decalogue itself, is the Law, and that it brings condemnation when men attempt to fulfil it in their own strength, and according to the inward motive.

"When he said 'except by faith' he means all those things which are not faith, and therefore also the works of the decalogue." [3]

"And this is most specially to be noted, that 'works of the Law' in this place (Gal. 2[16]) means not only the ceremonial law, as some wish, but all things, even the decalogue if they are done according to the letter, when they are done without grace are properly called 'works of the law,' ... but the law commands, with terror of penalties or promises of future good, and thus extorts them from the outward man without the agreement of the will. Therefore are they called works of the law, not

[1] W.A. 57 (ed. K. A. Meissinger), VII.   [2] W.A. 57.14.19 (Galatians).
[3] W.A. 57.17.28.

because they are according to the law, but because they are done from the law, by ourselves, but unwillingly." [1]

It is fundamental for Luther that Christ alone has perfectly fulfilled the law, though he never elaborates this doctrine as later classical Protestant orthodoxy was to do.

"For nobody fulfils the law, except Christ, therefore nobody can be justified outside Christ (extra Christum)." [2]

The distinction between the Law and the Gospel is clear, though it has not yet become the powerful dialectic of his mature theology.

"Law and Gospel properly differ in this, that the law preaches what is to be done, or not done, nay rather our commissions and omissions, and by this alone gives knowledge of sin. The gospel on the other hand preaches remission of sins, and the fulfilment of the law already made by Christ (per Christum). Thus the voice of the law is 'Pay what you owe': of the gospel, rather 'Your sins are forgiven' . . . this preaching of the remission of sins is the gospel." [3]

Because of this, it is the Gospel which reveals sin more profoundly than the law.

"Christ in the gospel taught many things, and gave a clearer knowledge of the law, and through this a greater knowledge of sin, so that by so much as grace is sought more ardently, and bestowed more largely, and served more diligently, by so much sin is more profoundly known." [4]

The law was instituted that it might bring men to knowledge of their sin, and of their need of salvation.

"The law was not put into our hand, that we should fulfil it, but rather into the hand of Christ who was to come, that he himself should fulfil it. Wherefore it was given, not that it might justify, but rather that it might the more convict sinners, and that it should require the hand of a Mediator." [5]

It is this righteousness of the law which a man sets up against the saving righteousness of Christ.

"Thus it is a terrible thing to set up one's own righteousness, for this is 'to be transferred' from Christ and to fall from the grace and truth of God." [6]

Thus it is that Christ came to establish the law by making men aware of sin, and at the same time, fulfilled the law itself, and made possible the destruction of sin through faith.

"For sins are only destroyed when the law is fulfilled, which happens

[1] W.A. 57.69.1.   [2] W.A. 57.37.10.
[3] W.A. 57.59.18.   [4] W.A. 57.60.10.
[5] W.A. 57.84.14.   [6] W.A. 57.56.14.

through the righteousness of faith. Therefore by faith the law is established and sins are destroyed . . . therefore whoso shall say that the law is fulfilled, by this he destroys and takes away sins, for he says they no longer exist (ea nusquam esse?). But this he does who preaches faith in Christ. Whoso says that the law is still to be fulfilled, by this both revives and rebuilds sins, which the other destroyed." [1]

This brings Luther back to the scholastic argument which he attacked so vehemently in his "Romans."

"Some make a distinction and say that it is one thing to act against the law, and another thing to go against the intention of the law: whoso acts against the law, they say, commits sin, but who really acts against the intention of the law does not sin, but comes short in a certain manner. These are human comments and to be removed as far as possible from the Holy Scriptures. For they prove their case in this way: if men were held to the intention of the law, it would follow that existing apart from grace they would sin without intermission while not killing, not committing adultery, not stealing, etc. O most brilliant argument! But the reply to that is: nobody sins outside grace by not killing, not committing adultery, etc., but he sins within himself, in his heart by his hatred and his lust, which are forbidden with such commandments . . . yet without such hatred and lust nobody can remain, unless he is cured by grace. Therefore it is not the intention of the law, that it should be kept in grace, as though to have grace itself were a new kind of exaction beyond the law: but the law is intended to be kept. But since it cannot be kept without grace, thus it forces us to seek grace." [2]

Luther continues:

"The rude and uninformed exposition of those who only understand the ceremonial or figurative law as though moral things and the decalogue were 'from faith.' But truly all law is the law of death, wrath and sin, insofar as it is the letter teaching, but not assisting, and thus it is not 'of faith.' For faith takes away sin, wrath and death, because it justifies, brings peace and makes alive in Christ who is made to us righteousness, peace and life. Wherefore whoso believes in him, does not sin, is not put to confusion, shall never die: and even if he dies, he lives, and if he sins, he is justified, and if he is put to confusion, he is at peace. Thus it follows that faith is to be distinguished from the law." [3]

The theme of the law leads to the theme of faith, faith which is always closely associated with the object of faith, God in Christ.

[1] W.A. 57.72.11. [2] W.A. 57.80.6.
[3] W.A. 57.80.21.

The liberty of a Christian man is that which is "through faith in Christ, who is bound to no works." [1]

On Gal. 2[16] he writes:

"A wonderful and new definition of righteousness, which is generally described as 'Righteousness is that virtue which renders to each his own.' But this says 'Righteousness is faith in Jesus Christ . . . a man does not live because he is just, but he is just because he believes . . . whence it follows that the just man does not render to each his own, out of his own resources, but from another, that is from Christ, who alone is so just that he gives to each what is due, nay rather all things are owed to him. Thus whoso believes in Christ not only satisfies all requirements, but does them in such a way that all things are owing to him, since by faith he is made one with Christ.' " [2]

"Since faith is universal justice, it follows that all sin is reduced to infidelity, which does not believe in Christ.' " [3]

Thus Luther affirms that faith really includes all the beatitudes since all the hopes of a Christian are laid up in Christ.

"From which it follows that faith is itself poverty of spirit, meekness, purity of heart, peace, patience, mourning, hunger and thirst after righteousness, and all the beatitudes since it involves the death of the old man, and the life of the new, as he says 'I live, yet not I, Christ liveth in me.' " [4]

Luther raises the objection, "Then are we not free? There are no more good things to be done, or bad things left undone, for faith in Christ and his righteousness are sufficient?"

He replies:

"They are sufficient indeed, but the faith of none is so great that it cannot be, nor ought to be increased. Thus for its increase good works are to be done, and bad ones avoided. For faith is a thing of the widest extent and differing with many degrees, until all things are perfectly despised save Christ. Which even if it were perfectly accomplished, which rarely happens, there would still be good works to be done, not that anything should be sought by them, but that the Lord might be served with the utmost freedom, that Christ might be his sufficiency, and there should be no obedience save the will of Christ his Lord." [5]

Again, Luther's recurrent theme that the will of God had to be performed from spontaneous, loving obedience.

"It is impossible for this love in man to be born from Adam, for he is

[1] W.A. 57.13.12.   [2] W.A. 57.69.15.
[3] W.A. 57.70.5.   [4] W.A. 57.70.15.
[5] W.A. 57.70.26.

'prone to evil, doing good with difficulty' and by this, empty of love of good. The works of the law are not therefore bad since they are imposed by God: but they are to be rejected, because confidence was put in them and the end of the law. So in this way fasts, prayers, vigils, labours, works, in the worship of God are such various works of the law, nor can anybody be justified by them: but yet they are so needful that righteousness cannot stand inwardly, unless these things are done outwardly, especially in the time of youth, and in the status of a beginner. Thus the whole active life 'troubles Martha about many things' and prepares the rest of Mary, i.e. the interior life. . . . thus salvation and righteousness may not be had without works, or because of works, but with works, with this distinction that by so much as the interior life progresses, by so much outward works are diminished." [1]

"For righteousness is twofold, of flesh and spirit, figure and thing signified, shadow and truth, exterior and interior, old and new, works and faith, servile and free, forced by fear, and led by joy, drawn by love of things, led by the love of words . . . 'of faith,' i.e. not of works, that is, we are, we live, and we act, and thus acting we expect the hope of that spiritual righteousness." [2]

Thus faith is closely allied with the work of grace.

"For this grace is spiritual and hidden, because it removes sin, and covers the most secret offences, but by itself it brings in the attacks of men, the flesh and the devil. For when the grace of God is given to a man, at once the wrath of the devil is roused, nay rather of the man against his own self . . . therefore while grace persists wrath at once follows and then war, war without and peace within." [3]

There is one important reference to what we have called Luther's doctrine of the "whole man," at Gal. 3⁹.

"This shows most plainly, that 'flesh' is not only the sensual man, or sensuality with its lusts, etc., but everything which is outside the grace of Christ. For it is certain that he says that the Galatians have ended up in the flesh, not because they are given up to luxuries and feastings, but because they seek the works and righteousness of the law." [4]

In a remarkable comment on Gal. 4¹⁹ on "Christ being formed in us," Luther says:

"For the life of the Christian is not of himself, but of Christ living in him . . . it is to be noted that it is true that Christ is not exactly 'formed' in anybody 'personaliter,' and thus the gloss is correct which says that faith in Christ or the knowledge of Christ should be taken

[1] W.A. 57.68.16.   [2] W.A. 57.98.11.
[3] W.A. 57.55.1.   [4] W.A. 57.77.18.

here for 'Christ' . . . but beware most carefully lest this be taken as a kind of speculative knowledge, with which Christ is known as a kind of object . . . for this is dead and even the demons have this . . . but it is to be taken practically, as life, essence and experience of the example and image of Christ, that Christ may be no longer an object of our knowledge, but rather we are the object of his knowledge." [1]

Luther here turns to the great Pauline passives, which stress the divine initiative and action.

"For thus the apostle in the briefest compass teaches that our knowledge is that we are known of God. . . . And as the instrument of the craftsman when he works, is rather acted upon by the workman, how much more the creature when he acts, is acted upon by the creator!" [2]

As in "Romans" Luther stresses the growth and movement of the Christian life.

"From which it is evident that the Christian life does not consist in being, but in becoming, not in victory, but in the fight, not in righteousness, but in justification, not in comprehending, but in stretching forward, not in purity, but in purification." [3]

There are three stresses especially called forth by the material of Galatians. The first is the emphasis on the ultimate unity and equality of all believers in Christ. Thus the gloss on Gal. 3[28].

"These 'persons' make an outward difference, but inwardly in the spirit there is no difference and you are one person." [4]

"Thus there is neither cleric nor layman, nor status of this or that order, not he who prays nor he who reads, but to all these things he is indifferent, doing or not doing as these things shall help or take away from charity." [5]

"For 'person' is properly speaking only 'face' or 'countenance' or 'mask' . . . and is that quality or quantity by which a man may be considered from without, and the meaning of 'God is no respecter of persons' is that he does not regard who, what kind, how much. What then does he regard? The answer is: the heart." [6]

"Therefore there is neither priest nor layman, canon nor vicar, rich nor poor, Benedictine, Carthusian, Friar Minor or Augustinian, for it is not a question of this or that status, degree or order. All these things are such that they do not make a believer if they are present, nor an infidel, if they are absent, nay, they much more frequently hinder the Christian man when they are present, as is evident in this century of moral landslide, where seas and rivers of the most arrogant hypocrites have flooded in glorying in their professions and bandying words against one another with incredible fury." [1]

The second and third stresses are closely linked, the theme of Christian liberty, as being the law of love.

"For Liberty in Christ is bound to no outward work, but holds itself free and indifferent, save where brotherly love requires as Rom. 13, 'Owe nothing, save to love one another.'" [2]

"'Liberty' is in this place to be understood theologically, as is also 'servitude' and these are duplicated according to the double nature of men. Liberty of the spirit or of the new man is the loosening from the old man, or from the servitude of sin. Liberty of the flesh or of the old man is contrariwise a loosening from the new man and the service of righteousness. The servitude of the spirit is the liberty of the spirit itself, and the servitude of the flesh is the liberty of the flesh itself. Nor do they differ in respect of the 'terminus a quo' and 'ad quem' because it is called liberty in respect of sin from which it is set free, and the service of righteousness to which it leads." [3]

Luther expounds in this way the fact that "there is no law" against the fruits of the Spirit (Gal. 5[23]).

"Here once again the Apostle theologizes in his own way . . . lest we foolishly imagine that a just man ought not to live well and do good. But the just man has not the law, in the sense that he owes nothing to the law, for he has that love and grace which the law requires. Thus we cannot say that three and seven ought to be ten, but that they are ten already, as B. Augustine says . . . thus a vessel full of wine does not need filling, for it is full. Thus the just man does not need to live well and to do good, for he lives well and does good. But it is of the unjust man that we may say that he ought (debet) to live well and to do good." [4]

Third, most striking of all, Luther treats love of neighbour (at Gal. 5[14]). Here he repudiates the doctrine of a proper self-love.

"We ought not to please ourselves or seek our own things, nay, we ought rather to hate ourselves and deny ourselves and always turn from ourselves to our neighbour. Therefore 'ordered love' (charitas ordinata) means hatred of self and love of neighbour." [5]

This brings him to a passage which goes to the heart of Luther's doctrine of love.

"For it is true that carnality finds pleasure in its neighbour, yet frequently denies true charity: for it judges only in terms of its own

---

[1] W.A. 57.28.15. [2] W.A. 57.63.25.
[3] W.A. 57.99.13. [4] W.A. 57.105.21.
[5] W.A. 57.100.25.

experience, which is temporal and particular. That is, it picks and chooses not only the persons which it loves, but even the qualities (mores) which it loves in them and thus it only loves its neighbour when masked (larvatum) and 'personated,' i.e. because he is learned, rich, merry, attractive, and it dislikes and despises whatever is commended under another label, the unlearned and the fools and the sinners, etc." [1]

Then comes the positive statement:

"But true charity is round and universal, nay, eternal (1 Cor. 13) and without picking and choosing it loves all men in God, with a single eye, and it treats its neighbour without respect of persons" (impersonalem).[2]

Though we must make allowances for the fact that we have not Luther's own lecture material, it must be confessed that his first lectures on "Galatians" are to our mind, the least rewarding of all his early works.[3]

The Lectures on Hebrews, on the other hand, contain some of his finest utterances.[4] He seems to have begun them in March 1517 and to have finished them just before Easter, i.e. at the end of March 1518.[5] The first term must have been reasonably quiet. But the next! Almost at the beginning of the semester the ninety-five theses were posted on the Schlosskirche, 31st October 1517. The end of the course saw their professor threatened on all sides by mighty enemies of Church and State, on the eve of an ominous and fateful journey to the Augustinian Chapter in Heidelberg. We shall see how the lectures themselves seem to gain from this "existential" reference.

It seems probable that Luther lectured two days a week, Mondays and Fridays, at 6-7 a.m., carrying on when necessary in the period after lunch, 12-1. In the case of these lectures, as with the Galatians, we are dependent on student copies, the reasonably complete Vatican MS. and the so-called Dessauer MS. (of the first five chapters of the Scholia).[6] The number of Biblical references are impressive: there are upwards of a thousand direct citations in the index of the Weimar edition. Next to Scripture, his major authority was the Homilies of St. Chrysostom on the Epistle to the Hebrews. One curious trait may perhaps be detected, that the scholastic references, to Biel, to

---

[1] W.A. 57.101.23.   [2] W.A. ibid. 102.1.
[3] On this, see Holl. Ges. Aufs. iii.134.
[4] W.A. 57, ed. J. Ficker. E. Hirsch and H. Rückert. Luthers Vorlesung über den Hebräerbrief. Berlin, 1929. Luthers Hebräerbriefvorlesung. Deutsche Übersetzung. E. Vogelsang. Berlin, 1930.
[5] W.A. 57.XIX. Böhmer. Luthers erste Vorlesung, 6. Hirsch-Rückert, xxvi. Easter in 1518 was 4th April. Term must have ended by 28th March.
[6] Bibl. Vat. Pal. Lat. 1825. Dessau. Landesbücherei Georg. 1049.

Lombard and to pseudo-Dionysius are more frequent, and, on the whole, more polite, than in the earlier commentaries. Is it too subtle to see in this fact the reflection of the outward conflict of these months, that being plunged into what was thought to be a dangerous and revolutionary attack on authority outside the lecture-room, he should stress within it those themes on which he could still accept conservative authorities? [1]

In addition there is evidence of Luther's growing mastery of the humanist tools, the texts of Erasmus, Faber and Reuchlin, and his developing facility in Greek and Hebrew. [2]

Again, the Biblical material determines the main themes: and in the Epistle to the Hebrews there are two of especial significance for Luther's own theology, the person and work of Christ, and the motive of faith. His thought of the person and work of Christ in the great duel of redemption blends some of the great patristic themes with his own stresses, and brings them into line with his developing "theology of the Cross." Faith is a master word, and it is now linked much more closely with another growing theme, that of the Word of God.

The Biblical material accounts for the paucity of material in which sin is diagnosed, but the repudiation of "amor sui" is maintained.

"For no mere teaching, whether civil or canonical or of the philosophers or of any other human kind, can direct a man in the right way . . . and so necessarily can only make pretenders and hypocrites, because the dregs of the heart and the bilge of the old man remain, namely love of self (amor sui ipsius)." [3] .

"For none loves righteousness save this one, Christ, all others either love money or comfort or honour, or else despising these things, they seek glory, or if they are the best of all people, they love themselves more than righteousness . . . thus while love of self remains, a man cannot love righteousness or do its works, though he may pretend to do so, and the consequence is that the so-called virtues of the philosophers, and indeed of all men, whether the lawyers or the theologians, may appear to be virtues, but are really only vices." [4]

---

[1] It should be noted that in two places of the Table Talk Luther placed his Hebrews as given before Romans. W.A.TR. 3.3644, ". . . promotus in doctorem theologiae. . . . mox legi Psalterium, epistolam ad Hebraeos, deinde ad Romanos, Titum." WA.TR. 4.4323, " Doctoratus Martini Lutheri anno 12, deinde 13 anno legit Psalterium, 15 anno epistolam ad Hebraeos, Romanos, ad Galatas et Titum."
[2] Some time in the first days of the autumn semester, his colleague, Karlstadt, paid him a compliment before the students. " Epistolam illam ad Hebraeos, rarae et mirae eruditionis Pater Martinus Luder qui ut sanctitate et ingenii acrimonia, bellissime convenientibus, pollet plurimum, ita probissime nec sine magna scripturarum non modo latinarum, sed et graecarum et hebraicarum copia explicat." Quoted Hirsch-Rückert, xxiii.
[3] W.A. 57.109.9.   [4] W.A. 57.110.3.

P

"Thus the Christian man begins to hate iniquity and to love righteousness, but he only loves through Christ, that is because Christ, who is the true lover of righteousness, supplies through his love that love of ours which is only beginning." [1]

"For those who please God cannot please themselves. They are two contrary wills. Therefore to do the will of God is nothing less than to destroy our own, simply more and more to be conformed to the will of God and this is 'to crucify the old man, with Christ.'" [2]

"For thus Christ, exhibited to the whole world through the gospel as a kind of display (spectaculum), by knowledge and contemplation of himself draws his own, and abstracts them from those things to which they adhered in the world. And thus, that they may be transformed and made like him. For thus Christ is said to be the cause and captain of salvation, because by himself he leads and draws his sons to glory, so that the common phrase is that Christ is the instrument and medium with which God draws his sons . . . for not by force or fear does God force us to be saved, but he moves and draws whoever he will save, by this sweet spectacle of his mercy and charity." [3]

"We are a house, which Christ builds (fabricat), but this act of building is nothing else than the tension and pressure and all the cross and sufferings which are in Christ." [4]

Closely linked with sin as "self-love" is the theme of our own human "proper righteousness."

"For our own righteousness and wisdom most of all deceives and hinders faith in Christ, for if we love the flesh and the mind (sensus) of the flesh, things, riches, and the like, we love nothing more vehemently than the judgment of the flesh (sensuum judicium) and of our own will, especially when they appear in the disguise of goodness . . . why cannot they believe? Because the 'deceptions of sin,' i.e. love of their own righteousness blinds them and hardens them while they think it good to glory and find pleasure in their own righteousness, and this is the worst of all vices, the most contrary thing to faith, which only finds pleasure and glory in the only righteousness of God (in sola Justitia Dei), i.e. in Christ." [5]

At Heb. 9[14] ("how much more shall the blood of Christ . . . cleanse your conscience from dead works"), he returns to the theme of the fugitive and anguished conscience.

"For, since past sin cannot be changed, nor future wrath by any means avoided, it is necessary that wherever it turns to flee, it is shut

[1] Ibid. 21.   [2] W.A. 57.91.20.
[3] W.A. 57.125.2.   [4] W.A. 57.141.2.
[5] W.A. 57.150.12.

up and troubled. Nor from these straits can a man be freed save by the blood of Christ, which if it shall be known by faith, a man believes, and understands his sins are washed and taken away in Him. Thus by faith he is at the same time purified and pacified, and now he does not fear the penalties for joy at the remission of his sins." [1]

"For nothing stains the conscience save sin. From which most solemn word it seems to follow that good works done outside grace are sin, so that they are called 'dead'. . . . it is certain that this does not mean venial, but rather mortal impurity . . . otherwise, if 'dead works' were the same here as 'non-meritorious,' as some say, it would follow that the blood of Christ purified, not sinners, but those who do good works 'in their kind' (as they say). Consequently they would be forced to say 'impure,' 'sin,' 'trespass' is the same as 'non-meritorious,' which is nothing else than to turn the whole scripture inside out by a new signification of words. It follows from all this, that a good, pure, quiet, joyful conscience only comes from faith in remission of sins, which nobody can have save in the Word of God which preaches to us that the blood of Christ is shed for the remission of sins." [2]

The distinction between Law and Gospel is sharpened in these lectures.

"This is the strength of the law, to commemorate and make manifest sin. The virtue of grace, however, is to hand sin over to oblivion, i.e. to purge it out." [3]

"The law and the gospel differ also in this way, that in the law there are many works, but they are all external, but in the gospel there is in truth only one work, and internal, and that is, faith. The one makes an external righteousness, but the other a righteousness hidden in God . . . and thus the whole substance of the new law and its righteousness is that unique faith in Christ but not simply a sterile human opinion, since Christ is alive, and not only lives, but is working, and not only works, but reigns. Thus it cannot be that faith in him is otiose, but it lives and works and triumphs and thus its works flow spontaneously outward from faith, for thus our patience comes from the patience of Christ, our humility from his, and other good things in similar fashion, if only we firmly believe that he has done all these things for us, and not only for us, but unto (coram) us, that is, as B. Augustine says, not only as a sacrament, but as an example." [4]

"For thus by the Spirit we are freed from the law, not that it should not exist, but that it should not be feared, and thus we are freed from

---

[1] W.A. 57.207.21.   [2] W.A. 57.208.6.
[3] W.A. 57.55.18.
[4] W.A. 57.113.21. Also W.A. 57.113.12: 192.16.24. " The grace of Jesus Christ who is the fullness of the Law."

the Devil, not that he should not be, but that we should not be afraid of him, and so from death, not that death should not be, but that he should not be feared." [1]

Luther takes from Isa. 28[21] the thought of the "strange work" by which God, by the office of the Law, brings men under God's "own work," the liberation by Christ through the Gospel.[2]

This thought of the apparent contradiction between God's saving purpose working through the Law, sin, death and the Devil, and his "own proper work," by which he comes to men in Christ through the Gospel, is powerfully applied by Luther to the thought of the Cross as a mighty duel. Luther here follows the theme of the great mediaeval hymns, and of the patristic writings of the Greek Fathers, the forceful Athanasian view of the Cross as a great struggle in which the Devil was deceived and vanquished.

"For God's proper work (opus proprium Dei) is 'life, peace, joy' and the other fruits of the Spirit. Yet in this God made marvellous his holy one, and is made wonderful in his saints, that he destroyed the Devil, not with the work of God, but even with the work of the Devil himself. For this is the most superb of all victories, to confound the adversary with his own weapon, and slay him with his own sword, as we sing, 'Prostrate he lies with his own dart.' For thus God sets forward his own work and fulfils it by means of his 'strange work' and with wonderful wisdom forces the Devil, by means of death to work nothing other than life, and thus when it seems to work most against the work of God, it works with his 'own work' for God. For thus it was with the work of Christ, his death, which Christ through the immortality of his divinity swallowed up altogether and gloriously rose from the dead." [3]

The "Justitia Dei" is defined in terms similar to those of the Romans commentary.

"Righteousness and peace in the scriptures are always understood as divine righteousness and peace, and thus righteousness is that grace itself with which a man is justified, that is, faith, hope, love.... for Rom. 1[17] is badly expounded of the Righteousness of God with which he himself is righteous, unless it is thus understood; for faith so lifts up the heart of man and turns him from himself to God, that he becomes one spirit from his heart with God and thus divine righteousness is the righteousness of the heart in that manner which some call 'informing,' as in Christ the humanity by union with the divine nature is made one person." [4]

---

[1] W.A. 57.135.9.   [2] W.A. 57.79.15.
[3] W.A. 57.128.7.   [4] W.A. 57.187.5.

Luther asserts that the grace of the sacraments must be received "in the fullness of faith." "But faith is already justifying grace." [1] "The sacraments of grace justify the heart, discerning between heart and heart, conscience and conscience, faith and faith, hope and hope, love and love." [2]

Luther speaks of prevenient grace along orthodox lines.

"To desire Christ, and to ask for him, to look and to knock is the gift of prevenient grace, and not of the choice of our will." [3]

But Luther prefers to speak of the Righteousness and Grace of God in terms of Jesus Christ. Here is one of the great, characteristic stresses of Luther's developing "theology of the Cross."

"It is to be noted that he speaks of the humanity of Christ before he names his deity, and by this approves that rule of knowing God by faith. For his humanity is our Scala Sancta, by which we ascend to the knowledge of God, our Jacob's Ladder . . . who wishes safely to ascend into the love and knowledge of God, let him leave human and metaphysical rules for knowing the deity, and let him first exercise himself in the humanity of Christ. For it is the most impious of all temerities when God himself has humbled himself in order that he might be knowable, that a man should seek to climb up some other way, through his own ingenious devices." [4]

The mighty work of Christ by which, in the conflict of the Cross, he overcame the devil, sin and death, is something into which the Christian man enters into conformity with Christ.

"So it pleases the most pious God now to destroy death and the works of the devil in us . . . we Christians ought to learn how to die with joy for as it is impossible that Christ, the victor of death, should die again, so it is impossible that he that believeth in him should die . . . as Christ by union with immortal deity died and by dying overcame death, so the Christian by union with the immortal Christ (which is by faith in him) even in dying overcomes death and thus God destroys the Devil by himself, and perfects 'his strange work.'" [5]

"Whoever fears death or does not want to die is not yet a sufficient Christian, for he fails in resurrection faith, so long as he loves this life more than that which is to come . . . for it is true that only the conscience aware of sin makes death horrible, for the 'sting of death is sin,' but this conscience of sin nothing takes away save faith in Christ who giveth us the victory." [6]

The work of Christ "for us" has to be carried through in us. The fearful Christians "are to be consoled and exhorted, first, through Christ himself, who left out nothing that could be desired from the

[1] W.A. 57.191.24.   [2] W.A. 57.192.2.   [3] W.A. 57.116.1.
[4] W.A. 57.99.1.   [5] W.A. 57.129.14.   [6] W.A. 57.131.5.

best kind of priest, who not only underwent death for us, that when it was conquered it might be despised by us, but even, on account of the weak in faith, took upon himself the fear of death, and overcame it and sanctified it that such fear might not be thought by us to be unto damnation. For it is another kind of sin, to be afraid of death, and not to want to die. See, therefore, what more could the most merciful Saviour have done, beyond what he has done?" [1]

The "theology of the Cross" means not only that Christ's humanity and extreme humiliation are the way by which we know God: not only that his work "for us" is the ground of our salvation, and his work "in us," that we too are to conquer sin, death and the devil. The Christian man and the Christian Church must also share the sufferings of Christ, that "form of a servant" which brings an ambiguity and contradiction into all their earthly existence.

"For there is, on the face of it, nothing more dissimilar to the throne of God than the people of Christ, since theirs does not seem to be a kingdom but an exile, and they seem not to live, but always given up to death, not to glory, but put to shame, not in riches, but put to extreme poverty, as whoever wants to be a sharer in this kingdom is forced to experience for himself. For the ornaments of the Christians are their poverties, tribulations, ills . . ." [2]

"For to have Christ crucified in oneself is to live full of temptations and sufferings, and thus be, in bodily things, 'a sign to be spoken against' . . . 'for verily Christ always comes in that form which he took when he emptied himself of the form of God." [3]

That Christ is both priest and Host brings comfort to those tormented by the final fear, of judgment to come.

"For those who are terrified by fear of that eternal judgment . . . there is only one refuge and asylum, Christ our priest in whose humanity alone we are protected and saved from judgment . . . wherefore the Apostle shows Christ here rather as priest than as Lord and judge that those who are fearful might be consoled." [4]

"These things most sweetly commend Christ to us, that he is, in the first place, not a vindicator of sins, or a judge, but a priest, who destroys sins: he is set forth to us as the author of righteousness and salvation, and that sad consciences might be the more comforted, not present with us, but 'coram Deo,' in God's presence, where was his greatest work, and where we are most accused and most guilty." [5]

---

[1] W.A. 57.133.9 : also 136.9.   [2] W.A. 57.107.17.
[3] W.A. 57.122.18.   [4] W.A. 57.164.14
[5] W.A. 57.54.13 : also 178.1. " The man Christ is the mediated cause of salvation " (alternative reading. Hirsch-Rückert, 182, " meritorious "). The motive for this offering of Christ is " the fire of his love." (50.10.)

Luther goes on to say that it is not enough to believe that Christ takes away sins in general.

"Nay, rather it is not enough to believe that his blood was shed for the remission of sins, unless you believe that he has shed his blood for your own sins. For it is in this way that only the shed blood of Christ purifies the conscience through faith in Christ's word. . . ." [1]

Those who simply meditate on Christ's passion as an event in past history, and without faith, "do so in a fruitless and Gentile manner."

"For who, even among the Gentiles, would not sympathize with Christ in his sufferings? But his passion ought to be thought upon with such study, that thereby faith is increased, so that the more frequently it is meditated, the more fully it is believed that the blood of Christ is shed for a man's own sins. This is that spiritual eating and drinking, that is, with this faith to be joined to and incorporated into Christ." [2]

"Note that it is not enough for a Christian to believe that Christ was instituted for men, unless he believes that he himself is one of those men." [3]

Inseparable from this emphasis on the conformity of the Christian with Christ, is the doctrine of the Word, through which living faith is evoked. The Word of God is the Gospel.[4] But it is God rather than human eloquence who is operative.

"For Christ does not need to be preached with a furious tempest of words, nay, he cannot be preached, save peacefully and calmly." [5]

The Word and faith may not be separated when we think of this divine activity in our salvation.

"For without faith it is impossible for God to work or to be with us, as he himself never does anything without his Word. Therefore none can co-operate with him, unless he adheres to the Word, which happens through faith, as an instrument cannot co-operate with the craftsman unless it is grasped in his hand." [6]

It is the Word of God which refreshes and sustains us amid the multiplicity of human cares (we think of Luther's own business at this time).

"When therefore we are in the midst of enemies, and drawn away by innumerable enticements, hindered by cares, occupied in business affairs, through all of which things we may be withdrawn from purity of heart, on that account one thing is left to us, that with all care we should exhort ourselves and excite our lethargic spirit with the Word

[1] W.A. 57.208.29.
[2] W.A. 57.209.18.
[3] W.A. 57.169.10.
[4] W.A. 57.15.14 : 108.14.
[5] W.A. 57.136.20.
[6] W.A. 57.143.2.

of God, by meditating, reading and listening assiduously to it . . . which unless it is done, certainly we shall be thrust against that multitude of things, and tepidity and dryness of spirit will overwhelm us." [1]

"For faith in the word purifies, for the Word of God is most pure and the best of all things." [2]

"For these three make one: faith, the Word and the heart. Faith is the glue or bond, the Word and the heart are two extremes, but by faith are made one spirit as a man and wife are made one flesh." [3]

Upon the evil and the unbelievers the Word of God is shown in judgment as a two-edged sword.

"As the Word of God (sermo) is above all things, outside all things, within all things, before all things, behind all things, and thus it is everywhere, it is impossible to escape it anywhere . . . this is that fear and confusion of which the scriptures speak so often." [4]

It is the office of the Holy Ghost to bring home the word.

"The Holy Spirit teaches the word of life, grace and salvation" . . . "for it does not suffice for the law to be objectively spoken to the soul, but formally, that is through love of the law written in the heart and so to be the law." [5]

"For nobody understands his precepts unless it be given him from above . . . you understand them, however, because the Holy Spirit teaches you . . . therefore those most sadly err who presume to understand the holy scriptures and the law of God by taking hold of them with their own understanding and study." [6]

"How then can a man understand or love God when all his own counsels and thoughts are condemned? But thus to understand the invisible will of God in such darknesses is the work of none save the Holy Spirit." [7]

We turn from the Word to Faith, about which Luther has more to say than in any commentary thus far. The expression "sola fide" recurs (but is not disproportionate to "sola misericordia" and "sola gratia" (135.20)).[8] Faith and Grace are inseparable, "for all the works of faith impossible to nature, but made easy by grace, because they are done to us who receive them, while God alone works them." [9]

"All the works of the whole Bible are described as works of faith." [10]

That the precepts of God are fulfilled by faith is described as "words of consolation, with a necessary reason to those who suffer, lest they

---

[1] W.A. 57.148.19.   [2] W.A. 57.147.20.
[3] W.A. 57.157.1.   [4] W.A. 57.162.2.
[5] W.A. 57.196.5.   [6] W.A. 57.185.21.
[7] W.A. 57.186.25.
[8] W.A. 57.19.4, "Sola enim incredulitas separat a Deo, sicut sola fides conjungit." 22.10 : 65.1 : 171.4.   [9] W.A. 57.69.15.   [10] W.A. 57.70.15.

fail since faith, i.e. the life of a Christian is much more the operation of God than of ourselves, i.e. is most truly our passion. For nobody is purged without vexations and buffetings. 'The more we suffer and are oppressed, the better Christians we are.' Thus the whole life of a Christian is in faith, i.e. in the Cross and in passions." [1]

Luther describes the sensual man, and the rational man, and comes to the spiritual man, "who rests from outward things in the Word and faith, positively, because the object of faith, i.e. the Word will remain fixed in him. He is troubled from without in the danger of faith (as it is called) and the withdrawal of the Word, as happens in the temptations of faith, hope and love: for this is the man who lives in the Word of God. For he is at rest from within, when he rests 'privatively,' raised up by faith and the Word into the essential work of God, which is the birth of the uncreated Word itself, as it is said, 'This is life eternal, that they should know thee, the true God and Jesus Christ whom thou hast sent,' i.e. the procession of the Son from the Father." [2]

"For if you ask a Christian what is the work with which he is made worthy the name of Christian, he can give no other answer than that hearing of the Word of God which is faith. Thus the ears alone are the organs of the Christian man because not by the works of any other members, but by faith he is justified and judged as a Christian." [3]

The emphasis on the hearing of faith is joined with an emphasis on the hiddenness of faith itself, for faith consists in the apprehension of that which is invisible but not inaudible. Luther can use the language of mysticism and of the "negative way" in this regard, but it is always in connection with faith, and with the work of the Holy Ghost, and never an intellectual and spiritual exercise within a man's unaided power. Of the Christian's advent to the Heavenly Jerusalem (Heb. 12) he says:

"All these things are indeed invisible, but they are amiable, as those other things were visible but terrible. And he comes to these by faith in the Spirit . . . for it is most joyful that this is performed through faith, that with us, nay, ours should be God, Christ, the Church, the angels, the saints and everything else." [4]

"All these things are so abhorrent from all sense, in order that it may be the most robust exercise of faith for those who wish to understand their truth." [5]

"You be the listener, and I will be the preacher, for the things which Christ has spoken about heaven and the future life, can only be caught hold of by hearing, since they are not only above the height of all

[1] W.A. 57.60.29.
[2] W.A. 57.159.15.
[3] W.A. 57.222.5.
[4] W.A. 57.83.18.
[5] W.A. 57.107.15.

intellect, but are even wider than the capacity of all desire. Therefore the testimony of the Lord is the word of faith, a hidden wisdom, the understanding of babes. Which is called audible by Isaiah 53. 'Lord, who hath believed with our hearing?" that is, with the voice which we make heard by evangelizing." [1]

"Therefore the hardest of all things is faith in Christ, which is being rapt and translated from all things of sense, within and without, into those things beyond sense within and without, namely into the invisible, most high and incomprehensible God." [2]

"For faith causes the heart to be fixed and to adhere to celestial things, and thoroughly to be rapt and turned towards invisible things." [3]

"To adhere to God means to be deprived of the world and of all creatures, as to carry the image of Christ is to live after the affection and example of Christ . . . but all these goods, as they are invisible, incomprehensible and entirely hidden, nature cannot attain to or love, unless it be raised by the grace of God. For the same reason, the spiritual man can be judged, known, seen, by none, not even by himself, since he dwells in the most high darknesses of God . . . this begins in this life, but is made perfect in the next." [4]

There follows one of the loveliest utterances of Luther in this period.

"O it is a great thing to be a Christian man, and have a hidden life, hidden not in some cell, like the hermits, or even in the human heart, which is an unsearchable abyss, but in the invisible God himself, and thus to live in the things of the world, but to feed on him who never appears except in the only vehicle of the hearing of the Word." [5]

The eleventh chapter of Hebrews forms the text for the most exciting of all the expositions in this commentary. Its theme is that heroic faith, of which the patriarchs were the historic emblems. But the whole treatment is conceived and uttered under the pressure of those hastening great events which Luther's own actions had initiated, and they reflect his own conflict; the battle against fears within and enemies without, out of which, in these months, his own courage was marvellously kindled. If ever passages deserved the comment of Pinomaa, "existential," these are they.

The chapter begins with the discussion of faith along the lines of the previous commentary.

"Faith is nothing else than the adherence to the Word of God, and it follows that the possession of the Word of God is that of eternal goods, and at the same time the removal . . . of all present goods." [6]

[1] W.A. 57.139.6.
[2] W.A. 57.144.10.
[3] W.A. 57.185.2.
[4] W.A. 57.214.20 : also 160.15.
[5] W.A. 57.215.1.
[6] W.A. 57.228.17.

Then, at 11.6 comes a passage which E. Hirsch says "leaps over the traditional debate about explicit and implicit faith . . . faith is "existential."[1]

"For to believe that God exists seems easy to many and they attribute it to poets and philosophers, as Rom. 1 . . . such faith is human, like any other reasoning, art, understanding of dreams, etc., but as soon as temptation comes along, all these fall. Then neither reason nor advice nor human faith can overcome . . . for such faith believes nothing of itself but simply of other people, for if he believes that 'God is the rewarder of them that seek after him,' yet he does not believe that God is his God and will reward him. This is faith about God and not faith in God. Wherefore the work of faith is a different thing, namely that we believe that we are of the number of those for whom God is, and is their rewarder. But this faith does not come from nature, but from grace. For nature dreads and flees from the face of God, believing him to be not God but a tyrant and a torturer and a judge . . . as a candle exposed to the wind not only loses its rays, but light altogether, but when the sun shines again it is not disturbed by the winds in its beams nor in itself, thus the first kind of faith is extinguished, the second never."[2]

"Some know Christ speculatively, others practically: the one says 'Christ appears before the face of God for others' but the others say 'Christ appeared before the face of God for us.' That is why a Christian ought to be sure, nay absolutely certain (certissimum) that Christ has appeared for him and is a priest before God. For as he believes, so it is to him . . . that is why we must be very careful and wary of the sentence of those who refer Eccl. 9, 'No man knows whether he is worthy of hatred or of love,' to the state of this present moment, and by this means make a man uncertain of the mercy of God and the confidence of salvation. This is to turn Christ and his faith upside down. For Ecclesiastes does not speak of the present time, but of our perseverance and of that future state of which nobody is certain, as the apostle says 'Who stands, let him take heed lest he fall.'"[3]

Then Luther comes to the patriarchs. Not least among the trials of Luther in the next months was the experience of isolation: he had to fight a battle in which his friends and admirers could only partly comprehend what the fuss was all about. He had to meet his own doubts and hesitations, which echoed the taunts of his enemies far more terrifyingly than they could ever guess. Here Noah "contra mundum" brought inspiration.

[1] Hirsch-Rückert, 269 n. [2] W.A. 57.232.26.
[3] W.A. 57.215.16.

"The whole ways of the world were vehemently embattled against the faith of this one man. For there is hardly any greater battle than this, since to know oneself to be one among many, nay, one against many, is judged the highest folly; that is why the faith of Noah was not that quiet quality of soul (as we are accustomed to dream of faith) but the life of the heart . . . as a lily among thorns . . . for to have faith in things invisible is to have a heart surely purged and separated from visible things. Which purity of heart is perfect righteousness." [1]

The figures of these pioneers of faith relying solely on God, were a source from which Luther was to draw courage and inspiration throughout troubled years.[2]

"For as the place of Enoch and Elijah is situated for us in darkness, and mists, and ignorance, in the invisible things of God, so is this place whither Abraham was called, entirely hidden. But this is the glory of faith: not to know where you go, what you do, what you are to suffer, and with all things made captive (sense and intellect and virtue and will) to follow the naked voice of God and rather to be led than to go . . . and so it is plain that Abraham with this obedience of faith shows the highest example of the evangelical life, who left all to follow the Lord, preferring the Word of God to everything else and loving it beyond all things, and willingly becoming a pilgrim (sponte peregrinus) and was subject at all hours to perils of life and death." [3]

Such faith is immediately assaulted by the Devil.

"For the temptation of faith is the greatest of them all, against which the Devil uses all his own strength and those of men and things." [4]

And so, even when Abraham reached the promised land, "Not only were his temptations not ended, but a new variety of temptation of faith began." [5]

Then the greatest of all temptations was that he should offer up Isaac, his beloved son. The Jews missed altogether the true significance of the life of Abraham, since they judge all these things externally.

"That is why it is the highest of all high temerities to judge one's neighbour, since even the elect are hidden and are saved through sins which appear most openly." [6]

Then the MS. breaks off, at Heb. 11^{27}, at the moment when Moses forsakes Egypt, forced to flee into Midian. It may be that the lectures continued, and that Luther finished the epistle, and that it is simply our MS. which is defective. But the student finished with plenty of room on his page. This suggests that Luther may have stopped at this

[1] W.A. 57.235.4.
[2] H. Bornkamm. Luther und das Alte Testament (1948), 18 ff.
[3] W.A. 57.235.25.   [4] W.A. 57.236.11.
[5] W.A. 57.236.23.   [6] W.A. 57.237.20.

point. And if so, how appropriately. And if not, was ever MS. broken at a more significant point?

Luther was now in deep waters. A process against him for heresy had been set on foot in Rome, from the Archbishop of Mainz, and more recently from the Dominicans, who were openly boasting that Luther would soon be disposed of. On 14th March [1] he had spoken openly about the abuse of excommunication. On 17th March his own students had aggravated his danger, by seizing the colporteur who had come to Wittenberg with copies of Tetzel's counter-theses, man-handling him, and burning the offending literature. The pro-magistrate of the Augustinians, Della Volta, had probably been in touch with Staupitz and had demanded that some action be taken on behalf of the order. It may be that it was at this very time that Luther received a visit from some of his brethren, seeking to dissuade him from obstinately persisting in this novel teaching, and begging him to refrain from bringing disgrace upon the order.

Now, in a few days, he must attend the Chapter of the Order at Heidelberg. The way lay through enemy territory, and already his friend Spalatin had told the Elector Frederick of the danger that he might be seized by his enemies en route, and indeed that if he went to Heidelberg, he might never return. Luther must have known how precarious was the protection of his Prince, if once an authoritative condemnation was set in motion. He may have thought of flight, and he must have known that the only place where he could hope for safety would be distant Bohemia.

We know the rest of the story: it takes an effort of imagination to put ourselves back into Luther's shoes in the last days of March 1518. It was one thing to have made something of a reputation as a younger theologian, in the vanguard of the fight against an outworn scholastic method. It was another to face disgrace and ignominy, while one's own friends and brethren turned away with clouded faces. The Diet of Worms has become the epitome of Luther's courage. But by then, he knew that giant forces were at his side. The real torment, the real trial lies within this period from Easter 1518 to the interview with Cajetan at Augsburg, in those two journeys which he had to adventure alone (save for a silent "socius itinerarius") and on foot. Faith was for him at each day and each step an adventure into the unknown.

That is the context. Menaced by great enemies, uncertain of his friends, he took up the tale of Moses, who, by faith, endured the con-tradiction of his brethren, and counted the reproach of Christ as greater riches than the treasures of Egypt.

[1] Boehmer. Road to Reformation, 224.

"Not on account of visible things which were greater than, or equal with them, but on account of the Cross, and those things which are only calamities; and he chose the wisdom or rather the foolishness of the Cross that he might reprove the wisdom with which he had been endowed . . . but greatest of all, he was repudiated by the very brethren on account of whom he despised all these things, and underwent these dangers, as Acts 7, 'Who made you a ruler over us?' . . . and so he was forced to flee into Midian." [1]

It was a wonderful exit line. If it were intended, if indeed this is the place where the lectures ended, perhaps for some accidental academic reason, but at least as if they had reached a logical conclusion, it must have been a memorable, hushed moment when the voice stopped, the volume closed, and the footsteps echoed down the long room. His enemies were saying that he would be dead in a few months. He could not know that that last "temptation" would be postponed for many years. Nor could he know that between that moment and this, such events would intervene that, at his death, and over his dead body, men would speak of another Moses, would sing another "In exitu Israel." He went out, by faith, alone.

[1] W.A. 57.238.1.

Chapter

10

THE HEIDELBERG DISPUTATION (1518), THE "OPERATIONES IN PSALMOS" (1518-21) AND THE "RATIONIS LATOMIANAE CONFOTATIO" (1521)

> "Verily, Luther is a strange sort of Antinomian ! Yea, he belongs to that great Antinomian multitude which comprises the glorious company of the apostles, and the goodly fellowship of the prophets, and the noble army of martyrs."
> JULIUS HARE. " Vindication of Luther."

IT all went much better than he had feared. There was the long, exhausting tramp, but the bright, lovely cheerfulness of spring kept breaking in. Spalatin had provided him with a series of comically elaborate passports. At Würzburg he was most heartily welcomed by the courteous Bishop Lorenz. He got a lift for the rest of the journey with old friends from the Erfurt Augustinians. The Chapter became a great personal triumph. If Lang succeeded him as District Vicar it was, it seems, in the line of duty, and unconnected with the scandal, and the change would be a great relief.

Then he presided at the disputation, about his chief theological concerns, against his chief theological enemies, and the practical bother of Indulgences was set aside. It is no wonder that he carried all before him, winning notable allies among the younger men, including Martin Bucer, John Brenz and Theodore Billicanus. For the theses are among his most succinct expositions, and summarize that development which we have traced and which can now merit his own term, "the theology of the Cross."

These theses sum up the development of ten years of theological study and teaching. There are the themes of the Romans and Galatians commentaries, the contrast between the righteousness of God and the righteousness of men, between the justice of human works and that of faith: the doctrine of the impotence of the human will, apart from grace. To these we may add the new stresses of the Lectures on Hebrews, the concentration upon Christ and his work, and the application of that work to the believers through faith, the thought of the conformity of the Christian with Christ. Then there is a growing awareness of the tension between the Law and Gospel, and the magnetic development of the conception of Faith. The whole movement by which a man is brought to awareness of his sin, to the accusation of himself, to accept-ance of the divine judgment, to humility, and so to the abandonment of his own righteousness, and to embrace the mercy of God, is now summed up in the dialectic of the Law and Gospel, the tension between God's "strange" and God's "proper work." Faith, so closely linked with the Word, and with Christ, becomes the secret of the whole approach of men to the invisible God. All these find a new focus in the theme "theology of the Cross." [1]

There are twenty-eight resolutions directed against the scholastic teaching about salvation, and setting forth Luther's own doctrine, and these are followed by twelve philosophical theses.[2] Many of them had been the subject of comment and digression in the commentaries of the last five years. More important for our purpose is the more extended "proofs of the conclusions." For here is laid open the whole movement to salvation as we have described it. The paragraphs which deal with the specific "theology of the Cross" occur significantly midway.

Luther begins with the assertion that "The law of God, that most healthful doctrine of life, cannot bring man to righteousness but rather hinders," "how much less can the works of man, according to the dictates of nature": the "works of men though they always seem to be good in appearance, yet are probably mortal sins." [3] Then Luther comes to the work of the Law, and to his distinction between God's "proper" and his "strange work."

"The Lord humbles us and terrifies us with the law and with the prospect of our sins, so that in the presence of men, and even in our own eyes, we seem to be nothing, fools, evil, nay, rather that is what we really are. So that when we acknowledge and confess that there is no form nor comeliness in us, but we live in the hidden God (that is in naked confidence of his mercy) we have in ourselves the answer to sin, folly, death and hell . . . and this is what Isa. 28 calls 'the strange work of God, that he may work his own work' (that is, that he may humble

---

[1] W. v. Loewenich. Luthers Theologia Crucis. Munich, 1933. "The 'theology of the Cross' is not a chapter in theology, but a certain kind of theology," 12. It is true that in a real sense Luther's theology was always a "theology of the Cross," but it is also true that there are special stresses in his thought at this time which later drop into the background. The chapter vi., "The theology of the Cross" in Miegge, Lutero, 141-77, is an exceptionally able survey of this period of Luther's life.
[2] W.A. 1.353.   [3] Werke Cl. V, 377-8.

us in ourselves, making us despair, that he may exalt us in his mercy, causing us to hope)." [1]

Luther reaffirms that all men sin, for all seek themselves, and give themselves the glory.

"For this is all perversity, to please oneself and to enjoy oneself in one's own works and so to adore an idol." "Such is the entire behaviour of the man who is secure, and without the fear of God." [2]

"For where there is no fear, there is no humility, where no humility, there is pride, there is the wrath and judgment of God." [3]

As in the Lectures on Hebrews, Luther attacks the distinction between "dead works" and "mortal works." On the contrary, "a man cannot avoid presumption nor come to true hope, unless in all his works he fears the judgment of damnation." [4] He then attacks the catchwords of his opponents. "'Free Will' after sin is a thing of words only, and when a man 'does what in him lies' he sins mortally!" [5] "A man who thinks that he can come to grace by 'doing what in him lies' adds sin to sin, and makes a double crime." [6]

All this means that there is no escape from the condemnation of the Law by human power or merit. All attempts to set up our own righteousness simply thwart our salvation, for we can never be saved until we learn to turn from ourselves to God. "The law humbles us, grace exalts us. The law works fear and wrath, grace works hope and mercy." [7]

"Through the knowledge of sin, however, comes humility and through humility grace is acquired. Thus God brings in his strange work that he may at length bring in his own work, when he makes a man a sinner, that he may make him just." [8]

To the taunt that this is a counsel of despair, Luther adds, that on the contrary it is the way of hope. "For that preaching of sin is the preparation for grace, or rather the knowledge of sin, and the faith in such preaching" [9] . . . "thus to say that we are nothing, when we do what in us lies, is not to make men despair (unless they are fools) but to seek to bring them to the Grace of our Lord Jesus Christ." [10]

It is in this context that Luther comes to speak of the knowledge of God. It is evident that "knowledge" here is not speculative intellectual perception, but "saving knowledge," that apprehension whereby men as living persons apprehend the Living God Himself. We come then to the important paragraphs XIX, XX and XXI.

[1] Ibid. 382.
[2] Ibid. 383.
[3] Ibid. 384.
[4] Ibid. 385.
[5] Ibid. 385.
[6] Ibid. 386.
[7] Ibid. 387.
[8] Ibid. 387.
[9] Ibid. 387.
[10] Ibid. 387.

"He is not worthy to be called a theologian who understands the invisible things of God, by the things which are made." [1]

"But (he is worthy to be called a theologian) who understands the visible and 'back parts of the Lord' and the prospect of passions and the Cross." [2]

This is expounded:

"The back parts and visible things of God are opposed to the invisible things, that is humanity, weakness, foolishness, as 1 Cor. 1 calls the 'weakness and foolishness of God.' For because men abused the knowledge of God by works, God wished on the other hand to be known by passions, and to condemn that invisible wisdom through visible wisdom, that those who did not worship God made manifest through works, might worship him hidden in passions. Thus he says, 1 Cor. 1[21], 'For seeing that in the wisdom of God, the world through its wisdom knew not God, it was God's good pleasure through the foolishness of the preaching to save them that believe.' So that now it will never be any good or use for him to know God in his glory and majesty, unless he knows him at the same time in the humility and shame of the Cross. Thus, 'he destroys the wisdom of the wise' and, as Isaiah says, 'Verily thou art a God that hidest thyself' (absconditus)."

"Thus in John 14, when Philip asks, according to the theology of Glory, 'Show us the Father,' then Christ withdrew him and his volatile thought of seeking God elsewhere, to himself, saying 'Philip, whoso hath seen me hath seen the Father.' Therefore in Christ crucified is the true theology and knowledge of God, and John 10, 'No man cometh to the Father save by me,' 'I am the door.'" [3]

XXI follows with the enigmatic sentence, "The theologian of Glory says bad is good, and good is bad, the theologian of the Cross says what is the fact."

"Whoso is ignorant of Christ," Luther explains, "is ignorant of God as he is hidden in passions." . . . "But God is not to be found save in passions and in the Cross. . . . Thus the friends of the Cross say the Cross is good and works bad, because by the Cross works are destroyed and Adam is crucified who is rather built up by works." [4]

Luther is not here discussing our modern problems of "Natural Theology," seeking to provoke a whole series of Gifford lecturers to rise up against him. What he has to say is important and meaningful in the scholastic context in which it is set, as long as we remember that what is at stake here is that "knowledge" of God whereby men are saved from sin and brought to eternal life. That is why he can

---

[1] Ibid. 388.   [2] Ibid. 388.
[3] Ibid. 838.   [4] Ibid. 389.

turn from these paragraphs to the theme of the Law, in the light of the revelation given in the Cross. XXIII, "The law works wrath, kills, curses, makes guilty, judges, damns whatever is not in Christ."

Thus Luther turns to the Righteousness of God. "The Righteousness of God is not acquired by frequently repeated acts, as Aristotle taught, but it is infused by faith."

"Not that the just man does not work, but that his works do not make him righteous, or rather his righteousness does the works. For grace and faith are infused apart from our work, and when they are infused, then the works follow." [1]

"For Christ is in us, nay rather is one with us through faith. But Christ is righteous and fulfils all the commands of God wherefore we fulfil them through him when he is made ours through faith . . . when Christ dwells in us by faith, then he moves us to good works through that living faith in his works. For the works which he himself does, are the fulfilments of the commands of God given to us, by faith, and when we behold them we are moved to imitate them." [2]

Thus Luther comes from Law to Gospel, from the saving revelation in the Cross, to the work of Christ for us and in us, and so to a remarkable paragraph on the nature of Love.

"The Love of God does not find, but creates the object of its love, whereas the love of man is created by the object of its love." [3]

This Luther explains:

"The second clause is evident, and is agreed by all philosophers and theologians that the object is the cause of love. For they lay down, according to Aristotle that every 'potency' of the soul is passive and 'matter' (materiam), and that it acts by receiving—and by this furthermore he bears witness that his philosophy is contrary to theology, inas much as it seeks its own in all things, and receives rather than confers good. The first clause is evident—since the Love of God living in man loves sinners, bad people, fools, weaklings that it may make them just, good, wise, strong and so it rather flows forth and confers good. For thus sinners are attractive (pulchri) because they are loved, and not loved because they are attractive (pulchri). So human love shuns sinners and evil men. Thus Christ says, 'I came not to call the righteous, but sinners.' And this is the love of the Cross, born of the Cross, which takes itself not to where it finds a good to enjoy, but where it may confer good on the bad and needy. For 'it is more blessed to give than to receive' says the Apostle, and so Ps. 41, 'Blessed is he that considereth the poor and needy.' Yet since the object of the understanding cannot

---

[1] Par. XXV, p. 390.   [2] Par. XXVI, XXVII.
[3] Par. XXVIII.

naturally be that which is nothing, i.e. poor and needy, but that which
has being, and is true and good, therefore it judges according to the
appearance and accepts the persons of men and judges according to
the things which appear." [1]

In a preparatory memorandum for the Disputation Luther has an
extended argument concerning the scholastic doctrine that a man could
love God above all things, by his own natural powers, and that he
could fulfil the law, not according to the "intention" but according
to the "substance of the deed." This Luther attacks, as he had attacked
it in his "Romans" on the ground that grace itself then becomes an
additional burden of law.

"Christ then is freely (superfluously?) dead for us, but he suffered
for the intention of God. We did not need him, but the 'intention of
the law giver' . . . 'for we could fulfil the law, but God was not content,
and demands grace beyond the law." And thus not Pelagius returns,
but a worse blasphemer than Pelagius. For thus we find we can by
natural powers love God above all things, and he is not ashamed to say
'above all things.'"

"But let us stop chattering and consult experience. Let a man 'do
what in him lies' when he is angry, excited, tempted, nay, rather, let
him prepare himself for that illumination of what he is ignorant, and
let us see where he gets. Let him do this, I say, and let him begin,
and we shall see what he does and what happens." [2]

The positive argument is given, however, in another paragraph.

"For this is the most sweet mercy of God, that he saves real sinners,
not imaginary sinners, that he upholds us in our sins, and accepts
our works and our life, which are worthy of all rejection, until he perfects and consummates us. Meanwhile we live under the protection
of the shadow of his wings. And we escape his judgment through his
mercy, not by our righteousness' . . . 'for he himself is our sole righteousness, until we are conformed to his likeness." [3]

The theology of the Cross therefore takes up the paradox of St.
Paul in 1 Cor. 1, that the Cross is a scandal, and that it is foolishness,
under which lie hidden the wisdom and power of God to salvation.
The theology of the Cross is therefore a stress on the practical, saving
revelation of God to men in the Incarnate Lord who is the object and

---

[1] Par. XXVIII. On the capital importance of this paragraph for Luther's doctrine
of Love. Nygren. Agape and Eros, ii.2.507 ff. Burnaby, "Amor Dei," 275, does
not expound the whole paragraph which shows clearly the difference between Luther
and St. Thomas and Scotus. He also seems to misconceive the relation between Luther
and Scotus. In particular the differences between Scotus and Luther in the teaching
about "resignation" are much more important than the similarities.

[2] W.A. 1.373. Werke Cl. V, 401.   [3] W.A. 1.370. Werke Cl. V, 397.

author of Faith. And this is opposed to the speculative, mystical way of "eminent" and "negative" analogy. We are to begin with the humanity of Christ, and so by faith we apprehend deity, nay rather, are apprehended, for, like St. Paul, Luther turns to the great passive voice.[1]

The "veiled" character of this revelation is not the Divine Incognito of modern dialectical theology, but the contradiction of the earthly life of Jesus, and the consummating scandal of the Cross whereby the glory of God is hidden in humiliation, power veiled in apparent shame and weakness. Finally, as von Loewenich has said, "The Cross of Christ and the Cross of the Christian are inseparable." The Christian man, and the Christian Church militant here on earth are called upon to share this contradiction, of poverty, weakness, shame, humiliation, suffering.

This brings us to the doctrine of God's "hiddenness." Luther uses the same phrase as the mystics, about the "Deus absconditus," but, as usual, he adapts the phrase to his own purposes. Here, in this period, his insistence is on the contradiction of revelation and on the essential "hiddenness" of the things of Faith.[2]

The Heidelberg Disputation sums up a good deal of Luther's theological development over ten years. It also expresses the special stress on conformity with Christ in suffering, and on the good fight of faith which was to sustain Luther himself in the lonely decisions of what Miegge calls "his terrible revolutionary vocation." That loneliness of Faith Luther had beautifully expressed before the outbreak of the Church conflict.

"The World is a house . . . but I am outside the house, on the roof, not yet in heaven, but also not in the world. I have the world beneath me, and the heavens above me, and so I am suspended in faith, alone, between life in the world and eternal life." [3]

This emphasis on the isolation of Faith is not in contradiction to the

[1] Von Loewenich distinguishes, 1. The theology of the Cross is a theology of revelation in contrast to speculation. 2. The revelation is indirect and veiled. 3. The revelation is not known through active works but through passive suffering (the double sense of " passio " is sustained here, as suffering and passive reception). 4. This knowledge of the veiled revelation is an affair of Faith. 5. This knowledge of God is joined to the practical emphasis on suffering in the " theology of the Cross," 18.

[2] Von Loewenich points out (p. 22), 1. The thought of Deus Absconditus is closely linked with the " theology of the Cross." 2. The God who is hidden is none other than the God who is revealed. " God is absconditus, for the sake of revelation." He quotes W.A. 1.138.13, " Homo abscondit sua ut neget, Deus abscondit sua ut revelet . . . sua absconsione nihil aliud facit quam ut impedimenta revelationis tollat i.e. superbiam." 3. The " Deus absconditus " is no tool for speculative knowledge. Luther uses the phrase, I believe, in a different way, in his " De Servo Arbitrio " (1525), but does not contradict his use of it in this period.

[3] W.A. 1.199.3.

theme of Christian solidarity in the Church, a theme which is a growing preoccupation of the next months and which we shall reserve for separate consideration. But in our examination of Luther's theological development, we come to the point when we must pause, and select. For we are on the edge of the period of Luther's prodigious literary output, something like a writing a fortnight over twenty years. Even if we leave aside his preaching, his polemical tracts, his popular writings and his works dealing with practical abuses in the Church, we cannot begin to deal in detail with what remains.

We shall select from two works some passages which either extend or illuminate the expositions already made. The first, Luther's Lectures on the Psalms, which he began in 1518, and which he worked over in the next years and which were finally published as his "Operationes in Psalmos" (1519-21). Here we have also a fragment in the Vatican MS. of certain Glosses on Ps. 4 and 5 which were edited and published by Vogelsang in 1940.[1] Second, Luther's Latin polemical writing, "Contra Latomum," written after the Diet of Worms, when he was away from any books save his Bible, but one of his ablest works, and which contains material about justification which may serve to focus our sketch of his development.

Turning first to the fragment, we remember the extraordinary tension of these months for Luther, the culminating ordeal of the interviews with Cajetan at Augsburg, perhaps the most anxious period of his career.

We find in these Glosses the familiar stresses. First, the doctrine of "accusatio sui," humility and the abandonment of one's own righteousness.

"For to have compunction is to displease oneself, to judge oneself."[2]

"For all sin displeases and offends God, but only iniquity properly makes him angry, which is pride, the setting up of our own righteousness against the righteousness and truth of God."[3]

"And this is spiritual idolatry: to adore an idol of one's own heart. That is to make a lie of God, conflated out of holy scriptures. Thus every man who thinks about God otherwise than he really is, and wills, especially if he takes it from some authority of the scriptures (which he understands falsely) is an idolater. Thus I have said that arrogant confidence in one's own truth and righteousness is 'iniquity' that is 'idolatry.'"[4]

This is contrasted with the righteousness of God.

[1] Unbekannte Fragmente aus Luthers zweiter Psalmenvorlesung, 1518. E. Vogelsang. Berlin, 1940.
[2] Vogelsang. Unbekannte Fragmente, 52.24.   [3] Ibid. 67.8.
[4] Ibid. 72.32.

"O humble voice and pleasing to God. The Just man says I am not my righteousness, but it is the righteousness of God or from God. I confess myself a sinner, but from thy bounty, O God, I have righteousness." [1]

The movement within justification is more clearly stressed than ever.

"For in this life we do not apprehend righteousness, but we stretch out towards it, and we always seek and ask that we may be justified, our debts remitted and the will of our heavenly father be done, and that his name may be sanctified, and yet in this we are accounted just by God (reputamur) . . . so that the saints are at the same time sinners (simul peccatores et simul sancti) knowing themselves to be sinners, not knowing that they are saints, sinners in fact, saints in hope . . . and yet God treats sinners as though they were not sinners . . . simul sumus justi et injusti. . . . God counts us as just, who have not yet obtained righteousness but only seek it: at the same time sin and the absence of righteousness remain in us, and yet the sin is not sin and the un-righteousness not unrighteousness because of the reckoning of the merciful God (Dei reputatione miserentis) . . . therefore we are just with a righteousness outside ourselves (extrinseca) within we are unjust with unrighteousness, outwardly saints, inwardly sinners, in our lives and works unrighteous, only just by the reputation of God." [2]

"For simply to sin is a part of sin: but it is the whole iniquity to make sin righteousness and think righteousness is sin: a simple sin is three: the justification of sin is four." [3]

"In this life we are always beginning, always at the commencement, never at the end." [4]

"For this evil stays always in us, we are always prone to sin which by baptism and penance is not then abolished, but only begins to be cured. Therefore until we are perfectly cured and made whole (which is not done in this life) we are always bad, always sin, always are vain, always liars, and in this only are we just and holy, that we hate this in ourselves and confess, groaning through faith in Christ, hoping at last to be made perfect, since he is our righteousness, our sanctification, our wisdom." [5]

When Luther comes to the "theology of the Cross" he uses the striking figure of the "gemellus" (a word which means both twin and "double").

"'For first through the Cross every disciple becomes Christ's twin,' for in the flesh he is a fool, in the spirit he is wise, he is fair within, but of no comeliness without, rejected without, glorified within; rich

[1] Ibid. 32.24: also 64.21.　　　[2] Ibid. 85.1.
[3] Ibid. 78.25.　　　　　　　　　[4] Ibid. 41.11.
[5] Ibid. 44.23: also 58.17: 94.30.

and poor thus come together in one, the strong and the weak, the troubled and the quiet, the one who is alone, yet surrounded by many, reprobate yet elect, nay, even a timid man and God, as in Christ our 'double' (gemellus) and the form of all 'doubles' who through weak humanity makes weak men to be straitened, captive, slaves, but through the power of deity makes mighty sons of God, and Gods and free Lords." [1]

"For this is our twin and double (gemellus) . . . whom St. Thomas also (i.e. twin or Didymus) confessed saying 'My Lord and my God.' 'King' means that Christ is Lord on account of his humanity which he assumed: God on account of his eternal birth from the Father." [2]

The Christian man shares the cross of his Master.

"The spiritual man is exercised in many passions, and carries the cross of Christ in which the man who knows only carnal and earthly things is scandalized." [3]

"Therefore fools flee the cross and are frightened by suffering and seek the peace of the world." [4]

"For the good things of the Lord, the wicked call ills, which they flee and despise: but faith has its place hidden under adversities and sufferings." [5]

"For all good things are hidden in the cross and under the cross, and thus they are not to be sought or understood save under the cross." [6]

To understand this is very difficult, even for the "spiritual man," indeed it would be impossible "unless the Holy Spirit himself with his Gift, lay it bare, which can be known by no word, no teacher, no study nor any discipline . . . but with simple faith we believe." [7]

The practical stress reappears.

"Nobody can pray this psalm who is not straitened and in tribulation (that is, who is out of Christ)." [8]

"Therefore whoever wants to stand in adversities and passions has the work of faith, with which he despises visible things, and he pays attention to invisible things, lest falling back in the time of temptation he should say 'Who shall show us anything good?' and cease to offer the sacrifice of righteousness but rather rejoice that present things may be removed through the cross and passions which he undergoes, whose removal means that he is brought to eternal things." [9]

We turn from the fragment to the revised and published edition of

---

[1] Ibid. 45.20.
[2] Ibid. 70.29.
[3] Ibid. 32.11.
[4] Ibid. 33.7.
[5] Ibid. 53.13.
[6] Ibid. 88.28: also 89.6.
[7] Ibid. 46.22.
[8] Ibid. 33.16.
[9] Ibid. 55.26. At the beginning of this passage Luther refuses to expound " the light of thy countenance " as the synteresis, but affirms " this light is to be understood as ' faith.' "   54.26.

Luther's commentary on the first twenty-one Psalms (1518-21). We shall note two special features. First, the fuller development of his doctrine of Faith, and of the Word. Second, a more extended treatment of the subject of temptation (Anfechtung).

In the Fragment on the Psalms Luther had not repudiated the notion of "synteresis," though he had said that it was better to relate "the light of thy countenance" to Faith. But here is the full and final substitution.

"For faith is a light above all our faculties and powers. And hence, this lifting up is nothing else than pouring out upon us that light of faith . . . hence it is certain that this verse cannot be understood concerning natural reason (of the synteresis) as being the great director: according to the opinion of many who say 'that the first principles of morals are innate.' All such things are false. Faith is the first principle of all good works: and this is so hidden and unknown that all reason shrinks from it." [1]

Similarly decisive is his rejection of the mystical Theology.

"Many men have vamped up and fabled forth many things about mystical, negative, proper and symbolical theology, not knowing what they say, or whereof they affirm . . . nor can the commentaries of such men be read without peril: for such as the men are themselves, so are their writings: as they felt so they spoke: they felt everything the contrary to negative theology: that is, they never knew nor felt death and hell, nor loved such experience. . . . I wished to say these things because the commentaries of Dionysius on mystical theology are everywhere handed abroad both from Italy and from Germany, which are mere 'oppositions of science' vaunting and showing off. Let no man therefore consider himself a mystical theologian because he has read, understood and taught these things: or rather because he imagines he has understood and taught them. . . ." [2]

There follows the famous sentence:

"For a man becomes a theologian by living, by dying and by being damned, not by understanding, reading and speculating." [3]

There are numerous passages concerning Faith, and we can restrict the selection.

"For faith is not, as some of our moderns dream, a 'habitus,' quiet, snoring and sleeping in the soul: but it is always turned towards God with a straight and perpetually looking and watching eye: hence it comes to pass that it is the author and origin of all good works . . . and what

[1] Tr. Cole, iii.168. W.A. 5.119.7. The citations are vols. 3-4 of Henry Cole's translation of the " Operationes in Psalmos," checked and, where necessary, amended. This passage shows how Faith has replaced the synteresis in Luther's thought.
[2] Ibid. 242. W.A. 5.163.17.　　　　　　　　　　[3] W.A. 5.163.28.

else are all the Psalms but certain definitions of faith, hope and love?" [1]
There is an assurance of faith.

"Wherefore those doctors of theology (as they are called) are to be
utterly detested and condemned who teach us to remain in doubt
and uncertainty about whether we are in the grace and favour of God
or not, and whether God be our God and we his people or not . . .
away with all such most absurd and impious heresies. Let everyone
take heed that he be by no means in doubt whether or not God be for
him, that is whether or not he has God for his Father, Creator, Saviour
and the giver of all good things: that he may dwell securely alone,
and in hope, and that he may not be in a continual state of fluctuating
uncertainty 'like the troubled sea.' . . . For if thou believest concerning
the saints that they are safely secure and confident, why not believe
the same concerning thyself if thou desirest to be like them, and thou
hast received the same baptism, the same faith, the same Christ and all
else the same?" [2]
It is this living faith which joins us to Christ.

"For it is faith in Christ which makes him live in me and move in
me and act in me: in the same way as a healing ointment acts on a
sick body: and we are hereby not only made one flesh and one body
with Christ: but have an intimate, ineffable exchange of our sins for his
righteousness, as the venerable sacrament of the altar shows us, where
bread and wine are transformed into the body and blood of Christ." [3]

Imbedded in the commentary are two extended discussions, desig-
nated in Cole's translation as separate essays, on "Hope and Sufferings," and on "Faith and Works." The first, on "Hope and Sufferings,"
expounds faith, hope and love as the three dimensions of Christian
existence.

"Grace, that is faith, hope and love are not infused (infundi) without
sin also being poured out (effundi) at the same time: that is, the sinner is
not justified, unless he be first condemned: he is not made alive unless
he be first killed: he ascendeth not into heaven, unless he first descend
into hell . . . wherefore the infusion of grace must needs be attended
with bitterness, tribulation and suffering, under which the old man
groans, not being able to bear his casting out with any kind of patience.
But if under this tribulation a man be patient and wait for the hand of
him that is working in him and infusing grace (or communicating it)
unto him, he is thereby proved and shall find faith, hope and love." [4]
This is the rule for the whole Christian existence.

"This is the way in which grace is infused . . . not only at the first,

---

[1] iv.138. W.A. 5.460.9.   [2] iii.175. W.A. 5.124.20.
[3] Ibid. 496. W.A. 5.311.12.   [4] iii.244. W.A. 5.164.22.

but also at every communication. For the old man is always more and more crucified and sin is expelled as grace more and more enters in, until death, according to Rev. 22[11]." [1]

That is why the lessons of tribulation are more important than those of the active life.

"For tribulation, as it takes away all things from us, leaves nothing but God only: it cannot take away God but rather brings him closer to us." [2]

But this Christian hope has to be maintained in the fight with temptation.

"In these storms of conscience . . . hope fights against despair, and almost against itself: nay, even against God: whom hope feels to be angry with her, because she has no merits whatever." [3]

Thus the Psalms show us the great David brought low and made equal with us all.

"Before the face of the truth of God, David is nothing: and in the judgment of a just and righteous God he is as the greatest novice, the greatest sinner of all sinners. And this is the end of the law of faith and hope, to make us all the greatest and least instructed of all sinners: that is to make us all equal and yet to work the most unequal and most strange things!" [4]

"Other virtues may be perfected by doing: but faith, hope and love, only by suffering . . . by being passive under an inward divine operation . . . other virtues are occupied with grosser things, and things outward and carnal: but these inwardly about the pure internal Work of God: whereby the soul is taken hold of and does not take hold of anything itself: that is, it is stripped of its own garment, of its shoes, of all its possessions, and of all its imaginations and is taken away by the Word (to which it cleaves or rather which lays hold of it and leads it in a wonderful way) into the wilderness (Hos. 2[14]) to invisible things, into the vineyard and into the inner chamber . . . but this leading, this taking away, this stripping miserably tortures her . . . this leading or being led is what the mystical theologians call 'going into darkness' and 'ascending above entity and non-being.' But I must question whether such understand themselves: for they make all these things to be elicited acts, and do not believe them to be the sufferings of the cross, death and hell. The theology of the Cross only is our theology!" (Crux sola est nostra Theologia).[5]

[1] Ibid. 164.31.   [2] Ibid. 247.   W.A. 5.165.39.
[3] Ibid. 248.   W.A. 5.166.25.   [4] Ibid. 255.   W.A. 5.169.37.
[5] iii.258-60.   W.A. 5.176.1. Also W.A. 5.179.31.   "Crux probat omnia." This is an important passage for the similarities and distinctions between Luther's doctrine of faith and the technique of mysticism.

The essay on "Faith and Works" begins with the affirmation of the importance of the First Commandment.[1]

"The proper works of which commandment are to believe in, to hope in, to love and to fear God."

This involves the primacy of Faith.

"For as the first precept is the measure, standard, rule and virtue of all other precepts: from which first precept as from the head, all other precepts hang, and receive life and influence: so faith, the work of the same precept is the head, life and virtue of all other works and is in the greatest truth that universal reality which is the one thing needful in all things: so that no work is good unless faith be the operating spring of it. . . ."

"And there can by no means be faith unless there be a certain, living, and undoubting mind whereby a man is assured with all certainty that he pleases God and has him as a propitious and pardoning God in all things which he does and carries on: propitious in good things and pardoning in evil." [2]

Thus when a Christian man falls into sin, he is not lost in despair.

"And these things ought to be exactly as they are between a father and a son. For the son if he has at any time done wrong, fears indeed his father, but does not let go his confidence in his father's loving kindness: and yet he is ready with humble confession to bear his father's discipline." [3]

Thus the Christian knows confidence in the midst of godly fear.

"Faith in the mercy of God is more powerful for justification than the fear of the judgment of God, for the condemnation of our conconscience. Wherefore we have always a cause for fear, since all that we do of ourselves is evil and of itself damnable. But again under this fear we have always an occasion for believing and of fighting against the fear of the judgment of God by faith in his mercy, and glorying in that faith and its conquest." [4]

"Under all the changes and varieties of works, faith remains the same, believing and being confident in every work, that it pleases God, or rather that he is pardoning the propitious.

"It is an error, therefore, to put faith and its work upon a footing with the other virtues and works. For this faith must be held as being exalted above all these things and as being a sort of general and inac-

---

[1] There are numerous and close correspondences between Luther's treatment here in his two classic works of 1520. " Of Good Works " (W.M.L. 1.173 ff.) and " The Liberty of a Christian Man " (W.M.L., ii.297 ff.). Extracts, Rupp, " Luther's Progress " (1951), 73 ff., 86 ff.

[2] iv. 48.   W.A. 5.395.6.   [3] iv.58.   W.A. 5.400.13.

[4] Ibid. 59.   W.A. 5.400.35.

cessible influence above all works: by the moving and agency of which it is that all the works which are done by man, move, act and flourish and please God." [1]

The ultimate and fundamental need of man is to be right with God. Out of that relation, of which the human side is faith, and the divine grace, springs the Christian obedience. When two people are in love, and sure of each other, they do not think in terms of quantity, that is, they do not reckon up the size of their gifts to one another, or how expensive they are, nor do the things they do together and the places they visit, depend on quantitative measure, the best seats in the best theatres, the more costly flowers, etc. It is when the relationship is unsure, when two young people are uncertain of one another, that they begin to think quantitatively, and the one may seek to please by bigger and better gifts. This fact that faith does away with a quantitative measurement of services, is a profound comment on the nature of the Christian religion and cuts deep into the heart of the practical abuses of the late mediaeval Church, cluttered up as it was with practices and doctrines of merit, and "good works" which had become technical ecclesiastical performances.

"So in faith all works are equal, howsoever they may present themselves to us: for faith alone is the work of all works . . . for when a man believes God, whether he fasts, or prays or serves a brother, is all one and the same: for he knows that he serves and pleases God equally whether his works be great or small, precious or vile, short or long . . . but where there is not faith, there will be always found a fermenting toil of distinguishing, choosing and rejecting works . . . which iniquity is full of labour, toil and solicitude." [2]

Fundamental to Luther's whole doctrine is his emphasis on the spontaneity of Christian obedience, and love to God.

"Works and ceremonies are then done in faith and love, where they are not done from any constraining necessity, nor because they are commanded, but when they are done in the freedom of spirit." [3]

Set free from anxious preoccupation with ourselves, by faith, we are thus the more free and ready to serve our neighbours.

"And therefore all our life from henceforth should be lived to the benefit of our neighbour as Christ lived for us: and as we do all other things for their good, much more should we attend to these indifferent ceremonies for their good. And therefore we owe no man anything save to love one another." [4]

"Behold, therefore, how free all things are unto us by faith. And

[1] iv.51. W.A. 5.396.22.
[2] Ibid.
[3] Ibid. 62. WA.5.402.23.
[4] Ibid. 63. W.A. 5.404.9.

yet all things are subservient with us because of love: that there is at the same time the servitude of liberty, and the liberty of servitude since we owe nothing to any man, save to love one another. Thus Christ says, John 10[9], 'I am the door. By me if any man enter he shall be saved and shall go in and out and find pasture.' The 'going into' Christ is faith which brings us into the riches of the righteousness of God, by which righteousness we now satisfy God and are justified and righteous, wanting no works whatever to form a righteousness for ourselves. And this 'going out' is love which causes us, clothed with the righteousness of God, to lay ourselves out for the service and benefit of our neighbour and to the exercising of our own bodies in order to be enabled to supply the wants of another's poverty: so that they being drawn by us, may with us enter into Christ. For as Christ came out from God and drew us, seeking nothing of his own in all his life, but only ours: so when we have entered in by faith, we ought also to go in order to draw and attract others, seeking nothing else but that we may serve all, and save many, together with ourselves." [1]

This doctrine of the interdependence of faith and love is expounded even more clearly in the "Liberty of a Christian Man" (1521).

"This is the rule for Christians, that we should devote all our works to the welfare of others, since each has such abundant riches in his faith, that all other works and his whole life are a surplus with which he can by voluntary well-doing serve and do good to his neighbour." [2]

"My God has given me in Christ all the riches of righteousness and salvation without any merit on my part out of pure, free mercy. . . . Why should not I therefore freely, joyfully with all my heart and with an eager will, do all things, which I know are pleasing and acceptable to such a Father, who has overwhelmed me with His inestimable riches. I will therefore give myself to Christ as a neighbour just as Christ offered Himself to me." [3]

Luther expresses this in the striking affirmation that we should be "Christs" to one another.

"As our heavenly Father has in Christ freely come to our aid, we also ought freely to help our neighbour through our body and its works, and each should become as it were a Christ to the other, that we may be Christs to one another and Christ may be the same in all: that is, that we may be truly Christians . . . surely we are named after Christ, not because he is absent from us, but because he dwells in us, that is, because we believe in him, and are Christs one to another and do to our neighbours as Christ does to us." [4]

---

[1] Ibid. 64.   W.A. 5.407.42.   [2] W.M.L. 2.336.
[3] Ibid. 337.   [4] Ibid. 338.

It is the doctrine of the Word of God which binds the doctrine of faith to the doctrine of the Church, for Luther is by no means ready to isolate his doctrine of justification from that of the Church and of the sacraments.

"For it is by the Word alone that the people of God live, are fed and are preserved . . . for while the Word of God flourishes, all things flourish and go well in the Church—and what is the reason that, at this day the Church is not only withered away into luxury and pomp but is almost wholly destroyed? It is because the Word of God is disregarded, and the laws of men and the artful inventions of Rome are taught." [1]

"For we are to fight with weapons different from those of the ungodly. They contend with might and tumult, but we are to contend with prayer, the Word and patience." [2]

"And when it is said that he hath perfected praise and exalted his own glory out of the mouth of babes and sucklings: by that is doubtless signified the preaching of the Gospel and the word of the Cross, by which all these things ever have been and still are accomplished. For certainly the Word of the Cross, like a wine press, bruises and humbles the men of the world, and collects many into one body, as the wine is collected into one receiving vessel." [3]

When the Psalmist speaks of God rebuking the heathen, Luther comments:

"I was thinking . . . that we should hear the clash of arms and the galloping tumult of horses and riders. But behold it is the noise and the rebuke of the Word which makes all this terrible to do . . . he does all by the Word . . . in matters of faith the Word deals with the spirit, not a crafty but an invincible warrior whom none can resist . . . for who will not be turned back and will not fall and perish, whose conscience rebuked by the Word of God, gives a condemning sentence against himself? . . . we often find it among men that he whom neither judgment nor rebuke nor reputation or peril could subdue has been vanquished by the torment of his own conscience." [4]

"The Word will never cease to sound nor God to work with it and by it in the Church. For we are never to cease from the Word: it is to be in use, in motion and in flight that the Lord may always fly above and move in us by faith. Who although he can do all things by himself has decreed to do all these things by the ministry of the Word, that there may be an opportunity and occasion for faith and that he may

[1] iii.189. W.A. 5.131.23.
[2] Ibid. 363. W.A. 5.234.37.
[3] Ibid. 389. W.A. 5.249.32.
[4] Ibid. 468-70. W.A. 5.294.21.

thereby meet our infirmities which cannot endure Divine things unless covered and veiled by the Word." [1]

"For in the midst of so many perturbations within and without, and as it were, under and in the midst of this most dark tempest, we have no other star to steer by than the Word of God, by which all who are preserved and saved steer their course . . . and what is this candle of ours which is illuminated by the Word? It is without doubt our heart: and whether you call it the conscience or understanding it is all one and the same thing. . . . David calls all that prudence and human guidance which is without the operation of the Word 'darkness,' and this is the darkness he prays to have enlightened by the light of the Word. . . . It is the Word only that sustains a man and tells him what to do, namely that he is to trust in God and to expect deliverance and salvation from him." [2]

"The Word of God is such that, if you do not shut up, as it were, all your other senses and receive it only by hearing and believe in it, you cannot receive it . . . to understand this no one ever comes but in the day of tribulation, when a man is made destitute of all counsel whatever and simply cleaves to the Word and becomes teachable by, and attentive unto, the divine hearing." [3]

"In the Church it is not enough for books to be written and read, but it is necessary that they should be spoken and heard. Hence Christ wrote nothing, but said all things: and the apostles wrote few things, but spoke a great deal . . . for the ministry of the New Testament was not written upon dead tables of stone, but it was to be in the sound of the living voice . . . and now he speaks in the Church who before wrote in the synagogue and by his scriptures promised the Gospel, Rom. 1, but it is by the living Word that he accomplishes and fulfils the Gospel. Hence we are to be anxious that there are more good preachers than good writers in the Church." [4]

"Our standard is the Word of the cross, the triumphal ensign dyed purple with the Blood of Christ which the Church of Christ, who is terrible as an army with banners, opposes to all the powers of darkness. And to set aside the Word and fight without it, is nothing more than to play like children on holidays." [5]

We shall reserve Luther's doctrine of the Church for separate comment, but may insert a characteristic note at this point.

"For the Church is and can be nothing else but a congregation of spiritual men, gathered together not into any one particular place, but

---

[1] iv.211. W.A. 5.505.28.   [2] iv.241 : also 244. W.A. 5.525.8.
[3] Ibid. 259. W.A. 5.536.30.   [4] Ibid. 260. W.A. 5.537.10.
[5] iv.321. W.A. 5.574.31. Also iv.331.419.

into the same faith, hope and love of the Spirit . ∴. let us arm our understandings with the Word of God firmly believing and most surely knowing that the Church of Christ is nothing other than an assembly of spiritual and believing men collected together, in whatsoever part of the world they may be: and whatever of flesh and blood they may be: and knowing also that of whatever person, place, time they may be, and whatsoever things they may have which flesh and blood use, these things pertain not to the Church." [1]

We turn, finally, to Luther's doctrine of "Anfechtung." This is the trial of faith by various temptations.

"For in adversity it is a hard matter not to faint, not to complain, not to become impatient, and from fear of evil not to do things or to leave them undone, contrary to the commands of God: and thus by the fear of God to overcome the fear of the creature, not to yield to the senses, and to sensible objects, not to cleave close unto the Word of the Lord even unto death." [2]

"These are words not of nature, but of grace, not of free will but of the spirit of strong faith: which even though seeing God as in the darkness of the storm of death and hell, a deserting God, acknowledges him a sustaining God: when seeing him as a persecuting, God acknowledges him as a helping God: when seeing him as one who condemns, acknowledges him as a Saviour. This faith does not judge of things according as they seem to be or are felt, like a horse or mule which have no understanding." [3]

"For it is a hard matter and the power of divine grace to believe in God as the lifter up of our head and our crown, in the midst of death and hell. For this exaltation is a hidden thing and what is seen is only despair and no help in God. And therefore we are taught to believe in hope against hope, which wisdom of the cross is at this day deeply hidden in a profound mystery. For there is no other way into heaven, than this cross of Christ. And therefore we must take heed that the active life and its works, and the speculative life with its speculations does not delude us: they are each very pleasing and quiet and on that account the more perilous until they be disturbed and tempered by the cross. The cross is the safest of all things—blessed is he who understands!" [4]

"We are all taught that in the time of temptation we ought to hope for the divine help from above but that the time, manner and nature of the help are unknown to us: that so there may be room for faith and hope . . . thus the eye of faith looks towards the deep darkness and

[1] iv.125. W.A. 5.450.25.   [2] Ibid. iii.82. W.A. 5.71.24. Also iii.87.
[3] Ibid. 101.W.A. 5.82.14.   [4] iii.106. W.A. 5.84.36. Also iii.108.

R

blackness of the hill, and sees nothing . . . it looks on high and from on high expects a helper: but what this on high is or what help it will get, it does not know. For although Christ knew all things, yet he was himself tempted as we are: so in respect of his humanity, and in a certain sense, he had this hill unknown to him and incomprehensible during the hour of his passion . . . for as God is ineffable, incomprehensible and inaccessible, so are his will and his help also, especially in the time of desertion." [1]

Throughout, Luther shows a concern for timid and afflicted consciences.

"Thou art not even then to despair when thou feelest despair. For that is not despair when thou desirest not to despair and grievest that thou dost despair, it is only the trial and temptation of hope: though that is certainly by far the most heavy of all temptations, because it involves in its sensations the greatest and eternal hatred of God, blasphemies, curses and all the evils of hell which we dare not openly mention: in a word it involves the ever-blessed and glorious Majesty." [2]

"What . . . shalt thou do? Why, first acknowledge that thou deservest all this and that it is due unto thy sins. And herein thou art to be wise: thou art to praise and give thanks to God: and thou art to endure this infirmity and temptation . . . do all in thy power not to yield to this hatred, blasphemy and desperation: but that thou cry unto God . . . and I will say one thing more in my free and bold way —there are none nearer to God in this life than this kind of haters and blasphemers of him, nor any sons more pleasing to him and beloved by him. And thou mayest in this state make more satisfaction for sin in one moment than by repenting for many years together under a diet of bread and water. Hence it is true that in death (where this temptation prevails most) a Christian may in one moment get rid and shot of all his sins if he do but act wisely under the temptation." [3]

As generally, Luther's portrayal of the stricken conscience is vivid and sombre.

"The soul being left destitute of all confidence finds herself in a horrible condition as a guilty criminal, standing alone before the tribunal of an eternal and angry God . . . the conscience being reprehended and convicted immediately feels nothing else than that eternal damnation is its portion; nobody can understand this deep experience nor indeed the inferior kinds of it who has not tasted it: and therefore we cannot fully describe it when dealing with it. Job experienced it

---

[1] Ibid. 110. W.A. 5.86.30.   [2] Ibid. 256. W.A. 5.169-70.
[3] Ibid.

more than any other, and that frequently. And after him David and King Hezekiah and a few others. And lastly, the German divine Tauler makes frequent mention of it in his sermons." [1]

"What this sensation of death and hell is, in this conflict and perturbation is shown in the Psalm . . . to those who are exercised under this tribulation, there is nothing in the whole creation so pleasant as to be able to give relief even to one hair of the head, nothing so sweet in sound as to be able to soothe the ear, nothing delightful to eat, to drink or to touch that does not seem very bitterness. Death is in every thing that is either seen or touched." [2]

"What then is this being in death and hell? It is, first, to be in an eternal forgetfulness and oblivion of God: and next to be in eternal blasphemy. For here the care for the love of self reigns with a most powerful and most confused concern: and therefore it is impossible for such to have the mercy of God before their eyes. They seek refuge and escape and find none: and then they are presently involved in a most burning hatred of God. They first of all desire that there were another God and then that they themselves had no existence: and thus, they blaspheme the divine majesty: they wish (as I said) with all their heart that no such majesty existed: and if they could they would destroy his existence: and this fleeing from and this hatred against God is eternal . . . they are ever fleeing but never escape." [3]

This wrath of God against the sinner is reflected in the creation.

"In addition to being alarmed and terrified by the anger of God, he can find consolation in no creature and whatever he looks at seems to be against him. For the whole creation acts with its creator: and especially when a man's own conscience is opposed to God: and therefore everything is wrath: everything increases the tribulation: all things around are enemies." [4]

"In this state, hope despairs and despair hopes: and there is nothing remaining alive but that inward groan that cannot be uttered in which the Spirit rises, moving upon the face of these waters covered with darkness . . . no one can understand these things but he who has tasted them: they do not stand in speculations and fancies . . . they lie in the inmost feelings of the immortal life, that is, in the feelings of the soul . . . it is the immortal part that suffers and is afflicted, and they are immortal things which cause the oppression and affliction: namely, sins." [5]

The remedy, to call upon the name of the Lord, is hardest to apply in the midst of temptation.

[1] Ibid. 307. W.A. 5.203.5.   [2] Ibid. 314. W.A. 5.207.28.
[3] Ibid. 318. W.A. 5.209.36.   [4] Ibid. 323. W.A. 5.213.4.
[5] iv.31. W.A. 5.385.19. Also iv.37, 38-9.

"Who but he that has experienced it would believe that it was so difficult to call upon the name of the Lord? Who would believe this but he that has felt death, fear of shame, conscience and a thousand other perils attack the soul more violently than all the forces of the enemy can attack it from without? For it is in the midst of these things that the soul is so distracted in the midst of the perils which are within it, around it, and rushing upon it, that it is in danger of losing sight of the name of the Lord. Nor is it enough merely to think on and call upon the name of the Lord at the first, but we must remember the name of the Lord with a persevering and constant remembrance, yea even unto the end of the victory against all the perilous and terrible things that may oppose themselves unto us. For as it is impossible that the name of the Lord should be overcome as it is eternal and omnipotent, so it is impossible that he should fall who trusts in it and perseveringly cleaves unto it." [1]

"The time for hoping is especially at that time when many great, powerful and continual evils rush in upon us . . . for what display of divine power in us would that be, that should only help us to bear the punishment of our sins and should not overcome the sins in us? . . . nobody is ever delivered from evils by looking at and dwelling in bitterness upon those evils: he overcomes them only in cleaving close to God and looking at his goodness." [2]

The most moving and profound of all his expositions is that of Psalm 21 with the cry of dereliction uttered by the Lord upon his cross. Here Luther paints with terrible and sombre realism the horror of "Anfechtung" and sets over and against it the "angefochtene Christus," the Saviour who trod the whole grim path of "Anfechtung" for us.

"The first terror is when the eyes of the soul are opened and it feels that it stands naked and is made manifest in the sight of all creation, together with all the shame of its actions and its ill-spent life . . . for the soul, as it were, goes out of its former coverings and is stripped of all corporal creatures which were before its coverings and garments and is compelled to see and permit to be seen all the secrets of its shame." [3]

The second wave of attack is the scorn of the rest of creation.

"Every creature that is seen will seem to have a voice in reproaching the person and upbraiding him for his wicked life, and deriding him for his folly . . . holding him in derision in the sight of all. And the devils are here specially busy themselves and weary the soul with the most terrible cogitations."

The third terror is when the condemnations of scripture are brought

---

[1] iv.327. W.A. 5.578.16.   [2] iv.191-3. W.A. 5.493.27.
[3] iv.385. ff W.A. 5.620.10.

home to the mind. The fourth is when not only the Law but the Gospel adds terror. The fifth is when the soul turns away from Christ.

"Hereby Christ is denied to be the head, and hope is fixed in God alone, that he would cause Christ to be given. And here the matter is carried on without a Mediator (Hic sine mediatore agitur res), and there is a disputing about the good pleasure and will of God."

Thus the soul comes to the final temptation, concerning Predestination. "The soul concludes that he is not predestined to salvation."

"In this last temptation 'the soul seems to be wholly thrust into and swallowed up in hell and the pit seems to shut its open mouth upon it and it seems as if it were almost an inhabitant of hell . . . here these blasphemies and murmurings and cursings are almost within the very gates of hell, and God begins to be considered unjust, savage and cruel.'"

The remedy is silence. "Let it take heed that it dispute not with devils and with evil cogitations concerning all these things: let it give no answer, but remain dumb to all these things which are objected to it, and suffer them to pass by . . . let the one tempted never lose sight of the example of silence given us by Christ, and then let him fight with faith against faith." [1]

But the real remedy lies not in advice, nor in any technique, though Luther has advice which is in line with the best moral and practical theology of his age, but Christ.

"When we begin to view, with a contemplating heart, Christ hanging at the breasts of his mother, or lying in a manger, what evil is not put to flight, what infirmity is not strengthened. Only make the trial and you will understand what it is to behold the Divine Majesty engaged in such infantile things, in such scenes of weakness and puerility." [2]

Luther will not soften the sharpness of Christ's cry of dereliction on the Cross.

"In Christ there were at the same time the greatest joy and the greatest sorrow, the greatest weakness and the greatest power, the greatest glory and the greatest confusion: and so also there were the greatest peace and the greatest trouble: and again the greatest life and the greatest death, and this is shown . . . where Christ says that he is forsaken of God and yet calls God his God."

"What then shall we say here? Shall we not say that Christ at the same time was (as he stood in our stead) the most righteous person and the greatest sinner, or the greatest lies and the greatest truth, of the greatest glorying and the greatest despair, the most truly blessed and the most utterly damned? For if we say not these things, I know not

[1] Ibid. 388.　　　　[2] Ibid. 393. W.A. 5.626.11.

how he could be forsaken of God. For if in this way many saints were left of God such as Job, David, Hezekiah, Jacob, how much more shall it be said of Christ, the head of all the saints that he was left of God and carried and bore all our griefs and sorrows in himself . . . I say of necessity Christ himself suffered the dread and horror of a distressed conscience that tasted eternal wrath. . . . For the Apostle saith, Heb. 4[15], that he was tempted in all points like as we are, yet without sin . . . what absurdity is there in ascribing unto Christ a trembling and fearful conscience for a time, and thereby showing that he, though innocent, endured our misery for a time?" [1]

He will not minimize the realism of the Gospel picture of Gethsemane.

"(They say) he opposes his will to the will of God: and that he did in the garden when he said 'Not my will, but thine be done': wherein they say, he manifestly indicated that he had a will contrary to that of God: and so strong a will that he broke it by much force and even with a bloody sweat in order to subject it to the will of God . . . but here again this was a motion of the greatest and highest kind proceeding from an innocent and infirm nature . . . which motion we could not feel on account of the depraved leaven and sin of self-love: and if we did feel it, rebellion and disobedience would creep in through the leaven of this sin. A clean hand may touch clean linen and not pollute it, but an unclean hand cannot but pollute it. . . . Christ therefore loved his father with all his strength: but his torments as they were above his human strength forced his innocent and infirm nature to sigh, groan, cry, dread and shrink: in the same way, if you load a beam beyond its strength it must from natural necessity and not from any defect in itself crack and give way . . . though Christ suffers that which is beyond his strength that which he sends forth in cry is not blasphemy, but an innocent cry like that which is blasphemy in us." [2]

"It was not a matter of play, or jest, or hypocrisy when he said 'Thou hast forsaken me': for he then felt himself really forsaken in all things, even as a sinner is forsaken after he has sinned: though he was not in reality left as a sinner . . . all that Christ suffered he suffered in deed: nor are we to lessen or make void the meaning and force of the words of God." [3]

Thus "Christ for us" leads us to the delivering righteousness of God.

"And this is that mystery which is rich in divine grace unto sinners: wherein by a wonderful exchange, our sins are no longer ours but Christ's: and the righteousness of Christ is not Christ's but ours. He has emptied himself of his righteousness that he might clothe us with

<hr>

[1] iv.359 ff.   W.A. 5.602.21 ff.   [2] iv.364.   W.A. 5.605.13.
[3] Ibid.

it, and fill us with it: and he has taken our evils upon himself that he might deliver us from them. So that now the righteousness of Christ is not only ours objectively (as they term it) but formally also. . . . For in the same manner as he grieved and suffered in our sins, and was confounded, in the same manner we rejoice and glory in his righteousness." [1]

Our last group of citations from among Luther's early writings will be taken from his "Rationis Latomianae Confutatio" (1521). Latomus (James Masson) was a secular priest, and Professor at Louvain. He was prominent in that group of theologians who hated and were hated by Erasmus almost as cordially as by Luther. Latomus had participated in the condemnation of Luther's doctrines by the Universities of Louvain and Cologne at the end of 1519. To this Luther replied in the following March. Latomus spent many months preparing an attack on Luther which he published 8th May 1521, and which is among the ablest of the writings of the Catholic controversialists.[2] Luther, now exiled in his Patmos of the Wartburg, his sources almost confined to the Bible, replied in a Latin tract which he had finished by the end of June, and which appeared as the "Rationis Latomianae Confutatio." It is one of his best controversial writings, and though, seeking to meet a fellow Professor on their common ground of technical discussion, he is handicapped through being parted from his library, he handles the intricacies of the debate with skill.

What Luther has to say about the remnant of sin in Christians after baptism, and about its conquest, illuminates the whole development of his theology to this point, and brings his teaching about Justification, not to a final conclusion, but at least to a convenient halting-place for our purpose.

Luther affirms that what remains in a man after baptism is not the mere "tinder of sin" (fomes peccati) but is properly to be called sin, for the baptized Christian in this life is always a sinner. "For I wanted to say, and now say (what makes the hairs of our learned Masters stand on end!) that sin is present in a good work with the 'predication of perseity' as long as we live, as risibility is present in man, whereas food, sleep, death are in him 'per accidens.'" [3]

Sin remains as a "substance" which Luther expounds "not in the manner of Aristotle, but of Quintilian," i.e. not as an "ens" but as the answer to the question "What is it?" [4]

"This substantial sin . . . after baptism and infused power of God

---

[1] iv.369. W.A. 5.608.5. On this theme, Vogelsang, Angefochtene Christus.
[2] Luther regarded it as the ablest of all the attacks on himself. TR. 463, " Unus Latomus ist der feinst scriptor contra me gewest."
[3] W.A. 8.77.8.   [4] W.A. 8.88.15.

is such that it is not yet entirely reduced to nothing, but is broken and in subjection, so that now it can no longer do what it once could. For what could it do? It brought us in guilty 'coram Deo' and tyrannically infested the conscience, and brought us day by day into worse ills, and was potent in quantity, quality and action, in which it reigned when and where it would, for always and at all times, and in all our powers and at all hours, it prevailed. In the 'predicate' of passion indeed it was nothing, for it would not suffer the argument of the law, and refused even to be touched. Thence it had its dwelling in the heart, turned its face away and downwards and made ready haste towards hell. In short, it was the relation of all the worst things which were opposed to grace, subject to the wrath and fury of God. Thus it reigned and we were its slaves. But when the kingdom of God came, this kingdom was divided, the prince of this world was cast out, the head of this serpent bruised so that only certain dregs and remnants remain which by our care are at last to be exterminated. . . . It is the question between me and these sophists whether this remnant of sin ought really to be counted as sin or no." [1]

Luther appeals to St. Paul in Rom. 7 and refuses to accept the subtle distinctions of those who evade this direct apostolic testimony. St. Paul did not speak of "infirmity" or "imperfection," but he called it sin. [2]

"Sin through baptism is made captive in us, judged and thoroughly weakened that it can do nothing and is handed over to be thoroughly abolished . . . thus sin in us after baptism really is sin by nature, but in substance, not in quantity, or quality, or action, but wholly in passion. For the motion of wrath and lust is just the same in the pious and impious, the same before grace and after grace, as it is the same flesh before and after grace, but in grace it can do nothing, and outside grace it prevails." [3]

"For Christ indeed once and for all freed us all from sin and death when he merited for us the law of the spirit of life. What then did that spirit of life? It has not yet freed us from death and sin, but it will free us at length, for we have yet to die, yet to labour against sins. But he freed us from the law of sin and death, that is from the kingdom and tyranny of sin and death, that sin indeed should be present, but with the tyranny taken away, it can do nothing, and death is indeed present, but with the sting removed it cannot harm or frighten." [4]

"What then? Are we sinners? Nay, rather we are justified, but by

[1] W.A. 8.88.26.
[2] W.A. 8.89.15-25 : 97.28. " If you can prove that sin, as cited in these texts of St. Paul, is not really and truly sin, 'Ruit Lutherus!'" P. Althaus. Paulus und Luther, 41 ff.   [3] W.A. 8.91.24.
[4] W.A. 8.92.3. Luther quotes Rom. 8[13], Col. 3[5].

grace. Righteousness is not located in those forms of qualities, but in the mercy of God. It is true that if you take mercy away from the pious, they are sinners and really have sin, but because they believe and live under the kingdom of mercy, sin is damned and continually put to death in them, and therefore is not imputed. This is the most glorious remission of baptism, and certainly if you look at the matter carefully, it is almost greater to count him righteous who is still infected with sin, than him who is altogether pure. We do not say, therefore, that baptism does not take away all sins, it really takes them all away, not according to substance, but much of their substance, and the whole of its power, at the same time, taking it away according to its substance every day, until it is removed . . . it is sin even after remission, but it is not imputed." [1]

Luther distinguishes here between "peccatum regnans" and "peccatum regnatum." [2] The first is sin under the Wrath of God. The other is sin under Grace. In each case the whole man is placed under the judgment or under the mercy of God. Luther replies to the suggestion that he was erecting a new vocabulary at this point, with the disclaimer that he will not fight about words, though this particular thought of "sin reigning" he had taken direct from St. Paul. The scholastics themselves distinguish between the venial sin, which cannot hurt, reign or damn, and mortal sin.

"I ask nothing more than that they permit me to call sin that remnant after baptism which they call venial, which needs mercy, and which is by nature bad and a fault, to which if you consent, you have allowed it to reign, and are in its service and have mortally sinned." [3]

Luther then treats of the power and inwardness of sin.

"I am not sure whether sin in the Scriptures is ever taken for those works which we call sins. For it seems to be rather that radical ferment which bears fruit in evil words and deeds." [4]

That is why there is sin in "good works" apart from grace.

"The law alone therefore shows, not that these things are bad in themselves, for indeed they are the gifts of God, but they are bad in the use of them, on account of that radical sinfulness which is most secret (occultissimum) in which they trusted, and found pleasure and gloried with an insensible evil, as this intimate evil of sin always does, since we are to trust and please God only and give him the glory." [5]

---

[1] W.A. 8.92.38 : 96.6. "Baptismi symbolum pro testimonio habes, in quo verissime omnia peccata tibi remissa sunt, remissa inquam in totum, sed nondum omnia abolita." The whole problem of the relation of the eschatological character of salvation, and of the work of Christ and its appropriation in time by "homo viator" is involved here.
[2] On this, Prenter, 88.
[3] W.A. 8.96.28.   [4] W.A. 8.104.4.   [5] W.A. 8.105.13.

Luther is here working with the background of his doctrine of "the whole man" who is a sinner, and who is received in a new, saving, right relationship with God. This is shown by a distinction which he makes more clearly in this writing than in any other, between "grace" (gratia), which is the favour of God, that is, the new relation between God and the believing soul, from which all salvation springs, and the "gift" (donum), the sanctifying work of the Holy Spirit. Nowhere is the doctrine of the "whole man" and of direct personal relationship with God more strikingly asserted than here.

"You see, then, how the law incomparably exceeds natural reason, and how profound is sin, whose knowledge the law teaches. All are under wrath, for all are in sin.

"The gospel, on the other hand, treats sin thus, that it may take it away and thus most sweetly follows the law. For the law was introduced that it might overwhelm us with sin through the knowledge which it gives us, which causes us to seek to be delivered from it, and sigh for grace. For the gospel preaches and teaches two things, righteousness and the grace of God, and through righteousness heals the corruption of nature, that righteousness indeed which is the gift of God, i.e. faith in Christ, Rom. 3^{21}: 5^1: 3^{28}. And this righteousness which is the opposite to sin is generally taken in the scriptures for that intimate root whose fruits are good works. To this faith and righteousness the companion is grace or mercy, the favour of God (against wrath which is the companion of sin) that all who believe in Christ may have a propitious God." [1]

"For we should not be joyful enough in this blessing of righteousness, nor should we magnify this his 'gift' (donum) if it were alone and did not reconcile us to God by his grace (gratia). I take grace here to mean properly, the favour of God, as it ought to be taken and not for a quality of the soul, as our newfangled theologians taught, and this grace really works peace in the heart until at length a man is healed from his corruption, and in addition feels (se sentiat) himself to have a propitious God. This it is which stirs the bones, and gives a joyful conscience, secure, unterrified, in nothing not daring, in nothing not strong, and which even laughs at death in confidence of this grace of God. Whence, as wrath is a greater ill than the corruption of sin, so grace is a greater good than the healing of righteousness which we said is by faith. For nobody would not rather choose (if it might be) to be without the healing of righteousness than without the grace of God. For the remission of sins and peace are properly to be attributed to the grace of God, but the healing of corruption to faith. For faith

[1] W.A. 8.105.33.

is the gift (donum) and an internal good opposed to sin, which it purges and it is that evangelical leaven hidden in three measures of meal. But the grace of God is an external good, the opposite of wrath. Rom. 5, 'For if through the sin of one many died, how much more shall the grace of God and the gift (gratia dei et donum) of one man Jesus Christ abound to many.' The gift (donum) in the grace of one man he calls faith in Christ (which also he more often calls 'donum'), and this is given us in the grace of Christ, i.e. because he alone among men is welcome and accepted, to have a propitious and clement God that he might merit this 'gift' and also this 'grace' for us." [1]

Here the doctrine of the "whole man," is joined with a doctrine of divine activity, and the doctrine of justification by faith becomes a congruent whole, in terms of what Prenter calls "the Biblical realism" of personal encounter with God.

"Thus we have two goods of the gospel against the two ills of the law, the gift for sin, and grace against wrath. Now it follows that these two, wrath and grace, are such (as they are outside us) that they are poured out wholly (ut in totum effundantur) that he who is under the wrath is wholly under all wrath (totus sub tota ira), and he who is under grace is wholly under the whole of Grace—for wrath *and grace have to do with persons.*[2] Whom therefore God receives in grace he receives wholly, and whom he favours he favours wholly. On the other hand, if he is angry with a man, he is angry with the whole man (in totum irascitur). For he does not divide this grace, as gifts are divided: he does not love the head and hate the foot, nor favour the soul and hate the body. And yet he gives to the soul what he does not give to the body, and gives the head what he does not give to the feet. And thus it is in the whole Church (in tota Ecclesia) which stands in the same grace of God as Rom. 5. 'Through whom we have access into this grace by which we stand.' He is diverse and many sided in his gifts. Thus, on the other hand, whom he does not favour, he does not favour as a whole, and yet he does not punish the whole, nay rather, that one through the sin of one member remains wholly under wrath, and this one with one gift of the one work remains whole under grace, so that, as we said, grace and gifts are to be carefully distinguished, for grace alone is eternal life, Rom. 6, and wrath alone is eternal death." [3]

"Meanwhile while this happens, it is called sin, and is really sin by nature, but now it is sin without wrath, without the law, dead sin, sin innocuous, if only you persevere in the grace and his gift. For

[1] W.A. 8.106.8.   [2] Our italics.
[3] W.A. 8.106.35. The key to this difficult but capital passage is " ira et gratia personas respiciunt "—have regard to persons. Luther here is not using " persona " as he sometimes does, as an outward covering or mask.

sin is no different by nature before and after grace, but it differs in its treatment. For now it is treated differently from before. How was it formerly treated? That it might be, and might be known and might overwhelm us, but now it is so treated that it should cease to be, and is cast out." [1]

"Grace therefore has no sin to face, for the whole person pleases, but the 'gift' has sin to face, which it purges out and fights against, but a person does not please and has not grace, unless he has the gift, and in this way is labouring to cast out sin. For God does not save imaginary sinners, but real sinners, and he teaches us to put to death not imaginary but real sin." (Deus non fictos sed veros peccatores salvos facit.) [2]

We can now see the point of Prenter's argument against the doctrine of Holl and Seeberg,[3] who speak of a "declaring righteous" and a "making righteous" as the two parts of Luther's doctrine of Justification. We can also see that Luther avoids certain dangers in the later Protestant differentiation between Justification and Sanctification at this point. For Luther the divine activity which is our justification is the whole continuing ground of our relationship with God: it is a personal relationship in which we are always sustained by faith in that other righteousness than our own, which is given us in Jesus Christ.

"Without any doubt the righteous and believer has 'grace' and 'gift': grace which makes him wholly gracious—so that as a person he is entirely acceptable, and there is no place of wrath in him any more, and the 'gift' indeed which heals him from sin and the whole corruption of his soul and body. It is therefore most impious to say that the baptized person is still in his sins, or that all his sins are not fully remitted. For what sin is there where God favours and wills to know no sin, and totally accepts the whole and sanctifies it? But this is not to be referred to our purity, as you see, but to the sole grace of the favouring God. They are all remitted by grace, but they are not yet all healed by the gift. For the gift is infused, the ferment is mixed, and it is working that it may purge out sin, which is now allowed (indultum) in his person, that it may expel the bad guest, and to it leave is given for ejection." [4]

---

[1] W.A. 8.107.24: also 121.5. "Thus the sin is really sin, but because 'the gift' and 'grace' are in me, it is not imputed, not on account of its innocence as though it was not harmful, but because the gift and grace reign in me."

[2] W.A. 8.107.32: also 96.8. "For we believe all our sins are remitted without doubt, but every day we act and expect that there may be a complete removal and emptying away of sins."

[3] Spiritus Creator, 84 ff. See above, p. 31.

[4] W.A. 8.107.13.

Chapter

11

COMMENT

"O for a Luther in the present Age!"
S. T. COLERIDGE on Luther's " Table Talk."

IN our sketch of Luther's development in these critical years, we have
followed the sound method of Regin Prenter, and concentrated on
"what" Luther said. We have sought to allow the reader to hear
Luther himself, and have deliberately reduced comment and interpretation to a minimum. We have risked the effect of repetition, for in
Luther's theology there are themes to which he returns again and
again. But it is like the ascent of a spiral staircase, where the same
point is reached but at a new level and with a wider perspective. It
remains to offer some more general comment.

Modern historical writing is suffering from the "pattern historian,"
who compresses and disposes of intricate historical complexities in
some short formula or key word. And perhaps the evil does not lie
in our Toynbees and our Tawneys as in their lesser followers and
imitators, the journalist historians with their social, political or ecclesiastical party line. But prefabricated history of this kind is a misleading
and dangerous method of disposing of vast historical complexities.
To weigh the nations as dust in a balance and take up the isles as a
very little thing is a divine, not a human capacity. Often when we
test such interpretations with some period with which we have detailed
acquaintance, we discover the description to be a pattern of half-truths
of which we may well prefer the alternative portions. One approaches
historical theology, in consequence, with a mistrust of the growing
tendency to short formulae.[1]

The debt which students of Luther owe to Scandinavian scholars
and the method of "motif" research is such, as we have admitted, that
an English writer must speak of it with deference. Those who have
used it most fruitfully are aware of its limitations, and of the complexities
involved in historical truth. They know the difficulties which arise

---

[1] It sometimes seems as though any great figure in the Christian past, whether it
be Origen, Athanasius, St. Thomas, Zwingli, Calvin, can only be commended in
modern ecumenical conversation if he is shown to have a theology which is (i) theocentric, (ii) existential, (iii) eschatological ! All these formulae have been applied to
Luther.

when we put to Luther fundamental questions which are ours, rather than his, and the peril of selecting out of the wealth of sources, what we set out to find. For that is the sure way to miss the problems of the Reformation as they arose in the creative and destructive moments of their origin, concerning which Protestants and Catholics are still at odds, and more than either side will admit, at misunderstanding.

The word "theocentric" has been a great formula of modern Luther study. In Germany this was the welcome stress of Karl Holl [1]: it was in part a protest against a christocentric and subjectivist Protestantism on the one hand and a formal, Melanchthonian orthodoxy on the other.[2] Holl was able to stress that Luther's "religion was a religion of conscience" because he insisted on Luther's concern to give God the glory, and his constant awareness of the Divine Imperative. To the criticism that Holl found this theocentric emphasis in Luther because of his own earlier preoccupation with Calvin, Holl replied that in fact the study of Calvin reminds us of an original Reformation insight in Luther which later Lutheranism had blurred. None the less, there is something, we feel, in this criticism. A good deal of the modern discussion in Germany about the significance of the First Commandment in Luther's teaching seems to reflect a tension in modern Protestantism rather than a motive dominant in Luther himself. The more recent stress in Althaus and Iwand and others, on Luther's thought of "justificare" as the "justification of God" (in Forsythian phrase)—is based on genuine elements in Luther's writings, and notably in his Lectures on Romans.

Yet is not this emphasis something about which modern Protestants become tense, while Luther himself could relax, since here the Nominalist doctrine of the glory of God supported him? For it is just here that the formula "theocentric" as applied to Luther is usually brought into conjunction with the charge of "anthropocentric" levelled at the mediaeval theologians and the Nominalists in particular. Luther was concerned to give God the glory: the First Commandment had immense significance for him. It is a great gain in Luther study that we are now irrevocably aware of this stress. But I doubt if this is the differentia between himself and the Nominalists. The most recent scholarship (and in the case of the works of E. Gilson and P. A. Vignaux of the highest order) has modified the picture given of late mediaeval theology in the Protestant and indeed in Catholic text-books.

---

[1] See O. Wolff. Die Haupttypen der neueren Lutherdeutung. Stuttgart 1938, 322. Miegge. Lutero, 141 n. Holl. Ges. Aufs. iii.255.
[2] I cannot help feeling that Luther himself would have been amused at some of the modern wedges driven between Melanchthon's teaching and his own. And dare one suggest that German Luther scholarship will continue to miss something of the authentic Luther as long as it is dogged by a phobia towards Pietism ?

P. A. Vignaux has shown that a prime concern of Ockham and his school was to guard the Liberty of God. Could there be a more thoroughly "theocentric" phrase than their watchword "nullius debitor est"? Was not the opposition to Pelagianism in the fourteenth century (and here the criticism levelled at Peter of Auriol is important) directly opposed to the suggestion that men could have rights over and against God and somehow claim their salvation from him? The theocentric formula "Velle deum esse deum"—"Let God be God,"[1] is a Nominalist formula. It is true that as Mr. P. S. Watson's fine study "Let God be God" shows, Luther differs vastly from the Nominalists as to the grounds and character of divine and human liberty. But it is plain that the formula "theocentric" itself offers no adequate differentiation. In fact, the whole careful structure of mediaeval theologies, in Aquinas, Scotus and Ockham, was concerned to set human freedom and the liberty of the creature within the sovereign action of the grace of God. We have noted Luther's drastic and violent criticism of that structure. But one can hardly dismiss the whole of late mediaeval theology as "anthropocentric" or "egocentric."

The most celebrated modern exponent of the theocentric character of Luther's thought is Anders Nygren in his seminal study "Agape and Eros." He speaks of Luther's "Copernican Revolution." This was the insistence of Luther, "in opposition to egocentric forms of religion, upon a purely theocentric relation to God." In late mediaeval piety the dominant motive is a man-centred "eros," which finds its clearest expression, however, in the Renaissance Platonism of Marsilius Ficino. In the piety of the later Middle Ages, "salvation is transformed from something God gives into something a man achieves. At the same time everything centres on a man's own interest. . . . Against the egocentric attitude which had come to mar the Catholic conception of love, Luther sets a thoroughly theocentric idea of love."[2]

It must be noted that Nygren recognizes that the matter is more complex than his formula suggests. Positively, it does justice to the greatness and originality of Luther's thought. It was a great weakness of the school of Denifle that while on the one hand it stressed the enormous tragic disturbance Luther had brought to sixteenth century Christendom, it was at pains to demonstrate, at the same time, that he was a bit of a fool, and as a theologian a very second-rate thinker who muddled and misunderstood when he did not deliberately fake. Against this can be set the theological and liturgical and poetical and institu-

---

[1] Luther. " Contra scholasticam theologiam," 17. P. A. Vignaux. Sur Luther et Ockham, 30.
[2] A. Nygren. Agape and Eros, 463-5.

tional achievements of four centuries of Protestantism, a rich and many-sided tradition stemming from Luther's themes. For when polemic has said all it has to say, and when it prophesies, as it has done every twenty years since the Reformation began, that Protestantism is about to die, it can still be said, after the order of Copernicus, "Eppur si muove"!

Nygren skilfully delineates the tension in mediaeval thought of a "eudaemonistic" element which penetrates into the orthodox doctrines of salvation and which is the object of some of Luther's most devastating criticism. Luther's attack on the doctrine of "doing what in one lies," and on the doctrine that man can love God and obey Him "according to the substance of the deed" is directed against an "anthropocentric" element which is really there.

None the less, here too, a word of caution is necessary. In the first place, though this proves nothing, it is worth noticing that "egocentric" and "anthropocentric" are precisely the charges which modern Catholic polemic has brought against Luther himself and against the doctrine of "Justification by Faith." [1] M. Maritain's essay on Luther in "Three Reformers" [2] discusses Luther in terms of "the arrival of the 'Ego,'" and Joseph Lortz, on a more reputable level, evaluates him in terms of a one-sided subjectivism.

Moreover, such formulae lend themselves to facile over-simplification. Thus a recent study of the development of Ulrich Zwingli shows him as moving towards an "existential—theocentric" conversion, for which only the most slender documentary proof is given. One feels that if it were a just description, the value of such a formula would be very small, if it gave no indication of the vast differences between Luther's and Zwingli's theological outlook. [3]

Furthermore, the formula does not point to the differentia of the "theology of the Cross." I do not think we can say of the Nominalists that they did not give God the glory. But I am sure that to turn from their discussion of Justification to that of Luther is to encounter another atmosphere. The word "christocentric" may have unfortunate associations in British and Continental theology, but at least no descriptive formula will do justice to Luther which does not point to the christological centre within his theological circumference.

Nor, especially when used as equivalent to one another, are the formulae "anthropocentric" and "egocentric" entirely satisfactory.

---

[1] The extent to which Protestant and Catholic theologians make precisely the same charges against one another is a subject worthy the attention of the ecumenical conversation.
[2] Three Reformers. Sheed and Ward, 1938.
[3] A. Rich. Die Anfänge der Theologie Huldrych Zwinglis. Zurich, 1949, 97 ff.

"Anthropocentric" may mean a system of salvation in which the human will and a man's own selfish need is the fulcrum on which all depends. But it might be used to distinguish a system which is concerned with mankind [1] from a system where, as in the thought of Origen, cosmological factors and angelology play an important part. Egocentric may mean that a man is morbidly self-obsessed or that he seeks his own interests in the manner of that rather pleasantly self-centred person, the Lord Chancellor in "Iolanthe."

The formula "existential" brings out another facet of truth. We have suggested how ably Lennart Pinomaa has used it to elucidate very important elements in Luther's conception of faith, and the whole of Luther's writing about "Anfechtung." But is it not possible, is it not a corollary of this very demonstration, that a system may be theocentric in the formal sense, and yet practically be dangerously anthropocentric? Is not this Luther's repeated and justified charge? We have seen how he appealed to the Scholastic theologians who thought they could fulfil the law of God by their natural powers. "Try and see how you fare in the moment of temptation!" But the same thing is true of Protestant orthodoxy, and indeed of all formal patterns of theology. A man might hold a Protestant orthodoxy which gives glory to God and trusts in God's election and disowns all human merit, and yet have a religion of self-centred subjectivism: and we suspect that it is here that the Catholic counter-charge against Protestantism can find real evidence. That is not at all to detract from the positive value of such great Luther scholars as Holl and Nygren, or to deny the importance of their criticism of those elements in scholasticism which Luther himself attacked, and of which Capito had appealed to theologians in the first edition of Luther's works (1518). "May they no longer drag Christ to the earth, as Thomas Aquinas always does, but may they instruct the earth in the doctrine of Christ."

In the light of recent developments and confusion about the meaning of "existential" we may note that Pinomaa is concerned to define "existential" in the case of Luther as "the theology of the tempted conscience." He traces the change in Luther's use of the word "humility" and in the employment of the conception of the "synteresis" and the changed use of them apparent in the "Romans" commentary. He finds that it was in 1515 and 1516 that the subject of the tempted conscience laid its imprint on Luther's thought, and that he

---

[1] "The orientation of Luther's thought is anthropocentric. The centre of his theology is the salvation of man : and (a very important point) this salvation is seen from man's point of view." This judgment by E. Molland (The Conception of the Gospel in the Alexandrian Theology. Oslo, 1938, 172) may be provocative, but it illustrates our point.

had now broken through to a theology which involved a man's real, practical relation with the Living God. The essay is most illuminating, and skilfully documented. When we put it beside Vogelsang's classic little essay, "Der angefochtene Christus," we can see how at this time Luther's doctrine of "Anfechtung" developed alongside his Christology and his "theology of the Cross."

Pinomaa demonstrates the importance of "Anfechtung" in Luther's whole development and not least in relation to the conception of Faith. Nobody can read what Luther has to say upon temptation, and on the "Tempted Christ" without realizing the absurdity of supposing that Luther means by faith, and by salvation by faith, a salvation dependent on a man's intellectual notions and human sentiments of confidence.

It is evident that Luther takes his place among the moral theologians who have dealt with problems of the tempted conscience. Just as, as a vernacular writer, Luther has more in common with other sixteenth century vernacular writers than we might suppose when we study him in isolation, so there is no doubt a large element of continuity between Luther and Gerson, Nider and Biel (who has far more "existential" things to say about tempted and afflicted consciences in his sermons than might be supposed).

Luther is the father of Protestant moral theology because his religion is indeed a religion of conscience. The doctrine of faith, of the assurance of faith, prepared for a new kind of casuistry. It is true that when we turn to the great Puritan casuistries of seventeenth century England it is the Calvinist emphasis, pattern, framework which is most apparent. Indeed, when we find the great William Ames transcribing whole passages from William of Paris, we realize the element of continuity between the Middle Ages and the seventeenth century, the extent to which Puritanism itself was the continuation of mediaeval asceticism by other means. But it was Luther who drew attention to the terrible primacy of the fight of faith, of the Christian warfare, to the "bruised conscience," and who in his writings provided a whole armoury of comfort for afflicted souls. And if it is apparent that the Calvinist patterns provided something more stable and more practical than Luther's moral theology, it is also true that Luther's stress on the spontaneity of the Christian ethic, on the creative ferment of the new life and liberty of the Christian man, might have saved Protestantism from the intermittent petrification of its religious life into the recurrent moralisms of the last centuries.

Thus the "existential" element is real and important. But it is not the whole Luther, nor the whole of what he has to say about the Righteousness of God, and indeed simply to evaluate Luther in terms of the "existential" would seem, in the end, to make him the father of modern subjectivism, in its latest phase.

Regin Prenter speaks of Luther's "Biblical realism" in contrast to the mediaeval and post-Augustinian notions of "infused charity." Prenter is most careful not to mis-state Catholic theology and expounds St. Thomas sympathetically. He shows how Luther succeeded in simplifying (without over-simplifying, in the manner of the humanist "philosophy of Christ") the complicated mediaeval structure of the plan of salvation. Luther swept away the intricate distinctions and qualifications of the Aristotelian psychology and philosophy (though he never ceased to use them in what he considered their proper place). He returned, it goes without saying, inaccurately, but at least more accurately than his opponents, to the Biblical categories and terms.[1] His doctrine of the flesh and spirit, his anthropology of the "whole man," his doctrine of grace as the personal favour by which a man is received into fellowship with God, these return to the Biblical world of personal encounter with the Living God. Grace here is much more than the Nominalist "acceptatio." It is a living personal relationship, and it may not be separated from the "gift," the transforming power of Faith, the work of the Holy Spirit. But apart from that personal relationship, the "gift" becomes an impersonal and sub-personal influence, and it is notable that modern Catholic apologists, Roman and Anglican, stress the personal quality of grace in a way that few theologians did in sixteenth century Germany. As we have said, we must not make Luther too modern, and must beware of using the terms "personal relationship" and "persons" as though Luther used them in our way. I am not sure that he can be said to be wholly on the side of those who in our day stress the existential "Real Life is Meeting" against the "Real Life is Being" of neo-scholasticism. His concern would be with "Real Life is God" (Pure Being and Pure Act!) and with a salvation begun, continued and ended in God's own saving action.

We have listened to Luther. Those first writings of his with which we have been concerned are like the first firm, opening solo notes of a great concerto, soon to be taken up and repeated and varied until the soloist is overborne by a swelling crescendo of sound. But here is

---

[1] Spiritus Creator. That there is a difference between Luther and St. Paul in the interpretation of man is made plain by Althaus in his discussion of Romans 7 in the light of Luther's exegesis. Althaus. Paulus und Luther über den Menschen, 41-95. But despite differences, Luther returns more accurately and more nearly to the Biblical anthropology than the Platonic dualism of " soul " and " body," and of " visible " and " invisible " things. And Luther's teaching is concerned with " the whole man " : this is the real key to all his expressions of the tension and movement within justification, in the formula " simul justus, simul peccator," and the more adequate " semper peccator, semper penitens, semper justus."

the great theme: the Righteousness of God. It would have gone ill with Christendom had it been a lesser one, and those fail to understand whole ranges of sober historical fact who attempt to evaluate the story with any meaner key. Luther is speaking about the work of God: the God who sought men from the beginning of their ways: who left nothing undone that a merciful God could do: the God who gave men his Law and his Gospel to bring them to salvation. For he has used their folly, disobedience, ingratitude, self-idolatry to bring them to a guilty recognition of their plight, and their horrified awareness of what they have done, willingly and without constraint, with themselves and God's ordered creation. They have been brought through the accusation of their conscience, through their apprehension of the Wrath of God, to acknowledge the justice of that judgment which has come upon them, and at length to that humility which rejects all its own self-righteousness. But when God brought men to this point through his Strange Work of the Law, it was that they might believe his own, Proper Work of the Gospel. Once for all, God came to men in his Son Jesus Christ, who prefectly fulfilled the Law on behalf of his brethren: who identified himself with humanity, in accepting the consequences of sin, enduring the pains and torments of soul which are the very pains of hell, to the extremity of agony, in the cry of dereliction on the Cross. There, in dying, he conquered death in a mighty duel, and risen from the dead, he sheds his victory abroad. Jesus Christ is the Righteousness of God, the divine verdict upon sin and the remedy for sin. Men cannot believe this good news, cannot receive it save when God himself comes to them in the power of the Holy Spirit, when they hear the Word which is the living Gospel. Then by faith they partake in the Divine Righteousness. All the Righteousness of God is freely bestowed on them. All their unrighteousness is assumed by God that it may be utterly destroyed. Henceforth they live by faith, hope and love under that covering mercy which gives them happy and victorious power. They are able to fight victoriously against the temptations of sin and death and the devil. In this most intimate relation with Christ they share that love which is "round and universal and common" to all, without distinction of persons. One with him they are united in the Church, the people of God, the communion of saints. But the Church shares in this world the contradiction involved in the "form of a servant." Life in the Church means life "under the Cross." It is life within the constant orbit of the Word, from which faith springs and by which the Church is guided and nourished. Thus God is the beginning and end of the whole economy of blessedness. And within the circumference of salvation, the centre is Jesus Christ. "The Cross is our Theology." And if a man say "this is not 'Luther's theology' but the common Christian Gospel, in Luther's accents!" that is how Luther would have had it. So be it. We have spoken of a "crisis of vocabulary." Luther did not take himself as seriously as some of his disciples did and do, and he had no love for those who consciously flaunted new jargon in the faces of their opponents. It is perhaps heresy to say so, but I think Luther sometimes toyed with a phrase, a word, or a theological distinction, and then let it fall again when it had served its particular purpose. None the less, he provoked a crisis of vocabulary of immense significance. The autonomy of Protestant theology as an expression of the Christian Gospel was possible on the basis of technical terms and categories which derive from Luther's development in the period we have considered. We have noted some important changes in his vocabulary, as he abandoned the traditional language of the schools, and turned to the Biblical setting. Above all, we have watched the growth of "Faith" into a great master Word: magnetically attracting to itself a rich complex of meaning.[1] For Faith comes to embody for Luther that double movement involved in the doctrine of Justification. On the one hand, Law—judgment—"accusatio sui"—humiliatio—humilitas: for there can be no living faith, until a man turns from himself, and is stripped of his own self-righteousness. On the other hand, there is the dynamism of Justification itself, by which the eschatology, the perfect Righteousness of Christ is appropriated by the believer, in time; the movement "semper peccator, semper penitens, semper justus," "grace" and "the gift"—"justificetur adhuc"—"magis et magis"—until the new day of resurrection. Although the word "eschatology" is as dangerously fashionable as "theocentric" and "existential" we may say that Luther's doctrine of Justification is an eschatology of Faith,[2] that it does recover that important element in

[1] Some words may be likened to single notes in music : they have one clear and distinct definition. It was one of the merits of scholasticism that it had achieved a technical vocabulary of such precision. But there are other words which are more like chords of music, rich complexities. Many of the great Biblical notions are of this kind, and for Luther " Righteousness," " Word," " Faith " are such master words. Luther fills them with meaning almost to the point of overloading, and it is perhaps understandable that his successors lost something of the balance and many-sidedness of his conceptions. But at least " Faith " is not in Luther to be restricted within former Augustinian and mediaeval definitions, or in those of sixteenth century Protestant confessional definition.

[2] Luther's eschatology has a threefold reference. First, in his view of history as bounded by the Divine intervention, the apocalyptic horizon. Here the differences as well as the similarities between his view and that of a mediaeval chronicler like Otto of Freising are important. Second, his vocabulary of time recovers the stress on the critical interval of fulfilled time, time not as mere succession, but as the vehicle of divine action, which is Biblical. Here Luther's use of " Stündlein " is important : as the " hour " when God breaks the empires of proud tyrants, or when a driven

the New Testament eschatology, in which faith, hope and love are recognized as the dimension of Christian existence, by which men draw their life from God's Mighty Acts in his Son, who reigns over and in us as Head and Lord.

Luther's theological development (1509-21) has its own coherence and integrity. Those will misunderstand it entirely who pick out elements of Protestant or Catholic orthodoxy, and dismiss the rest as muddle. Like the other great voyagers and pioneers of that century of explorations, Luther's thought has the fresh quality of wonder. He has, after all, the Copernican touch,

> "Like some watcher of the skies,
> When a new planet swims into his ken."

The great pioneers were followed closely by the great map makers, and these in turn gave way to the real epigoni, the map readers. It seems to us bracing and exhilarating to turn to Martin Luther from the addled orthodoxies and the stale rebel patterns of our time. If we will listen to him, patiently, without rushing in with our own wooden preconceptions, it may be that at the end of the day it will be found that this Son of Thunder is, more than he could know, or the Church has yet understood, a Son of Consolation in Israel.

---

leaf becomes the vehicle of the Wrath of God, and armies flee before it, and most notable of all, of the " hour " of death, including the anticipated " Anfechtung " of his own death. Third, and most important, the affirmation that our salvation lies in the perfect and final righteousness of God in Jesus Christ, achieved once in his death and resurrection and apprehended by us here and now, really and truly, in the dimension of faith, hope and love. But in this life, faith may never be turned into sight, and since it is in this good fight of faith, constant, unremitting, that the tension between " then " and " now " becomes acute, we call his doctrine an eschatology of Faith (as, we should argue, John Wesley's doctrine posits an eschatology of Love).

PART

III

LUTHER AND . . .

Chapter

12

LUTHER AND ERASMUS, 1525

"Such utter unlikes cannot but end in dislikes and so it proved
between Erasmus and Luther."
S. T. COLERIDGE on Luther's "Table Talk."

WE may take our history penny plain, or twopence coloured. The cheap
way, all black and white, formulae and catchwords. To search out
the fading tints, the mingling colours, the subtle perspectives, is the
more costly discipline, the craft of the true wayfaring historian. In
writing of Luther and Erasmus it is impossible altogether to avoid the
kind of "compare and contrast" antithesis. But even when men so
notable as these come into head-on collision, as they did in their controversy of 1525, it is our duty to recognize the intricacies of their separate
historical setting, and to avoid the over-simplification which would
affix to the one the label "Reformation" and to the other "Renaissance."
Be it confessed, this will be a one-sided account of the matter,
and we shall be more concerned with what Luther believed about
Erasmus than to give a detached appraisement of him. For, after all,
the case for Erasmus can hardly be said to have gone by default in this
country. There have been far more learned and sympathetic writings
about him than about Luther. What needs to be said on his behalf
has been written in the magisterial studies of Dr. P. S. Allen,[1] and told
with superb skill. Dr. J. P. Whitney has given us a characteristically
learned and choicely phrased essay.[2] There are the Hulsean Lectures
(1921-2) of Dr. Elliott Binns, entitled "Erasmus, the Reformer," [3]
and further described as a "Study in Re-Statement." From the angle of
the doctrine of toleration there has been Dr. R. H. Murray's "Erasmus
and Luther." [4] The American historian Preserved Smith produced
a valuable study in Erasmus which suggested that he was more at home
with him than with Luther, his first love.[5] More recently the fine
Dutch study by Huizinga has been made available in English. There

---

[1] P. S. Allen. The Age of Erasmus. 1914. Erasmus. Opus. Epist. Des. Rot.
1906.
[2] J. P. Whitney. Reformation Essays, 41.
[3] J. E. Binns. Erasmus the Reformer. 1923.
[4] R. H. Murray. Erasmus and Luther. 1920.
[5] Preserved Smith. Erasmus. 1923.

have been the learned and distinguished studies in Erasmus by A. Renaudet,[1] a Life by the German scholar Dr. K. A. Meissinger,[2] and an admirable sketch by Miss Margaret Mann Phillips, "Erasmus and the Northern Renaissance." [3] Neither here nor on the Continent has there been any adequate account of the theology of Erasmus, and an article by Stupperich [4] which suggests that Erasmus turned more and more from the liberal opinions of his youth and is the real father of the mediating theology of Pighius and Gropper seems to deserve to be treated with caution.

Erasmus was Luther's senior by seventeen years. The difference of generations is important. He was coming into his own as the first scholar in Christendom at a time when Luther was still an unknown academic. For this European prestige and for the physical means to carry on his studies, Erasmus had to labour through long, anxious and uncomfortable years. The original Flying Dutchman, the last great wandering scholar of the Middle Ages, and the first modern journalist, he moved from place to place, fleeing from bad food as from the plague (he departed from both with irritable haste); he found in Europe no abiding city, though he was perhaps happiest of all in Basel. In an age without research fellowships, he could do no other. His regular and too often irregular income came from a complicated array of pensions, gifts and subsidies: so many princes and potentates came to have a vested interest in him that he almost resembled that Duke of Plaza Toro who turned himself into a limited company. But it involved Erasmus in more than the usual amount of literary touting, which could not fail to cramp his style. There was enough truth to sting in Tyndale's gibe that "Erasmus maketh of little gnats great elephants and lifteth up above the stars whoever giveth him a little exhibition."

What shall we say about the man who wrote to the Lady Anne of Veere, that merry widow, comparing her with the four great Annas of sacred story. "Would that posterity might know of your snow-white purity. . . . I send you some prayers to the Virgin. She is ever ready to hear the prayers of virgins, and you I count not a widow, but a virgin," and on the same day could write about the same lady, "The minx! She neglects her property, to dally and flirt with her fine gentlemen!" [5] A certain canniness in money matters belongs perhaps to the Dutch temperament. But it is characteristic that Erasmus

---

[1] A. Renaudet. Érasme. 1926. Études Érasmiennes. 1939.
[2] K. A. Meissinger. Erasmus von Rotterdam. 1948.
[3] M. M. Phillips. Erasmus and the Northern Renaissance. 1950.
[4] R. Stupperich. Der Humanismus und die Wiedervereinigung der Konfessionen. (Ver. Ref.) Leipzig, 1936.
[5] P. S. Allen. Age of Erasmus, 131-2.

should go to almost extravagant lengths to get legal sanction for his will (his birth and his dispensation from his habit may partly account for the anxiety) with a whole row of certificates from Pope, Emperor and town councils, while Luther, who distrusted lawyers, wrote out his own will and nearly jeopardized the family for which he intended to provide.[1]

His greatest admirers have admitted something slapdash about his best work. There was that extraordinary edition of his letters in which half the dates were wrong, in which dates were altered, facts suppressed, and in which Justus Jonas was startled to find a letter to himself, expanded out of all recognition, and with at least one incorrect statement inserted. We had better admit that classical humanism lacked some of the methods and canons of modern scientific scholarship. It seems probable that Erasmus may be acquitted of the gravest charge against his integrity, the authorship of the satirical dialogue against Julius II, the "Julius Exclusus." [2]

But it would be superficial to write off Erasmus as the Mr. Facing-Both-Ways of the Reformation, and not rather to begin with Dr. Allen's judgment that the greatness of Erasmus consisted of "a combination of brilliant intellectual gifts with absolute sincerity and enduring purpose." There is something fine and moving about the way in which Erasmus pursued the end of true humanism amid a dissolving world, preparing his New Testament texts and paraphrases, his erudite and massive editions of the Fathers, his picaresque essays, the lucid correspondence with all its profound and sparkling premonitions of a coming age. As he put it, he had rather be a spectator than an actor, and as he hated Julius II, the warrior Pope whose trumpets shattered his dream of a golden age of scholarship, so he never forgave Luther for the Church struggle which was made inevitable by the revolutionary call to arms of Luther's tracts of 1520.

Erasmus stood for the combination of good letters (bonae litterae) and sacred letters (sacrae litterae), a Christian humanism purged of Italian paganism. "I wished," he wrote, "that good letters should find that Christian character which they have lacked in Italy and which, as you know, ended in glorifying pagan morality." [3] And though the humanists, like every intelligentsia, lacked coherence, this was the good cause which enlisted most of the forward-looking minds in the first half of the lifetime of Erasmus. It was primarily a concern for letters and scholarship, for despite his own early taste for painting

[1] P. Smith. Erasmus, 262. Life and Letters of Luther, 369.
[2] C. Stange. Erasmus und Julius II. Berlin, 1937. Also Z. für Syst. Theol., 1936, 339-52.
[3] Eras. Epist., 1581, 113-18.

and singing, Erasmus shows little appreciation of the amazing artistic achievements of the age,[1] and none of that appreciation of natural beauty and of music which was so marked in Luther. But this empire of letters was no island: it ran alongside Philosophy: the revival of Platonism in the Florentine Academy, and in the work of Ficino and Pico della Mirandola (that early enthusiasm of Sir Thomas More)— and the revival of Cicero, significant in an age like our own, bedazzled with rhetoric, though Erasmus poked fun at the more rigid Ciceronians.[2] The critical exposure of the Donation of Constantine and the pseudonymous character of the writings attributed to Dionysius the Areopagite had repercussions well beyond the field of letters. But it was the new programme of theological simplification, the return to the Biblical tongues of Greek and Hebrew, to the "philosophy of Christ," which brought the humanists into fierce collision with the scholasticism entrenched in the religious orders. The humanists defended themselves with the potent weapons of brilliant invective and biting wit, which ate like an acid, corrosively and destructively, into the accumulated weight of anti-clericalism which had come to permeate all levels of society. The Reuchlin affair brought it to a head. Erasmus, watching, saw how an attack launched by obscurantists, aided by ecclesiastical log-rolling in high places, could bring irretrievable damage to the career of the greatest scholar in Germany. I do not think Erasmus ever forgot that warning.

There followed the devastating repartee of the "Letters of Obscure Men." One would like to believe the story that when Erasmus read them he fell into such a fit of laughing that an abscess burst in his face which else should have been opened by a physician—if only for Bayle's comment, "This ought to be reckoned one of the benefits of reading!"[3] Luther, on the other hand, was not amused. He felt that the hurt of the Daughter of Zion was beyond laughter, and would have agreed with Tyndale that "It doth not become the Lord's servants to use railing rhymes."

But Erasmus was the spiritual father of all the great scholars of the 1530's and '40's. In 1527 Zwingli (who had taken a knock or two from Erasmus by then) compared Erasmus and Luther, "Saul has slain his thousands, but David his tens of thousands," but he still thought of them in terms of a single warfare. Erasmus was the devoted friend of Fisher and of More: but it was his Enchiridion which was the prentice translation of William Tyndale, and his New Testament

---

[1] " What he was after in Italy was books!" says Huizinga, quoted Meissinger, 119
[2] W. Rüegg. Cicero und der Humanismus. Zurich, 1946, 117 ff.
[3] Stokes. Epistolae Obscurorum Virorum (1925), intr. 50.

(especially in its Latin version) which launched the Reformation movement in Cambridge. When Bishop Stephen Gardiner was grown to great dignity he wrote to Erasmus how in Paris, in 1511, "there was a boy who every day prepared at your order, a lettuce cooked with butter and vinegar, and you used to say you never had them so tasty anywhere else," and this friendly feeling towards Erasmus was almost the only mental habit of Gardiner to survive from what were, in a rather special sense, his salad days. But Gardiner's fiery antagonist, Robert Barnes, had gone off to Louvain in 1517 because the great Erasmus was there.

It was not Erasmus who changed. It was the world, which was moving fast and far. Erasmus had to endure a new and dangerous combination of events, not of his willing or contriving, in which he must take decisions which either way must lose him friends and divide his public. In that new world, Luther was a portent.

It is not easy to define Luther's relation to the humanists. But it is not easy to define the humanists themselves. Groups of forward-looking scholars were to be found in most of the University centres of Europe, each group a ferment of criticism and speculation, among whom, on the one hand, the zest for classical antiquity turned back to the inspiration of the classics of Greece and Rome, while on the other there was an evident impatience with the reigning scholasticism, and a bent towards new tools, and the new intellectual disciplines, history, geography and the like.[1] In the waning years of mediaeval unity, the learned world was still a great whispering gallery, and the gossip filtered across Christendom with remarkable swiftness via the journeying scholars, the book fairs, and an extraordinary network of semi-private, semi-public correspondence, which afforded them a sixteenth century premonition of the modern quarterly journal. As always, the intelligentsia was divided by the impact of dire, practical events, and enthusiasm, interest, concern, anxiety were among the changing moods to be detected among them, as events began to march, from 1517 onwards.

Luther went into the monastery hugging his Plautus and his Virgil. But in 1508 he made some violent comments against the Alsatian humanist Wimpfeling, who had aroused the fierce enmity of the Augustinians by denying that the African Father had ever been a monk. But he was whole-heartedly on the side of Reuchlin, and rejoiced when, in 1518, that great scholar's nephew, the prodigy Philip Melanchthon, came to teach in Wittenberg. We know that he was eager to make use of the latest critical tools, the Le Fevre edition of the Psalms,

[1] See H. S. Bender. Conrad Grebel (1950), 9-53.

Reuchlin's Hebrew grammar, and the New Testament of Erasmus. He worked hard at Greek and, unlike Erasmus, acquired a working knowledge of Hebrew. But a letter of his, in October 1516, shows penetration into the differences between himself and Erasmus.[1] "In the exposition of the Scripture I put Jerome as far behind Augustine as Erasmus puts Augustine behind Jerome." Yet he could still say, "I am reading 'our Erasmus,'" though he adds, a little later, "I am moving more and more away from Erasmus. He doesn't give sufficient room to Christ, or the glory of God." In January 1518 he wrote, "I find much in Erasmus which seems strange and unhelpful to the knowledge of Christ, if I speak as a theologian, rather than as a grammarian." [2]

With the opening of the Church struggle, Luther needed every friend he could find. It was with profound relief that Luther heard that the greatest scholar of the age approved his Theses and was inclined to speak on his behalf. He was not mistaken. Erasmus never changed or withheld his opinion that there was much he must approve in the writings and protest of Luther. He also cordially detested the narrow fanaticism of scholastic bigotry which had dogged him from his youth and was almost to encompass him with ruin in later years. He had himself claimed that wayfaring Christians should be trusted with the Scriptures. In inimitable fashion, in the "Praise of Folly" and in the "Colloquies" he was to attack the superstitions of a religion which had run to seed in a riot of externalities, which had allowed inward, spiritual life to ossify beneath a veneer of ecclesiastical customs. We need also to remember that theological confusion and uncertainty about many points of controverted doctrine from "Indulgences" to the "plenitude of power" of the Papacy to which Joseph Lortz has drawn attention, perhaps a little too sharply.

Thus though it was a deep and far-reaching distinction between Erasmus and Luther, that for Erasmus "the Law" from which Christians were freed was the outward ceremonial law of custom and observance, while for Luther the profound problem of the divine imperative and of all law was in question, there was a large common field of practical abuse which both detested and attacked.

Melanchthon, whose Inaugural at Wittenberg took the form of a programme of humanist studies, hugely admired Erasmus and remained his friend and correspondent throughout. He brought a softening influence to bear at the time when Luther himself was becoming

---

[1] M. Richter. Desiderius Erasmus und seine Stellung zu Luther. Leipzig, 1907. (Quellen aus Gesch. der Ref.), 5.
[2] Ibid. 6-9.

sharply conscious of the differences between himself and Erasmus, and in the next years he did what he could to soften the buffets which each gave the other, by conversation with the one, and correspondence with the other.

In March 1519 Luther wrote to Erasmus a letter which marks the summit of his good relations with him. "Who is there whose inmost being Erasmus has not penetrated, whom Erasmus does not reach, in whom Erasmus does not reign . . . wherefore dear Erasmus, learn to know this little brother in Christ also . . . he is assuredly your very zealous friend, though he otherwise deserved on account of his ignorance, only to be buried in a corner, unknown even to your sun and climate." [1] Erasmus sent a polite reply in May beginning, "Dearest brother in Christ . . . your epistle, breathing . . . a Christian spirit, was most pleasing to me." [2]

It was more than unfortunate that this private letter was published and taken up by the enemies of Erasmus at Louvain. As Luther persisted in his defiance, and as the consequences of his stand were more and more evident, the humanist circles buzzed with admiration and with speculation. "About Luther there is no more certain news . . ." wrote Beatus Rhenanus to the eager enquiry of Zwingli in 1518. They thought of him at this time as a cross between Hercules and David. But as his public condemnation by the Church became more and more likely, their enthusiasm was tempered by caution. Zwingli's biographers have had to note that though he bought most of Luther's works in 1519 he carefully and unwontedly refrained from making his usual marginal annotations. In July 1520 Zwingli was saying loudly, "I read almost nothing of Luther nowadays." [3] At the same time Erasmus could write (Nov. 1519) to Albert of Mainz, "Luther is as unknown to me as to anybody, nor have I yet had time to read his works, except that I have glanced at them hastily"; [4] and in September 1520 he wrote still more tactfully (and still less truthfully?), "I do not know Luther nor have I read his books, except ten or twelve pages, and those hastily." [5]

None the less, at a fateful and dangerous moment in Luther's affairs, Erasmus did him greater service than he ever fully realized. At the end of 1520 considerable pressure was exerted on the young Emperor Charles V to accept the ecclesiastical condemnation of Luther without any further consultation of the forthcoming Imperial Diet. Even the

[1] Preserved Smith, 219.   [2] Ibid. 222.
[3] A. Rich. Die Anfänge der Theologie Huldrych Zwinglis (1949), 73.   O. Farner. H. Zwingli. Zurich, 1946, 334 ff.
[4] P. Smith. Luther's Correspondence, 238.
[5] Ibid. 355.

Elector Frederick was in considerable perplexity about the matter. While he lingered in Cologne in November, laid up with gout, Erasmus visited him at his hotel. Frederick asked him straight out what he thought of the Luther affair. Erasmus paused: then, a frosty twinkle in his eyes, gave his epigram: "He has committed great sin—he has hit the monks in their belly, and the Pope in his crown!" He was presented with a damask gown for this consultation, and Frederick seems to have felt that this was indeed a high specialist's fee, for he grumbled to Spalatin, "What a wonderful little man that is; you never know where you are with him." [1] None the less, at a time when the Papal Nuncios were exerting maximum pressure to get Luther condemned unheard, it counted for much in stiffening the Elector Frederick that Erasmus had not flung his great prestige against his "Sorgenkind."

Erasmus did what he could to assuage the dangerous heat of the conflict, and at the request of the Princes wrote down some "Axioms" which in the light of his later hostility are surprisingly bold on Luther's behalf. Thus:

"The evil root of the matter is hatred of 'good letters' and tyrannical ambition."

"The matter is pursued with clamour, intrigues, bitter hatred and poisonous writings."

"The affair is more critical than many imagine."

"Only two Universities out of many have condemned Luther."

"All fair-minded people believe that Luther wants a fair deal: he asks for a public disputation and will accept the judgment of impartial judges."

"Luther is not self-seeking and ambitious and is the less suspect."

"Vested interests have a hand in this game."

"The world is thirsting for the truth of the Gospel, and history seems to be moving on this side (fatali quodam desiderio videtur huc ferri), therefore perhaps such desires ought not to be opposed with so much hatred." [2]

Erasmus proposed in a memorandum that the Emperor, the Kings of England and of Hungary might form an impartial tribunal. It is doubtful whether these academic blueprints had much effect upon the statesmen and the politicians. Erasmus was now involved in a dangerous dispute of his own at Louvain, where his old enemies had received powerful reinforcement from the Papal nuncio, Jerome Aleander. Aleander as a University Lecturer had been the success of the century. At his inaugural in Paris in 1511 he spoke to a thousand students for

---

[1] TR. 4899 (Cl. 8.243). Meissinger, 264. Bainton. Here I Stand, 170.
[2] Meissinger, 265.

two and a half hours, and on the third day all seats were taken at eleven for a lecture which began at one. One feels that the rest of his career was an anti-climax, and he was not the last don turned diplomat to be badly outwitted by German politicians. But he was convinced that Erasmus was a more dangerous foe to the Church than Luther (a view to which at least one modern Catholic scholar, Joseph Lortz, has returned). He wrote to the Cardinal de Medici in Rome that "I have long known that Erasmus is the source of all this evil . . . he is the corner stone of this heresy." [1]

Thus, the fact that Erasmus did not fling himself against Luther counted at this time. And Erasmus himself knew what might happen if he came out whole-heartedly on Luther's side.[2]

But that he could not do. He did not understand Luther's theology, which he had not widely read or deeply pondered, and he deplored Luther's violence and intransigence, which he felt to be in the worst scholastic and mendicant tradition. Moreover, he was by temperament a neutral. In July 1521 he wrote some revealing sentences to Richard Pace:

"Even if he had written all things well, I should not have courage to risk my life for the truth. All men have not the strength for martyrdom. I fear lest if any tumult should arise I would imitate Peter. I follow the just decrees of Popes and Emperor because it is right. I endure their evil laws because it is safe. I think it is allowable to good men if they have no hope of successful resistance." [3]

We must recognize the introspective frankness of one who, like the Vicar in Crabbe's "Borough,"

> "Was his master's soldier, but not one
> To lead an army of his martyrs on."

It was perhaps aggravated by his own cult of the enigmatic epigram. It is not only Luther who arraigned this deliberate ambiguity when he said, "Erasmus is slippery as an eel. Only Christ can grab him!" Duke George, the Elector Frederick, and humanist scholars complained of his "amphiboliae." [4]

The honest suspicion got abroad among Catholics and Reformers that Erasmus's own real convictions were more negative than his formal statements implied, and that his scepticism was much more radical than he allowed to appear.

[1] P. S. Allen. Age of Erasmus, 112. Smith. Luther's Correspondence, 454.
[2] Epistolae, Vol. V, 1263, "Si voluissem tribus verbis me declarare Lutheranum, videremus alium ludum apud nos et Germanos quam nunc videmus." 1274, " Si Luthero vel tantulum favissem, nolo jactare quid potuerim in Germania."
[3] P. Smith. Erasmus, 243.
[4] TR. 446. " Erasmus est anguilla. Niemand kan yhn ergreiffen denn Christus allein. Est vir duplex." Also 4905.

The result was that Erasmus was attacked from both sides. At one time he was not only accused of writing Luther's "Babylonish Captivity," but the reply written by Henry VIII! The time was to come when the theologians of Paris and Louvain, the inquisition in Spain, and an important party at the Curia were to demand his own impeachment, and Erasmus had to reckon with an element of fierce hostility against himself which was not to be assuaged by the half-hearted sops which he proffered, of which his writing against Luther was his greatest act of appeasement. [1]

Luther's revolutionary tracts of 1520 ruined the hope of bringing the affair to a peaceful conclusion, though Erasmus continued to write and work towards that end. [2]

Meanwhile the patrons and friends of Erasmus, the Pope, Henry VIII, Duke George of Saxony, pressed him to enlist his mighty pen in the service of the faith. The suspicion, openly voiced by Latomus, that he was a secret Lutheran made his danger evident. [3] Luther was alarmed at the prospect of such an intervention, which must make a division among friends and allies and must bring decision to many waverers. In 1522 he wrote, "I will not provoke Erasmus, nor will I when provoked, return the blow." Luther does deserve some praise, in fact, for the books he refused to write, and the challenges he did not accept, of which he could write to Amsdorf, "You know my methods, of holding such authors to silent contempt. For how many books of Eck, Faber, Emser and Cochlaeus . . . have I by my silence brought utterly to nought." But there was a "We don't want to fight, but by jingo if we do! . . ." ring about his letter which did no good, when inevitably it got round to Erasmus.

When it became clear, beyond rumour, that Erasmus was going to write, Luther's anger boiled over. For him this meant that Erasmus had made the "great refusal." He had rejected the good cause. We have recognized the sincerity of the good neutral. Let us admit the equal integrity of the fighter.

"By the grace of God, I am not so great a fool or madman, as to have wished to have to sustain this cause so long, with so much certitude and firmness, which you call obstinacy, in the face of so many dangers of my life, so much hatred, so many traps laid for me, in a word, in face of the fury of men and devils.

"I have not done this for money, for that I neither have nor desire: nor for vainglory, for that, if I wished, I could not obtain in a world

[1] Renaudet. Études, ch. 5.
[2] Epistolae, Vol. VI, 1688, to Luther, "quasi studio tibi sit ne tempestas haec aliquando vertatur in laetum exitium : in quam occasionem ego semper intentus fui."
[3] Renaudet. Études, 191.

so enraged against me, nor for the life of the body, for that cannot be sure for an hour . . . do you think you alone have a heart that is not moved by these tumults? But I am not made of stone . . . but since it cannot be otherwise, I choose rather to be battered in temporal tumult, happy in the Grace of God, for God's Word's sake . . . for how much better is it to lose the world than to lose God the creator of the world, who can create innumerable worlds and is better than infinite worlds." [1]

Thus Luther wrote to Erasmus a final and disgusted letter:

"Hitherto I have controlled my pen and told my friends in writing which you have seen, that I would control it until you publish something openly . . . we see that the Lord has not given you the courage or the sense to tackle these monsters openly with us." [2]

It was this letter from Luther that lay on Erasmus's desk when he received an interview from the Polish nobleman, Laski, who tried to appropriate the letter. "Pretending not to notice what he had done," said Erasmus, "I took it from his hands and placed it on the table. I said, 'I will give you this autographed letter and two others, and by these you may show the Emperor (for he was ambassador to the Emperor) that my relationship with Luther is not so close as some declare.'"

It seems that Erasmus made the decision to attack Luther in September 1523. The choice of subject must have exercised him. It must not be one of those subjects still undefined and controverted among the orthodox, yet it must be a theme in which the orthodoxy of Erasmus could emerge as beyond dispute. It seems that the mathematical English bishop, Tunstal, suggested the theme of "Free Will," [3] which would be as a watchword of orthodoxy to all who heard, even if they never read or understood the intricacy of the dispute.

In February 1524 Erasmus informed Clement VII that he was writing against Luther on this subject. Next month, he sent a copy of the completed work to Henry VIII, and by July could tell his friends that publication was imminent. It appeared in the beginning of September. The work was well received by his patrons, and acclaimed by that band of controversialists whom Erasmus had hitherto avoided and despised, but among whom he must now company with fastidious

[1] W.A. 18.625.19.
[2] P. Smith. Erasmus, 344.
[3] Renaudet. Études, 44. But see also Sturge, C. Tunstal, 122-4. In an earlier letter, Tunstal had written, " You say that I find fault with Luther and the Lutherans, but I find no worse fault with them than does God himself, whom Luther makes the author of all evil, while he at the same time deprives men of free will and maintains that everything happens by the fixed laws of fate, so that no one is free to do right if he wishes to do." That Luther made God the author of evil and believed a doctrine of fatalistic determinism were common charges against the Reformer, circulated in England by Sir Thomas More and Henry VIII, as well as Tunstal.

disrelish. The theologians were not very pleased, and in a few months Erasmus was meditating writing on the Eucharist. As his admirer M. Renaudet says, "He was no theologian."

There followed a long interval in which it seemed, after all, that Luther would let the case go by default. Then 1525 brought dire and crowded events. There came the upheaval of the Peasant War and Luther believed his own death to be imminent. With frantic and violent haste he wielded his pen like a clenched fist in face of the rebels. Then he married a wife and therefore could not enter the arena. Luther began to write in September 1525, and the work "De Servo Arbitrio" appeared in December.

As a controversy, it is not one of the great literary duels.[1] Both writers have an eye over their shoulder at the listening world. Erasmus is too bent on clearing his own reputation. Luther suffers from major and minor inhibitions: angry and disappointed and alarmed, still, by the defection of Erasmus, engaged in a subject touching some of his deepest convictions, yet restrained at the entreaties of such friends as Philip Melanchthon, who had to keep friends with both parties: and perhaps with a too lively inferiority sense about his own Latin style when contrasted with the magisterial elegance of Erasmus.

Erasmus wrote with his inevitable grace and clarity. He is shrewd, and in comparison with Luther almost urbane (I think one may say, from Luther's point of view, maddeningly and provocatively calm), but he points carefully the deadly, poisoned barb. It was, as he said, something of the conflict between a wasp and an elephant. As M. Renaudet says, "His knowledge of psychology and of the metaphysic of grace is less profound than that of Luther, and he has less solid knowledge of the texts." Yet many readers of it as a controversy would, I imagine, give Erasmus a victory on points.

For, as we have hinted, the "De Servo Arbitrio" shows Luther at his most exasperating. For one thing, he made huge efforts to be calm and courteous, with the result that every now and then this repressed vehemence explodes with all the sudden violence of a New Zealand blow-hole. "You not only surpass me in the powers of eloquence and genius . . . you conduct this discussion in a most specious and uniform modesty by which you have met me and prevented my being angry with you"—and then, "What shall I say, Erasmus? To me you breathe out nothing but Lucian and draw in the gorging surfeits of Epicurus." Most of what Luther says and much of the way he says

[1] There is an excellent French edition, Érasme de Rotterdam. Essai sur le Libre Arbitre. Pierre Mesnard. Alger, 1945. The most reliable English translation of Luther's reply is still that by the Rev. Henry Cole. W.A. 18.597 gives the Latin text with a very good introduction.

it must set the modern Protestant mind on edge. And yet Luther himself thought that of all his writings, this and the little Children's Catechism best deserved to survive. More striking still is the fact that some of the most interesting theological discussions of recent years have centred on this writing. Impulsively, incoherently, if you like wrong-headedly, alive it is, and, unlike the essay of Erasmus, has a far more than antiquarian interest. The book contains some excellent astringent medicine for modern Protestants in England and America.

Tribute from an unexpected quarter comes from M. Berdyaev's "Freedom and the Spirit." He writes, "It was the Jesuits who knew nothing of the pattern of spiritual freedom and rejected liberty of conscience who became the most ardent champions of Free Will. The Jansenists who like Luther denied Free Will and attributed everything to Grace recognized religious liberty far more than the Jesuits. See Luther's remarkable book, 'De Servo Arbitrio.'" [1] It is a salutary reminder that the man who wrote of the bondage of the human will through sin should have penned "The Liberty of a Christian Man." It was those who charged Luther with inflaming social revolution by putting little people in notion of their prodigious dignity before God, who arraigned him for reducing men to the status of mechanical automata.

We shall not resume the controversy in detail here. A great deal of the discussion turns on the interpretation of texts of Scripture. But there were two positions of Erasmus which roused Luther's strongest reprehension. The first was an unwise admission of Erasmus which confirmed his enemies in their convictions that he was at heart a sceptic.

"For my part, I have so little pleasure in dogmatizing that I would rather put myself on the side of the Sceptics, whenever I am allowed to do so by the inviolable authority of Holy Scripture and by the decisions of the Church, to which I always submit freely my judgments, whether I understand the reasons for what she ordains or no."

"If I were convinced that Christ did not institute confession . . . I should fear to publish that opinion . . . there are some errors which are concealed with less harm than by making them known. . . . If I were sure that a Council had defined the point as erroneous . . . I would prefer to say that it no doubt appeared to them useful in their time, but that at present the same reasons proclaimed its abrogation."

That is a recognizable attitude to truth, and there is a great deal to be said for it.[2] But it is certainly not that spirit of the Renaissance to

[1] N. Berdyaev. Freedom and the Spirit, 118.
[2] Yves Congar (Vraie et fausse Réforme dans l'Église (1950), 375) notes how with the Nominalists " among those who have done so much to undermine the authority of the Church, their positive criticism and practical scepticism is counter-balanced by a certain ecclesiastical fideism—a recourse to the authority of the Church."

which those appeal who are wont to sigh for a Reformation which might have been "along Erasmian lines." Is it, after all, Luther and Tyndale, not Erasmus, who pave the way for the "Areopagitica" of John Milton?

The word "scepticism" enraged Luther. The temper of his own fighting faith emerges in tumultuous polemic, and again and again in fine epigrams, notably the memorable "Take away assertions and you take away Christianity," [1] and the great "Spiritus Sanctus non est scepticus."

"For the Holy Spirit is not a Sceptic, nor are what he has written on our hearts our own doubts and opinions, but assertions far more certain and firm than life itself and all human experience." [2]

The other vulnerable argument used by Erasmus was that Scripture contains dark mysteries.

"There are some sanctuaries in the Holy Scriptures into which God has not willed that we should enter too soon, and if we try to penetrate them we are surrounded with darkness."

"We ought not, therefore, to precipitate sacrilegious controversy upon these obscure questions, whether God knows future contingents in advance, if our will contributes in any way to salvation, or if it is limited to the reception of grace, if we really do all we perform of good or ill, or if we submit to it from sheer necessity."

There are many passages in Scripture so obscure that nobody has ever unravelled them, and such are the distinctions between the Persons of the Trinity, the intimate union of divine and human natures in Christ, and the Unforgivable Sin. On the other hand, Erasmus affirms, returning to the simple gospel, "the precepts destined to regulate our existence" are patent and evident in the Scriptures.

Luther was quick to point out that Erasmus, by stressing the obscurity of Scripture, was relapsing into the very trick of orthodox apologetic which he had himself withstood in a famous passage of the Paraclesis to his New Testament. There he had "vehemently dissented" from those who would not put the Scriptures into the hands of the unlearned, and he had hoped rather that they might be read, not only by the Scots and Irish, but by the Turks and Saracens, by the ploughboy in the field, and the workman at the loom. [3]

"The Scripture," said Luther, "is not abstruse . . . it is with such scarecrows that Satan has frightened men away from reading the Sacred Writings, and has rendered the Holy Scriptures contemptible, that he might cause his poison of philosophy to prevail in the Church." [4]

[1] W.A. 18.603.29.   [2] W.A. 18.605.32.
[3] Desid. Erasmus. Ausgewählte Werke. Ed. Hajo Holborn. 1933, 142.10-24.
[4] W.A. 18.606.19.

It is true that God has not told us "how" many mysteries of the Gospel have been performed, but of the "what," of the fact, the Bible leaves us in no doubt at all. We know that God is Three in One and that human and divine nature are one in Jesus Christ, even if we cannot explain them. (But Luther's central affirmation is that Christ himself is the key to the Scriptures and in his light we see the truth.)

"What of importance can remain hidden in the Scripture, now that the seals are broken and the stone rolled away from the sepulchre, and that greatest of all mysteries brought to light, God made man, that God is Trinity in Unity, that Christ suffered for us. . . . Are not these things known and sung even in our streets. Take away Christ from the Scriptures and what else will you find in them?" [1]

On the other hand, Erasmus has spoken about truths of Scripture which are self-evident. But none can understand the Scriptures without the aid and operation of the Holy Ghost.

"If you speak of the internal clearness of the Scripture, no man sees an iota of the Scripture but he that hath the spirit of God . . . for the Spirit is required to the understanding of the whole of Scripture and of every part of it. If you speak of external clearness, nothing whatever is left obscure or ambiguous but everything that is in the Scripture is by the Word brought forth into the clearest light and proclaimed in the world." [2]

Luther also scores a point when he affirms that Erasmus believes in peace at any price. He himself is moved by the prospect of war in Christendom, but he knows that Our Lord came to bring the sword of truth, and he announces his own premonition, which was to be terribly fulfilled:

"To wish to silence these tumults is nothing else than to wish to hinder the Word of God and to take it out of the way. For the Word of God, wherever it comes, comes to change and renew the world . . . you do not see that these tumults and dangers increase through the world according to the counsel and the operations of God. And therefore you fear that the heavens may fall about our ears. But I by the grace of God see these things clearly, because I see the other tumults greater than these which will arise in ages to come, in comparison with which these appear but as the whispering of a breath of air, and the murmuring of a gentle brook." [3]

As is the case with most sixteenth century controversial writings, Luther's reply is a point by point rebuttal of successive passages in his opponent. The notion that in the "De Servo Arbitrio" Luther is incon-

---

[1] W.A. 18.606.24.   [2] W.A. 18.609.5.
[3] W.A. 18.626.25.

sistently relapsing into a scholastic theology which he had in theory repudiated seems to rest upon a complete misconception of Luther's attitude
to tradition. Here, and in his subsequent treatise against the eucharistic
doctrine of Zwingli, he makes more use of theology than his opponent
because he is himself more of a theologian. Unlike Erasmus and
Zwingli, Luther was by calling and by training a theological Professor.
It is true that for Luther the paramount authority was that of Holy
Scripture: that his new awareness of this criterion of orthodoxy led
him to drastic criticism of the tradition in which he had been trained.
But, subject to the over-riding authority of Holy Scripture, he in no
wise repudiated either the language or the categories of Christian
theology. P. A. Vignaux has suggested that at the very end of his life
Luther could use arguments about the Trinity which are to be found
in his earliest writings. The truth is that the two elaborate theological
disputes with Erasmus and Zwingli enabled Luther fully to deploy
theological resources which he never repudiated. Because Luther
deplored the aggressive intrusion of philosophy, and its abuse in the
wrong place, it did not mean that he could not use it himself with effect.
And Luther can use a doctrine of deity, e.g. "the Immutability of the
Divine Will and Promises," without the slightest hesitation and with
no sign of any inconsistency. His theology appears piecemeal in
irregular and isolated blocks. It will be convenient, therefore, to look
more closely at what he has to say about three major themes, Free Will,
Providence, Predestination.[1]

The title "De Servo Arbitrio" responds to the title of the Diatribe
of Erasmus, but his own title is taken from St. Augustine, and represents a theme affirmed and expounded by Luther in various disputations and writings. (For Erasmus this subject seemed remote and
peripheral. For Luther it brings into play the whole economy of Grace.)

1. FREE WILL.

"Sir, we know our wills are free, and there's an end on't." As usual,
there is truth in Johnsonian common sense, and as usual, theological
truth is more intricate than any epigram. But Luther does not deny
at all what most people nowadays mean when they speak about Free
Will. In the first place he goes a great deal further than many modern
philosophers and psychologists in the room he leaves for psychological

[1] J. Iwand. Studien zur Problem des unfreien Willens. Z. für Syst. Theol.,
1930-1, 216-50. C. Stange. Die Gottesanschauung Luthers. Z. für Syst. Theol.,
1931, 45. M. Schüler. De Servo Arbitrio. Z. für Kg., 1936. L. Schott. Luthers
Lehre vom Servum Arbitrium in ihrer theologischern Bedeutung. Z. für Syst. Theol.,
1929-30, 399-430. F. Kattenbusch. Luthers Lehre vom unfreien Willen. 1905.
E. Schweingruber. Luthers Erlebnis des unfreien Willens. Zurich, 1947.

freedom. He is not concerned with whether we are free when we choose marmalade instead of jam for breakfast, with why we walk down a road instead of up another, with why we choose our wives, or run our businesses. These are great and important areas of human life in which he concedes human freedom.

"I know," he admits, "that Free Will can by nature do something: it can eat, drink, beget, rule, etc."

For Luther, in the classic tradition, man has a special place within the enormous pyramid which is the hierarchy of creation. Man was created to have dominion over all things, and though, through sin, his mastery over things has got out of gear (as Luther's commentary on Rom. 1-2 powerfully expounds) he still can exercise a genuine freedom in respect of what Luther calls "things below him," even though, in relation to God, above, he has lost his freedom.

"We may teach a Free Will of man, not in respect of things above him, but in respect only of those things which are below him, that is, he may be allowed to know that he has, as to his goods and possessions the right of using, acting and omitting according to his Free Will." [1]

"In respect of things beneath him, here he has dominion and is Lord, as things are left to his own counsel. Not that God so leaves a man that he does not co-operate with him, but he commits to him the free use of things." [2]

Moreover, Luther concedes not only psychological but ethical freedom.

"I grant that Free Will can by its own endeavours move itself in some directions, we will say unto good works, or unto the righteousness of the civil or moral law, yet it is not moved unto the Righteousness of God." [3]

He is concerned to make it clear that however bound and paralysed the will of man may be, men do not cease to be men.

"If we call the power of Free Will that by which a man is fitted to be caught by the Spirit or to be touched by the Grace of God as one created to eternal life, or eternal death may be said to be: this power, that is fitness or as the sophists call it 'dispositio,' this quality and passive aptitude this also I confess." [4]

Or better, in the forthright, famous phrase, "God didn't create the Kingdom of heaven for geese." [5]

---

[1] W.A. 18.638.5.
[2] Ibid. 672.8. This is a view put forward by Luther in his earliest ethical disputation. W.A. 1.365.25, " respectu aliorum suorum inferiorum non nego quod sit, imo videatur sibi libera." P. Vignaux. Luther Commentateur, 7 n.
[3] W.A. 18.767.40.
[4] W.A. 18.636.16.   [5] Ibid. 21.

Luther therefore concedes a Free Will in the sense in which most people think of it. What then does he deny? He denies that man is able, in his fallen state, to turn from his sin to God. If Free Will be "the power of the human will which can of itself will or not will to embrace the Word of God by which it is led to those things which are beyond its capacity and comprehension," [1] then Luther denies that fallen man has this freedom.

"The will cannot change itself and turn itself to another way, but the more it is irritated to will, the more it resists . . . on the other hand, when God works in us, the will being changed and sweetly breathed upon by the Spirit of God desires and acts not from compulsion, but responsively from pure willingness inclination and accord, so that it cannot be turned any other way by any thing contrary, nor be compelled nor overcome even by the gates of hell." [2]

Orthodoxy stressed also the need for grace, and indeed had gone so far in the condemnation even of semi-Pelagianism that Erasmus proved too much by the texts which he cited in Scripture. Luther had little difficulty in proving that they went far beyond what Erasmus desired, if once they were interpreted in his way. But it is true that orthodoxy, and especially Nominalism, tried to combine its emphasis on the Liberty of God with such a doctrine of the liberty of the creature, despite the Fall, as should allow free play for the doctrine of merit. Luther is concerned to show, as his earlier writings had abundantly made clear, that for him too there are two great freedoms. Like the great Nominalists, he too is concerned to emphasize the Liberty of God, since God alone is truly free.

"It follows, then, that Free Will is clearly a Divine Name (esse plane Divinum Nomen) which is attributed to men no more justly than if you attribute divinity itself to them." [3]

He, too, is concerned with the liberty of the creation. But in this fallen world, the only true human liberty is the "Liberty of a Christian Man," that glad, spontaneous service of God which comes when a man is set right with his creator and at peace with him, whereby the will is freed from the deadly paralysis of its own selfish preoccupations. The Bible, Luther says, shows us man apart from grace as bound in servitude.

"The Scripture," says Luther, "setteth forth such a man as is not only bound, miserable, captive, sick and dead . . . but who . . . to his other miseries adds that of blindness: so that he believes that he is free, happy, at liberty, powerful, whole and alive. For Satan knows well that if men knew their misery he could not retain one of them in

[1] W.A. 18.664.1.   [2] W.A. 18.634.30.
[3] W.A. 18.636.27.

his kingdom: because it could not be but that God would immediately pity and succour their misery and calamity seeing that he is with so much praise set forth throughout the whole Scripture as being near to the contrite heart . . . wherefore the work of Satan is to hold men so that they cannot know their misery." [1]

This tragic dilemma of sinful man is no merely private affair. Luther sees our human existence as the arena of a tremendous conflict where, in the very nature of the case, there can be no neutrals.

"For there is no medium between the Kingdom of God and the Kingdom of Satan: they are mutually and continually opposed to one another." [2]

"For Christ said, 'He that is not for me is against me.' He did not say 'He that is not for me is—somewhere in the middle!'" [3]

It is rather like the traditional picture of St. George and the Dragon, say in the Leningrad Raphael. The captive maiden has to await the issue of a mighty duel in the outcome of which she is vitally concerned, but which in the end depends upon the great champion who will kill the beast and set her free. The mighty duel of redemption was wrought by Christ upon the Cross, but for Luther that is not simply an isolated struggle in the past: our human existence and all human existences in history belong to that drama of salvation, and our liberation, our bondage is part of that situation into which God has come. Luther says to us as well as to Erasmus:

"You put God and the Devil at a distance as it were as spectators. . . . But God has not gone off to an Ethiopian banquet." [4]

Thus Luther comes to the not very happy illustration, which, however, he did not invent.

"The human will is like a beast between the two: if God sits thereon, it wills and goes where God wills to go as the Psalm says, 'I am as a beast before thee.' If Satan sits thereon it wills and goes where Satan wills. Nor is it in its power to choose which rider it will ride to or seek, but the riders contend which shall have it or rule it." [5]

To those who eagerly scent the brimstone of Manichaeanism, it may be said that Luther has no doubt at all of the power of God as against the power of Satan. "A Word shall quickly slay him." And if we ask, then, whether the great conflict must not be a sham fight, we must ask that question of the Bible as well as of Luther, and indeed of any Christian interpretation of history which reckons seriously with the power of evil.

[1] W.A. 18.679.23.   [2] W.A. 18.743.34.
[3] W.A. 18.670.5.   [4] W.A. 18.750.8.
[5] W.A. 18.635.17.

Moreover, Luther's motive here is religious, to safeguard the freedom of the Grace of God, and to strike at the nerve of all self-righteousness.

"A man cannot be thoroughly humbled until he comes to know that his salvation is utterly beyond his own powers, counsel, endeavours, will and works and absolutely dependent upon the will, counsel and pleasure of another." [1]

That man's repentance, his conversion, his turning to God is a divine work; that Faith itself is a miracle and a gift, the work of the Holy Spirit; these are truths that modern English and American Protestantism, sometimes far more Pelagian and anthropocentric than late mediaeval Nominalism, has good need to ponder. Most of us feel that to deny "Free Will" as completely as Luther is to cut the very root of the meaning of human personality (but in the theological sense, are we persons because of innate qualities or because we are treated by God as responsible before him, even in our sins? Are we not persons because of our standing "coram Deo"?).

Luther believes that to speak of a man as free in this realm of the Spirit, to be able to apply or not to apply himself to salvation, to embrace or not to embrace the Gospel, is in the end to make the universe irresponsible and to make salvation turn not upon God's loving will and saving initiative but on the changes and chances of unpredictable spontaneity. Thus his thought upon Free Will is bound up with his doctrine of Providence.

2. DIVINE PROVIDENCE.

The famous gardener who said, surveying his ruined crops, "That there Providence has a lot to answer for, but there's one above will teach him his business," had doubtless never heard of Marcion, like a good many other Christians who have been driven by two centuries of scientific controversy to an unconscious dualism which sets God over and against nature and history. The God of modern men who has ceased to intervene in human affairs is not the God of the Bible or of Luther, though the thought of man as imprisoned behind a barbed-wire fence of natural law is yet another symptom of the modern return to Gnosticism. Fate on the one hand; chance on the other. Luther has a horror of a universe where the loving purposes and promises of God can be frustrated or mocked by chance, contingency or accident.

Perhaps the one outstanding impression one receives from Luther's letters, from the very beginning to the end, is this reliance and waiting

[1] W.A. 18.632.30.

upon the providence of a Living God. Luther sees God always at hand, wonderfully close, using all the changing panorama of his creation as the instrument of his kindness, in a profound and often beautifully expressed theology of the natural order and of creation. He sees God at work behind all human history, sustaining all things by his will so that even the evil could not work their tragic infamies save by the permission (Luther, like the Nominalists, distrusts secondary causes and will say outright, the will) of God.

"All things which we do, though they may appear to be done by change and chance, are yet done necessarily and immutably if you have regard to the will of God." [1]

"For God foreknows nothing by contingency, but he foreknows purposes and does all things according to his immutable, eternal and infallible will." [2]

Here Luther touches an ancient and intricate mediaeval debate, whether God foreknows contingent future happenings, and if he does, whether they must take place, simply because God foreknows them. The elaborate distinction had been suggested between "necessity of the consequence" and "consequential necessity"—that is between a necessity in the natural and logical sequence of events, and a necessity caused by the divine will. In this debate the philosophers of the Middle Ages tended to emphasize the reality of contingency, leaving others to explain how God could have a knowledge of contingent things if they were really and truly contingent. The theologians reproached the philosophers with underrating the reality of the divine prescience and undermining the divine prophecies of Scripture.[3] Luther is on the side and tradition of the theologians, but he will have nothing to do with these elaborate distinctions. They only wrap up the real question which is whether, whatever may seem to us to be the truth, God really holds the final, all-powerful, all-seeing guardianship and control of his creation.

On the other hand, Luther does not like either the words "contingency" or "necessity" in this connection.

"Being done by contingency does not signify in the Latin language that what is done is contingent, but that it is done according to a contingent and mutable will . . . moreover a work cannot be called contingent unless it is done by us unawares by contingency and chance, that is, by our will or hand catching at it as it is presented to us by

---

[1] W.A. 18.615.31. [2] W.A. 18.615.12.
[3] L. Baudry. La Querelle des Futurs Contingents. (Louvain, 1465-75.) Paris, 1950. Nominalism laid great stress on contingency and Ockham seems to have left room for the so-called neutral contingencies of three-value logic. See Ph. Böhner. The Tractatus de Predestinatione . . . of William of Ockham. New York, 1945.

chance, we thinking nothing of it, nor willing anything about it before hand." [1]

Luther says, "God foreknows nothing by contingency but he fore-knows, purposes and does all things according to his immutable, eternal and infallible will." [2]

This stress on the unchangeable will and goodness of God is in the Nominalist tradition, but Luther has an evangelical reason for his insistence.

"How else can you believe confidently and trust to and depend upon God's promises? . . . For the greatest and only consolation of Christians in their adversities is the knowing that God lies not, does all things immutably, and that his will cannot be resisted, changed or hindered." [3]

When Luther speaks of necessity on the other hand he does not mean a constrained and forced necessity, as though man were taken by the scruff of the neck and made to do evil.

"Necessarily I say, but not a necessity of 'coaction' as they call it, but necessity of immutability, not of coaction, that is, a man who is void of the Spirit of God does not do evil against his will, as by some kind of violence, as though caught hold of by the neck, unwilling to commit it, as a thief or robber is led to punishment, but he does it with a spontaneous and consenting will." [4]

God therefore sustains all men by his power.

"God cannot do evil, though he works evil through evil men. Being good himself he cannot do evil, but he uses evil instruments which cannot escape the sway and motion of his omnipotence. . . . The fault is in the instrument." [5]

Thus he acts even in Satan and the impious.

"God acts in them as they themselves are, and as he finds them: that is, as they are averse from God and evil, being carried along by his omnipotence they cannot but do what is averse and evil. Just as it is with a man driving a horse lame on one foot or lame on two feet: he drives him just as the horse is: the horse moves badly. But what can the man do? He is driving along this kind of horse along with other horses." [6]

Thus God moves the whole course of history and gives life and breath to all things, superintending and working out his own purposes through good and evil. Luther believed that this is the view of the Bible. But this doctrine of the unchangeable will of God, so comforting in its assurance that the promises of God can never be altered, so infinitely

[1] W.A. 18.616.7.   [2] W.A. 18.615.12.
[3] W.A. 18.619.3.   [4] W.A. 18.634.21.
[5] W.A. 18.709.29.   [6] W.A. 18.709.21.

more comfortable than the ever-recurring "perhaps" of scholastic logic, becomes a terrible temptation if once a man doubts his own place among the promises of salvation. The question immediately involved the theme of Predestination.

3. PREDESTINATION.

Here Luther must be set against a debate already a thousand years old in the Western Church, and about which as severe things had already been said as Calvinism was to say in the next century, or Jansenism in the century after. A doctrine of Predestination is in any case an integral part of both Protestant and Catholic divinity, as it must always be part of any gospel which gives God the glory, and which maintains the divine freedom and initiative in creation and redemption, and which acknowledges that the ultimate judgment is not our verdict upon God, but his upon us. And even where a disciple of John and Charles Wesley must confess himself most restive with Luther's treatise, there is wisdom profitably to be studied. That mankind is divisible into elect and reprobate, that the number of those saved are the smaller portion of mankind, these were ideas to be found among the mediaeval disputations from the time of Augustine. Though the Council of Orange had refrained from asserting a double Predestination, isolated theologians had taken up the statement of Isidore of Seville that "There is a double predestination, to life and to death. Both are concerned with a divine judgment, so that he makes the elect follow internal things and things above, and permits the reprobate always to be damned by being delighted with external things and things below." [1]

Here the whole question arose of human merits, whether God predestinated men on their account, or whether he foresaw those merits, or whether the sole cause of predestination was in God's own sovereign freedom.[1]

But let us listen to Luther at his most uncongenial and hardest saying.

"This is the highest degree of Faith: to believe him merciful who saves so few, and who damns so many: to believe him just who according to his own will makes us necessarily damnable so that he seems, as Erasmus says, rather to delight in the torments of the miserable and to be an object of hatred rather than of love." [3]

The "pessimism of Grace," as M. Rondet calls it, which thought of

---

[1] Rondet. Gratia Christi. Paris, 1948, 172. Also ch. 8, 10.16-17. H. de Lubac. Surnaturel. Paris, 1946. Gilson. Introd. à l'étude de S. Augustin, 201-5.

[2] P. A. Vignaux. Justification et Prédestination au XIVe siècle. Paris, 1934.

[3] Normann. De Servo Arbitrio. Z. für Syst. Theol., 1937, 303-338, 332. W.A. 18.633.15.

the elect as a small number compared with the damned was a common mediaeval theme, and even St. Thomas inclined to the view that "the smaller number" would be saved. The subject received some horrible elaboration in both Protestant and Catholic preaching in the seventeenth century. It was one of the great achievements of the Evangelical Arminianism of the Wesleys that it replaced this with an "optimism of Grace."

We have then to recognize, as Bishop Normann of Oslo says, "that Luther teaches a double predestination."

But not only did Luther not invent this teaching, it had been for him the cause of the most terrible "Anfechtungen" which, as we have seen, he had so vividly described:

"That the God who is full of goodness and mercy should of his own will harden men, leave them and damn them as though he delighted in such eternal torments of the miserable: to think thus of God seems iniquitous and intolerable, and it is this which has given offence to so many and great men in so many ages. I myself have been offended more than once even to the abyss of despair, nay so far as even to wish that I had not been born a man: that is before I knew how beautiful that despair was, and how near to Grace." [1]

And here Luther comes to one of his most interesting theological distinctions, between God hidden (Deus absconditus) and God revealed (Deus revelatus). [2]

The doctrine and fact of predestination is to be accepted, Luther believed, because it is asserted in the Scriptures. But we are to leave it alone. We are not to speculate about it. We have to hold to the revealed truth that Christ's mercy is to be preached.

"We are to argue in one way, concerning the will of God preached, revealed and offered to us and worshipped by us: and in another concerning God himself not preached, not revealed. In whatever therefore God hides himself and wills to be unknown to us, that is nothing to us: that sentiment stands, 'What is above us does not concern us.'" [3]

"God is therefore to be left in his own nature and majesty: for in this respect we have nothing to do with him, nor does he wish, in this respect, to have anything to do with us: but we have to do with him insofar as he is clothed and delivered to us by the Word: and that is his beauty and glory." [4]

Luther has no thought of two Gods, or of two wills in God. If we have God Incarnate in Jesus Christ then we have God, Deus abscond-

---

[1] W.A. 18.719.5.
[2] F. Kattenbusch. Deus Absconditus bei Luther. Festgabe für J. Kaftan, 1920, 170-214. W. v. Loewenich. Theologia Crucis, 27 ff.
[3] W.A. 18.685.3.   See also W.A. 43.403.9.   [4] W.A. 18.685.14.

itus and revelatus. And for our hope and certainty we are to turn, as long ago Staupitz had told him to turn, to the Cross of Christ and to the Wounds of Jesus.

Moreover, this is not to posit an irrational will in God though it is to admit that God's will is beyond our yardsticks. Like St. Augustine and St. Thomas, Luther affirms that at the end of the day we shall perceive that God's judgments are righteous.

He develops the common distinction between the three layers of our knowledge, "the light of nature, the light of grace, and the light of glory," and suggests that on the one plane we cannot conceive of the true explanation, which is given to us in terms of the new dimension of superior revelation.

"So," says Luther, "by the light of nature it is insoluble how it can be just that the good man can be afflicted and the wicked prosper, but that is solved by the light of grace. By the light of grace it is insoluble how God can damn him who by his own powers can do nothing but sin. Both the light of nature and the light of grace say that the fault is in the injustice of God . . . but the light of glory will show that God to whom alone belongeth the judgment of incomprehensible righteousness is of righteousness most perfect and most manifest." [1]

Schott is perfectly right when he insists that for Luther the doctrine of Predestination is subordinate to the doctrine of Justification. The body of the elect does not play the part in his ecclesiology which it does in the doctrine of Wyclif and of Huss. At the end of his life Luther told how he tried to console a woman in distress who was suffering from this terrible form of "Anfechtung," the temptation about predestination. As Staupitz had turned him so now he turned her thoughts to the one healing remedy. "Hear the Incarnate Son, He freely offers thee himself as Predestination." [2]

In the next centuries both Protestant and Catholic theologians were to be exercised by these intricate problems. We have learned some things about the workings of grace and the nature of human personality since then, and I do not think many would state even Luther's positive truths about this matter exactly as he stated them. But I hope it can be seen why this treatise "De Servo Arbitrio" still lives and why it is, as Bishop Normann has it, "the finest and most powerful Soli Deo Gloria to be sung in the whole period of the Reformation."

.   .   .   .

It is a sound advice to those entangled in controversy to stop with the first round. Luther did not know how hard he hit, and Erasmus

[1] W.A. 18.785.28.
[2] Volz. Wie Luther in der Genesisvorlesung sprach. Theol. St. u. Krit., 1927, 187.

U

did not like what he received.   But having entered the lists he could
not expect to enjoy the status of a non-belligerent.   That he was deeply
hurt and offended by Luther's work was shown by an angry letter
which he wrote him after Luther (no doubt solicited by Melanchthon)
had written a half-apologetic letter.[1]

Erasmus wrote a reply, the "Hyperaspistes" in two volumes, one of
300, the other 500 pages.[2]   They remind us of that dreary and inter-
minable second Dialogue of Sir Thomas More.   It is at least one point
to the Reformers, William Tyndale and Martin Luther, that they
forced the two greatest wits of the age to perpetrate two ponderous
diatribes from which all the sparkle and wit had withered and which
bored even their most devoted admirers.   Luther replied only by an
open letter in which he said things which were bitterly unfair, but which
was perhaps the best to be made of a bad job.   From this point onwards,
Erasmus was to him as an heathen and a publican.   The Table Talk
is full of the kind of bitter comment which shows that as with
Müntzer and Zwingli, Luther had hardened his heart and mind, with
that implacable obstinacy which was no doubt a defect in his make-up.[3]

"Such utter unlikes cannot but end in dislikes, and so it proved between Erasmus and Luther," said Coleridge.[4]   In their controversy they
were strangely at cross purposes. We are told that as young men, Erasmus
painted, while Luther played the lute, and something of the difference
underlies their controversy. "How thin, how superficial!" cries Luther.
"How confused, how lacking in perspective," complains Erasmus.

In the National Gallery there is a Flemish landscape.   The artist,
Patinir, had never seen real mountains, and he practised with shards of
rock which jut grotesquely from the level plain.   Erasmus's handling
of this controversy was a little like that.   His gospel was smooth and
pleasantly even as his native Holland.   When compared with Luther's
grim expositions of the tempted Christian and the "angefochtene
Christus," his "Enchiridion" is an arm-chair study of the Christian
warfare.   Nobody has yet satisfactorily expounded his theology,[5] and

---

[1] Epistolae, Vol. VI, 1688. 11th April 1526.
[2] Part 1, March 1526. Part 2, Sept. 1527.
[3] TR. 1.352.432.3.3795.4.3963.4905. The defects of the two men were as various
as their temperaments, for Luther would have been incapable of the action of Erasmus
in refusing to receive the desperate, disgraced and dying Hutten. And if Luther's
comments on the death of his enemies sound callous, they are different from Erasmus's
peevish remark on hearing of Hutten's death, that it would spoil the sales of his
"Spongia adversus aspergines Huttenii" which had just appeared.   Renaudet.
Études, 310-16.
[4] He also said, "That Luther was practically on the right side in this famous controversy and that he was driving at the truth, I see abundant reason to believe . . . but
it is no less evident that he saw it in a mist, or rather as a mist with a dissolving outline
. . . but Erasmus " was " equally indistinct : and shallow and unsubstantial to boot."
[5] Not even J. B. Pineau. Érasme, sa pensée religieuse. Paris, 1924.

the exact content of that "philosophia Christi," though it seems to be a compound of classical philosophy and the "devotio moderna," and smacks a little of that ever recurrent fallacy the "simple Gospel," which rejects theology in favour of practical piety, rational intelligibility and devout mysticism.

He did not understand the great heights and depths of the Christian faith: what it meant, with Luther and Augustine, to peer steeply down into the nauseating "abyss of the human conscience," with Luther and Bunyan to tremble in the Valley of Humiliation, and to weep upon the Delectable Mountains at the brave prospect of distant Zion. It cuts deeply between the two men that while Erasmus never exercised spiritual direction, never had cure of souls, for Luther the souls of men and women were a charge which came upon him daily, and of which that last, scribbled note of his bears witness.

"Nobody can understand Virgil who has not been a shepherd or a farmer for five years . . . nobody can understand Cicero who has not been a politician for twenty years . . . nobody can understand the Scriptures who has not looked after a congregation for a hundred years. We're beggars, that's the truth."

Well, there is a high road and a low road where comparisons are blasphemous. In that fine volume of his own letters, Dr. P. S. Allen has words about Erasmus which seem to apply to both these great men, and deserve to be our final word about them both.

"You detect weakness? He had marvellously little care for his personal reputation. But I don't believe the weakness can have counted for much, or he wouldn't have been so beloved by people whose judgment was sound."

In the end, the Spirit of the Pities is a sounder guide to historical truth than the Spirit of the Furies, and we err least when we judge men, as we ourselves might hope to be judged, by the verdict of their friends.

Chapter

13

LUTHER AND GOVERNMENT ("REGIMENT")

"Yes, heroic Swan. I love thee even when thou gabblest like a
goose: for thy geese helped to save the Capitol."
S. T. COLERIDGE on Luther's "Table Talk."

AMONG the lesser figures surrounding the giant Luther in the famous
memorial at Worms are the figures of the Elector Frederick the Wise
of Saxony, and of the Landgrave Philip of Hesse. They are salutary reminders that there is no merely ecclesiastical reading of the Reformation.

Luther did not forget that, humanly speaking, he owed the safety
of his person and of the good cause to the Elector Frederick (not to
forget Mr. Secretary Spalatin who deserves a chapter in the unwritten
history of the influence of Court Chaplains and Private Secretaries). [1]
He owed it to his Prince and his advisers that in the critical months
(1517-21) he did not go the way of John Huss, and that Wittenberg
remained the strange, calm centre of the destructive cyclonic whirlwind.
When the first Protestant martyrs died in Brussels, Luther wrote a
fine hymn in their honour, and when his English friend (almost the
only Englishman we might call his disciple) Robert Barnes was burned
in London, he wrote him a splendid obituary notice: but in his own
case what was literally a "war of nerves" was never consummated in
his flesh. It was a strange turn which made Frederick, the extravagantly
devoted collector of relics, into the first patron of the Reformation,
and more is needed to account for it than the pride of an ambitious
ruler in the pet theologian of his pet University.

It was that practical, common-sense astuteness (which Luther so
much admired, akin as it was to his own wisdom) and a certain obstinate
integrity which enabled Frederick the Wise to turn the bribes, threats,
entreaties, the twists and turns of Papal diplomacy to his own and to
Luther's advantage, even though there were moments, as immediately
after Luther's interviews with Cajetan in 1518 and in Cologne in
November 1520, when it was touch and go. Philip of Hesse, a tragic
and less noble figure, and of a younger generation, is a different kettle
of fish. Luther generally left Melanchthon, with Martin Bucer, to

---

[1] A useful sketch has been provided by I. Hoess. Georg Spalatins Bedeutung für
die Reformation und die Organisation der lutherischen Landeskirche. Archiv für
Ref., vol. 42, 1951, 101-36.

deal with him, and he represented all the ominous political pressures and interests which Luther distrusted on his own side, and which in the last decade of his life he watched mounting in power and influence.

But if Luther had good cause to be grateful to his princes, the gibe of undue subservience comes a little oddly from the lips of Erasmus. It must always be remembered that one of Luther's key texts was "Put not your trust in princes," and he frightened his friends and disgusted his enemies by addressing potentates in Church and State with the same measure that they meted out to him, and in the case of Henry VIII epithets in full measure, pressed down and running over. And this, it would be easy to prove, is a constant element in his career, as marked after the Peasant War of 1525 as before it.

It takes us deep into his theology and its application (for the practical application of Biblical exegesis to the affairs of the contemporary world always seemed to Luther a solemn part of the calling of a theological professor) that the last mission of his life was concerned with his rulers, the attempt to mediate in the territory of which he was a "Landeskind" in an ugly affair of brotherly enmity which stimulated the worst vices of the German gentry. The last sermons of his life are therefore concerned to speak plainly of the vices of governors and their need to obey the laws of God.[1]

No teaching of Luther has been more misrepresented than his teaching about the nature, extent and limits of temporal power.[2]

Partly this has been due to an attempt to by-pass Luther's theology. Thus Professor Pascal tells us that the real key to Luther lies, not in his theology and his ideas, but in the "consistency of class interests," and proceeds to tie Luther up into knots which in the end are of his own contriving, since while the sociological element is really present in the story of the Reformation, it does not account for nearly half the story of sixteenth century Europe, let alone Martin Luther.[3]

Nor can we explain Luther in terms of the classical problems of

---

[1] W.A.Br. 11.273 ff. W.A. 51.186.189.
[2] Harald Diem. Luthers Lehre von den zwei Reichen. 1938.
Hermann Diem. Luthers Predigt in den zwei Reichen. 1947.
K. Holl. Luther und das Landesherrliche Kirchenregiment. 1911.
F. Kattenbusch. Die Doppelschichtigkeit bei Luthers Kirchenbegriff. 1928.
G. Törnvall. Andligt och världsligt Regemente hos Luther. Stockholm, 1940, and German tr. Geistliches und Weltliches Regiment bei Luther, 1947. See also Th. Lit. Z., 1949, 97.
O. Scheel. Evangelium, Kirche und Volk bei Luther. Leipzig, 1934.
C. G. Schweitzer. Luther and the State. Theology. 1943, 196-203.
P. S. Watson. The State as the Servant of God. 1945.
P. S. Watson. Luther's Doctrine of Vocation. S.J.T., Dec. 1949, 364.
G. Wingren. Luthers Lära om Kallelsen. Lund, 1948.
E. Wolf. Politia Christi (Ev. Theol., 1948-9).
[3] R. Pascal. The Social Basis of the German Reformation. 1933.

political philosophy. Luther was no political philosopher: he was, in P. Congar's phrase, "a man of the Word," a preacher and a professor of Biblical theology, with strict views about the need for parsons to mind their own business. If his dwelling-place in the middle of the sixteenth century Saxony was indeed a watch-tower from which a man might survey the heavens, it did not permit him to overlook the corners of the earth. Though, as we shall see, he had a theology of politics, he was at all points removed from the systematic, doctrinaire theoretician. His political judgments were those of a keen, common-sense empiricism, and he had a distrust of the high-sounding slogans of contemporary idealism, whether of so-called wars for righteousness— of Pope Julius II against Venice, or Duke George's Friesland campaign,[1] or the "Christian" manifestos of the Peasant War.

He stands midway between the long, intricate, mediaeval disputation between the Spiritual and the Temporal powers in Christendom and the modern dilemma of Church and State. He will not easily fit into either group of problems.[2]

A fertile source of English misreading of Luther has been the translation into English, in 1931, of Troeltsch's great "Social Teaching of the Christian Churches." Yet no part of Troeltsch has been more damagingly criticized in Germany and Scandinavia than this. In three major positions, his interpretation has been demonstrably defective. He misunderstood and mis-stated Luther's attitude to Natural Law: he read back into Luther his own too rigid dichotomy of "Church" type (versus "Sect" type) and he wrongly interpreted Luther's teaching on the relation of the Ten Commandments to the Sermon on the Mount.[3]

We may mention at the outset the most common criticism of Luther's teaching, that he sets up a baneful dualism between private and public morality, which paved the way for the divorce between religious and political morality in modern Germany, and indeed made possible the terrible infamies of the modern secular State. We shall concentrate on a positive exposition of Luther which may deal with this criticism on the way.[4] We may and must admit that the distinction between

---

[1] W.A. 56.448.
[2] G. de Lagarde, Recherches sur l'esprit politique de la Réforme, misreads Luther by cramping him within these alien themes.
[3] K. Holl. Ges. Aufsätze. Luther, 243-4, 261-2, etc.
[4] Among writings especially concerned with " Obrigkeit " are :
     " To the Christian Nobility of the German Nation." 1520.
     " Of Earthly Authority " (Von Weltlicher Obrigkeit). 1523.
     The writings against the " Fanatics " and concerning the Peasant War.
     " Can Soldiers be Christians ? " 1526.
     " On Keeping Children at School." 1530.
     The 82nd Psalm (1530). Psalm 101 (1534).
     The Genesis Commentary. 1535-45.

two, Kingdoms, and two kinds of Rule, is fundamental to Luther's view of God's government of the world.

1. THE TWO KINGDOMS: SPIRITUAL AND TEMPORAL.

As in the case of the Biblical word "Basileia" in the phrase "Kingdom of God," so Luther's thought is better expressed in terms of the "rule" than the realm of government.

Gustav Törnvall has clarified the issue by insisting that we look at this doctrine from the aspect of God's own rule. It is when we look from below, in terms of the spheres of the operation of that rule, that misconception arises and we misinterpret Luther either in terms of one "Corpus Christianum" (Sohm) or in terms of a too spiritualized conception of the Church (Holl?). But like so many other of Luther's teachings, it is clarified only when we think "coram Deo." Luther has a profound doctrine of Providence and of creation. He insists that God is always active in all his works, manifesting his bounty and goodness' through all his creatures, and that in fact all creatures are his "veils" or "masks" (larvae) [1] through which he disguises his own unbearable Majesty and yet deals with his world and with his children. The two kinds of rule are ways by which God himself runs his world, without ever abdicating his own present authority, and his own laws. The idea that there are areas of life where God has no control, and where men can rule by their own will, and make up the rules as they go along, the whole notion of the modern omnicompetent and secular State, is not only foreign to Luther's thought but would have appeared to him as a deadly blasphemy.

Törnvall is equally, and justifiably, insistent that this rich doctrine of God's creation, and continuously creative Providence, cannot be cut off from his doctrine of redemption in Christ. Luther knows what Isaac Watts has told us in his hymns, but what English Protestants have often forgotten, that the kingdoms of nature and of grace are one in Christ.

"There is not a God of general Providence who stands behind secular government, and who as such is separated from the revelation in Christ. He is not a certain, more abstract aspect of the Divine Being, who finds his expression in Creation, nor can this be understood as a preparatory disposition for the side of God seen in relation to Redemption, but he is the same God who comes to us in spiritual government who is Creator and Lord of all the orders of human society." [2]

---

[1] " Ideo universa creatura ejus est larva." W.A. 40.1.174.3. See also F. Lau. "Äusserliche Ordnung" und "Weltlich Ding " in Luthers Theologie. 1933.
[2] Törnvall, 79.

And because this is a doctrine "coram Deo," it is an apperception of God's rule given by revelation and embraced by Faith.

The distinction between the Kingdom of Christ and the Kingdom of this world is classical in Christian history, and goes back to the New Testament.[1] Luther says:

"We must divide the children of Adam into two classes: the first belong to the Kingdom of God, the second to the Kingdom of the world. Those belonging to the Kingdom of God are all true believers in Christ, and are subject to Christ. For Christ is the King and Lord in the Kingdom of God (Ps. 2) . . . all who are not Christians belong to the Kingdom of the world and are under the Law. Since few believe and fewer live a Christian life . . . God has provided for non-Christians a different government outside the Christian estate and God's Kingdom and has subjected them to the sword, so that even though they would do so, they cannot practise their wickedness, and that if they do, they may not do it without fear nor in peace and prosperity . . . for this reason the two Kingdoms must be sharply distinguished and both be permitted to remain: the one to produce piety, the other to bring about external peace and to prevent evil deeds: neither is sufficient in the world without the other." [2]

"God separates his spiritual kingdom sharply from his temporal. . . . St. Peter and St. Paul had not a foot-breadth nor a straw to call their own or by which they might keep themselves, let alone be rulers or lords. Yet at that time there were both Kingdoms at Rome: one ruled by Emperor Nero against Christ: the other Christ ruling through his apostles Peter and Paul against the Devil." [3]

The second quotation reminds us of a fact which blurs all theorizing and prevents a smooth and rounded doctrine in this matter, the conflict and dynamism in history, the ferment of evil, to which Luther's doctrine of the Devil bears witness.

God's spiritual government is that of the "Kingdom of God," the "Kingdom of Christ," and is exercised through the Gospel, as a "Kingdom of Hearing" (through Faith). If all men were truly Christian that would be sufficient, and there would be no need of the secular government.

"If all the world were composed of real Christians, that is, true believers, no prince, king, lord, sword or law would be needed. For what were the use of them, since Christians have in their hearts the Holy Spirit who instructs them and causes them to wrong no one, to love everyone, willingly and cheerfully to suffer injustice and even

---

[1] A. Nygren. Luthers Lehre von den zwei Reichen. Th. Lit. Z., Jan. 1949, 1.
[2] W.M.L. 3.234-7.   [3] W.A. 51.238.35.

death from everyone. Where every wrong is suffered and every right is done, no quarrel, strife, trial, judge, penalty, law or sword is needed. Therefore it is not possible for the secular sword of law to find any work to do among Christians for of themselves they do much more than its laws and doctrines can demand . . . a man would be a fool to make a book of laws and statutes telling an apple tree how to bear apples and not thorns, when it is able by its own nature to do this better than man with all his books can define and direct." [1]

But Christians are rare birds, "among thousands there is scarcely one true Christian," [2] hence "Christ's rule does not extend over all but Christians are always [3] in a minority and are in the midst of non-Christians." It was one of the grave counts which Luther had against the Peasants that they attached the name "Christian" to their own banner, and thought in terms of a "Christian" movement. "But, dear friends, Christians are not so common that they can get together in a mob." [4] "You ask, who are the Christians and where does one find them? I answer, They are not many, but they are everywhere, though they are spread out thin and live far apart, under good and bad rulers." [5]

"It is true that Christians so far as they are concerned are subject to neither law nor sword and need neither: but first take heed and fill the world with real Christians before ruling it in a Christian and evangelical manner. This you will never accomplish: for the world and the masses are and always will be unchristian, although they are all baptized and are nominally Christian. . . . Therefore it is out of the question that there should be a common Christian government over the whole world, nay, even over one land or company of people since the wicked always outnumber the good. Hence a man who would venture to govern an entire country or world with the Gospel would be like a shepherd who should place in one fold, wolves, lions, eagles and sheep together and say 'Help yourselves, and be good and peaceful among yourselves; the fold is open: there is plenty of food: have no fear of dogs and clubs.' The sheep indeed would keep the peace and would allow themselves to be fed and governed in peace—but they would not live long! Nor would any beast keep from molesting another." [6]

God rules the two spheres of his world by two instruments.

"God has established two kinds of government among men: the one is spiritual: it has no sword but it has the Word by which men . . . may attain everlasting life. The other is Worldly government through the

[1] W.M.L. 3.234.   [2] W.M.L. 3.236.
[3] Ibid. 237.   [4] W.M.L. 4.231.
[5] W.M.L. 5.89.   [6] W.M.L. 3.237.

sword which aims to keep peace among men and this he rewards with temporal blessing." [1]

This earthly government is a kind of parable of the spiritual Kingdom.

"For God wills that the temporal rule (Weltregiment) should be an image of the true blessedness and of the Kingdom of heaven, like a conjurer's mirror or mask." [2]

God rules the temporal "regiment" through the law, of which the symbol is the sword.

"The law is given for the sake of the unrighteous that those who are not Christian may through the law be externally restrained from evil deeds . . . since however nobody is by nature Christian or pious God places the restraints of the law upon them all so that they may not dare give rein to their desires and commit outward wicked deeds." [3]

Luther believed the confusion of the two Kingdoms to be pernicious. He believed that the Papacy had entangled the spiritual vocation of the Church in political and economic and juridical pressures to the detriment and destruction of the souls of men. He believed the religious idealists who were the ideological leaders of the Peasant War were equally pernicious. Zwingli (and Oliver Cromwell!) holding Sword in one hand and Bible in the other is as much a contradiction of the Gospel as Boniface VIII claiming to be the fountain of both kinds of jurisdiction.

"For the Devil is always trying to cook and brew the two Kingdoms into one another. The temporal ruler tries to teach and rule Christ in the Devil's name and tell him how he ought to run the Church and the spiritual power. The false Papists and the fanatics are always trying to teach and run the temporal order: so the Devil gets busy on both sides and has quite a lot to do. But God'll teach him!" [4]

"God's Kingdom is a kingdom of Grace and mercy, not wrath and severity, but the kingdom of the world is a Kingdom of wrath and of severity . . . now he who would confuse these two Kingdoms . . . as our fanatics do, would put wrath into God's Kingdom and mercy into the world's kingdom." [5]

2. GOVERNMENT "REGIMENT."

Our world, which has moved nearer the edge of things than the late Victorian age could understand, is better fitted to understand Luther's

---

[1] W.M.L. 5.39.

[2] W.A. 51.241.39. Luther, whose vocation was the Spiritual Kingdom, the ministry of the Word, thought this was the really hard work. Discussing the " sweat " which came to man through Adam's Fall, he says it is "magnus " with "oeconomia," " major " with " politia " and " maximus " with " ecclesia." Cf. Kattenbusch. Theol. St. und Kr., 1928, 326.

[3] W.M.L. 3.235.

[4] W.A. 51.239.24.

[5] W.M.L. 4.265.

insistence on the fact that ordered government and stable peace are God's good gifts and blessings to be reverently accepted and solemnly guarded. These are gifts which God as creator has bestowed on his children.

"Earthly government is a glorious ordinance of God and a splendid gift of God, who has established and instituted it and will have it maintained as something that men cannot do without. If there were no worldly government no man could live because of other men: one would devour the other, as the brute beasts do . . . so it is the function and honour of earthly government to make men out of wild beasts and to prevent men from becoming wild beasts. . . . Do you not think that if birds and beasts could speak they would say 'O ye men, you are not men but Gods compared with us. How safe you live and hold your property, while among us no one is sure for an hour . . . because of the others. Out upon your unthankfulness.'" [1]

"So we see that God scatters rule and kingdoms among the heathen . . . just as he does the dear sun and rain. So he calls such earthly rule among the heathen his own ordinance and creation." [2]

"God is a mild, rich Lord who scatters gold, riches, authority, kingdoms among the heathen as though they were spray or sand, also he throws among them reason, wisdom, languages, oratory so that his dear Christians look plain children, fools and beggars compared with them." [3]

"God calls Nineveh city of God, for he has made and makes all communities: he still brings them together, feeds them, increases them, blesses and preserves them . . . the worldly wise know not that a community is God's ordinance and creature, but think it has come into being by accident by people keeping together and living side by side in the same way that murderers and other wicked bands come together."[4]

The gifts of God are more than gifts, for they are the instruments of the Providential activity of God:

"For what is all our work in field, garden, house, war, ruling, towards God but child's play, through which God gives his gifts to field and house and all the rest? They are the masks (larvae) of our Lord God through which he will remain hidden and yet do all . . . God bestows all good things but you must take the bull by the horns, you must do the work and so provide God with an opportunity and a disguise." [5]

In his great "Social History," Troeltsch has shown that two principles live side by side in constant tension throughout Christian history, world renunciation and world acceptance. On the one hand, there

[1] W.M.L. 4.159. [2] W.A. 51.238.19.
[3] W.A. 51.242.15. [4] W.M.L. 4.292.
[5] W.A. 31.1.436.7.

are those who have heard the divine command to come out and be separate, and to keep unspotted from the world. Often they have obeyed by abandoning civilized society as evil and contaminating, and have sought to solve their ethical problems by contracting out of those offices and responsibilities of political and economic life where the ethical conflict between the Sermon on the Mount and natural law is most acute. This was the way of many of the sects of the Middle Ages, of the Reformation, as it is still the attitude of sects and parties in the modern Church. The religious Orders of the mediaeval Church were a series of valiant attempts, among other things, to prevent the spiritual life from becoming entangled in things, in great and small possessions. Their distinction between the precepts and counsels of the Gospel softened something of the sharpness between the "religious" and the "secular" life, for at least in theory it did not acquiesce in a double standard of morality. On the other hand, there was the attempt to bring the Christian gospel into direct and permeating influence upon the vast areas of political and economic and cultural life, the attempt, impressive and even magnificent, at a Christian civilization.

The working out of this in mediaeval society, with the delicate and always changing balance of spiritual and temporal powers at every level of the intricate pyramids, from Pope and Emperor at the top to priest and squire or municipality and monastery at the bottom, was reflected in a whole theological literature concerning the relation, under God's Providence, of the two powers. The later mediaeval prospect in which the growing ferment of nationality and the bursting energies of separate kingdoms threatened to burst the mediaeval unity, and where the spiritual power presented a shocking parody of spiritual leadership by becoming entangled and immersed in legal, financial and political affairs, showed something of the peril of the principle of world acceptance, once the spiritual vocation was neglected. That was Luther's charge. He did not foolishly imagine that politics and economics and law were bad things, or that the world could get on without them, or that a church across the world could escape complicated practical problems. But his charge was that the two powers had become confused, and that the Church as a spiritual entity had forsaken its prime vocation.

When M. de Lagarde quotes Luther's saying, "Since the time of the Apostles no doctor, no exegete, no theologian or lawyer has so truly and clearly confirmed, comforted and consoled the conscience of the Temporal estate as I," he takes Luther to task for arrogance, and if not for arrogance, for ignorance of a whole range of Imperialist literature.[1]

---

[1] Lagarde. Recherches, 209. See also Naissance de l'esprit laïque, vols. 1-6, for a survey of mediaeval political theology.

But that is to misunderstand what Luther said. Luther's claim is to have comforted the conscience of the Temporal Ruler. Here is something more than a mere annotation to a long debate already powerfully discussed from the secular side in the eleventh century by the "Anonymous of York," or in terms of the Aristotelian political theorizing of Ockham or Marsiglius, or even the new sixteenth century insistence on the "godly Prince" responding as it did to new pressures of history, and in itself an inevitable and obvious emphasis once the Church had been cleared from a vast no-man's-land of competitive claims and jurisdictions.

Luther sought to reject three false solutions of the problem of Christian existence in the world. First, he denied the mediaeval distinction between the precepts and the counsels of the Gospels and insisted that the Sermon on the Mount has meaning for the wayfaring Christian in the world. Second, he rejected the fanatical and sectarian repudiation of law, which contracted out of the obligations and responsibilities of government. At the same time he sought to avoid the disaster which had overtaken the institutional Church, by returning to the distinction between the things pertaining to Caesar and those belonging to God (though in another sense Caesar also belongs to God). Thus he explained his object in the Preface to his "Von Weltlicher Obrigkeit " (1523).

"I hope to instruct the.... secular authorities in such a way that they shall remain Christians and that Christ shall remain Lord, yet so that Christ's commandments need not for their sake be changed into 'counsels.'" [1]

The problem of the relation between public and private morality belongs to all ages. Can a Christian be a magistrate, executioner, policeman, soldier? The sectarian, modern and mediaeval, says "No," and by taking refuge in personal or group piety, he contracts out of the obligations of society and erects the very dualism of which Luther himself is sometimes charged.

On the other hand, as human life shows, problems continually arise. A Christian man may have several official capacities: he may be a Christian man, a father of a family, a master of a business, a local magistrate, a town councillor, and may well be confronted during the week with differing ethical decisions which he is tempted to solve in terms of the reflex of the social pattern in which he is engaged. This tension runs through all civilized life, and it is acute for the Christian who is concerned with the loftiest of all ethics, the Christian doctrine of love. But what Luther has to say is not, in the first place, concerned

[1] W.M.L. 3.229.

to grapple with this ethical tension, though something so fundamental is bound to be reflected in his exposition. Luther, we have seen, is thinking primarily of the Rule of God through his creation, and through that ordered government which in his bounty and kindness he has provided for his children.

Luther distinguished between a man's "person" and his "office": "person" is what a man is "coram Deo." As persons we are all equal before God, since in Jesus Christ there is neither male nor female, cleric nor layman. In his sight and in this relation, all human righteousness is condemned [1] and we can stand before God on the ground only of God's own Righteousness in Christ. But God has provided "offices" in the world, through which the orderly use of creation is carried on. These are not abstract entities, to be considered apart from the people who are called to occupy them. But in them a man may fulfil his vocation as father, husband, magistrate, teacher, farmer, and the like. When a man serves God and his neighbour in such an office, it is not to be evaluated in terms of accident, self-interest or opportunism, but it is a " Calling." [2]

A man's calling, his vocation, is the place where he fulfils the concrete, particular reference of the will of God. By faith, hope and love, the Christian man lives in the Kingdom of Christ and he serves God and his neighbour with the glad and creative obedience of a Christian man. But God has not left the majority of men, who are not Christians, to their own devices. They, too, are under God's provident care, and the ordered life of home, society and state are part of his provision for them, and his rich, good gifts. Nor is the kind of righteousness they own a mere sham righteousness, nor God's oversight of them a kind of lower level of justice. Luther, as Törnvall has demonstrated, teaches that "justitia civilis" is a real righteousness, and genuinely related to God's own righteousness in Christ, even though our human apprehension of this righteousness is imperfect and vitiated by sin.

A Christian man is called to endure and suffer wrong, without reprisal. But as a magistrate or policeman he may be called on to enforce drastic (and in the sixteenth century that often meant savage) sanctions on evil doers. These are not two sets of moralities, for love is the meaning and vindication of both sets of righteousness, for the end of both is the service of our neighbour and the glory of God.

"Christians among themselves," says Luther, "need no law or sword . . . but since a true Christian lives not for himself but for his

[1] " Justitia politica, id est coram Deo reproba."
[2] K. Holl. Ges. Aufs., iii. 189. Die Geschichte des Wortes " Beruf." G. Wingren. Luthers Lära om Kallelsen. P. S. Watson. Luther's Doctrine of Vocation. S.J.T., 1949, 364.

neighbour and . . . the sword is a very great benefit and necessary to the whole world to preserve peace . . . to punish sin and to prevent evil . . . he serves, helps, and does all he can to further the government . . . he considers what is for the profit of others." [1]

"Therefore should you see that there is a lack of hangmen, police, judges, lords or princes and find that you are qualified, you should offer your services and seek the job, so that necessary government may by no means be despised and become inefficient or perish." [2]

"But you ask, whether the policemen, hangmen, lawyers, counsel and the like can also be Christians and in a state of salvation. . . . I answer: if the State and its sword are a divine service as was proved above, then that which the State needs to wield the sword must also be a divine service . . . when such duties are performed not with the intention of seeking one's own ends but only of helping to maintain the laws there is no peril in them . . . for as was said, love of neighbour seeks not its own, how great or small, but considers how profitable and needful for neighbour and community such works are." [3]

"Worldly government through the sword aims to keep peace among men and this God rewards with temporal blessing . . . thus God himself is the founder, lord, protector and rewarder of both kinds of righteousness. There is no merely human ordinance in either but each is altogether a divine thing." [4]

So far from leaving politics to itself and free to make its own laws, Luther would have regarded the attempt to establish a secular state apart from the laws of God as the summit of human folly and pride. Here is an extract which we might call "The Planners":

"For such godless people are so sure and secure in their own wisdom as if our Lord God must sit idle and not come into their clever counsels. And so he has to chat for a while with his angel Gabriel and says, 'Friend, what are the clever ones planning in that council chamber that they won't take us into their counsel? Perhaps they're planning to build another Tower of Babel. . . . Dear Gabriel, go down, and take Isaiah with you and give them a little reading in through the window and say "with seeing eyes shall ye not see, with hearing ears shall ye not hear, with understanding hearts shall ye not understand. Make your Plan and nothing will come . . . for mine is not only the Plan but the deed."'" [5]

Thus we are not to think that God is only interested in Christians and has left the world to its own devices. God has given all men the light of reason and the law of nature. Luther accepts the fact that

[1] W.M.L. 3.239.
[2] Ibid. 241.
[3] W.M.L. 3.249.
[4] W.M.L. 5.39.
[5] W.A. 51.203.26.

natural law is reflected in the legal systems of mankind, in the accumulated wisdom of the past, and in the common proverbial wisdom
of the people. In a passage which will surprise many people, he
says:

"Let whoever wants to be wise and clever about earthly government
read the pagan books and writings . . . out of which our own Imperial
law has come. . . . And it is my conviction that God has given and preserved such pagan books as the poets and histories, as Homer, Virgil,
Demosthenes, Cicero, Livy and also that fine old lawyer Ulpian . . . so
that the pagan and godless should have their prophets, apostles, theologians or preachers for their earthly governance . . . so they had Homer,
Plato, Aristotle, Cicero, Ulpian as God's people had Moses, Elijah,
Isaiah, and their kings, and princes Alexander and Augustus as their
David and Solomon . . . and where could anybody make a finer book
of heathen wisdom than the common, simple children's book of Aesop's
fables? Yes, because the children learn it and it is so common it counts
for nothing, and yet it is worth four doctors who have never been able
to grasp one of the fables in it." [1]

Yet Luther distrusts lawyers (he had some reason to in the context
of his time and he puts in a plea for equity and natural wisdom).

"So the heathen Plato writes that there are two kinds of Law:
Justum Natura: Justum Lege. I will call the one sound law and the
other sick law, for that which flows out of the power of nature flows
freshly without need of law, although it runs also through the law.
But where nature is absent and all things have to be done by written
law, then all is poverty and patchwork." [2]

Luther's stress on equity and his reference to Aristotle's "Epieikia"
is his own adaptation of a frequent late mediaeval reference. He
regards much of the work of government as a kind of "make
do and mend." "Civil law and righteousness is a real beggar's
cloak." [3]

In this connection Luther can even use the Nominalist formula
which in connection with "justitia christiana" he had fiercely repudi-

---

[1] W.A. 51.242.36.   [2] W.A. 51.214.15.
[3] W.A. 40.2.526. 1. "Noster Rex habet verbum Dei purum, etiam ad punctum
mathematicum. Jurista, magistratus, trifft den Zweck nicht, punctum indivisibilem.
Sufficit petiisse sapienter, si non tetigit. Punctus physicus ein ganzer wal, quidquid
bonum, propius punctum physicum, kan man nicht wohl feylen, alium nicht treffen.
Nullus Jurista magistratus in terris, qui sine vitio administrat. Hoc tempus non patitur.
Satis est quod jura humana, ponuntur, attingere scopum. Ideo Juristarum studium
est infinitum, data una lege, sequuntur X exceptiones etc. Sicut numquam possunt
redigi leges civiles in punctum mathematicum, fallen ymer casus, actiones zu, quae
variant illam legem. Ideo ista civilis justitia per se vitiosa. . . . Ideo opus Epieikia,
man mus lappen und flicken, ist ein rechter petler mantel lex civilis et justitia."
Törnvall, 147.

ated. Here, in the matter of "civil righteousness" a man must "do what in him lies" (facienti quod in se est).[1]

The following passage shows how differently Luther conceives of this "Law of Nature" from the mediaeval philosophers, and the democratic rationalism of Marsiglius in the fourteenth and Priestley in the eighteenth centuries.

"For if natural law and reason were in all heads and all human heads alike, then idiots, children and women could rule and make war as well as David, Augustus, Hannibal . . . yes, all men would be alike and none would rule over another. And what an uproar and wild state of affairs would be the upshot of that? But now has God so created them that men are unlike one another, and that one should rule and another obey. Two can sing together (that is, praise God alike) but they cannot speak together (that is, rule), for one must speak and another listen. So you'll find among those who brag and boast about their natural reason and law there are a good many thorough and big natural idiots. For that noble jewel which is called natural law and reason is a rare thing among the children of men." [2]

In his later writings Luther speaks often of the "Three Hierarchies": "The first is the Houschold, the second the State, the third the Church." [3]

In his last great commentary on Genesis Luther drew the lesson from the stories of the Patriarchs, who served God in the world in their vocations as parents and as husbands and as economic men, and he pointed the contrast with an over-clericalized contemporary society where these humbler callings were often disparaged. What he has to say about home and government is not to be dissociated from his

[1] " Ultra posse viri non vult Deus ulla requiri. Bona quidem sententia est, sed in loco dicta, scilicet de politicis, oeconomicis, et naturalibus. Ut si ego existens in regno rationis rego familiam, aedifico domum, gero magistratum et facio, quantum possum vel quod in me est, ibi sum excusatus. Hoc enim regnum habet suos terminos ad quod etiam proprie pertinent ista dicta: Facere quod in se est, vel: facere quantum possum. Sed sophistae ea trahunt in regnum spirituale in quo homo nihil aliud potest quam peccare. 'Est enim venundatus sub peccatum.' In externis illis autem, hoc est in politicis et oeconomicis rebus, homo non est servus sed dominus illarum corporalium rerum. Ideo impie fecerunt sophistae quod dicta ista politica et oeconomica traxerunt in Ecclesiam. Regnum enim rationis humanae longissime separandum est a spirituali regno, 19." W.A. 40.1.292. E. Wolf. Politia Christi, 67.
[2] W.A. 51.212.14.
[3] "Of Councils and Churches" (1539). W.A. 50.652. W.A. 39.2.34. E. Wolf. Politia Christi. Ev. Theol., 1949, 60. It is interesting to note that E. G. Selwyn in his Commentary on 1 Peter, 98 ff., and Essay II, treats these sets of human relations as the primitive Christian ethical pattern. He comments, " It indicates a disinclination on the part of the Apostolic writers to express direct moral judgments on all or any issues that arise in human affairs. The broad principles they enunciate are applicable to every sphere of life, but the application is to be made not directly by Church authority, but by Christians conversant with the sins and conditions of various social groups."

X

teaching about the Church. Taken as a whole, his teaching about the "Earthly Rule" and "Spiritual Rule" makes an impressive unity, showing how presently and actively God carries out His provident care of His creation, in and through Jesus Christ. Luther did not try, as we sometimes do, to fob off laymen's problems with parsons' solutions. "Why should I teach a tailor how to make a suit?" says Luther. "He knows it himself. The same is true of the Prince. I shall only tell him that he should act like a Christian." [1]

The last actions of his life illuminate his teaching. His loyalty and reverence for lawfully constituted authority made him accept the call to make a terrible and costly journey in mid-winter to advise and mediate in a quarrel between two nobles. He did not meddle with the lawyers and the politicians, though he gave his advice when asked. At the same time he preached plain and outspoken expositions of Scripture which went to the root of the high matter of the Christian duties of the parties to the quarrel.[2] Thus the spiritual "office" of the preacher was by no means confined to purely "spiritual" matters, but gave the practical, outspoken application of Holy Scripture to the condition of a place and time.

Luther's doctrine of the two forms of rule, taken as a whole, bears impressive testimony to the unity of all life, of creation and redemption. "The created world and justitia civilis," profoundly comments Törnvall, "are not two different things, but it all makes a unity together, one living, concrete reality which embraces men and in which men are installed by God. Luther sees all these things, ideas, principles, laws and morals, as one indivisible whole, as constituting one creation." [3]

The created orders, the callings of human society, the "justitia civilis," and the law, are themselves the instruments of God's own personal action. We are not to think of them as abstract entities or impersonal instruments. God does not conceive these "offices" as like the holes in a solitaire board into which in due season he puts persons, like marbles. Nor may we drive a wedge between creation and redemption as though in the one case God were concerned with making things, and in the other with bringing men into fellowship with himself. "God is the author of both kinds of righteousness." And the end of all righteousness is to bring God's creation home where it belongs. The Law is the "strange work" of God—and this means that all the orders of creation are part of God's active, personal moving redeeming action. All God's Birnam Woods come at last to Dunsinane. The splendid pageant of creation, all nature, all history, groaning and

[1] W.A. 10.iii.380.10.   [2] W.A. 51.173.26.
[3] Törnvall, 152.

in travail until now, belong to the grand theme of the universe, the Righteousness of God.

3. AUTHORITY ("OBRIGKEIT ").

Luther's doctrine of obedience to authority is rooted for him in the Biblical doctrine of Christian obedience and Rom. 13^1 is its locus classicus. ("Let every soul be subject to the higher powers, for the powers that be are ordained by God.") But it is to be balanced by Acts 5^{29}. "We must obey God rather than men." That is why Bishop Berggrav could write, "In the fight against Nazism Luther was a magnificent arsenal of weapons for our Church."

We have already noted how strongly Luther was impressed as a monk with the duty of holy obedience, and how vehemently he opposed those who sought to evade its responsibilities in the supposed or pretended interests of the Observants. He believed that God willed and intended law and order, and it was not the least part of his spiritual agonies during the period 1517-21 that his own conscience charged him with going against accredited authority and bringing disorder and chaos into Christendom. Luther expected citizens to obey their magistrates for the same reason that he expected University students to obey their proctors. In Erfurt in 1510 he had experienced the effect of a minor revolution in which the town council had been violently expelled, and the Volksjustiz hanged. Some days later some mercenary soldiers were involved in a brawl which developed into an ugly riot between town and gown, in which the arts buildings of the University, the library, and two student hostels were looted and burned. Luther had first-hand experience of the inability of a people's government to handle its own extremists, and only inadequate and tardy measures were taken. We have no direct comment of Luther on the business, but when a similar town and gown affair blew up in Wittenberg in 1520 he took drastic and unpopular action with regard to his students. Amid threats to his person and life Luther went into the University Pulpit and spoke "against the tumult as though I were partial to neither side: I simply spoke of the evil of sedition in the abstract whether supported by the citizens or students and I commended the power of the magistrates as one instituted by God. Good heavens, how much hatred I won for myself! They shouted out I was taking the part of the Town."[1] Here, in 1520, was Luther making the same unpopular stand that he made in 1525 against the Peasants.

Thus he thought of "obedience" as the "crown and honour of all

[1] Smith. Luther's Correspondence, 339-40. July 1520.

virtue," and he thought that the ideal situation for any land was where all classes served one another in love. But he was only too aware, though, like most of his contemporaries, the causes and extent of the disturbances were unknown to him, that existing society was straining under great new social pressures, that there was a dynamism of unrest, and that a new and, it seemed, cynical resentment was filtering into Germany through the cities of Italy and their warrior bands, through returning mercenaries, and from the preaching of the "fanatics" in Bohemia and Switzerland.

Luther believed that it was the Christian duty not to resist evil but to endure it. We have seen how integral a part it was of his "theology of the Cross" that the Christian is called upon to suffer with Christ all the shame and agony of injustice and wrong. His saying to the Peasants "Leiden! Leiden! Kreuz! Kreuz!" of which Figgis made so much, was written precisely because the rebels claimed that theirs was a Christian movement and a Christian revolution.[1]

In 1520 Luther made his "Appeal to the Christian Nobility," which included the knights and the Free Cities of the Empire, as well as the Princes. He appealed to the secular arm on precise theological grounds, in a state of emergency in which the spiritual arm, refusing a free, Christian Council, had repeatedly failed to amend. He appealed to the authorities on the ground of the common priesthood of all believers, and because the office of the magistrates, to bear the sword, fitted them to intervene on behalf of the community. He has been criticized for not recanting at Worms and putting himself at the head of national resistance to Rome, on the basis of the Gravamina of the German Nation. That shows little understanding of Luther. He refused that temptation, though he was aware of it—"Had I desired to foment trouble, I could have brought great bloodshed upon Germany. Yea, I could have started such a little game at Worms that the Emperor would not have been safe. But what would it have been? A mug's game. I left it to the Word."[2] Luther evaded the almost desperate wooing of the Knights under Hutten and von Sickingen. He can hardly be blamed for fearing that the even more dubious political revolt of the Peasants, led by his deadly foes against whom he had written for several years, would ruin all his work and drown the Reformation in a welter of bloodshed, destruction and anarchy.

---

[1] The problem of Luther's attitude in the Peasant War is too complex to be disposed of in a paragraph and I shall hope to attend to it elsewhere. But at least, as they framed their cause, Luther never " let down " the Peasants, for he never took them up. Nor did he " go over to " or " fling himself into " the arms of the Princes afterwards.

[2] W.M.L. 2.399.

Luther was convinced that revolution and rebellion were contrary to natural as well as to divine law and that revolution could not only endanger the whole fabric of society but must result in worse evils than those it tried to remedy. So he says, and it is a timely thought for us all to meditate:

"Changing a government is one thing. Improving a government is another."

And again:

"I take and always will take his part who suffers from rebellion, however unjust his cause may be: and will set myself against him who rebels, let his cause be ever so just, because rebellion cannot take place without injury and shedding of blood." [1]

At any rate, had Luther's teaching been followed the frightful events of the next century and a half of European history might have been greatly mitigated. Certainly Luther did not have to face the cruel dilemma of tyrannicide as it had to be faced later in the century. But perhaps we think too academically, and I do not think we ought too easily to assume that there is a Christian right or duty to participate in revolution, especially when that involves the bloody overthrow of organized government. And certainly the heroic modern German Lutheran, Dietrich Bonhoeffer, knew real agony of mind before actively joining in the resistance to Hitler through which he lost his life.

Luther did not approve of the examples of tyrannicide in the history of Greece and Rome. But he insists that the Christian duty of non-resistance is not a counsel of despair. In the first place, "tyrants cannot injure the soul," but are only injuring their own: "do you not think that you are already sufficiently revenged upon them?" And perhaps we can agree with Luther, even after the Nuremberg trials, that the most dire retribution for wicked men is that they should be "wicked men" given up, as St. Paul says, to "reprobate minds." In the second place, there can be worse things than tyranny: "a wicked tyrant is more tolerable than a bad war." In the third place, God is at hand and he is able to deal with tyrants. "God is there," says Luther. In the fourth place, since most men were not Christians there was the probability that other subjects would rise in revolt. And last, God could raise up other rulers to make war on the tyrant.[2]

Nevertheless there is a point when, at all costs, the Christian must disobey. Luther's treatise "Of Earthly Authority" was written to meet just this situation in which the Catholic rulers were forbidding

---

[1] 1522! Admonition to all Christians to beware of Insurrection and Rebellion.
[2] "Can Soldiers be Christians?" W.M.L. 5.49.

men to read Luther's Bible and demanding that such Bibles be surrendered. Luther tells Christians:

"You should say, 'It does not become Lucifer to sit by the side of
God . . . if you command me to believe and to put away books I will
not obey: for in this case you are a tyrant and over-reach yourself and
command where you have neither the right nor the power.'" [1]

Again:

"Never remain silent and assent to injustice, whatever the cost," for
he who remains silent makes himself an accomplice. [2]

Luther tells a soldier impressed into an unjust war:

"You should not fight or serve. 'Nay,' you say, 'my lord compels
me, takes my fief, does not give me any money, pay or wages, and
besides I am despised, put to shame as a coward, nay as a faith-breaker
in the eyes of the world, as one who has deserted his lord in need.'
I answer, 'You must take that risk.'" [3]

If need be, the Christian preacher must allow himself to be deposed
rather than be silent.

"It is not rebellious to let oneself be deposed, but it would be
rebellious if one who preaches the gospel did not chastise the vices of
the authorities. For such is the behaviour of lazy and useless
preachers." [4]

Luther had no room for doctrinaire democracy, and for him Herr
Omnes was no abstract "common man," but a peasantry which he saw
with the shrewd eyes of a Pieter Brueghel, partly because he had sprung
from among them. He had only scorn for Karlstadt, that model of a
left-wing intellectual, who, dressed as a peasant "Brother Andrew,"
tilled his plot of land while continuing to draw his professorial stipend.
Luther himself undertook a dangerous trip at the height of the Peasant
War into Thuringia, where he was threatened with physical violence
from the peasantry.

The emphasis upon the godly prince and the power of the magistrate
in Western Europe was the inevitable counterpoise to the clericalized
church-state. But you will find in Luther none of the subservience
discoverable in the Henrician Bishops in England. When all is said
and done, the passages in which Luther criticizes the crowd are far
outnumbered by those in which he delineates the vices and temptations
of the Princes. Nearly four centuries before Lord Acton, Luther speaks
of the corrupting effect of power:

"For power, honour, riches, authority . . . to have these and not to be
conscious of it, and not to be proud against one's subjects is no achieve-

[1] W.M.L. 3.257.   [2] E. Berggrav. Luther Speaks (1946), p. 10. See W.A. 28.286.359.
[3] W.M.L. 5.68.   [4] W.A. 31.i.196.

merit of common reason or simple human nature, but it needs the virtue of a Hercules or a David inspired by God." [1]

"The heart of man . . . is itself prone to presumption: and when beside this power, riches and honour fall to his lot, these form so strong an incentive to presumption and over-confident security as to move him to forget God and despise his subjects. Being able to do wrong with impunity he lets himself go and becomes a beast, does whatever he pleases and is a ruler in name, but a monster in deed." [2]

"But if a prince . . . lets himself think that he is a prince, not for his subjects' sake, but because of his beautiful blonde hair, as though God had made him a prince so that he may rejoice in his power and wealth and honour, take pleasure in these things and rely upon them, he belongs among the heathen, nay, he is a fool. That kind of prince would start a war over an empty nut and think of nothing but satisfying his own will." [3]

And in a memorable saying:

"He who wants to be a ruler, must have the Devil for his godfather." [4]

As in 1523 he had said that "a prince is a rare bird in heaven" and that "princes are usually the greatest fools or the worst knaves on earth, therefore one must constantly expect the worst from them, and look for little good," [5] so in 1534 he extends the judgment, "For if a prince is a rare bird in heaven, then councillors and men about court are still rarer birds in heaven." [6] If we feel sometimes that Luther's heaven must be as full of space as Sir James Jeans' "Mysterious Universe," we might remember his poignant comment on infant mortality in the sixteenth century, that he thought heaven must be full of little children!

Moreover, Luther was as certain as the Thirty-nine Articles, and a good deal more certain than some of the Caroline divines, that rulers must not interfere in spiritual things. This was his reason, in 1522, for disobeying the plain and express command of the Elector Frederick that he should remain in hiding on the Wartburg, and for his famous letter of Ash Wednesday 1522, in which he told the Elector:

"I come to Wittenberg under a far mightier protection than that of an Elector. Far be it from me to desire protection from your Grace . . . in this cause no sword can or shall afford counsel or succour." [7]

In 1534 he states clearly the dangers of secular interference:

"When temporal princes or lords in a high-handed manner try to change and be masters of the Word of God and decide themselves what

[1] W.A. 51.252.7.   [2] W.M.L. 3.124.   [3] W.M.L. 5.60.
[4] W.A. 51.264.6.   [5] W.M.L. 3.258.
[6] W.A. 51.254.12.   [7] 5th March 1522.

shall be taught and preached—a thing which is as forbidden to them as to the meanest beggar: that is seeking to be God themselves . . . like Lucifer." [1]

Or, as he said five years later, like Henry VIII!

But Luther does not think only of the temporal ruler under natural law, but of the Christian ruler.

"I say this not because I would teach that worldly rulers ought not to be Christians or that a Christian cannot bear the sword and serve God in a temporal government . . . would God they were all Christians or that no one could be a temporal prince unless he were a Christian." [2]

Again:

"It would indeed be good and profitable if all princes were real and good Christians, for the sword and government as a special service of God belong of right to Christians more than to all other men on earth." [3]

The ruler "should picture Christ to himself and say, 'Behold, Christ the chief ruler came and served me . . . I will do the same, not seek my advantage in my subjects, but their advantage' . . . thus a prince should empty himself in the heart of his power and authority and interest himself in the need of his subjects, dealing with them as though it were his own need. Thus did Christ with us: and these are the proper works of love." [4]

A whole section of Luther's tract of 1523, "Von Weltlicher Obrigkeit," is devoted to the theme of the Christian ruler, and Luther gives him four guiding principles:

1. He must seek his inspiration from God.
2. He must seek the good of his subjects before his own.
3. He must not allow his sense of equity to be obliterated by the lawyers.
4. He must punish evil-doers with measured severity (Luther says elsewhere that in case of doubt, mercy must always take precedence of justice).

Thus Luther left a good deal of room for Christian influence to be brought to bear upon the political order, and not only in his teaching about the office of the ruler, but in his doctrine of the calling of all Christians to serve God in the common life, not only in their vocation, but through their vocation.

One of Luther's most remarkable political writings is his exposition of Psalm 101, which he wrote in 1534 for the new Elector John Frederick. He lacked the wisdom of the Elector Frederick the Wise and the piety of the Elector John, was known to be self-opinionated and to have

---

[1] W.A. 51.240.30.   [2] W.M.L. 5.84.
[3] W.M.L. 3.245.   [4] W.M.L. 3.265.

surrounded himself with friends and flatterers who whispered to him the same Italianate notions which Henry VIII had greedily imbibed. Rumours of the great changes at court reached Wittenberg and gossip told of a ruler susceptible to the pleasures of the table. Luther's tract is as outspoken as any tract he ever wrote. It gave great offence to the court at Torgau. If John Frederick had been wondering what his predecessors had that he hadn't, Luther left him in no probable, possible shadow of doubt. But the tract is more than a tract for the times, more than the devotional exposition of a Psalm (Luther thinks of David as the type of the best Christian ruler): it contains material for an interpretation of history. Luther was very interested in history and had read a good deal, besides being saturated in the Biblical history. In accordance with his conception of temporal government as under God's general providence for all men, Luther's illustrations in this writing are drawn almost equally from Scripture and from secular history (classical and mediaeval), and in accordance with his high rating of common wisdom it is notable that in these few pages there are some 170 proverbial sayings quoted.

Luther believed that the great operative changes in history and ameliorations of human law were the work of great men, men called and moved by God, what he calls the "Wundermann" or the "Vir Heroicus." That this doctrine is opposed entirely to the doctrine of the Führerprinzip, was wistfully admitted in a German-Christian essay by Otto Scheel in 1934, who said rather ruefully that Luther's doctrine could not be fitted to the modern thought of the Führer.[1] Nor is there much affinity with Carlyle's "Heroes and Hero Worship." If Luther had some regard for heroes, he had none at all for hero worship, and believed the man who takes action on the basis of his own will and pride is not a hero, but a fool.

Says Luther:

"God has made two kinds of people on earth, in all estates : some have a special fortune before God which he teaches and awakens as he wills to have it. They have, as we say, a fair wind upon earth, luck and victory. What they start comes to a good end, and even if all the world withstand them yet the work goes through without hindrance. For God who put it into their hearts moves their mind and courage and gives them hands so that it must come out well . . . so it was with Samson, David, Jehoiada and the like . . . and not only those, but also among the heathen, and not only princes but among townsfolk, peasants and craftsmen. As in Persia King Cyrus, in Greece the princes Themis-

[1] O. Scheel. Evangelium, Kirche und Volk bei Luther (Schrift. Ver. Ref., 1934), 69. Also O. Scheel. Hist. Z. 1940. Z. für Syst. Theol., 1939, 216.

tocles and Alexander the Great, Augustus and Vespasian among the Romans . . . such men I do not call trained, or educated but created and moved by God to be princes or rulers." [1]

Such "viri heroici" do not need books or instructions to tell them what is just, for in them natural law and reason work out of their very nature. Such a prince, in point of wisdom, Luther considered Frederick the Wise to have been, but he makes it clear that he takes no such view of John Frederick. Luther calls those who imitate real greatness fools and apes put up by the Devil. They can only achieve folly and had better confine themselves to written precepts and the advice of good councillors. At the time the imitation hero may seem to carry all before him in his pride, but when his "hour comes" (Luther's eschatological word "stündlein") the imitator of true greatness falls in utter shame and disaster. The real hero, or better, the great man, for the word is not used in the Romantic sense, is like the exception in grammar, like the word "poeta," which is not to be explained in terms of the common rules.[2] Luther realizes that for most of the time such great men are not available. What goes on then is a kind of gradual patch-work improvement. "For the world is a sick thing . . . like a hospital [3] . . . or it is like a fur pelt or skin, the hair and skin of which is in poor condition." If the ruler is not a hero who can make a new skin, he must patch the old and make do and mend until the time comes when God will raise up a great man under whose hand everything goes better and who either changes the laws, or so administers them that "all is green and blooming in the land with peace, virtue, protection and sanctions so that it can be called a healthy government." [4] When one considers the historical writing at Luther's disposal I do not find this theory fanciful or eccentric.

Finally, Luther's thought about temporal rule is bounded by eschatology, like all the classical Christian interpretations of history. Like many of his contemporaries, like the first Christians and a notable succession of Christian leaders down the centuries, Luther believed himself to be living on the edge of history. He had no notion of our modern themes of progress, organic development and automatic self-contained historicism. He had no Utopianism. He had no thought of a gradual moral and physical improvement of one particular culture as a primary objective of Christian attention. We cannot even claim for him that he conceived of a political machinery for social change, though he hit hard at specific social and economic evils. We might find in this that mediaeval pessimism so vividly exemplified in Otto

[1] W.A. 51.207.21.   [2] R. Seeberg. Luther, iv. 157, n. 1.
[3] W.A. 51.214.29.   [4] W.A. 51.215.3.

of Freising and his Tale of Two Cities, if we did not remember all
that Luther has to say of Faith and of the Word of God. And at least
Luther's is not the pessimism of our modern secular eschatology,
without faith, without hope and without love. Luther finds this a
sick world, but not without a remedy, not without a Good Physician.
"The Plan of Our Lord God is better, who intends to bring heaven
and earth into one heap—and make a new world." [1]

[1] W.A. 51.261.20.

Chapter

14

LUTHER'S DOCTRINE OF THE CHURCH

"Well and nobly said, thou rare black swan! This, this is the
Church. Where this is found, there is the Church of Christ,
though but twenty in the whole of the congregation: and were
twenty such in two hundred different places the Church would be
entire in each. Without this, no Church."
S. T. COLERIDGE on Luther's "Table Talk."

MUCH has been written about Luther's doctrine of the Church, not
without much controversy and some confusion.[1] Part of the difficulty
arises from the theme itself. One wonders whether there is any ecclesiology which does not somewhere blur its edges. P. Congar has profoundly suggested that there is a "certain duality" in all doctrines of
the Church because of the difficulty of relating the reality of a spiritual
and eschatological salvation to the means of grace which are sensible,
social and which exist on the earth.[2] Luther, we have repeatedly
affirmed, was no doctrinaire, and what he had to write was called forth
by some particular occasion, or within the context of some specific
point of Scriptural exegesis. There were many questions which were
raised after his lifetime which he did not treat. Thus, as we shall see,
he was vitally concerned to determine the centre of the existence of
the Church, and so with the doctrine of Word and Sacrament: but
it was not until after his death that Protestantism really grappled with
the intricate question of the circumference, and added to Word and
Sacrament another dimension, "The Discipline of Christ." And
though I believe there is a coherent and consistent core to Luther's

[1] K. Holl. Die Entstehung von Luthers Kirchenbegriff. Luther und das landes-
herrliche Kirchenregiment. Ges. Aufs. Luther, 288-381.
K. Müller. Kirche, Gemeinde und Obrigkeit nach Luther. 1910.
R. Sohm. Kirchenrecht Deutschlands.
E. Foerster. Fragen zu Luthers Kirchenbegriff aus dem Gedankenwelt seines
Alters. Festgabe für Julius Kaftan. 1920.
F. Kattenbusch. Die Doppelschichtigkeit in Luthers Kirchenbegriff. Theol.
St. u. Kr., 1927-8.
E. Rietschel. Das Problem der unsichtbar-sichtbaren Kirche bei Luther. 1932.
O. Monsenheimer. Der Kirchenbegriff und die Sozialethik Luthers in den
Streitschriften und Predigten,'1537-40. 1930.
P. Althaus. Communio Sanctorum. 1930.
H. Strohl. La Notion d'Église chez les Réformateurs. Rev. d'Hist. et de Phil.
Rel. 1936.
W. Pauck. Heritage of the Reformation, ch. 3. 1950.
[2] Vraie et Fausse Réforme, 368.

teaching in this matter, a mind so fertile and intuitive as his cannot be regimented into a smooth and tidy and wholly consistent method of expression. None the less, Luther was concerned with the Church and wrote and thought about it throughout his life. Karl Holl showed in a famous essay how firm and developed was his doctrine of the Church in the first Lectures on the Psalms, and in those on Romans. Nor is this some early preoccupation, a mere remnant of Catholicism from which he disentangled himself. The lovely hymn (1535), "Sie ist mir lieb, die werte Magd," is a daring exposition of the Church as the mother and bearer of the Son of God—for Luther thought of Christ as Head of the Church in his humanity. In the last part of his life, "Of Councils and Churches" (1539) is a great treatise almost wholly devoted to this subject. The polemic against Duke Henry of Brunswick—"Wider Hans Worst"—is a lively statement of the claim that the evangelicals are the "true, old Church."

Luther's doctrine was no improvisation in 1517, but it was affected by the public controversy. He became plunged in a theological war. In the critical months before the Leipzig disputation he read the historians and the Canonists and became acquainted with a whole current of critical ideas which in his early ardent Papalism he had not known or heeded.

In two learned studies,[1] Walter Ullmann has shown, first, how extravagant were late mediaeval Canonist claims in the matter of the Papal "plenitude of power," and second, the almost breath-taking daring of the criticism of that theory from the time of the Great Schism onwards.

"This trend of opinion was not only illegal: it was, above all, against a fundamental article of Faith. And that is another strange phenomenon in the history of thought, namely, that measures palpably against law and dogma were thus propounded by Canonists and theologians of the highest repute. Furthermore, not a single writing can be produced which would show that the illegal and anti-dogmatic character of the proposed measures was recognized. Anti-Papalism became the watchword, defended by cardinals, theologians and Canonists generally." [2]

One result was what P. Congar calls "a liquefaction of the certitudes of Catholic conscience on the elements essential to the structure of the Church." [3]

It is not our purpose to trace the stages in Luther's rebellion against ecclesiastical authority, 1517-21, and the hardening of his mind and

---

[1] W. Ullmann. The Origins of the Great Schism. 1948. Mediaeval Papalism. 1949.
[2] Ullmann. Origins, 183. [3] Vraie et Fausse Réforme, 377.

heart against what he came to regard as an apostate Church. Almost immediately after the Diet of Worms he was forced to turn attention to Church problems of another kind, the whole practical business of Reformation. Here a series of writings emerge, dealing with practical and changing problems. There were cities where the evangelicals were in a minority (as in Prague), and others where (as in Altenburg and Leisnig) they were strong enough to influence the town council: there was the important but difficult question of the manner in which reforms should be carried out, and from the time of the Wittenberg disturbances of 1522 the conflict between the Reformation Left and Right. There came the problem of the authority of the "Obrigkeit" in the matter of Reform, and the vexed question of Luther's attitude to the visitation of Saxony. But the preoccupation never ceased, and he continued throughout his life to watch prayerfully and anxiously the progress of the great Church struggle, as one who must one day give an account.

We shall speak of Luther's doctrine in relation to three main issues:

1. His doctrine of the Church as "Communio Sanctorum."
2. His relation of the visible and invisible Church.
3. The question whether Luther believed in a State Church or free Church ("Volkskirche" or "Gemeinde der Gläubigen").

1. THE CHURCH AS A "COMMUNIO SANCTORUM."

The charge of "Individualism," long laid at the door of Protestantism, and of Martin Luther, has been a little too successful. We are beginning to think rather wistfully about the nineteenth century nowadays. One might even prophesy that among polemical writers there will soon be a change of party line. We may expect to hear of the sinister Group Mind of the Protestants—that mass-mindedness, that tyranny of the small group which in the "Gemeinde," presbytery, church meeting and class, foreshadowed the corporative engines of modern secular despotism. We may expect an exposition of the view that John Calvin was Joseph Stalin's spiritual ancestor, and in due course the inevitable volume from M. Maritain, "True Individualism."

Protestants have often deserved the reproach. There have been expositions of the "Right of Private Judgment," which mean almost exactly what Martin Luther intended by "Original Sin." But no doctrine of Luther's is more plain than his early insistence that the Church is the "Communion of Saints." [1]

[1] F. Kattenbusch. Die Doppelschichtigkeit in Luthers Kirchenbegriff. Theol. St. u. Kr., 1927-8. "It is an established finding of Luther research that Luther's fundamental principle in this matter is the 'Communion of Saints.'"

So far from Luther's challenge of 1517 being a proud defiance of Christian solidarity, it was a protest in the name of the true Christian catholicity against the degradation and perversion of that grand affirmation. For if every abuse in the Church involves, theologically, a defect of charity, a return to the self, then individualism was running riot in that mediaeval Church where the whole vast machinery of pastoral care had become the tool of thousands of competing private commodities, where the institution of Private Masses had become the antithesis of true Christian brotherhood, and where the Indulgence racket had turned the ineffable mystical commerce between heaven and earth into the venal exploitation of frantic, foolish fears on the part of countless individuals the horizon of whose charitable concern was narrow indeed.

Luther turned again and again to the simple affirmation of the Creed, which he rendered, "I believe in a holy, Christian Church, a communion of saints." He insisted that in the first place the "Communio Sanctorum" is a fellowship of persons, and that meaning has priority before the other possible interpretation, a sharing in holy things.

Thus (1520):

"I believe that there is on earth, through the whole wide world, no more than one holy, common Christian Church, which is nothing else than the congregation (Gemeine) or assembly of the saints, i.e. the good, believing men on earth, which is gathered, preserved, ruled by the Holy Ghost and is daily increased by means of the Sacraments and the Word of God." [1]

And (1539):

"The Creed indicates what the Church is, clearly, namely: A Communion of Saints, that is, a group or assembly of such people as are Christians and holy." [2]

Luther takes the word "saint" in its Biblical usage for the man who is called to sanctity, and it is one of his constant thoughts that the Church is a hospital.

But Luther admitted that he did not like the word "Kirche," which he regarded as ambiguous and "Un-German."

"The Creed calls the holy Christian Church 'Communio Sanctorum' a fellowship (Gemeinschaft) of saints: . . . but this is badly and confusedly translated into German 'Gemeinschaft der Heiligen,' if it is to be plainly rendered it must be put into German in a different way. For the word 'Ecclesia' means properly, in German, an assembly. But we are used to the word 'Church,' which simple people suppose means not an assembled company but a dedicated house or building

[1] W.M.L. 2.372.   [2] W.M.L. 5.264.

. . . therefore it should in good German and our mother tongue be rendered 'a Christian congregation or gathering.' And so also the word 'communio' should not mean 'Gemeinschaft' but 'Gemeine.'" [1]

"The word is not German and does not convey the sense of idea that is to be taken from this article. . . . If the words had been used in the Creed, 'I believe that there is a holy Christian people,' it would have been easy to avoid all the misery that has come in with this blind, obscure word, . . . for the common man thinks of the stone house which we call a Church. 'Ecclesia' ought to mean the holy Christian people, not only of the time of the apostles . . . but right to the end of the world, so that there is always living on earth a Christian holy people in which Christ lives, works and reigns 'per redemptionem' through grace and forgiveness of sins, and the Holy Ghost 'per vivificationem et sanctificationem' through the daily purging out of sins and the renewal of its life." [2]

The theme of Christian solidarity has rarely found more powerful expression than in Luther's tract "On the Blessed Sacrament" (1519), for the Sacrament of the Altar was for him the great treasure of the Church and the climax of Christian brotherhood. It is significant that he coupled this with a slashing attack on Brotherhoods, those innumerable late mediaeval sodalities which Luther believed to have become a caricature of true fellowship.

"Christ and all the saints are one spiritual body, just as the inhabitants of a city are one community and body, each citizen being a member of the other and a member of the entire city." [3]

"All the spiritual possessions of Christ and the saints are communicated to him who receives this Sacrament: again, all his sufferings and sins are communicated to them and love engenders love and unites all." [4]

"If any one be in despair . . . let him go joyfully to the Sacrament . . . and seek help from the entire company of the spiritual body and say, 'I have on my side Christ's Righteousness, life and sufferings with all the holy angels and all the blessed in heaven and all good men upon earth. If I die I am not alone in death. If I suffer, they suffer with me.'" [5]

We have already suggested how deeply the Psalms affected Luther's mind and outlook. We know that in the lonely years of crisis he found deep comfort in the solidarity of all the People of God, and in the stories of the great patriarchs of Faith.[6] So Luther calls the Psalms

---

[1] Der Grosse Katechismus. Munich ed. Werke, 3.246.
[2] W.M.L. 5.264-6.   [3] W.M.L. 2.10.
[4] W.M.L. 2.10-13.   [5] Ibid. Althaus. Communio Sanctorum.
[6] H. Bornkamm. Luther und das Alte Testament. 1948.

"A book of all saints" (1530), and says that the reader "becomes sure that he is in the Communion of Saints and that it has gone with all the saints as it has gone with him since they all sing one song with him. The Psalter holds you in the 'Communion of Saints' . . . and you think and speak as all the saints have spoken . . . in a word, would you see the Holy Christian Church painted in living form and put in one little picture . . . then take up the Psalms." [1]

Finest of all is the passage in that "Fourteen of Consolation" in which he attempted to provide a more Biblical spiritual consolation than the customary invocation of the Fourteen Auxiliary Saints.

"For Christ has so cared for us that we do not need to tread the way of death alone, but walk with the attendance of the whole Church . . . and the Church bears it more strongly than we ourselves, so that we know that the word of Elisha applies to us, which he said to the timid young man, 'Fear not, for those that are with us are more than those who are against us': and Elisha prayed and said, 'Lord, open the eyes of the young man that he may see,' and the Lord opened the eyes of the young man, and he saw, and lo! the mountains were full of horses and chariots of fire round about Elisha. So it happens with us too, that we ask that our eyes may be opened and we should see, with the eyes of faith I mean, that there is nothing to fear, for 'as the mountains are about Jerusalem so the Lord is round about his people now and for ever.'" [2]

Thus Luther's primary insistence is that the Church is a solidarity of persons, and that every other aspect of the meaning of the Church is subordinate to this fact. And Luther makes it plain that we become persons when we stand "coram Deo." It is when we enter into redemption through faith that we become one in Christ, and one in each other so that in that ultimate situation, grasped by faith, Christ is all, and in all, and there is neither male nor female, bond nor free, and as Luther insisted in his first lectures on Galatians, "neither cleric nor lay." Thus there is one ultimate Christian estate (Stand), though to each Christian there may come a different office (Amt). It is this ultimate estate in which all Believers are counted priests and Kings. The Priesthood of All Believers never means for Luther what it has sometimes meant in degenerate Protestantism, the secularization of the clergy, the doctrine that we are all laymen.

In the volume "The Apostolic Ministry" the Bishop of Oxford speaks of the meaning of the "Priesthood of All Believers" as the refusal of the Christian "to have any man standing between himself and God." But Paul Althaus pointed out long ago, that in Luther's usage the

<hr>

[1] W.M.L. 6.387.　　　　　　　　　　[2] W.A. 6.132.13 ff.

doctrine stands for the responsibility of the Christian on behalf of his brethren.

"In addition, we are priests, which is a far greater thing than being Kings, for priesthood makes us worthy to stand before God and pray for others. For to stand before God's face is the prerogative of none except priests. Christ has so operated on us that we are able spiritually to act and pray on behalf of one another, just as the priest acts and prays bodily on behalf of the people." [1]

"As many of us as have been baptized are all priests . . . without distinction for thus it is written in 1 Peter 2, 'Ye are a royal priesthood and a priestly kingdom.'" [2]

None the less, the Priesthood of All Believers is compatible with, nay demands, a called and consecrated ministry.

"Let everyone therefore who knows himself to be a Christian be assured of this, and apply it to himself that we are all priests and there is no difference between us: that is to say, we have the same power in respect to the Word and Sacraments. However, no one may make use of this power except by consent of the community or the call of the superior. For what is the common property of all, no individual may arrogate to himself, unless he be called." [3]

The minister is called to his office (Amt) even though the call is attested and confirmed by the Christian congregation.

"Thus it follows that there is really no difference between laymen, and priests, princes or bishops, spiritual and temporal, except that of office and work, but not of estate (Stand): for they are all Christians —true priests, bishops or Popes—though they are not all engaged in the same work. . . . For Christ has not two bodies, one temporal, one spiritual. He is one head and he has one body." [4]

"Therefore when a bishop consecrates it is the same thing as if he, in the place of the congregation, all of whom have like power, were to take one out of their number and charge him to use this power for the others: just as though ten brothers, all king's sons and heirs, were to choose one of themselves to rule the inheritance on behalf of them all —they would all be kings and equal in power, though one of them would be charged with the duty of ruling." [5]

2. THE VISIBLE—INVISIBLE CHURCH.

It was inevitable and proper that Luther should emphasize the personal and spiritual nature of the Church, against the extravagant claims made for the Papal "plenitude of Power" and its intrusion into

---

[1] W.M.L. 2.324.   [2] W.M.L. 2.279.   [3] W.M.L. 2.282.
[4] W.M.L. 2.69.   [5] W.M.L. 2.67.

a whole continent of secular pressures. But we are not to suppose that Luther spiritualized the Church away.

When, in 1530, Melanchthon denied that he made the Church an abstract spiritual idea, he was but echoing what Luther had said to Emser in 1521.

"When I have called the Church a spiritual assembly, you have insultingly taken me to mean that I would build a Church as Plato builds a state that never was." [1]

Luther's thought of the Church as invisible save to faith was no product of the Church conflict, but, as Holl showed, is to be found in the early Lectures on the Psalms.

"For the deeds and works of the Church will not appear outwardly but all her structure is from within, invisible, 'coram Deo.'" [2]

"For Christ is concealed in the Church which is hidden from men but manifest to God." [3]

"For the Church is invisible and is recognizable by faith alone." [4]

Luther prefers such phrases as "bodily" and "spiritual" or "inward," to "visible and invisible."

We misunderstand if we suppose that because a thing is "sola fide perceptibilis" it is therefore purely inward, or in some sense unreal. But it is only faith, Luther insists, which can recognize the Church for what she is. Ernst Rietschel is surely right when he says that Luther's judgments about the Church are "Glaubensurteile"—judgments of faith.

"Therefore, as this rock (Christ) is invisible and only to be grasped by faith, so too the Church (apart from sin) must be spiritual and invisible, to be grasped only by faith." [5]

In the Preface to the Apocalypse (1530) Luther says:

"I believe one holy Christian Church . . . this article is as much an article of faith as the others. So no reason may perceive it, no, not if everybody were to put on spectacles. She will not be perceived but only believed. For faith is of those things which are not seen." [6]

And in "Wider Hans Worst" (1540):

"Oh, it is a high, deep, hidden thing is the Church, which nobody

---

[1] W.A. 7.683.9. "His view of the Church as a spiritual-corporeal communion of believers was thus a Biblical theological re-interpretation of the Roman Catholic idea of the Church as the 'Mystical Body of Christ.' The correction of the impersonalizing that was implied in the Roman Catholic ecclesiology was of special importance to him." Wm. Pauck. Heritage of the Reformation, 40.
[2] W.A. 4.81.12. Also 3.183.24, 203.22. W.A. 4.450.39. Other passages, Holl. Luther, 296 ff.
[3] W.A. 3.124.36.
[4] W.A. 4.189.17.
[5] W.A. 7.710.1.
[6] Pref. Apoc. 1530.

may perceive or see, but can only grasp by faith in Baptism, Word and Sacrament." [1]

It is fundamental for Luther that the Christian life is a battle school for faith:

"It is necessary that the love and fellowship of Christ and all the saints be hidden, invisible and spiritual, and that only a bodily, outward and visible sign of it be given us, for were this love, fellowship and help known to all, like the temporal fellowship of men, we should not be strengthened nor trained thereby to put our trust in the invisible and eternal things or to desire them, but should much more be trained to put our trust in temporal and visible things and to become so accustomed to them as to be unwilling to let them go and follow God onward." [2]

The Church, then, is a present, spiritual reality.

"The Church is a gathering of all the Christians upon earth."

"The being, life and nature of the Christian people is not a bodily assembly together but an assembling together of hearts in one faith."

"Though they be separated a thousand miles from one another they are still an assembly in the spirit . . . that is, properly speaking, a spiritual unity which by men is called a fellowship of saints and this unity suffices to make a Christian people."

"As a man is of two natures, body and soul, so he is not reckoned a member of the Christian Church according to his body, but according to his soul, yes, according to faith." [3]

But it is precisely because of this need for faith that the Church has an outward form.

"It is certain that man with his wisdom cannot find out God. . . . Against such danger we are ensured when we follow the visible form or the visible signs which he himself has given us. In the New Testament we have as visible form, the Son of God, in the lap of Mary his mother, and who suffered and died for us, as the Creed teaches us. In addition we have other additional forms, Baptism, the Lord's Supper, and the spoken Word itself . . . but you must receive and follow as a sure and unfailing rule that this is the ordinance of Divine Wisdom, to reveal himself to men under a sure and visible form, which can be seen with the eyes, grasped by the hands, and apprehended by the five senses." [4]

Of exceptional interest is a letter from Luther to his friend Amsdorf in 1542. Amsdorf's feeble "Nolo episcopari" had been brushed aside by the Elector, and he had been torn from his own devoted

[1] W.A. 51.507.9 ff.   [2] W.M.L. 2.25.
[3] W.A. 6.293-6.   W.A. 3.103.9.   199.28.   W.A. 4.24.35.
[4] W.A. 42.625.30.

congregation to be Bishop of Naumberg. Luther sent a note of encouragement.

"Be strong therefore and fear not!" Even if Amsdorf is going to
be treated like a prince, and to suffer the temptation of dignity, it is a
mere outward matter. "Larva est, non res seria." The episcopal office
will be an outward thing, a covering or mask (Luther's favourite
expression "larva"), like Luther's own offices of Married Man and
Economic Man. But Amsdorf should know that God does not worry
about such outward things, in which the Kingdom of God does not
consist, since, Gal. 2[6], "God is no respecter of persons." Then comes
this striking paragraph:

"For the Church must appear in the world. But it can only appear
in a covering (larva), a veil, a shell, or some kind of clothes which a man
can grasp, otherwise it can never be found. But such a mask is
a married man, somebody in political or domestic life, John, Peter,
Martin, Amsdorf, etc., yet none of them is the Church, which is
neither man nor wife, Jew nor Greek, but Christ alone." [1]

In that ultimate situation we are all one, and Christ is all and in all,
and the Church is one person, Christ.

That does not mean that the "larva" of a man's calling is unim-
portant in the divine scheme of things. On the contrary, these "larvae"
are the instruments by which the Living God superintends his own
creation, the only way in which his majesty can come into contact
with sinful human beings, who otherwise could not bear his glory.
We may repeat here a passage already referred to in the discussion
of Luther's doctrine of our human, earthly authority.

"For what is all our work in field, garden, house, war, rule, towards
God but child's play, through which God gives his gifts to field and
house and all the rest. They are the masks (larvae) of our Lord God
through which he will remain hidden and yet do all things . . . God
bestows all good things, but you must take the bull by the horns and
you must do the work and so provide God with an opportunity and a
disguise." [2]

But how is this spiritual reality which is mediated to the world made
plain to men? A clue is to be found in Luther's simplest yet profound
definition in the Schmalkaldic Articles of 1537.

"Thank God, a child of seven years old knows what the Church is,
namely the Holy Believers and the lambs who hear the Shepherd's
voice."

[1] W.A.Br. 9.608, n. 3709, 3rd Feb. 1542.
[2] W.A. 31.1.436.7. Also W.A. 51.241.41. W.A. 30.ii.554.10. W.A. 40.1.174.3.
W.A. 40.1.462.3. W.A. 40.1.175.3. W.A. 40.1.173.8. W.A. 40.1.176.13. W.A.
40.1.174.8. W. Koehler. Dogmengeschichte, 149. Törnvall, 89.

Here are the two poles of Luther's Ecclesiology, the Word and Faith.

In the matter of the Church, the Word is Luther's magisterial and ruling doctrine, for it sums up all the activity of God to usward. It is for him a rich and many-sided complex, a master word which, like that other master word " Faith," is not to be restricted to any one definition. It is the whole divine revelation, it is the revelation in Jesus Christ, it is the apostolic Kerugma, it is the living and preached Gospel, the whole witness of the Scriptures, mediated by the whole apparatus of institutional religion. But we must begin with the widest and most sublime connotation.

"Now we see from where the Apostle gets his speech, in that he calls Christ an image of the Divine Being . . . every word is a sign of that which it means. But here that which it means is by nature a sign or word which has no other sign, and is therefore called an essential image or sign. . . . So it is with God. For his Word is so like him that his whole Godhead is wholly within it, and he who has the Word has the whole Godhead. But here all comparisons fall away, for the human heart does not bring forth the very nature of its heart, but only signifies it, but here in God the Word is not only the sign and image but also the whole Being with it . . . wherefore the Word of God is above all other words." [1]

"When we come to heaven we shall see him in another fashion without intermediary or darkness, but here on earth you will not see him with your senses and thoughts, but as St. Paul says, we see him in a dark word or covered image, namely in Word and Sacrament that are at once his "larvae" or masks and the clothes whereunder he is hidden. But he is most surely there and present and himself does miracles, preaches and gives the Sacraments, hears, strengthens and helps and we also see him yet as a man sees the sun through the clouds. For we cannot yet suffer the clear sight and showing forth of his Majesty, and so it must be covered and veiled and behind a thick cloud. So it is decided that he who would grasp them both, the Father and the Son, must do so through the Word." [2]

Luther never tires of the thought which he derived from Augustine, that the Word it is which creates the Church and the Scriptures.

"The Church does not make the Word of God, but she is made by the Word of God." [3]

"In short, the whole substance and life of the Church is in the Word of God." [4]

[1] W.A. 10.1.1.187 ff.
[2] W.A. 45.522.7 ff.
[3] W.A. 8.491.34. W.A. 3.259.18: 139.19: 454.25. W.A. 4.173.34. W.A. 4.179.14.
[4] W.A. 7.721.12.

"For God's Word cannot be without God's people, and God's people cannot be without God's Word." [1]

"We know that Jacob . . . sees in a dream the same Church which he had seen and heard at home, even though he is quite alone here. So we learn that the Church of God is present wherever the Word of God is spoken, whether it be in the middle of the Turk's land or in the Pope's land or in hell itself. For it is the Word of God which builds the Church, which is Lord over all other spaces: where that is heard, where Baptism, the Sacrament of the Altar, and the Forgiveness of Sins are administered there hold fast and conclude most certainly that there is the house of God and that here is the gate of heaven." [2]

Here the thought of the Word as revelation passes into the thought of the Word as the Gospel, as the preaching of God's Mighty Acts and of the benefits of Christ.

"I do not now speak of the written Gospel, but of one spoken by the mouth, the common and immediate word which teaches the true faith of Christ." [3]

"The Gospel is simply a crying and preaching aloud of the Grace and compassion of God . . . and is properly not that which lies in books and is put down in letters, but much more the preaching through human lips and the living word. . . ." [4]

"The Gospel is the unspeakable goodness of God which no prophet, no apostle, no angel has ever been able to express, no heart can ever sufficiently admire, or comprehend, which is the great fire of the Love of God to us-ward with which our hearts and consciences become joyful, certain and at peace, and that is the preaching of Christian faith." [5]

Luther answers the charge that it would be a new thing to choose and create bishops.

"Yet even if it were a thing of the highest novelty, since the Word of God shines here and issues its orders, and at the same time the necessity of souls demands it, the thing that matters is not the novelty but the majesty of the Word. For what, I ask, is not new that faith does? Was it not a novelty when the apostolic ministry was constituted? Was it not new when Abraham offered his son? Was it not new when the children of Israel crossed the Red Sea? Will it not be a new thing when I shall pass from death to life? But in all things, it is the Word of God, and not the novelty which is to be regarded." [6]

The Word is the source of all that is creative in the life of the Church.[7] By it, as by a banner, the army of Christ is to be discerned.

---

[1] "Of Councils and Churches." W.M.L. 5.271.
[2] W.A. 43.596.38 ff.   [3] W.A. 7.721.15.   [4] W.A. 12.259.8.
[5] W.A. 10.i.11.18.   [6] W.A. 12.192.34.   [7] W.A. 12.192.

"For just as a man tells by the banner of an army as by a sure sign what manner of Lord or army is in the field, so may a man tell surely by the Gospel where Christ and his army are present. So have we the sure promise of the God of Israel. 'My Word shall not return unto me void.' So we are sure that it is impossible that there should not be Christians wherever the gospel is, however weak and sinful they may be."[1]

Thus the Word is for Luther the integrating principle of his doctrine: Preaching and Sacraments, Scripture and tradition, the ministry, all are the vehicles of God's own present, creative, renewing activity.[2] One way and another almost all of Luther's own massive creative achievements is concerned to let the Word go free, conquering and to conquer.

In his "Of Councils and Churches" (1539), and again in the "Wider Hans Worst" (1540), Luther gives a list of the notes of the Church, the outward marks by which it may be discerned. Such signs are:

1. The Preaching of the Word.
2. The Holy Sacrament of Baptism.
3. The Sacrament of the Altar.
4. The Keys of Christian discipline and forgiveness.
5. A called and consecrated Christian ministry.
6. Public thanksgiving and the worship of God.
7. Suffering, the possession of the Holy Cross.

Yet the visible Church is recognized by Faith. Ernst Rietschel has suggested the analogy of music. The sounds of music may be audible by all, but to the tone-deaf or the musically ignorant they are only a series of sounds without pattern and meaning. So with the Church, and with Faith. What seems a mere collection of people, a human institution, is recognizable by Faith alone. Faith is not deceived by Cinderella-like rags, the form of a servant, but knows the Church to be the Bride.

3. A "STATE CHURCH" OR "FREE CHURCH" ("VOLKSKIRCHE" OR "GEMEINDE DER GLAUBIGEN").

The German word "Volkskirche" does not translate well. It stands for the combination of Church and nation which is the notion of a Christian realm expounded in England by Stephen Gardiner in the

---

[1] " Das eine christliche Gemeine " (1523). Werke (Munich), 3.93.
[2] In a valuable essay on Luther's doctrine of the Church which reached me after these pages had been written, Wm. Pauck distinguishes, following his statement that the Word is the constitutive principle of the Church: 1. The distinction between the " internal " and " external " or visible/invisible nature of the Church. 2. There is a Church in the general sense (the universal character) and the specific " Gemeinde," the local church congregation. 3. This local Church is organized round the preaching of the Word and related to the priesthood of all believers. 4. The Church with the family and the political order is one of the hierarchies through which the Church expresses its life. (Heritage of the Reformation (1950), 31.)

beginning of the English Reformation, and in classical phrase by Richard Hooker.

"There is not any man of the Church of England but the same is also a member of the commonwealth, nor any man a member of the commonwealth which is not also of the Church of England."

It is the mediaeval idea of the "Corpus Christianum" translated into national terms, and of course disintegrated in the process. Many of the great Lutheran churches in the past four centuries have embodied the "Volkskirche," though the hard lessons of the modern Church struggle and the gallant story of the resistance movements have made many good Lutherans turn more kindly to the "Confessing" Church idea, and to show an interest in the story of the origins of the historic English Free Churches, with their ideal of the "gathered Church" and their emphasis on the Church as a fellowship of believing Christians.

Luther has been claimed for both conceptions, though perhaps both are ideals which belong to a later age than his and represent questions which we cannot profitably ask of his ecclesiology. In 1908, Drews said that Luther was the great exponent of the Church as a "fellowship of Believers." He believed that Luther, in 1520, appealed to the rulers of the German nation because, with a "naïven Optimismus," he thought them to be earnest, believing Christians. He thought that after the Diet of Worms Luther was disillusioned and turned for Reform to the individual Christian congregation.

He found Luther's dream expressed in the Preface to the "Deutsche Messe" (1526), where he speaks of the separation of a congregation of earnest Christians from the mass of nominal Christians about them. They would have a simpler, more mature form of Christian worship "which would not be held in a public place for all sorts of people, but for those who mean to be real Christians, and profess the gospel with hand and mouth. They would record their names on a list, and meet by themselves, in some house, in order to read, pray, baptize, receive the Sacrament and do other Christian works. In this manner those who do not lead Christian lives should be known, reproved, reclaimed, cast out, excommunicated according to the rule of Christ . . . if one had the people and persons who wanted to be Christians in deed, the rules and regulations could easily be supplied." [1]

At the other extreme, Sohm and Riecker asserted that Luther thought against the common background of Christendom, the one society of a "Corpus Christianum." [2] In 1910 Karl Müller [3] produced a series of

[1] W.M.L. 6.173.
[2] Sohm. Kirchenrecht, 1.
[3] K. Müller. Kirche, Gemeinde und Obrigkeit nach Luther (1910). Christliche Welt (1910), 510 ff.

studies which admitted that Luther began by thinking of one Christian society, but said that a new situation arose during Luther's stay on the Wartburg, and when, during his absence, the extremists tried to carry out a violent reform in Wittenberg. Luther had already realized that the evangelicals would have to separate from the Catholics, but he now saw the danger of a new and Protestant legalism on the other side. From then on, Müller suggested, Luther began to think more and more of building an evangelical core within the wider parish community, a theory of two concentric circles of Christians. He said that these ideas had most influence on Luther in 1525, that they reappear in his correspondence in 1527 and then disappear.

It is generally agreed that Müller misunderstood Luther, and did not allow for the occasional nature of Luther's writings, and for the changing practical situation. As usual, Karl Holl greatly clarified the problem.[1] As against Sohm and Riecker, he pointed out that Luther never used the expression "Corpus Christianum" and that by the doctrine of the Word and of Faith Luther had broken the conception of a society into which a man could be born and baptized. Yet, although he could say that "Luther knows no more of a Christian State than a Christian shoemaker," he thought that Luther did think along the lines of a Volkskirche. Holl said that Luther turned to the Princes not because of the failure of the Peasant War, but because the progress of the Reformation in Saxony made possible the formation of one evangelical order for the whole territory and brought with it a number of grievous practical problems, the question of Church property, the relation to the Papists on the one hand and the Anabaptists on the other. None the less Holl thought that Luther was apprehensive about the encroachments of the secular power and he saw in Luther's Preface to the "Instructions" for the Visitation of Saxony a protest against the terms of those instructions.

More recently, Erich Foerster drew attention to the significance of Luther's later writings, and as against Drews and Müller pointed out that Luther could never have written as he did in "Wider Hans Worst" (1540) had the Saxon Landeskirche been the antithesis of his own hopes.[2] For in that tract Luther justifies the claim of the evangelicals to church property on the ground that they are the true, old Church.

"The former old Church shines forth again now as the sun out of the clouds behind which was that same sun all the time but not clearly."

---

[1] K. Holl. Die Entstehung von Luthers Kirchenbegriff. Luther und das landes-herrliche Kirchenregiment. Ges. Aufs. Luther.

[2] E. Foerster. Fragen nach Luthers Kirchenbegriff aus der Gedankenwelt seines Alters. Festgabe für Julius Kaftan. 1920. O. Monsenheimer. Der Kirchenbegriff und die Sozialethik Luthers in den Streitschriften und Predigten, 1537-40. 1930.

"For our part we have never desired a Council to reform our Church, for God the Holy Ghost has through His Word sanctified the Church . . . so that we have (God be praised) all pure and holy, the pure Word, pure Baptism and Sacrament, the Keys pure and all that belongs to the true Church pure and holy, free from all adulteration of human teaching." [1]

Luther sharply distinguishes the Papists, however, from the Turks. It is indeed the one qualification in our mind to Ernst Rietschel's insistence that for Luther the Church is always "sola fide perceptibilis" —that Luther here says of the notes of the Church "nobody can deny . . ." and seems to make of Papists a class different from believers and unbelievers.

Luther never unchurched the whole Roman Church, though he thought that those only were saved in it who had relied wholly on Christ's merits for salvation: "some children, and some old people (but very few) who at the end of their lives turned to God." [2]

Luther frankly admits that the life of the evangelical Churches has not caught up with the purity of doctrine.

"I confess that we have the pure teaching of the Divine Word and such a fine pure Church as ever there was in the time of the Apostles in all respects that pertain to salvation, yet are we not better or more holy than Jerusalem, God's own city, wherein were so many evil people and yet all the time the Word was kept pure by the prophets. So there is among us flesh and blood." [3]

Thus Luther's doctrines of the Word and of Faith are complex. It can be seen how easily his successors might fail to do justice to their comprehension. The Word, especially when set over and against a one-sided doctrine of the Spirit (Luther himself never split the two great dimensions of Word and Spirit) might easily become an emphasis on written Biblicism or "pure doctrine." Faith might become an arid intellectualism or subjective emotionalism. The whole rich notion of God close at hand and using the whole creation as his instrument, linking the kingdom of God with the earthly ordinances and uniting nature and grace as Protestant doctrine over four centuries has often sadly failed to do: in these matters Protestantism has much to learn by returning to what Luther had to say.

He did not exhaust all the problems of ecclesiology: indeed, he was perhaps hardly aware of some of those which were beginning to take shape in his lifetime, and we do no service to Luther studies when we

[1] W.A. 51.529.1.
[2] W.A. 51.506.5. Also W.A. 39.2.167.20.
[3] W.A. 51.536.10.

assume that all he had to say is true, and that all he had to say is the whole even of the truth which he asserts.

It is the great strength of Luther's doctrine of the Church that he returns to the true centre of all ecclesiology, to Christ himself living and reigning in the midst of his people, exercising active and present sovereignty which he needs to delegate to none, since he is always at hand, through the Holy Spirit in the Word and in the Sacraments which are the visible Words. The first generation of Protestantism had to get its centre right, as against the disruptive tendencies to split apart the Word and the Spirit, and the Word and the Sacraments. It was in the next generation that the problems of circumference really arose, in that enormous ferment, 1550-1660, when the third dimension of the Church is the object of attention, Word, Sacraments, and the Discipline of Christ.

We saw that Luther's primary stress in considering the universal Church was upon it as a "communio sanctorum"—in the sense of a fellowship between persons. The same emphasis is important when we turn to the local congregation, the "Gemeinde." Here was a life-long pastoral concern of Luther. It evoked some of his most splendid achievements, the classical Children's Catechism and the fine longer catechetical works, the hymns, and the liturgical experiments and orders. In the years 1521-5 he had to deal with delicate and rapidly changing situations as the Reformation movement spread and as various congregations sent to him for advice. And in 1528 he had to face the difficult task of advising the Elector how to carry through the visitation of Saxony.[1] There is nothing of a Johnny Head-in-the Clouds about Luther's doctrine of the Church, and we must never forget the practical context of the ever-widening Church struggle, and his constructive, genial provisions for the edification of those Churches which he saw to be sustained and directed by the Word and by the Spirit.[2]

---

[1] See especially, Die Wittenberger und Leisniger Kastenordnung. 1522-3. " Dass eine christliche Versammlung oder Gemeine Recht und Macht habe alle Lehre zu beurteilen und Lehrer zu berufen, ein und abzusetzen " (1523), and the Unterricht der Visitatoren (1528). See Luthers Werke, vol. 3 of the Munich ed., 1950. Schriften zur Neuordnung der Gemeinde, des Gottesdienstes, und der Lehre.

[2] Luther's repudiation of Canon Law and of the Papal authority created a practical vacuum. He was able to emphasize, particularly in his writings 1522-5, the important autonomy of the particular " Gemeinde." But despite Luther's careful and profound distinctions, the " Obrigkeit " inevitably played a large role in the reorganization of the life of the Church along territorial lines. In some valuable comments on this situation in which Melanchthon, Bugenhagen and Amsdorf prepared the way for a Protestant form of ecclesiastical jurisdiction, Ritter says, " As long as Luther's mighty personality dominated the Saxon court, there was no serious danger of the misuse of the new ecclesiastical jurisdiction for political ends. But for the future of the new ' Landeskirchen ' it was a question how long the spiritual and theological interest could hold out, in these little states, and the needs of secular power politics be restrained " (G. Ritter. Die Neugestaltung Europas, 119).

It has sometimes been said that Luther does not sufficiently allow for the activities of the Church as a fellowship, or "Gemeinschaft," as against the worshipping community of the "Gemeinde" or congregation. But we must remember Luther's difficulty of finding a way between the clericalized hierarchical, swollen structure of the Church of Rome and the intense group piety of the "Schwärmerei." It is true, I think, that Luther would have had little patience with some of the apparatus of modern Protestantism, cluttered up with dozens of organizations which absorb a frightening amount of Christian energy, and which are kept going long after the original theological idea (if any) has disappeared. But Foerster rightly points out that Luther found a full-time programme for the Church in daily life, in the Christian vocation, in obeying the commandments in the light of the Sermon on the Mount, and of the supreme Law of Love. The Church is a fellowship of people, but people in what the Germans call their "Lebenszusammenhang," their whole life-setting.

"For," says Luther, "I am not only a prince or a landlord, man or woman, who does his work among other estates. But I am baptized. . . . Where now such faith and recognition of the grace of God is, you can go further and say surely that such work is well pleasing to God and brings forth true Christian fruits in temporal and bodily matters, as ruling a land or people, bringing up children and serving and working and through these things comes fruit to eternal life." [1]

"For Christ has not two different bodies, one temporal and the other spiritual. He is one head and he has one body." [2]

Finally, the eschatological boundary remains. The Church is the Church "under the Cross." A great deal of the matter of the Great Divide may be found in the fact that, according to Cardinal Bellarmine, a note of the Church is "of the temporal felicity of the true Church," whereas for Luther this would rather be a sign of the False Church. For Luther the Church on earth is always militant and suffering. History is the royal progress of the Word, but because of that, it offers Christian men, and the remnant of Christendom in our time, a warning and a hope. There is a quotation which is almost hackneyed in Germany but which may have salt in a different context, in that English and American world which needs to beware lest it posits a univocal relation between its culture and the Christian faith.

"Let us consider the former darkness and misery in which we sat, if we permit God's Word to pass by. It is to be feared that we shall suffer still more darkness and plague. Buy, dear people, while the fair is at the doors. Gather in the harvest while it is sunshine and fair

[1] W.A. 45.661.25.   [2] W.M.L. 2.69.

weather; use the Grace and the Word of God while they are still here.

"For know this: that God's Word and Grace are like a passing rainstorm which does not return where once it has been. It came to the Jews but it passed over; now they have nothing. Paul brought it to the Greeks, but it passed over; now they have the Turks. The Romans and the Latins had it . . . and you must not think you have it for ever; for ingratitude and contempt will not suffer it to remain. Take hold and hold it fast, whoever can." [1]

But that is not his final word. The one prophetic word to which again and again he returned is a word of triumph and of promise.

"For as the rain cometh down and watereth the earth . . . so shall my Word be that goeth forth out of my mouth: it shall not return unto me void, but it shall accomplish that which I please, and it shall prosper in the thing whereto I send it."

[1] W.M.L. 4.108.

Chapter

15

LUTHER ON THE TRUE AND THE FALSE CHURCH

"They who do not rightly estimate and feel thankful for the Reformation cannot rightly understand Luther or attain to that insight into his heart and spirit which is never granted, except to love."

JULIUS HARE. "Vindication of Luther."

(An examination of P. Congar's critique of Luther's ecclesiology, with special reference to his exegesis of Gen. 25.)

IN "Vraie et Fausse Réforme dans l'Église," [1] P. Yves Congar has added an impressive volume to modern Roman Catholic expositions of the doctrine of the Church, and a work which ranks with the signal achievements of P. P. Mersch and De Lubac. These are works which deserve to be carefully studied by Protestants, and perhaps their authors might be surprised at the extent to which students on the other side of the Great Divide can admire and assent to many of their arguments and conclusions. Our present concern is not with P. Congar's whole argument, but with his detailed and careful critique of the doctrine of Martin Luther.

He has taken pains to be exact and knowledgeable. The citations are many and accurate, and in the main set in their proper context. Like Denifle, P. Congar has taken care to read Luther at first hand, but, unlike Denifle, he has also studied the best Protestant secondary studies on his subject. It is true that his essay has a slightly self-conscious air: he is a little eager, in the manner of one reading a brilliant and provocative paper, to adventure generalizations beyond his book, as when he tells us that "if Luther had formulated a theory of knowledge he would have held a doctrine of illumination in the manner of Roger Bacon": [2] when he imports a whole strategy of divine operation into half a dozen words of Staupitz which could equally bear a conventional meaning: [3] and when he interprets Luther's Christology

[1] Éditions du Cerf. Paris, 1950.   [2] Ibid. 399.
[3] Ibid. n. 87b, 91b.

in relation to the Eucharist in a way which would seem to render unintelligible Luther's sustained argument against Zwingli in this very matter.[1]

Though the argument is lofty, and the way lit by flashes of insight, there are moments when—like a sudden clearing of the mists—it is revealed that this is an ecumenical conversation across a deep crevasse. Thus when he devotes a separate note to the question, concerning the economy of Grace, "Have Protestants read the doctrine of the Church, solemnly formulated by the Council of Trent?"[2]—one wonders if this is more than a rhetorical flourish—and if it is more, what an ignorance it reveals of the innumerable Protestant histories and theologies which grapple with those canons, even though, like Harnack (to name but one), Protestants have had the temerity to examine those decrees on their strictly theological merits, and have not failed to observe some notable reticences and ambiguities. And when having (as we shall try to show) misinterpreted Luther at a critical point, he cries of Luther's errors, "My God, how are such lamentable and tragical misconceptions possible?"[3] we feel that this is a rhetorical question the author is better fitted to answer.

There are two lapses from a persuasively rational method of argument. Having claimed that Luther was not a Reformer, but a revolutionary, a conscious innovator in the field of doctrine (P. Congar does not shrink from speaking of the braggadocio ("hâblerie") of the Reformers)[4] he admits that Luther and his friends did in fact claim that so far from being merely innovators, they were restoring the true, original and apostolic testimony. This latter claim (to which a whole literature in sixteenth and seventeenth century Germany and England was devoted) is dismissed with the remark that "Marcion also pretended to restore original Christianity."[5] Poor Reformers! If they claim originality, they are braggarts: if they claim to restore what has been overlaid and lost, they are "just like Marcion!" Either way, the great question is begged.

The other lapse comes when the author sketches the critical currents of thought in the later Middle Ages, and their attack on the temporal power of the Papacy, its entanglement with "dominium" and with possessions. "Certainly," says P. Congar, "it would have been better had the Church freed itself from these solidarities, but when can you see a man jump out of his own shadow?"[6] Thus he rides off on a metaphor from a grave matter: as though between an entirely spiritual-

[1] Ibid. n. 91. " Vom Abendmahl Christi Bekenntnis " (1528). W.A. 26.261.
[2] Vraie et Fausse Réforme, n. 88.   [3] Ibid. 396.
[4] Ibid. 312, 363.   [5] Ibid. 367.
[6] Ibid. 373.

ized Church (which was a practical impossibility) and an irretrievably
secularized Church there were not a thousand intermediary degrees
and possibilities, as though the problem did not offer different degrees
of intricacy and open up different measures of solution in the ninth,
thirteenth and fifteenth centuries, as though the whole point is not
whether but at what point a reformation is possible without catastrophe?
Thus a figure of speech evades the perennial dilemma, how the Church
can be immersed in human cultures without being submerged by them
("absorptus" is Luther's word).

P. Congar begins with a sketch of the antecedents of the doctrines
of the Reformers, from the time of St. Augustine in whose doctrine
of the Church a "certain duality," not to be exaggerated, is to be
observed. There is little to criticize here, save an over-simplification
of Wycliffe's ecclesiology, which was more intricate (it had to be in
face of the situation provoked by the "Captivity" and Schism) than
P. Congar's description would suggest. When he lumps together "the
Cathari, Vaudois, Poor Men of Lyons, Joachimists, Spiritual Franciscans, Wycliffe, the Lollards, John Huss and the Bohemians," [1] and
says that the "continuity reaches to Luther and even the humanists
and the Erasmian Reform," he himself admits that this is a "strange
genealogy," but he affirms that it represents a coherent, continuous and
serious criticism of the Church. If all that is meant is that this amalgam
of influences, with the ideological currents from Nominalism and from
the Conciliar Movement, powerfully affected the "climate of opinion"
in the sixteenth century, in regard to its anti-clericalism and its readiness to call in question the Papal claims, the comment is wise. Only
we must be careful not to mistake this as in any sense a pedigree for
Martin Luther.

The caveat is necessary since at one point [2] it is hinted that Marsiglius
of Padua anticipated some of Luther's notions, though it is demon-
strable that Luther's doctrines are based on utterly different premises
from those of the democratic Aristotelian. P. Congar also affirms that
Luther was thoroughly Ockhamist. [3] On this point [4] it may be said
that there seems no evidence that Luther knew Ockham's anti-papal
and political writings: that Catholic writers have hailed Biel, the more
direct source of Nominalist influence, as impeccable in loyalty to Rome,
and that we have Luther's own and repeated statements that he grew
up, not in an anti-papal milieu but as a zealous adherent of papal
claims. [5] When P. Congar finds in Luther's appeal to Scripture and to

---

[1] Ibid. 372. [2] Ibid. 386.
[3] Ibid. 425 : 366, n. 34. [4] See above, p. 88.
[5] W.A. 50.472.31. W.A. 51.543.6. TR. 5.657.4.

z

evident reason, a plainly Ockhamist trait, and when [1] he couples this
with the remark that this was characteristic of the school also, that
it combined scepticism with a "certain ecclesiastical fideism," we are
left wondering what other weapons were left to the Ockhamists beside
reason, scripture and tradition? But that this emphasis of Luther
was no Ockhamism but common ground between himself and his
opponents is demonstrated by the "Seven Swords" of the Franciscan
Alveldus, against Luther (1520)—the first, "recta ratio": the second,
"canonica scriptura": and the third "vera scientia" (which includes
the tradition).

We are in accord with P. Congar when he says that in the main
Luther's doctrine of the Church is coherent and that it is continuously
held. We would add that we must not expect Luther to answer questions which are those of a later age. We cannot ask of him a smooth
and tidy doctrine with no rough edges or loose ends, though we can
ask of all expositions that they make sense of most of Luther's writings,
and do not leave out of account themes and actions which cover many
years. Père Congar is careful to cite all the most important documents
from many different levels, though he hardly touches the important
group of practical treatises, 1522-5, in which Luther attempted to
grapple with the practical problems of Reform. Yet here is evidence
that Luther's thought about the Church could really be positively
and practically applied and was much more able to be rooted in worshipping, believing Christian congregations, than P. Congar is able
to believe.

P. Congar rightly begins with what, since Holl, has been the needful
first word, that a firm doctrine of the Church is to be found in Luther's
earliest Lectures on the Psalms and on the Epistle to the Romans. He
also very properly draws attention to the importance of the public
Church struggle. Luther's doctrine was no hasty improvisation, but
it was bound to be affected by the new questions to which his attention
was forced by the Indulgence controversy, by the excommunication,
and by the events leading to the Diet of Worms. Here we must notice
(a point perhaps insufficiently stressed by P. Congar) the effect upon
his mind of intensive study of the Church historians and the Canonists,
in the months before the Leipzig Disputation (1519)—a study far more
catastrophic in its consequences than his reading, many months later,
of the "De Ecclesia" of Huss. But if P. Congar fails to bring out the
importance of the Canonist interpretations of the "plenitude of power"
which provoked Luther's violent reaction, he gives a lucid exposition

---

[1] Vraie et Fausse Réforme, 375. That Biblical authority held a specially important
place in Ockhamism is not questioned. Cf. Ritter. Studien zur Spätscholastik I, 148.

of what Luther meant by "Church," of his preference for "Christen-heit" to "Kirche" and the theme of "Communio Sanctorum."

But the heart of P. Congar's criticism, formidably buttressed by citation, is concerned with what he calls "Luther's great dialectical opposition between exterior and interior" [1]—"the great idea of two orders of reality and two births." [2] He finds this dichotomy running through all Luther's doctrine and embodied in the following sets of expression:

"Exterior—corporal—visible—reason—nature—first and carnal birth—political laws—disciplines—thing—place—body.

"Interior—spiritual—invisible—faith—second birth—by vocation and the word—spirit—'being from God.'" [3]

The opposition of two kinds of birth is found by P. Congar in Luther's last Lectures on Genesis, and at Gen. 25^{21}, and we must be grateful to him for centring attention on this important passage. But P. Congar writes as though "prima nativitas" were some constant category of Luther's thought, a technical expression which he used throughout his life. It is, of course, nothing of the kind, but it is an exegetical expression used in connection with a particular passage, which Luther takes up for a moment and then relinquishes, as he did with many such expressions, e.g. the thought of Christ as "gemellus" in the 1518 commentary on Psalms, and the distinction of "donum" and "gratia" in the "Contra Latomum" (1521). We are not to exaggerate the technical importance of this paragraph in Luther's very last commentary.

P. Congar thinks that Luther drew this dichotomy, first from the Epistles of St. Paul, and especially from the Epistle to the Galatians, and second, from St. Augustine's "Spirit and Letter." If this be intended as an historical pedigree, it will not do. Luther's later statements about the importance of Galatians for his thought, stem from the period following his mature enunciation (from 1518 onwards) of the dialectic of Law and Gospel. Luther did not begin with a view which he found in Galatians and then move on towards a one-sided Augustinianism. He derived much profit from Augustine's tract, but he spoke of it with qualified praise. It can be demonstrated by examination of Luther's vocabulary in the period between his Marginal Notes on Peter Lombard (1509) and his Lectures on Romans (1515-16) that Père Congar has inverted the true order of his developing thought. He did not begin with the Bible, and then under Augustinian influence move towards a Neo-Platonic dualism between "the world of images and the world of realities." His firm grasp of an anthropology of the "whole man" in his Lectures on Romans shows that here he has

---

[1] Ibid. 382.　　　　　[2] Ibid. 381.　　　　　[3] Ibid. 383.

grasped the Biblical dialectic of "flesh" and "spirit." The famous antithesis with which Luther's "Liberty of a Christian Man" (1520) begins its argument can be understood only against this Biblical background. P. Congar quotes the view put forward by Hunziger long ago, that Luther's early lectures are strongly Neo-Platonic (but did Hunziger ever apply this to Luther's early ecclesiology?), but the recent attempt to revive this view by Erich Seeberg has found very little favour among the experts.[1]

P. Congar suggests that the Platonism ought to be distributed into a "certain Johannism," "certain Augustinian themes" and an "Ockhamist formation"! How all these elements could be combined, P. Congar does not inform us. At one moment Luther is accused of an exaggerated Paulinism, at the next of being too Johannine (a new argument in Luther studies!), and this is combined with Augustine and Ockham. Thus Luther gets the worst of both worlds: his ancestry is at one moment Realist and Platonist: in the next breath, Nominalist and Aristotelian. This is incredible. P. Congar can make Luther an "Ockhamist": he will then have to explain how Luther, trained in a school which emphasized the concrete and particular, which has been hailed as anticipating modern empiricism, could produce a spiritualist mentality which is for ever running away from all contact with physical reality. Or he can call Luther a Platonist, in which case it is hard to see how the label "Ockhamist" can have any meaning at all.

But the confusion is not Luther's but his critic's, who does not pause to disentangle the two kinds of dualism, the Biblical tension of "flesh" and "spirit" and the Platonic and Neo-Platonic dualism of soul and body. Getting Luther wrong at this point, he consequently blurs Luther's doctrines: just as two lenses in field-glasses, wrongly focussed, affect the whole landscape which is viewed through them. It is perhaps significant that P. Congar does not quote one famous statement of Luther about the Church:

"That I have called the Church 'a spiritual assembly' you have insultingly taken to mean that I would build a Church as Plato builds a state that never was."

Naturally, he is not so crude as to suppose that Luther never spoke of the visibility of the Church in Word and Sacraments, and he does indeed quote Luther on these subjects. But he returns to the charge. Luther has added to the Biblical contrast between nature and grace "an identification in practice with another opposition, that between exterior and interior," "sensible and corporeal, and spiritual." This,

[1] E. Seeberg. Luthers Theologie, vol. i. (1929). Luthers Theologie in ihren Grundzügen, 1950.

he claims, leads Luther entirely to misapprehend the apostolicity of the Church, and the true significance of its sacramental life, reducing everything to the "purely interior." The sum of the matter is that Luther pursued an idea of a Church which should be "pure Gospel, pure Grace, pure interiority . . . a Church which was a new creation," a "reality of the other world, completely spiritual." [1]

This is indeed a blurring of the landscape. P. Congar's argument has proved far too much. It leaves too much of Luther unexplained and unintelligible,[2] as, for instance, the whole conflict with the Left Wing Reformers [3] in the matter of the objectivity of Word and Sacrament. Even if we could suppose that the definition of the Church in the Augsburg Confession represented Melanchthon rather than Luther we should still have to reckon with the firm stress on the visible Church in Luther's own Schmalkaldic Articles.

P. Congar quotes from the important tract "Wider Hans Worst" (1540): but if Luther held the views attributed to him, how confused and indeed unintelligible becomes his claim in this writing that the evangelicals have a just claim to Church property, since they are the "true, old Church." It is true that Luther was, as the author says, "a man of the Word," that he knew his own vocation to be that of a theological professor and a preacher, and that he studied to mind his own business, and left others, like Bugenhagen or Amsdorf, to exercise an office of administration. Yet how massive was his own concentration on the visible Church: the Bible, the Catechism, the hymns, the correspondence on ecclesiastical problems from every quarter of Christendom, the cure of souls, and the care of the Churches, that preoccupation with the wider Church struggle which breathes through his correspondence up to the very last. P. Congar leaves all this unaccounted for.

We turn to what the author calls "the truly capital text," Luther's exegesis of Gen. 25^{21}.[4] The passage is for Luther a veritable conjunction of planets, for it is where the narrative of the Patriarchs coincides with St. Paul's discussion at Rom. 9^{10-12}, or the contrast between Israel "after the flesh" and Israel "after the calling and the promises of God." [5]

---

[1] Ibid. 397.

[2] P. Congar shows some uneasiness (p. 408) on this account and admits that many Protestant writers have brought forward evidence that Luther thought of the visible Church as a mode of divine action. But he takes refuge in the support of M. Strohl. Yet M. Strohl's treatment of Luther's doctrine of the Church is the weakest point in his fine Luther studies. In any case, there is a mass of evidence which is not to be brushed away. [3] W.A. 51.174.23.30.

[4] W.A. 43.380 ff. We must waive the delicate question how far these reported lectures can be taken as evidence for Luther's vocabulary.

[5] " Hic locus maxime insignis et memorabilis est."

Like St. Paul, Luther finds deep symbolic significance in the struggle between Esau and Jacob in the womb, and in the setting aside of the physical primogeniture of Esau, on the ground of the calling and promise of God.

Luther says that, with St. Paul in Romans, we must distinguish a birth after the flesh (nativitas ex carne), from spiritual birth (nativitas spiritualis). Despite Adam's sin, God allowed him to bring all his sons, pious and impious, into the world, but he decreed that it would not be sufficient for them to be born in a physical way, since beyond this (ultra nativitatem) they needed re-birth, renovation and regeneration through the Holy Spirit.[1]

The Patriarchs did not, therefore, bear sons of the Kingdom by the first birth, but "vocation has to be added to creation" (ultra creationem addenda est vocatio). Thus the conflict of the two twins, Esau and Jacob, is a sign of a conflict which runs through the entire history of the People of God, "and of which the end is not yet" . . . "for it is the same conflict which was between Cain and Abel, and the posterity of the serpent and of the seed of woman . . . Ishmael and Isaac, Esau and Jacob, the Church of God and of the Devil." The Church of the Devil is always seeking to dominate, and this on two grounds: first, on account of physical pedigree (propter sanguinem et patres): second, on account of temporal blessings." [2]

These are the two claims of "Israel after the flesh": the historical pedigree and superiority of tradition, and the evident share in the power and glory of this world. A glance at the kind of polemic Luther had to meet from the Papalist side, and at the kind of Catholic practices admitted by such historians as Joseph Lortz, will show that what P. Congar calls Luther's "one-sided Galatianism" responded to what Gilbert Burnet memorably named "superannuated Judaism." [3] But, continues Luther, St. Paul deals a death-blow to such human pretensions in Rom. 9^{12}. "The Word and Promises of God are necessary."

If all that counts is "prima nativitas," the natural order of creation in fallen history, what need is there of God? The Turks are "the most wise, the most honest, and the most religious of men . . . who exercise the most severe discipline." In addition, they are endowed by God with wealth, wisdom, glory, reason and the most outstanding victories

---

[1] W.A. 43.383.24.30. P. Congar does not object to this argument which he finds to be Biblical and correct, " would that Catholic theology and preaching drew nourishment from it more frequently." But he complains that Luther perverts this distinction by importing his dualism between external and internal, bodily and spiritual. Vraie et Fausse, 392.

[2] W.A. 43.384.

[3] We do not regard either of these descriptions as necessarily definitive.

... but all this is "prima nativitas." It is all under judgment, when it is viewed "coram Deo."

The second kind of boasting after the flesh is to glory in tradition and historical pedigree. "The Jews gloried in their blood, that they were born of the Fathers and the Prophets." Thus the Turk boasts in the perquisites of totalitarian power: the Jews have the historical pedigree. But, asks Luther, "Where is the calling of God? Where is the Word?"

Now comes the point. Luther believes that the Papacy has relapsed into an "Obrigkeit," a secular power. Losing the promise and calling of God, it has only the two impressive glories of temporal power and of historical pedigree. Like the Turk, the Papacy is "absorbed" in the same "first birth."

Illustrations of this are the papal stress on the Sacrament of the Altar as an "opus operatum" and the demand for unconditional obedience to ecclesiastical authority.

We may think Luther was wrong: but it is an intelligible and well-argued position, and it goes to the heart of what Protestantism meant by its violent repudiation of "Popery." And Luther has intuitively grasped a question fundamental in the Protestant-Catholic dilemma. The distinction between "Israel after the flesh" and "Israel after the Spirit" is fundamental to the Christian apologetic against Judaism. St. Paul knew it to be a delicate argument. The danger is to split the historical continuity of revelation, and to turn the Christian pedigree within the People of God into a series of isolated pockets of purely spiritual religion (a kind of ecclesiology to which many Protestants have turned, and of which P. Congar wrongly accuses Luther). St. Paul at this important point in Rom. 9⁴ refuses to snap the link between the two Israels. But neither St. Paul nor Luther deny the truth of apostolicity. Luther is not saying that history, time and place are irrelevant. But he faces the awful possibility that in the New Israel, as in the old, there may be sin and rebellion and apostasy, and that the Church (though never the whole Church) may become an "Israel after the flesh." I do not think Roman and Protestant ecclesiological conversation will get very far until this question is seriously faced. And at this point P. Congar goes off into righteous indignation.

Thus, when Luther asks, of the Turks, "if the first birth were sufficient, what need would there be of God?" P. Congar comments "who ever said such a thing? Here is one of those mortal misunderstandings introduced by Luther." But P. Congar can hardly blame Luther for a use of rhetorical questions in the light of his own fondness for them, and the point at issue here is the vital connection between Gen. 25

and Rom. 9. In another place he blames Luther for not realizing that it would be possible for the Church "to have an hierarchical organization, an institution and a head . . . with the will of God and a real vocation, in conformity with the great Biblical vocations, even to the point where, like them, a feeble man after the flesh should be, in the order of the divine promises, the foundation of the Church."

But Luther had wrestled with that possibility twenty years before, in the long agonizing months between the Indulgence controversy and the Leipzig disputation. This was not an idea he had never considered, but one shouted at him by all his opponents, a little late in the day, since he had begun by believing it, and had through long tribulation argued it within himself. But here, like a good exegete, Luther is concerned with the passage before him and its present application.

Luther's attack on Popery here is not simply objection to all outward forms and hierarchical organization, but that it had fallen from the promises of God and rested its authority on outward and empty symbols.

"Thus the Popish Church is not the true Church, because they fall into the 'first birth' and presume that salvation follows upon outward works. But where God adds vocation to birth (Deus ultra primam nativitatem addit) there you find the Church." [1]

P. Congar interprets Luther as though he insisted on a Church "*sine prima nativitate*," but it is integral for his whole argument that Adam begets both sets of sons in history, even though on this plane alone it would seem that the Church of Esau had the claim of primogeniture.

Thus Luther adds, "If you ask the Pope, why are you the People of God? he replies, 'Because I sit in the seat of the Apostles Peter and Paul I am their successor. Thence have I my cause in Scripture. Thou art Peter and upon this rock will I build my Church.' But a dog or a pig can sit in the seat of Peter. But to have vocation, that is, believe the Word, over and above (supra illam successionem) that succession, this constitutes the Church and the sons of God . . . but we do not doubt we are the Church, for we have the Gospel, Baptism, Keys, Holy Scripture, which teach that man is lost and damned in Original Sin and that it is required that he be born again through Christ." [2]

The point about the pig and the dog is characteristically blunt, but not frivolous. It is simply that historical continuity, alone and by itself, is not the differentiation between the true and false Church, but the divine vocation and promise. Here again P. Congar's treatment of "*supra* illam successionem," as though it meant "*without* any succession," misinterprets Luther into denying any historical continuity at all.

---

[1] W.A. 43.386.21.   [2] W.A. 43.387.14.

Abundant testimony could be given that Luther constantly believed in the need for a continual succession of believers on the earth, and, above all, for the continuity of the ministry of the Word. Thus:

"For if the office of Preaching and the rule (Regiment) of the Holy Ghost did not always persist in the Church, it would not be possible that Baptism, the Sacrament and the knowledge of Christ would remain, and who would keep it if it were not carried on through a public ministry?" [1]

"For (the Apostles) speak and carry no other word than they have received from his mouth . . . the same goes on from them, from the apostles to us, through right Bishops, Ministers and Preachers as they have received from the Apostles." [2]

But even clearer is a passage in this very commentary on Genesis:

"There is no difference, save that here in the Church, it is God who calls and there in the world and among the impious, God is silent. For the Turk has not one letter with which to show that the things he does are done justly. There God is not calling. Thus the Pope and Caesar hear nothing. They are in silence. But we have the calling of God, for he revealed himself to us, that we should have God visible, sensible and apprehensible. We have the Word, Baptism, the Keys, and we still suffer—and it is well indeed that we do suffer. But they will be servants of the Lord, and on the other hand, 'We shall remain, but they shall be submerged.' Our heirs (posteri), who are really ours, will abide even here on earth, as from time to time the other prophets have had their abode from the beginning of the world, and as with a kind of hereditary right (!) handed over to us the voice of God (quasi haereditario jure nobis vocem Dei tradiderunt.)" [3]

This hardly needs further comment, when placed alongside P. Congar's affirmation that Luther's "essential point of view . . . corrodes and destroys all affirmation of a true visibility and discernibility of the Church." [4]

We can only refer to three important subsidiary charges. P. Congar affirms that "an external element has no Christian value for Luther." Yet he will find in the famous Preface to the "Deutsche Messe," the favourite court of appeal for those who have contended that Luther's real ideal was a "fellowship of believers," Luther's clear affirmation not only of the vital importance of- the means of grace for sinners, but that such externals as organs and Church bells and the like have an educational value in the training and edification of Christians, even though a perfect Christian might dispense with these things. Nor is Luther opposed to outward considerations of time and place.

---

[1] W.A. 45.580.21 (1538).   [2] W.A. 45.521.6 (1538).
[3] W.A. 43.404.30.   [4] Vraie et Fausse, 410.

"Without place and body there is no Church (sine loco et corpore non est Ecclesia), and yet body and place are not the Church, nor do they belong to it." [1]

And again:

"The fellowship of believers is twofold, one inward and spiritual, the other outward and bodily. The spiritual consists in a unity of faith, hope and love to God. The bodily consists in sharing in the same sacraments, i.e. the signs of faith, hope and love, which, however, extends further to things, matters of use and language, buildings and other bodily circumstances." [2]

"The Church is the number or gathering of the baptized and believing people who belong to a pastor in a town, or in a whole countryside, or in the whole world." [3]

"This is our trust and glory, that with good ground we confidently boast and say: We are holy and holy brothers towards one another at Wittenberg, Rome, Jerusalem and where the Holy Baptism and Gospel are." [4]

When Luther comes to the differentia between the true and false Church, he does not deny, but affirms the continuity of history.

"For we have the same Baptism, the same Sacrament of the Altar, the same Keys, the same Scripture and Word. And then, we have arisen from the same apostles and Church, as from one mother Rebecca. Where then do we differ? We take hold of the Word in the Sacrament, we follow our vocation, and we treat things according to faith. They according to a visible appearance. We say that the Word is to be regarded 'in usu Sacramenti' and to be received in faith. They make it an 'opus operatum.' Thus that is the true Church which adheres to the Word, and faith which does not lean on works but which hears and follows the calling of God." [5]

P. Congar takes the narrowest reading of Luther's rich and complex doctrine of the Word, which he unjustifiably restricts to the "Preaching of Christ as 'My' Saviour." But though it was a needful and wholesome emphasis of Luther to stress the benefits of Christ, the doctrine of the Word embraces for Luther the whole content of divine revelation as given to men in history, in the Scriptures and in the tradition Luther's appeal to the "old Fathers" and his constant citation from theological tradition—even in these last lectures, and, with approval, from the "Vitae Patrum"!—show how he, too, accepted tradition). Nor does P. Congar hint, indeed in this section of his book he hardly

---

[1] W.A. 7.720.2.3. (Against Ambrosius Catherinus).
[2] W.A. 1.639.2.   Sermon on Excommunication (1518).
[3] W.A. 30.2.421.19.   [4] W.A. 45.617.27.
[5] W A. 43.387.42.

mentions the importance for Luther of the Holy Scriptures, not as an arbitrary collection of proof texts for some selected notions, or to support a "one-sided Galatianism," but as the massive background. Luther's mind and thought was saturated in the whole Biblical material. When he charges Luther with only being able to think of salvation as "from within to without," or "from above downward," he again fails to apprehend the objectivity of Luther's doctrines—even though it may be admitted that they are of another kind than those of orthodox Catholicism.

Finally, P. Congar has not explained the origin of, nor demonstrated the existence of, the "dualism" in Luther's dialectic of "visible-invisible." Luther's teaching is susceptible of an explanation in Biblical terms, in a way which does justice to more facts. But the author has done great service in calling attention to the passages in the Genesis commentary. For here Luther has raised a fundamental issue. What of the sins and disobedience and guilt of the Church, as the "New Israel"? Church historians, Catholic and Protestant, deal lightly with Christian failure in comparison with the rough handling of the Old Israel by the Psalmists, the Prophets and the Apostles. These could never write off the results of centuries of sin and disobedience in the manner of P. Congar (who in this respect is no worse than the rest of us), with a "malheureusement"—as though what is at stake can be discussed in terms of a series of regrettable accidents.[1]

And yet, surely, somewhere here lies the whole issue of true and false Reform? True Reform, Luther saw, does not mean reform which takes place obediently and quietly, without straining the structure of hierarchical authority: it may involve such obedience to the Word of God as involves disaster, catastrophe and tragic discontinuity. That is the patent story of ancient Israel. Violently, and if you will, one-sidedly, Luther grasped the relevance of this to the New Israel. Here, in these paragraphs (which are after all an "occasional" exegesis) Luther provides material for an interpretation of Church history. In the first years of the Reformation (though never guilty of "naïve optimism") Luther may have written, as though the story could be told in terms of the all-conquering and ever-fruitful Word. He lived to see many brave hopes frustrated and disappointed. We can sympathize, for in our time, too, men had believed that history might be

---

[1] " Malheureusement, rien de vraiment sérieux n'a été fait pendant deux siècles pour une telle Reforme " (376). In face of the gravity of these things, as the Bible and Luther viewed them, P. Congar's appendix on " Collective responsibility " (pp. 579-596) must be regarded as hardly grappling with the problem. It is significant that this, from a Protestant view, the heart of the matter, is relegated to a few pages (out of 650) in an appendix in this fine volume.

described in terms of the slow fruition of the good, and have seen their doctrine broken by hard facts, yielding to the truth that ferment and conflict are endemic in the human story.

St. Augustine, in his great "City of God," had interpreted history in terms of conflict, the collision between two great societies. Luther perceived that Church History, too, is not exempt from these conditions governing all human existence. Through the life of the People of God, in the old Israel and in the New, there runs conflict and tension. The two Israels, one "after the flesh" and the other "after the Spirit," do not simply co-exist side by side. They collide, like Esau and Jacob in the womb. It is noticeable that at this point Luther uses the Augustinian category of "cupiditas" and "dominium" as the operative factor in this story. Thus human egoism, lust for power and for dominion play their tragic part in Church History.

"The Holy Spirit wishes us to have the two brothers perpetually before our eyes, and as a daily proverb. For at all times we are either Esauites or Jacobites . . . and even if we were to conquer the Pope and his men, and if our doctrine, which is proper to the true Church were to triumph: yet from out of our own midst would arise Papists and Turks who would sell the title of 'Church.' Thus the Anabaptists and Sacramentaries have arisen . . . thus always, Cain or Abel, Esau or Jacob." [1]

Not that this conflict is a complete dualism without an end or as though the two solidarities were mutually exclusive.

"For we are certain of victory. For the Word or Promise will conquer without any doubt. Thus if any of our adversaries are saved, it will not be because they are papists, or monks or Turks, but because they belong to us, that is, to Abraham, Isaac and Jacob. And though they are not of our seed: yet they are grafted in. Thus not the whole mass are rejected, but the glorying and arrogance of the mass which glory in the fathers, the ceremonies and the law. And if he wishes to join us, he will be a holy mass (massa sancta) with us and with all the generation of the pious." [2]

Luther's doctrine of the Church at this point is indeed, to use P. Congar's penetrating phrase, "an ecclesiology of Crisis." [3] There is much to ponder in his further description of it as a "marginal gloss on traditional ecclesiology." But an "ecclesiology of Crisis" marks a return to the New Testament dimensions.

For Luther it is an essential note of the Church to be "under the

---

[1] W.A. 43.418.6.   W.A. 51.175.26.
[2] W.A. 43.401.13.   Also W.A. 51.174.16.
[3] Vraie et Fausse, 391.

Cross." It is the gravamen of his charge against the Papacy that it has sought to turn faith into sight, and so lapsed into the "prima nativitas." And by turning faith into sight, it has cut the knot of eschatology. And it is interesting to note how, as Luther closes the discussion of Gen. 25, the eschatological note returns:

"So today the Pope has the name of Church. We have not. But we know that we are the true Church, for we have the Word, Sacraments, Keys, which Christ left behind him, not that they might serve our power or our desires (cupiditatibus) in this life, but that they might prepare us for the advent of the Son of God." [1]

"Jacob knows that sacred things are the preparation for a future life, and that is why he magnifies them and ardently gives himself to them . . . for whoso wishes to be in the Church must magnify his primogeniture, not so much in this life as in that which is to come." [2]

"For we indeed have nothing other from God than the pure Word, that the Lord Jesus sits at the Right Hand of the Father, and is Judge of the Living and of the Dead, through whom we are kings and priests. But where can these things be discerned? Not in the indicative, but in the imperative and optative mood. For why he thus hides himself, we shall know in that Day, when all his enemies shall be put under his feet. Meanwhile we believe and hope. For if these things were now manifest before our eyes, there would be no work for faith (nihil opus esset fide) . . . thus he seems to have deserted us, for he ascends to heaven and sits at the Right Hand of the Father and yet he leaves us the Word and Sacraments. But what is this? The flesh objects: I see nothing, it is only a word. It is Word indeed, but in it is supreme and divine virtue, which you will experience, if with firm faith you cleave to it." [3]

[1] W.A. 43.425.6.
[2] W.A. 43.427.17 : 428.6.
[3] W.A. 43.393.6.

Chapter

16

LUTHER, A MAN

"In how many little escapes and corner holes does the sensibility, the fineness (that of which refinement is but a counterfeit, at best but a reflex), the geniality of nature, appear in this Son of Thunder."

S. T. COLERIDGE on Luther's "Table Talk."

"ALAS, gone is the horseman and the chariots of Israel." These were the words with which Philip Melanchthon broke the news of Luther's death to the hushed Wittenberg students. His words recalled how, at the departure of Elijah, Elisha was left alone with the disciples of the prophet. It was an apt, if characteristic comment, for Melanchthon could never quite get himself out of any picture, least of all in that moment of sharp bereavement when he must face the burden of the future without the man on whom he had always too heavily leaned. Some cynical student may have wondered whether Melanchthon anticipated a double portion of Luther's spirit. In the event it might be said that Luther's disciples and a good deal of later Lutheranism received a double portion indeed, but of the spirit of Melanchthon! But if you turn to what Luther's friends had to say about him, even those who during his lifetime criticized him very plainly, you will find them turning to the great measuring rods, to the patriarchal and prophetic figures, to Elijah and Jeremiah, to Noah and to David. We do not normally speak in this way, even from motives of party zeal, of real men whom we have known. Here, somewhere, was a giant.

It is, as we have admitted, almost impossible to dissociate Luther from his work. But we may claim for him the right to be considered, before the bar of history, as a private as well as a public person, as a human being. It is the second-rate historian who reads history with the faith of a moralist, approving and disapproving, acting the part of God. And perhaps that wrongs God, who, as has been said, "loves this human life of ours, not only as a moralist, but as a poet or artist loves it, because he cannot help loving a thing so strange, piteous and enthralling as the story of every human soul must be."

Thus the historian must always be seeking for the human stuff within the intricate pattern of history, and he will treasure each scrap of evidence: a few words scrawled in the dark by William Tyndale; the menu of the last meals shared by Ridley, Cranmer and Latimer in Bocardo, the entry in the diary of Gentleman Pensioner Underwood, which vividly shows us his gaunt, pale, sick figure staring at the procession of the new Queen Mary; the last petition of Captain Henry Bell from within the Gatehouse: those rare moments when we can look out through our subject's own eyes. Let us then consider Luther as a man, rather than a theological symbol.

We have watched the development of Luther's theology during the years of struggle, and of growth, before the outbreak of the dire Church conflict, and it has been to us as a shadow cast by his human presence. We have been aware of him in the background, but him we have hardly glimpsed. It would have gone ill with him in the critical years of his revolutionary vocation, had he not learned lessons from his spiritual struggles. "My son," Staupitz had said, more wisely than he could have known, "perhaps God is teaching you not to be afraid." It is one of the clues to the understanding of Luther that the man who appeared before the world as Mr. Standfast should be known within his city of Mansoul as Mr. Fearing. And, like Mr. Fearing, because his fears were about his acceptance at the last, he made light of the Hill Difficulty and was undaunted because of the lions by the way. But he was nothing, in Ritter's phrase, "of the academic bully": there was a point in the Erasmian "elephant," but its pertinence does not lie in the thickness of his skin. He could face the taunts of his enemies because he had met them all before, in his own conscience—"How do you know you are right? Perhaps God is hostile to you" . . . and this battle was never over and done with, but to be faced again and again in loneliness and in the night watches, when the whole moving tragedy of the sixteenth century schism seemed laid to his account, beside that which came upon him daily, the cure of souls immediately committed to his charge, and the conscience of his own sins.

In the years 1517-21 Luther became an operative factor in history. Had he given way, had he been induced to recant, and one way and another great influences were exerted upon him to do so, then vast ranges of European history must have been different. Most of the great persons of history have been, in the end, imps surrounded by giant forces, tides of history stronger than they have known. But the secret of their greatness has been their ignorance that the stars in their courses had made alliance on their behalf. John Buchan has said that the great strokes of the military art look very simple—afterwards. It is an effort of imagination to put ourselves back amid the loneliness of great decisions to be made and paid for, as Luther made them and paid for them in a toll of nervous and physical energy which left him a spent old man before his time.

It is a platitude, but perhaps worth pondering, that Luther was a Protestant before there was any Protestantism. He lacked that support and stay which a living theological, liturgical and devotional tradition brings to a Christian man, from within his own household of faith. That is partly why the Psalms meant so much to him, and the great Biblical figures, as emblems of the encompassing solidarity of the People of God. Like Abraham, like Jacob, he had to leave home. For him, by faith the clouds were cheering, beckoning chariots of fire, but sometimes he must have yearned, even with Melanchthon at hand, for closer comradeship. There was for him no "Matthew Passion" of J. S. Bach, no hymns of Rinkart or Gerhardt, none of that rich and many-sided tradition which was to stem from his own life and deeds. He had to make it up as he went along, and how he made it—a German Bible, a Children's Catechism, a few dozen hymns—all events in European history which counted for more than all the battles of Gustavus Adolphus and Oliver Cromwell. To speak thus is not to forget his deep debt to the past, the many signs that to the end of the days he was nourished by great debts incurred during his monastic training, the deep levels of mediaeval devotion and theology and liturgy to which he always owed more than he knew and more than most Protestant historians have ever brought themselves to acknowledge.

Lord Acton saw the decisive moment as that in which Martin Luther, in December 1520, burned the volumes of the Canon Law outside the Elster Gate in Wittenberg, and added, as a deliberate afterthought, the Papal Bull. All writers dwell on the dramatic climax to the Diet of Worms, when, like a Teutonic knight, he raised his arm victoriously and shouted "I am through." But by then Luther knew what forces were on his side. The moment of high danger was over, though it would never entirely disappear, and, at his death, would burst upon his widow and his children, his land and his prince. But now, though devils innumerable might be upon the tiles of the houses, the streets were full of men crying, as Aleander complained, "Long live Luther!" and "Death to Rome!"

The real testing time lies earlier, between the journey to the Heidelberg Chapter in the spring of 1518 and the interviews at Augsburg with Cajetan in the summer of that year. He arrived in Augsburg "pauper et pedester," with no safe conduct, not knowing whether he had not been sacrificed already as a gambit in the great game between the Empire and the Papacy. Rumours were rife that he would be arrested and sent in chains to Rome. It was then that Urban de Serra-longa sought him out, and with smooth guile, put into words all Luther's own fears:

Serralonga. Do you really think the Elector Frederick will take up arms to protect you?

Luther. I hope not.

Serralonga. Well, then, where will you go?

Luther. Under heaven (Sub Coelo).

Luther was not the last professor to draw more comfort from his own lectures than his students, and his studies in the Epistle to the Hebrews and the stories of the patriarchs gave him strength and encouragement at this time. And at this time, the anxieties of his timid friends were not the least of his afflictions. He wrote to Spalatin before the Leipzig Disputation:

"Let my friends think me mad. The affair will not reach an end (if it is from God) unless, as his disciples and acquaintances deserted Christ, so all my friends desert me, and the truth is left alone—truth which will save itself by its own right hand, not mine nor yours, nor any man's . . . if I perish the world will lose nothing . . . I, unhappy, fear lest perchance I should not be worthy to suffer in such a cause."

It is no accident that Luther's doctrine of the Devil really develops after the Diet of Worms. In the loneliness of the Wartburg there was the inevitable reaction of a mind held taut for long, now relaxed, and of a soul flung back upon itself. Luther's Devil is by no means to be disposed of in terms of superstition, catarrh, noises in the head and what are now fashionably described as "poltergeist phenomena." The theologians have described the importance for Luther of the theme of conflict, and of the dynamism and objectivity of evil. Here we remember the continuing significance for him of "Anfechtung." It is here that Luther reminds us again and again of the great English writer with whom he had most in common (far more than with John Wesley), John Bunyan. As Bunyan found his own heart written out in Luther's Galatians, so there is much of Luther in "Grace Abounding" and in the "Pilgrim's Progress." Here is Luther, thinking of the Christian man as a St. George against the dragon—and coming very close indeed to the immortal conference between Christian and Apollyon. In this case the Christian faces Sin personified, sin which entices the Christian to "lust or avarice or despair of hatred of God."

"Then Christian arouses himself and as though in admiration says, 'And art thou come at last? Welcome, Lord Sin. Where have you been? What have you been doing all this time? Where have you been living? Whence have you come to us? Avaunt, in the name of the

Cross! Not so, it shall not be so. I will serve my virgin, and that I may deal fairly with you, I will challenge you, and the more you torment me or entice me to dishonour, lust and despair, the more I will laugh you to scorn, and with a great and strong heart, relying on the aid of Christ, I will despise thee and bruise thy head. What have I to do with thee? I have another Lord, in whose camp I am now a soldier: Here I stand. Here I will die.' This is that glorious champion and strong St. George who makes mighty onslaught on the army of the Devil and gloriously conquers, as St. Paul says, 'In all these things we are more than conquerors through Christ Jesus,' nor does he suffer sins to devour his flesh." [1]

It is now when, for the first time, he had begun to put on weight, and when bearded like the pard, as "Junker Georg" he looked really fierce, that we get a glimpse of that unexpected gentleness which was a genuine deep element in his character, and was evidenced much more in personal contact than can be gauged from his writings. In search of needful exercise he joined a hunting party "to get a taste of the pleasures which fine gentlemen love." He was disgusted when the chase turned out to be, not after some animal of prey, but after hares, and when one of the terrified creatures ran his way, "With great pains I saved one of them—and let the live hare take refuge in the sleeves of my cloak." Luther let it stay there, and began to edge away from the group of huntsmen, but was soon the centre of the group of baying, leaping hounds who had scented "Poor Puss"—and when Luther uncovered his reddening sleeve he found that the silly hare's leg and throat had been bitten through the cloth. As he stared and shuddered, he saw the parable of his own situation and his own possible fate, and he had done for a lifetime with the hunting of innocent things.

While Luther grappled in his Patmos with great literary tasks, and with sharp physical illness, and with spiritual "Anfechtungen," he had to meet a crisis in Wittenberg, provoked by Karlstadt and a handful of extremists, the premonition of a century of baneful Puritan icono-clasm. Luther paid a secret visit to the town, and in defiance of the express order of the Elector that if he valued his life, he must at all costs remain in hiding, he entered the city. On Sunday, 6th March 1522, he re-entered his pulpit—his beard shaved off, his disguise put away and (the whole of his Reformation is in this touch) carefully habited as an Augustinian monk.

"Let us beware lest Wittenberg become a Capernaum . . . dear friends, a man must not insist on his rights, but must see what is useful and helpful to his brother. . . . I would not have gone as far as you have

[1] W.A. 39.1.505.6.

done if I had been here. What you did was good, but you have gone too fast, for there are brothers and sisters on the other side who belong to us, and must still be won. . . .

"Faith never yields, but Love is guided according as our neighbours can grasp or follow it. There are some who can run, others must walk, and still others who can hardly creep. Therefore we must not look on our own, but on our brother's powers, so that he that is weak in faith . . . may not be destroyed . . . let us therefore cast ourselves at one another's feet, join hands and help one another. . . . I will do my part, for I love you even as I love my own soul. . . .

"We must first win the hearts of the people. And that is done when I teach only the Word of God, preach only the Word of God, for if you win the heart, you win the whole man."

Thus Luther began his war on two fronts, against the legalism of the Papists on the one hand, and the legalism of the fanatics on the other. The new movements on the left had their own pedigree: the writings of Conrad Grebel and of Thomas Müntzer include a mystical terminology and an apocalyptic emphasis which did not derive at all from Luther's movement. That there were Anabaptists in that time of simple piety and gentle mien is undoubted, but we can hardly wonder if their still, small voice was swallowed in the fire and earthquake of the Peasant War and the Munster debacle. The great themes "Word —Spirit" were strained through the new tension, and as the radicals emphasized the voice of the Spirit within, so the conservatives stressed more and more the objective and written Word and prepared for the later uncompromising Biblicism. Thomas Müntzer repaid every hard word he received from Luther with interest: he was "a blind archdevil," "a poisonous worm with your dirty humility that you got out of Augustine" . . . "sleep softly, Mr. Soft Life . . . Asses' Flesh . . . Dr. Martin Liar . . . Mr. Sit on the Fence . . . His Holiness the Pope of Wittenberg . . . Mr. Cleverstick . . ." [1]

Luther's intolerance may have hardened in later years, and his original insistence that heresy can only be fought by the Word was reluctantly and half-heartedly compromised by the pressure of his friends and patrons and his concern lest the Reformation movement go completely astray. But there is about him little of the unlovely rigidity of some forms of modern Lutheranism in this matter, and he maintained as few in that age or since two convictions: first, that as he said, "one point in doctrine is more important than heaven and

---

[1] H. S. Bender. Conrad Grebel. E. A. Payne. The Anabaptists of the sixteenth century. Thomas Müntzer. Politische Schriften. C. Hinrichs, 1950. G. Ritter. Die Neugestaltung Europas im 16. Jahrhundert, 1950, 120.

earth"—and second, a conviction that the Word of God, not force, is only able to conquer in matters of truth. It was not simply obstinacy or fundamentalism which led him to write on the table the words which divided him and Zwingli, in the great matter of the Eucharist—"Hoc EST corpus meum." [1] It was the conviction that to turn that "EST" into "significat" was to turn the religion of incarnation into that docetism and subjectivism which has haunted and impoverished Protestant eucharistic life for four centuries over the greater part of Protestantism. He warned his generation as he warns the Ecumenical movement in our time, that the most urgent practical, political, reasons of expediency cannot justify a reunion which involves the weakening of obedience to the truth as God gives men to believe it.

By 1525 Luther was ceasing to stand out with the clear isolation of a Perugino painting. He becomes part of a crowded canvas. The Reformation was afoot, not so much a movement as a series of ever-multiplying, ever-divided persons, events, causes. As earlier on, the tides of history supported him, and his resistance in 1517-21 was, as Müntzer gibed, made possible by the support of German national anti-clericalism, so now he had the less pleasant experience of having to stand against the stream of public opinion, not only in the learned and public world but among the common people.

His consistency in the matter of the Peasants can be fully demonstrated, from a succession of writings in the preceding years. He had warned the rulers, he had warned the cities, he had warned the peasants, and, above all, he had raised his voice against the fanaticism of the parsons who provided the heady ideological leadership among them. The brutality of his terrible broadsheet against the Peasants springs from his alarmed apprehension that the whole Reformation might now be swallowed up in bloodshed and anarchy. But he wrote at a time when the Peasants were carrying all before them and when he had reason to expect that he might pay for his plain speaking with his life.

Moreover, it seems that the writing appeared originally at the end of an edition of his moderate appeal to both sides, as a kind of appendix added when negotiations had broken down and the insurrections were in full spate.[2] When it was over, and the dreadful reprisals were in swing, his words sounded harsh and provocative, and alarmed his friends, and enraged the defeated. His own obstinacy prevented him from retracting, though he made some bold comments against the

---

[1] F. Hildebrandt. Est. Das Lutherische Prinzip, 1931.
[2] See W.A. 18.376. Also K. Aland. " Auch widder die reubischen und mordischen rotten der andern Bawren." Eine Anmerkung zu Luthers Haltung im Bauernkrieg. Th. Lit. Z., May 1949, 299.

Junkers and made personal intercession for some of the sufferers. But it was not all obstinacy. It was his own doctrine of obedience, conscientiously sustained, and it was his special count against the rebel leaders that as their movement swept along with blood and fire they conscripted innocent men and women into what Luther regarded as a damnable cause.

Our immediate point is not to make special pleading on his behalf, but to point out that he deliberately refused to play to a very considerable gallery, as his friends urged him to do, and that his loyalty to the truth as he saw it, lost him a public support which affected his whole later life, and turned important currents of the Reformation into other channels.

At the height of the Peasant war he married, deliberately, partly to show that his conscience was clear. Marriage in the sixteenth century was a marvellously common-sense affair. Luther's wooing was not romantic, but it turned out very well indeed. Those who dismiss it in terms of runaway nun and apostate monk beg one of the biggest of sixteenth century questions. But certainly Luther needed looking after.

"Before I was married the bed was not made up for a whole year and became foul with sweat. But I worked all day and was so tired at night that I fell into bed without knowing that anything was amiss."

In the event his home life can stand comparison even with the home life of Sir Thomas More, and was in respect of the relations between husband and wife, a good deal happier. We have a vivid picture of their relations together in the letters with their roughly gentle banter, and Luther could ask no more effective testimony than the letter which his Kate wrote her sister, full two months after his death:

"Who would not be sorrowful and mourn for so noble a man as was my dear lord? Truly I am so distressed I cannot tell the deep sorrow of my heart to anybody and I hardly know what to think or how I feel. I cannot eat or drink nor can I sleep. If I had a principality and an empire it would never have cost me so much pain to lose them as I have now that our Lord God has taken from me this dear and precious man. God knows that for sorrow and weeping I can neither speak nor dictate this letter."

And as through the years he became a beloved father, and, like all in that age, watched children grow, and some of them die, and as he pottered about in the garden and tinkered with his clocks, and gave generously both goods and money which the home could ill afford and for which he was still more generously chided, he provided more than a theory of the ministry. If it be true that there are more sons of the Manse and Vicarage in the Dictionary of National Biography than from any other kind of home (and Professor Bainton says the same is true in the United States), then we need not be too apologetic about Luther's home and Luther's wedding.

We are all familiar with the portraits of Luther. The early engraving which shows him as a monk, and much as Mosellanus described him at the Leipzig disputation:

"Of middle height, with slender body worn out both by study and care, so that you can almost count his bones. He is in the vigour of manhood. His voice is sharp and clear."

There is the fine profile, which shows how very tough, and how very German Luther looked at the time when he was hailed as the "Hero of the German nation."

There are the series of Cranach portraits which show that, like Jabez in the Scriptures, Luther's coasts were continually being enlarged until he attained (let us admit it—since polemic has made so much of it) a Chestertonian girth almost as great as that of St. Thomas Aquinas, and from which Luther stares at us, with moody benevolence, or in one of his own favourite phrases, "like a cow staring at a new gate." That is a pity, for his eyes, flashing, quick, twinkling in fun or flaming in anger, were what all his contemporaries, friend and foe, remembered of him. The whole man was in them: the obstinacy and occasional malice, the unabating anger against those he believed to be the enemies of God, the humour and the gentleness and the unexpected timidities, and the charm which he could exercise, to melt even hostile, critical visitors.

But the fight never stopped and the strain was constant. And in the later years he had to watch the growing division among his friends, the growing power of his enemies, the evident and even growing strength of his Papal foes. There is the story of how, in 1535, when the English delegates were with him, he received a visit from the Papal Nuncio, and took Robert Barnes along with him to dinner, no doubt with long spoons used all round. And Luther put on his best clothes, and brushed his hair, carefully hiding all traces (he was fifty-two) of his age, lest it be whispered in the streets of Askelon that his strength was failing.

One of the legends of modern polemic has been of a great decline in Luther's last years. It is true that some of his fiercest polemic against the Papacy (but it was the edge of the Council of Trent) and against the Jews was written at this time. But there is nothing which cannot be paralleled from his earlier writings, and a great weight of fine, edifying, constructive writing to set against it. He came to be racked with chronic illness, and knew few hours without physical pain. He suffered much from stone. Ebstein's list of his illnesses includes: "Calculi, constipation, catarrh of the middle ear, piles, periostitis, stomach affections, weak heart, dysentery, cataract and rheumatism."

Whether he suffered from serious heart trouble, or whether his swoons and fainting periods from 1527 onwards are what are now described, but hardly explained as "psycho-physical," cannot be accurately determined. He was prematurely aged. There were times when he thought of death as a coming blessing and longed for rest— the famous "volo esse miles emeritus"—and the half joking:

"I am an old, tired, chilled, frozen man and now, to crown all, one-eyed, and now that I am already dead, so to speak, I might be allowed some peace . . . but no, I must be writing and talking as though I have never written a word."

When at last he brought his great course of Lectures on Genesis to a close, in November 1545, it was with the same sense of burdened relief, "May our Lord God grant to somebody else to make a better job of it. I can no more, I am too weak—pray to God for me that he will give me a good, blessed end (stündlein)." [1]

Here was no old reprobate, snarling in his cups, of polemical legend. But there were times when he had his tantrums and when his friends dreaded to bring him bad news (but always about the good cause of Reformation). [2] It was at this very time that, disgusted and disheartened at the moral laxity of Wittenberg, he shook its dust from his feet and declared that rather than live in such a place he would wander round Germany begging the bread of charity, until a scared deputation of town and gown came after him, begging him to return.

Then in January 1546 he was asked to mediate in a dispute between the two young lords of Mansfeld. He had every reason for not going, and he left his wife stiff with anxiety. But they were his "Obrigkeit" and Mansfeld was his home town. With two sons and with Justus Jonas he adventured the long eighty miles. He had taken pains that his wife should not be left destitute, and now he wrote her a series of frequent, homely, teasing, cheerful letters which are among his finest writings. They were halted by the flooded River Saale.

"We met a huge She-Anabaptist with great waves and huge blocks of ice, threatening to re-baptize us . . . we have had to wait." [3]

The negotiations were long and difficult, not least because of the implacable arrogance of the gentry, of whom Luther wrote bitingly to his wife. He found committees always a trial, and for him it was

[1] W.A. 44.825.10. [2] E. Wolf. Luthers Erbe. Ev. Theol., 1946, 82 ff. [3] W.A.Br. 11.4191. 25th Jan. 1546, 269.5.

always the hard thing to sit and watch. The Diet of Augsburg in 1530 had been for him a fidgeting torment when he had to wait outside in the Castle Coburg, leaving the care of the Churches to God and to Philip Melanchthon. But he did not forget his wife and her worries, and did what he could to tease her out of them.

"My Dear Wife, Doctoress, Director of the Wittenberg Pig Market. Dear Kate, read St. John and that little Catechism of which you once told me, 'Why there's all about me in this book' . . . you seem to have taken on God's own worries, as though God couldn't create ten Doctor Martins if the old one gets choked in the River Saale. . . . I have a better protector. He it was who lay in a manger and was nursed at a maiden's breast and sits at the right hand of God the Father Almighty—so be at peace." [1]

And again, three days later:

"Most holy Doctoress. We thank you most gratefully for your worry about us, which is so great that you can't sleep . . . since you started worrying we have been nearly burned to death by a fire outside the door of my room in the inn . . . then yesterday, no doubt in the might of your worry, a stone (as big as a long bolster and a good hands-breadth) . . . fell down and nearly crushed us like a mouse in a trap . . . no doubt in gratitude for your holy worry—I am now worried that if you don't stop worrying, the earth will just open up and swallow us and the elements will chase us. Are you learning that catechism and creed of yours? Say your prayers, my dear, and let God worry about me, for you and I are not commanded to worry, but as Ps. 55 says, 'Cast thy burden on the Lord for he cares for you, etc.'" [2]

There was one more letter, happy, serene, telling of a difficult mission wonderfully accomplished, of a reconciliation made and confirmed in a meal at Luther's table. His last words of his last letter to her echo the constant refrain of all his correspondence from first to last, "we will wait and see what God will do." [3] But now he was deathly tired. Afterwards his friends noticed a special solemnity about those prayers of his, which, after his wont, he made audibly by an open upper window. Then, a few hours later, he halted before a chill river more dreadful than the flooded Saale.

Like so many "Last Words" his recorded final utterances are conventional. [4] But years before he had written:

"If we believe the waters below us depart and . . . harm us not but flee

[1] W.A.Br. 11.4201.   7th Feb. 1546, 286.
[2] W.A.Br. 11.4203.   10th Feb. 1546, 290.
[3] W.A.Br. 11.4207.   14th Feb. 1546, 299.
[4] C. Schubart. Die Berichte über Luthers Tod und Begräbnis. Weimar, 1917.

from us. . . . And those above us stand up high as though they would overwhelm us: these are the horrors and apparitions of the other world, which at the hour of death terrify us. If, however, we pay no heed to them and pass on with a firm faith, we shall enter into eternal life dry shod and unharmed." [1]

It seems to be the fact that for him those last terrors, that final temptation so often anticipated, were wonderfully abated.

He passed over, as one seeking a strong City.

[1] W.M.L. 2.25.

SELECT BIBLIOGRAPHY

ALANEN, Y. J. E.   Das Gewissen bei Luther (A.A.S.F., XXIX, 2).   Helsinki, 1934.
ALLEN, P. S.   Erasmus.   Oxford, 1934
   The Age of Erasmus.   1914.
   Opus Epistolarum Des. Erasmi Roterodami.   Oxford, 1906-38.
ALTHAUS, PAUL.   Communio Sanctorum.   Gütersloh, 1930.
   Paulus und Luther über den Menschen.   Gütersloh, 1951.
ANDREAS, WILLY.   Deutschland vor der Reformation.   Stuttgart, 1948.
ARNOLD, F. X.   Zur Frage des Naturrechts bei M. Luther.   1937.
BAINTON, ROLAND.   Bernardino Ochino.   Florence, 1940.
   Here I Stand.   New York, 1950.
BAUDRY, L.   Guillaume d'Occam.   Tome 1.   L'homme et les œuvres (Études de Philosophie Médiévale).   Paris, 1950.
   La Querelle des Futurs Contingents (Louvain, 1465-75) (Études de Philosophie Médiévale).   Paris, 1950.
BENDER, H. S.   Conrad Grebel, 1498-1526.   Goshen, Indiana, 1950.
BOHATEC, JOSEF.   Budé und Calvin.   Vienna, 1950.
BOEHMER, HEINRICH.   Luther and the Reformation in the Light of Modern Research.   Eng. tr., 1930.
   Der Junge Luther (ed. Heinrich Bornkamm, 1939).   Eng. tr., "Road to Reformation."   1946.
   Luthers erste Vorlesung.   Leipzig, 1924.
BÖHNER, PHILOTHEUS, O.F.M.   The Tractatus de Praedestinatione et de Praescientia Dei of William Ockham.   New York, 1945.
BORNKAMM, HEINRICH.   Eckhart und Luther.   Stuttgart, 1946.
   Justitia Dei in der Scholastik und bei Luther.   Archiv für Ref. 39. 1942.
   Luther und Böhme.   1925.
   Luthers Geistige Welt.   Lüneberg, 1947.
   Luther und das Alte Testament.   Tübingen, 1948.
   Studien zu Luthers Anschauung vom Alten Testament (Archiv für Ref. 1948).
BRANDI, KARL.   Kaiser Karl V.   2 vols.   Munich, 1941.
BRING, RAGNAR.   Dualismen hos Luther (1929).
   Einige Blätter aus der Schwedischen Lutherforschung (Z. für Syst. Theol., 1931).
BÜHLER, P.   Die Anfechtung bei Luther.   Zurich, 1942.
BURNABY, J.   Amor Dei.   London, 1938.
CARLSON, EDGAR M.   The Reinterpretation of Luther.   Philadelphia, 1948.
CARRÉ, M.   Realists and Nominalists.   Oxford, 1946.
   Phases of Thought in England.   Oxford, 1949.
CLARK, JAMES M.   The Great German Mystics.   Oxford, 1949.
COLERIDGE, S. T.   Notes Theological, Political and Miscellaneous.   Table Talk.   1853.

CONGAR, YVES. Vraie et Fausse Réforme dans l'Église. Paris, 1950.
DAVIES, R. E. The Problem of Authority in the Continental Reformers. 1946.
DENIFLE, HEINRICH. Luther und Luthertum in der ersten Entwicklung, quellenmässig dargestellt. Mainz, 1904.
Die Abendländischen Schriftausleger bis Luther über Justitia Dei. Mainz, 1905.
DIEM, HARALD. Luthers Lehre von den zwei Reichen. Munich, 1938.
DIEM, HERMANN. Luthers Predigt in den zwei Reichen. Munich, 1947.
DREWS, P. Entsprach das Staatskirchentum dem Ideale Luthers? Z. für Theologie und Kirche. 1908.
DRUMMOND, A. L. German Protestantism since Luther. London, 1951.
EBELING, GERHARD. Die Anfänge von Luthers Hermeneutik. Z. für Theol. und K. 1951.
EELLS, H. Martin Bucer. New Haven, 1931.
ELERT, WERNER. Morphologie des Luthertums. Munich, 1931.
ERASMUS, DESIDERIUS. Ausgewählte Werke. Ed. Holborn. Munich, 1933.
Vertraute Gespräche. Köln, 1947.
Essai sur le Libre Arbitre. (Ed. P. Mesnard.) Algiers, 1945.
FARNER, OSKAR. Huldrych Zwingli. Vol. 1, Zurich, 1943. Vol. 2, Zurich, 1946.
Martin Luther. Zurich, 1946.
FEBVRE, LUCIEN. Martin Luther: a Destiny. (Eng. tr.) London, 1930.
FIFE, ROBERT. Young Luther. 1928.
FOERSTER, ERICH. Fragen nach Luthers Kirchenbegriff aus der Gedankenwelt seines Alters. In Festgabe für Julius Kaftan. 1920.
FRIEDENSBERG, W. Fortschritte in Kenntnis und Verständnis der Reformationsgeschichte (Schriften des Ver. Rcf. Ges., 1910).
FROUDE, J. A. Martin Luther.
GILSON, ÉTIENNE. The Spirit of Mediaeval Philosophy. London, 1936.
La Philosophie au Moyen Age. Paris, 1930.
Introduction à l'étude de saint Augustin. Paris, 1949.
GRAVIER, F. Luther et l'opinion publique. Paris, 1942.
GRISAR, HARTMANN, S.J. Luther (Eng. tr., vols. 1-6). 1913-17.
HAMEL, ADOLF. Der junge Luther und Augustin. Gütersloh, 1934-5, 2 vols.
HARE, JULIUS. Vindication of Luther. 1855.
HARNACK, THEODOSIUS. Luthers Theologie. 2 vols. Rev. ed. Munich, 1927.
HAUSRATH, ADOLF. Luthers Leben. 2 vols. Berlin, 1904.
HAYNE, THOMAS. Life and Death of Martin Luther. London, 1641.
HERTE, ADOLF. Das katholische Lutherbild im Bann der Lutherkommentare des Cochlaeus. Münster, 1943. 3 vols.
HESSEN, J. Luther in katholischer Sicht. Bonn, 1949.
HILDEBRANDT, FRANZ. Est. Das Lutherische Prinzip. Göttingen, 1931.
Melanchthon. Cambridge, 1946.
HINRICHS, CARL. Luther und Müntzer. Berlin, 1952.
HIRSCH, E. Initium Theologiae Lutheri. In Festgabe für Julius Kaftan. 1920.
HOESS, IRMGARD. Georg Spalatins Bedeutung für die Reformation und die

358 THE RIGHTEOUSNESS OF GOD

Organisation der lutherischen Landeskirche. Archiv für Ref., 1951, 101 ff.
HOLBORN, HAJO. Ulrich von Hutten. (Eng. tr.) 1937.
HOLL, KARL. Gesammelte Aufsätze zur Kirchengeschichte. 3 vols. Tübingen, 1948.
IWAND, HANNS JOACHIM. Rechtfertigungslehre und Christusglaube. 1930. Glaubensgerechtigkeit nach Luthers Lehre. Munich, 1951.
Studien zum Problem des Unfreien Willens. Z. für Syst. Theol. 1930-1.
JACOB, GUNTHER. Der Gewissensbegriff in der Theologie Luthers. Tübingen, 1929.
JOACHIMSEN, P. Die Reformation als Epoche der Deutschen Geschichte. Rev. ed. Munich, 1950.
JOLIVET, RÉGIS. Saint Augustin et le Néo-Platonisme Chrétien. Paris, 1932.
JOSEFSON, RUBEN. Ödmujkhet och Tro. Stockholm, 1939.
Den Naturliga Teologins Problem hos Luther. Uppsala, 1943.
KASSIRER, E. (and P. O. KRISTELLER). The Renaissance Philosophy of Man. 1948.
KATTENBUSCH, FERDINAND. Die Doppelschichtigkeit in Luthers Kirchenbegriff. Th. St. und Kr., 1927-8.
Deus Absconditus bei Luther. In Festgabe für Julius Kaftan. 1920.
KAWERAU, GUSTAV (and J. KÖSTLIN). Luther. 1903.
Luther in katholischer Beleuchtung. Ver. Ref. Ges. 1911.
KOEHLER, WALTHER. Dogmengeschichte. Reformation. Zurich, 1951.
Das Täufertum in der neueren kirchenhistorischen Forschung. Archiv für Ref. 1940, 1943 and 1948.
KOOIMAN, W. J. Maarten Luther. Amsterdam, 1948.
KÖSTLIN, JULIUS. Luther's Theology. (Eng. tr.) 2 vols.
KRISTELLER, P. O. Humanism and Scholasticism in the Italian Renaissance Byzantion. XIII. 1944-5, 346-74.
KRAMM, H. H. The Theology of Martin Luther. London, 1947.
LAGARDE, G. DE. Naissance de l'esprit laïque au déclin du moyen âge. Vols. 1-6. Paris, 1940-8.
Recherches sur l'esprit politique de la Réforme.
LAU, FRANZ. "Äusserliche Ordnung" und "Weltlich Ding" in Luthers Theologie. Göttingen, 1933.
LEY, ROGER. Kirchenzucht bei Zwingli. Zurich, 1948.
LILJE, HANNS. Luther. 1946.
Luthers Geschichtsanschauung. 1932.
LJUNGGREN, GUSTAV. Zur Geschichte der Christlichen Heilsgewissheit. Göttingen, 1920.
LOEWENICH, WALTHER VON. Luthers Theologia Crucis. Munich, 1933.
LORTZ, J. Reformation in Deutschland. 2 vols. Freiburg, 1947.
MACKINNON, JAMES. Martin Luther and the Reformation. 4 vols. 1925-30.
MARROU, H. I. Saint Augustin et la fin de la Culture Antique. 2 vols. Paris, 1949-50.
MAURER, WILHELM. Von der Freiheit eines Christenmenschen. Göttingen, 1949.
MCGIFFERT, A. C. Martin Luther, The Man and His Work. New York, 1919.

MEIER, L., O.F.M. Ein Neutrales Zeugnis für den Gegensatz von Skotismus und Ockhamismus im spätmittelalterlichen Erfurt. (Franz. Stud. 26 (1939), 167-182, 258-287.)

MEISSINGER, KARL A. Erasmus von Rotterdam. Berlin, 1948.
Zu Luthers Vorlesungstätigkeit. Heidelberg, 1920.

MESNARD, PIERRE. Érasme de Rotterdam. Essai sur le Libre Arbitre. Alger, 1945.

MIEGGE, GIOVANNI. Lutero. Torre Pellice. 1946.

MÜLLER, KARL. Kirche, Gemeinde und Obrigkeit nach Luther. 1910.

MÜNTZER, THOMAS (ed. HINRICHS). Politische Schriften. Halle, 1950.

MURRAY, R. H. Erasmus and Luther. 1920.

NYGREN, ANDERS. Agape and Eros. Eng. tr. Pt. I, 1932. Pt. II, i., 1938. Pt. II, ii., 1939.
Luthers Lehre von den zwei Reichen. Th. Lit. Z. 1949.

OBENDIEK, HARMANNUS. Der Teufel bei Martin Luther. Berlin, 1931.

PAUCK, WILHELM. The Heritage of the Reformation. Boston, 1950.

PAYNE, E. A. The Anabaptists of the Sixteenth Century. London, 1949.

PHILLIPS, MARGARET M. Erasmus and the Northern Renaissance. 1950.

PINEAU, J. B. Érasme. Sa Pensée Religieuse. Paris, 1924.

PINOMAA, LENNART. Der Zorn Gottes in der Theologie Luthers. Helsinki, 1938.
Der existentielle Charakter der Theologie Luthers. Helsinki, 1940.

PIRCKHEIMER, WILLIBALD. Briefwechsel. Vol. 1. Ed. Dr. E. Reicke. Munich, 1940.

PRENTER, REGIN. Spiritus Creator. Copenhagen, 1946.

PREUSS, HANS. Martin Luther. Gütersloh, 1947.

REITER (Dr. Med.), J. PAUL. Martin Luthers Umwelt, Charakter und Psychose.
Vol. 1. Die Umwelt. 1937.
Vol. 2. Luthers Persönlichkeit, Seelenleben und Krankheiten. Copenhagen, 1941.

RENAUDET, A. Érasme. Paris, 1926.
Études Érasmiennes (1521-9). Paris, 1939.

REU, A. V. Thirty-five Years of Luther Research. Chicago, 1917.

RICH, A. Die Anfänge der Theologie Huldrych Zwinglis. Zurich, 1949.

RIETSCHEL, ERNST. Das Problem der unsichtbar-sichtbaren Kirche bei Luther. 1932.

RITTER, GERHARD. Studien zur Spätscholastik.
1. Marsilius von Inghen und die Ockhamistische Schule in Deutschland. Heidelberg, 1921.
2. Via Antiqua und Via Moderna auf den Deutschen Universitäten des XV. Jahrhunderts. Heidelberg, 1922.
Luther, Gestalt und Tat. 1947.
Die Neugestaltung Europas im 16. Jahrhundert. Berlin, 1950.

RÜEGG, WALTER. Cicero und der Humanismus. Zurich, 1946.

SCHEEL, OTTO. Martin Luther. 2 vols. Tübingen, 1930.
Dokumente zu Luthers Entwicklung. Tübingen, 1929.
Evangelium, Kirche und Volk bei Luther. (Schrift. Ver. Ref., 1934.)
Die Entwicklung Luthers bis zum Abschluss der Vorlesung über dem Römerbrief. (Schrift. Ver. Ref., 1910.)

SCHLISSKE, OTTO. Handbuch der Lutherlieder. Göttingen, 1948.
SCHREY, H. H. Die Luther Renaissance in der neueren schwedischen Theologie. (Th. Lit. Z., 1949.)
SCHUBART, CHRISTOF. Die Berichte über Luthers Tod und Begräbnis. Weimar, 1917.
SCHWEINGRUBER, EDUARD. Luthers Erlebnis des Unfreien Willens. Zurich, 1947.
SCHWEITZER, C. G. Luther and the State. (Theology, Sept. 1943.)
SCHWIEBERT, E. G. Luther and His Times. St. Louis, 1950.
SEEBERG, ERICH. Luthers Theologie. 2 vols. 1929 and 1937.
    Luthers Theologie in ihren Grundzügen. Stuttgart, 1950.
SMITH, PRESERVED. Luther's Table Talk. Columbia, 1907.
    Luther's Development of the Doctrine of Justification by Faith Only. (Harv. Theol. Rev., 1913.)
    English Opinion of Luther. (Harv. Theol. Rev., 1917.)
    Decade of Luther Study. (Harv. Theol. Rev., 1921.)
    Life and Letters of Martin Luther. 1911.
    Erasmus. 1923.
SORMUNEN, EINO. Die Eigenart der lutherischen Ethik. Helsinki, 1934.
STANGE, KARL. Erasmus und Julius II. Berlin, 1937.
    Die Gottesanschauung Luthers. Z. für Syst. Theol., 1931.
STOKES, F. G. Epistolae Obscurorum Virorum. London, 1935.
STOMPS, M. A. H. Die Anthropologie Martin Luthers. 1935.
STRACKE, ERNST. Luthers grosses Selbstzeugnis, 1545. Schrift. Ver. Ref., 1926.
STRATENWERTH, GUNTER. Die Naturrechtslehre des Johannes Duns Scotus. Göttingen, 1951.
STROHL, HENRI. La Substance de l'Évangile selon Luther.
    L'Évolution Religieuse de Luther. Strasbourg, 1922.
    L'Épanouissement de la Pensée Religieuse de Luther. Strasbourg, 1924.
    La Notion d'Église chez les Réformateurs. (Rev. d'Hist. et de Phil. Rel., 1936.)
STUPPERICH, R. Der Humanismus und die Wiedervereinigung der Konfessionen. (Ver. Ref.) 1936.
TÖRNVALL, G. Andligt och världsligt Regemente hos Luther. Stockholm, 1940.
    German tr. Geistliches und weltliches Regiment bei Luther. Munich, 1947.
VIGNAUX, PAUL A. Justification et Prédestination au xive siècle. Paris, 1924.
    Dict. Théol. Cath. Arts. " Nominalisme." " Occam."
    Luther Commentateur des Sentences. Paris, 1935.
    " Sur Luther et Occam " in " Wilhelm Ockham." 1950.
VOGELSANG, ERICH. Der angefochtene Christus bei Luther. 1932.
    Die Anfänge von Luthers Christologie nach der Ersten Psalmenvorlesung. 1929.
    Unbekannte Fragmente aus Luthers Zweiter Psalmenvorlesung. Berlin, 1940.
    Luthers Hebräerbrief Vorlesung, 1517-18. Deutsche Übersetzung.
WATSON, P. S. The State as the Servant of God. 1946.
    Let God be God. 1947.

Luther and Vocation. (S.J.T., Dec. 1949.)
" The Significance of Luther for Christians of Other Communions."
(Essays presented to A. Nygren. World Lutheranism Today. 1951.)
WEIJENBORG, R., O.F.M. La charité dans la première théologie de Luther.
Rev. d'Hist. Eccl., vol. xlv. 3-4, 1950.
WENDORF, H. Der Durchbruch der neuen Erkenntnis Luthers im Lichte
der handschriftlichen Überlieferung. Historische Vierteljahrschrift.
1932.
WERNER, MARTIN. Psychologisches zum Klostererlebnis Martin Luthers.
Schweizerische Zeitschrift für Psychologie, vol. vii., 1948, 1-18.
WHITNEY, J. P. Reformation Essays. 1939.
WILL, R. La Liberté Chrétienne. Strasbourg, 1922.
WINGREN, G. Luthers Lära om Kallelsen. Lund, 1948.
WOLF, ERNST. Staupitz und Luther. Leipzig, 1927.
    Luthers Erbe. (Ev. Theol., 1946.)
    Politia Christi. (Ev. Theol., 1948-9.)
WOLFF, OTTO. Haupttypen der neueren Lutherdeutung. Stuttgart, 1938.
WOOD, A. S. Theology of Luther's Lectures on Romans. (S.J.T., 1950.)
ZEEDEN, E. W. Martin Luther und die Reformation im Urteil des Deutschen
Luthertums. 1. Band. Darstellung. Freiburg, 1950. 2. Band. 1952.
ZWINGLI, U. Hauptschriften. Ed. Blanke, Farner, Pfister. Zurich,
1941-

QUOTATIONS FROM THE WEIMAR EDITION
OF THE WORKS OF MARTIN LUTHER

SUBJECT MATTER AND TECHNICAL VOCABULARY

INDEX